THE SPIRITUAL LIFE

IN THE SCHOOL OF ST. LOUIS-MARIE GRIGNION DE MONTFORT:
A DOGMATIC EXPOSITION

ANTONIN LHOUMEAU

Superior General of the Company of Mary
and Daughters of Wisdom

† 1920

Translated by

HARRY B. OESMAN

UBI•CARITAS PRESS
www.ubicaritaspress.com
San Diego

2020

Previously published as *La vie spirituelle à l'école du bienheureux Louis-Marie Grignion de Montfort*, 2Ed., (Paris: Oudin, 1904).

Cover image: Unknown artist, *Matka Boża Serdeczna* ("The Mother of God"), c. 1600, Church of St. Alexius, Przedbórz on the Pilica, Radomsko County, Poland.

Cover design by Harry B. Oesman

Printed in the United States of America

ISBN: 9781699042892 (Paperback)

ISBN: 9781078732482 (Hardcover)

Library of Congress Control Number: 2019916243

CONTENTS

Translator's Note ix

Antonin Lhoumeau xiii

Foreword xv

The Act of Consecration to Jesus Christ, the Eternal Wisdom, through
    the Hands of Mary xix

Author's Preface 3

PART I: OUR END, OR JESUS CHRIST LIVING IN US

    Chap. 1: Jesus Christ 21
        Art. 1: The Grace of Union 22
        Art. 2: The Habitual Grace of Christ 26
        Art. 3: Capital Grace of Christ 28
    Chap. 2: Christ Living in Us 30
        Art. 1: Through Him 31
        Art. 2: With Him 36
        Art. 3: In Him 39
        Art. 4: Our Spiritual Growth in Christ 53
    Chap. 3: The Life and the Way of Union 56
        Art. 1: The Fundamental Idea 56
        Art. 2: A Brief Historical Review 59
        Art. 3: Characteristic Notes 61
    Chap. 4: On Holy Slavery 70
        Art. 1: What Should Be Understood by "Slavery" 71
        Art. 2: The Foundation of Holy Slavery 72
        Art. 3: Qualities of This Holy Slavery 81
        Art. 4: The Value of the Word "Slavery" 90

PART II: OUR MEANS, OR THE UNION WITH JESUS THROUGH
MARY

    Prologue 99
    Chap. 1: Mary is Our Mother 102
        Art. 1: Mary Conceives Us in Christ 103
        Art. 2: Mary Conceives Christ in Us 107
        Art. 3: Phases of the Spiritual Motherhood of the Blessed
            Virgin Mary 108
    Chap. 2: Mary, Treasurer and Dispenser of Grace 112
        Art. 1: Treasurer 112

Art. 2: Dispenser of Grace and Cooperator of the Holy Ghost 117
Art. 3: How the Blessed Virgin Cooperates or by which Acts
    She Exercises Her Mediation 121
Chap. 3: The Queenship of Mary..142
Art. 1: The Titles of Her Queenship..142
Art. 2: The Extent of her Queenship 145
Art. 3: Queen of Hearts 150

PART III: THE PRACTICE OF THE PERFECT DEVOTION TO
THE BLESSED VIRGIN

Chap. 1: The Spirit of Mary..161
Art. 1: The Handmaid of the Lord..161
Art. 2: The Enmities..167
Art. 3: Effects of the Spirit of Mary..171
Chap. 2: The Consecration..175
Art. 1: Scope of This Consecration and Its Practical
    Consequences 176
Art. 2: The Perfect Consecration Compared to Other Acts..........185
Art. 3: The Idea of This Consecration 187
Art. 4: The Riches of Our Poverty 192
Chap. 3: The Interior Exercise 202
Art. 1: To Act through Mary...204
Art. 2: With Mary 207
Art. 3: In Mary 208
Art. 4: For Mary 212
Chap. 4: Spiritual Childhood 217

PART IV: THE ASCETIC VIEW ON THE PERFECT DEVOTION

Chap. 1: Exercises to Prepare for the Consecration 227
Art. 1: The Twelve Preliminary Days 228
Art. 2: The First Week..232
Art. 3: The Second Week..235
Art. 4: The Third Week 237
Chap. 2: Acting in Union with Mary: Practical Observations............241
Art. 1: Applying the Interior Practice...241
Art. 2: The Renunciation Necessary to Act in Union with Mary ..245
Art. 3: How to Make Our Act of Union...250
Art. 4: Questions and Answers...255
Chap. 3: The Perfect Devotion and the Three Stages of Spiritual
    Life...261
Art. 1: The Purgative Way 262
Art. 2: The Illuminative Way..273
Art. 3: The Unitive Way 277
Chap. 4: The Path is Easy, Short, Perfect, and Secure 293
Art. 1: The Path is Easy..293
Art. 2: The Path is Short...303
Art. 3: The Path is Perfect..307
Art. 4: The Path is Secure 312

CONTENTS v

PART V: THE LIFE IN UNION WITH MARY

Prologue 319
Chap. 1: On Prayer 319
Chap. 2: The Examen and the Work 337
    Art. 1: The Examen 337
    Art. 2: The Work 339
Chap. 3: On Holy Communion 343
    Art. 1: The Virgin Mary and the Eucharist 344
    Art. 2: Holy Communion through Mary 347
    Art. 3: Holy Slavery and the Effect of Holy Communion 352
Chap. 4: Mary and the Holy Sacrifice of the Mass 355
    Art. 1: The "Virgin Priest" 356
    Art. 2: The Representations of Mary in the Objects of Sacred
        Liturgy 362
    Art. 3: The Liturgy of the Mass 364

Bibliography 375

THE MOST REV. ANTONIN LHOUMEAU
1852-1920
Superior General of the Company of Mary
and Daughters of Wisdom, 1903-1919.

TRANSLATOR'S NOTE

The book *La vie spirituelle à l'école du bienheureux Louis-Marie Grignion de Montfort*, by the Most Rev. Antonin Lhoumeau, was first published in 1901. I revised and copiously annotated the second edition that appeared in 1904, and the resulting product is available from the same publisher, with the title *La vie spirituelle à l'école de saint Louis-Marie Grignion de Montfort*, which is the basis of this translation, the first ever in English.

The name Louis-Marie Grignion de Montfort means that he was Louis-Marie of the family Grignion of the hamlet of Montfort-sur-Meu, in Brittany, France, and not of the family "de Montfort," for there is no evidence that he bore or claimed any relation to the either of the two noble houses of that name that thrived in the Middle Ages. His name should have been anglicized as St. Louis *of* Montfort. I used the name St. Louis-Marie, the one preferred by the Fathers of the Company of Mary, and kept the endearing "good Father de Montfort" wherever Fr. Lhoumeau uses it.

There are some places in *La vie spirituelle* where trains of thought end abruptly, or allusions are made but whose sources may be unfamiliar to readers, making it hard for them to make the connection, or the text needed rearranging to make the logic flow more smoothly. I tried to remedy this perceived shortcoming by adding, revising, deleting, or rearranging the text. The places where I added begins with the mark "⁝⁝"; where I revised, "⁝"; and both end with "|". The three places marked with "⁝|" are where I deleted the text completely or moved it nearby. All this I did, not with any assertion of even the slightest knowledge of the subjects in question, much less the authority, but merely on the feeble force of my lowly logic, and purely under the pretext of understanding the written word.

I ignored or summarized a few of the literary flourishes common to French writers at the turn of the nineteenth century.

Fr. Lhoumeau had some 300 notes. In most cases, the citations were rudimentary. I added some 600 more, and used standardized notations. All but a handful references are to published works freely available online. The text in the notes following the "♦" mark belongs to Fr. Lhoumeau. In the notes, I used the same marks for the same cases indicated in the preceding paragraph. Altogether, the notes take up some 50 pages, in small type and single-spaced. For reasons of economy, the majority of the time, I do not show the quotes in their original languages, preferring to give just translations of them. I believe the reader may readily benefit from my having done so.

St. Louis-Marie composed some 160 poems. The original French and their literal translations are available at www.monfortian.info. I have made my own of the ones Fr. Lhoumeau quotes. If they seem odd even to the novice poet, I beg pardon for my ignorance of meter and alliteration, for my only creative contribution, if it could even be called that, was to give them the same number of syllables, and make them somehow rhyme.

I have a bone to pick with the French "*l'esprit de*." Whether applied to an idea, thing, or person, it can mean a lot of things. "Esprit" itself in most cases refer to the mind proper, for which we may make use of certain locutions in English to translate "*l'esprit de*"; e.g., where the text implies, "to have a mind" to do something. Rather than resorting to the nebulous and facile "spirit of," and with a deliberate purpose of avoiding interjecting an agent into an action where none is warranted, or none can exist, and most especially to avoid imparting the rancid flavor it has taken of late because of its perverted use among the heterodox, "*l'esprit de*" is severally rendered, if to a subject: "essence," "heart," "principle," "proclivity," "specter," "substance," "tenor," "tone"; and if to the mind: "idea," "imagination," "thought," as the context requires, all of which, according to the *Académie Française*, are among its many documented received meanings. Where Fr. Lhoumeau is wont to say, for instance, that "*l'esprit de notre dévotion*" does one thing or another, I chalk it up to imprecise language, for there is no actor or agent called "the spirit of our devotion." Hence, I ignored *esprit*, and credit the act to the person who has the devotion.

Where *esprit* properly refers to *spiritus* as distinguished from *anima*, as in Hebrews 4.12, it is translated as "spirit," with the understanding that it should be taken to mean what Fr. Cornelius à Lapide says it means. In his *Commentaries* (18:389), he writes that "soul" comprises the faculties, senses, and passions; whereas "spirit" denotes her substance, independent of her powers. St. Teresa of Avila says that in the inferior degrees of the mystical life, God operates through the faculties of the soul; while in the mystical marriage, He acts directly on her substance. (*Interior Castle*, 7.1; *Life*, 18.4). It is with the foregoing in mind that I rendered "*l'esprit de Marie*," as "the spirit of Mary." In a few cases, I used "the heart of Mary," taking into consideration that in English, "heart" also means "substance," as well as all the other things Fr. Lhoumeau points out in Part 2.3.3, with the hope that in so doing, the reader somehow would be minded to rekindle his devotion to the Immaculate Heart of Mary. "*L'Esprit de Dieu*" needs no explanation.

The English translations of St. Louis-Marie's *Vraie Devotion* and *Secret de Marie* that I used seem to suffer from some inapt rendering of certain French expressions. For instance, "*entrer dans*" means what it literally is: "to enter into," as in a space or situation. But in some cases, it means "to begin." Without discriminating among them, we are left, for example, with the awkward "enter into this devotion." For this and other reasons, where Fr. Lhoumeau quotes from either work, I made my own or revised the translation as necessary, and the reader will know that I did, if he sees the notation "cf." before "*TD*" or "*Secret*."

I reproduced the style of quoting the Bible in both Latin and vernacular, wherever Fr. Lhoumeau does so. The translation I used is the Douay-Rheims version (1899).

The bibliography provides a list of all sources cited. A pdf file with live links is available for free upon request at the publisher's contact page, www.ubicaritaspress.com/contact. If I used an existing translation or modified it, I tacked its citation on to the listing of the work in the original language, otherwise all translations are mine.

HARRY B. OESMAN
Feast of the Holy Family
January 12, 2020.

ANTONIN LHOUMEAU

ndré-Antonin Lhoumeau was born on August 9, 1852, in La Mothe-Saint-Héraye. He first studied at the École Saint-Charles de Niort, and went on to the minor Seminary at Montmorillon. At the age of 19, he entered the major Seminary at Poiters and was ordained priest four years later, on September 18, 1875, and made the Pastor of Niort and Chaplain to the Daughters of Wisdom, the women religious of the Company of Mary, at their hospital in the same town.

Taking the advice of Charles Louis Gay, who two years later became Bishop of Poitiers, and very much drawn to the *Treatise on the True Devotion to the Virgin Mary*, at age 32, he entered the Company of Mary as a novitiate at Schimmert, Holland, and made his profession on May 4, 1885. He spent five years with the missionaries at Orleans, after which he was sent to England to establish the foundations of the missions of the Montfortians and the Daughters of Wisdom.

In 1893, he was called to Saint-Laurent-sur-Sèvre in the Vendée, where he directed the novitiate of the same women religious order. He was made general councilor of the Company of Mary in 1896, and in 1900, founded the journal *Le Règne de Jésus par Marie*, for the diffusion of the works of St. Louis-Marie. On April 3, 1903, he was elected Superior General of the Company of Mary and of the Daughters of Wisdom, the twelfth after their founder, St. Louis-Marie Grignion de Montfort.

He launched other periodicals: in 1904, *Messager de Marie reine des Cœurs*, in Canada; 1907, *La Revue des Prêtres de Marie reine des Cœurs*; 1908, *Onze missionarissen*, in Holland; and 1914, *Regina dei Cuori*, in Italy. During his term of office, the Company experienced tremendous growth. He brought back the general administration to

Saint-Laurent. He relinquished his office on April 22, 1919. But for the interruption of the Great War he would have retired sooner. Fr. Lhoumeau died August 10, 1920, and is buried at Saint-Laurent.

A brilliant and cultivated soul, Fr. Lhoumeau was a renowned musician and musicologist. He was a collaborator of Dom Joseph Pothier, the celebrated Benedictine liturgist and scholar, Abbot of Saint-Wandrille de Fontenelle, and pupil of Dom Prosper Guéranger himself. Fr. Lhoumeau published several studies on Gregorian chant and hymn books.

On subjects spiritual, Fr. Lhoumeau is associated with Charles Louis Gay, a prolific writer of spirituality. His favorite authors were St. Thomas Aquinas, St. Francis de Sales, St. Teresa of Avila, and Frederick William Faber, much of whose writings he quotes in *The Spiritual Life in the School of St. Louis de Montfort*.

Fr. Lhoumeau wrote a large number of articles in the periodicals mentioned above, but his seminal work is *Spiritual Life*. Previously, it had only been translated once: into Flemish in 1943, but is now, for the first time, available in English. Much of the interest in the book lies not in the teaching of St. Louis-Marie's as contained in *the Secret of Mary* and *True Devotion*, which became very well-known after it was discovered in 1842, some 125 years after the author died; rather, it is in the systematic manner in which Fr. Lhoumeau explains their theological foundations, and presents them as "a system of spirituality, a special form of interior life, and not merely a collection of pious practices."

Fr. Lhoumeau's other major work is *La Vierge Marie et les apôtres des derniers temps*, "The Virgin Mary and the Apostles of the Last Times" (Tours, 1919), inspired by the works of St. Louis-Marie. In the twenty-one meditations of *Elévations Mariales*, "Marian Elevations" (Tours, 1919), Fr. Lhoumeau speaks of his Marian soul, as faithful son of St. Louis-Marie. At the end, he said: "My life has been a celebration." No better commentary may be said of a life entirely devoted to Jesus with Mary.

FOREWORD

I t is not just any treatise on spiritual life that Fr. Antonin Lhoumeau claims to give us in this work. A fervent admirer and passionate disciple of St. Louis-Marie Grignion de Montfort, Fr. Lhoumeau set out to retrace the path of perfection that the great apostle of the western provinces of France, at the beginning of the eighteenth century, taught a large swath of the population by his sermons and writings and, by his zeal, brought all Christian virtues to be practiced. This path of perfection is none other than the devotion to the Mother of God, considered in the special form that it takes in the little book by St. Louis-Marie, which the first editors gave the title of *Traité de la vraie dévotion à la sainte Vierge*, "Treatise on the True Devotion to the Blessed Virgin." Fr. Lhoumeau took on the task to plumb its ideas, in an effort to bring the substance of the devotion to light. His is the first effort, in what he described in the subtitle of this work, at "a dogmatic exposition" of the teachings of St. Louis-Marie. Anyone who reads this work will confess that he has achieved his purpose successfully.

Fr. Lhoumeau himself alerts us in his preface that he has presented most of the dogmatic truths on which the perfect devotion to Mary rests. His motive for doing so was, at first, that he did not want to part company with St. Louis-Marie, who devoted most of his little treatise to the exposition of Marian dogma, before coming to the practice of the perfect devotion; but mainly because he was anxious to join the movement of reaction against Separatism which, in the prior centuries, too often isolated morality and spirituality from dogma, sucking the sap out of Christian piety, and ending up with life being mere impressions, sentimentality, nuances, and capriciousness.

Fr. Lhoumeau needed to summarize the theology of the devotion to the Blessed Virgin to illuminate the Christian faith. He devotes one part of his work to that purpose. But because the devotion to Mary, as conceived and practiced by St. Louis-Marie, is the most effective and the surest means of achieving the perfection of Christian life; that is to say, that it is the union which gives life to Jesus Christ in us, and us in Him, Fr. Lhoumeau judged that he should discuss this union at some length, and recall the theological truths on which its sanctifying virtue is based. Otherwise, we would know neither the purpose of the devotion to the Blessed Virgin nor its marvelous capacity as a means of leading us to the goal of holiness in Christ and through Christ.

Hence, the division of the book into three main parts. Part I explains how Jesus Christ, God made Man, being holy in Himself and being the fullness of grace, is also the principle of all holiness through the union we have with Him. Part II offers us Mary as the Mother of Mankind, their sovereign and, after Jesus Christ, their universal Mediator of grace; that is, as the predestined means of achieving perfect union with God made Man. Here, careful to follow step by step the doctrine of St. Louis-Marie, the author presents this two-fold union, one of which is the goal and the other the means, using the notion of "slavery."

To be the slave of Mary is to be the slave of Jesus. In short, such is the spiritual life learned in the school of de Montfort. But, when we speak of slavery, we have to reject everything base, constraining, and degrading, that the word may imply. The holy slavery signified by the words of the Blessed Virgin: *Ecce ancilla Domini*, is a slavery of total dependence with respect to Our Lord and His Mother, but one entirely to our advantage and founded on love.

In Part III, the author studies the practices of perfect devotion to the Blessed Virgin. He finds them summed up in these few words of St. Louis-Marie: "This devotion consists in giving oneself entirely as a slave to Mary, and to Jesus through her; then to do all things through Mary, with Mary, in Mary, and for Mary." In essence, the subject of this part of the book is to show the extent of this consecration and its consequences, and to clarify the meaning of the formula: "to act through Mary, with Mary, in Mary, and for Mary," as compared to the analogous formula: "to act through Christ, with Christ, in Christ, and for Christ." If needed be, the author could have stopped at this point.

However, the work would have seemed unfinished, had it not been expanded into the particular applications of the devotion, or had it not shown, in a final consideration, that the path to union with Jesus is through the union with Mary. Provided that it is well understood, it is in all truth "an easy, short, perfect and secure way" of attaining perfection in the spiritual life. Parts IV and V discusses the ascetic aspects of the perfect devotion to Mary.

As may be surmised by now, there is an abundance of doctrine in Fr. Lhoumeau's work, both on the theoretical and practical aspects. All those who have at heart the glory of their Mother, and the great business of their perfection in Christ, will have the pleasure and will gain edification by reading this book. The style is usually clear, lively, incisive, colorful. The author uses many analogies, comparisons, metaphors, illustrations—well-chosen all—that shed light on what may be too abstract a reasoning. Particularly to be recommended are the pages on the notion of Holy Slavery as taught by St. Louis-Marie, either so as to gain further understanding or to be rid of all acquaintance with certain spiritual practices not countenanced by the Church.

We end these few remarks with a wish that is a hope: It is that the diffusion of the *Spiritual Life at in the School of St. Louis-Marie de Monfort* will contribute towards gathering many more slaves at the feet of the our Queen of Heaven, in order to increase in the same proportion the number of the slaves of Christ the King.

JEAN-BAPTISTE TERRIEN, S.J.

Adapted from the review of "La Vie spirituelle à l'école du bienheureux L.-M. Grignion de Montfort," *Études*, Oct 20, 1902, 93 (2):273-276. Tr. Harry. B. Oesman. *Études* is a journal of the Society of Jesus in France.

THE ACT OF CONSECRATION

TO JESUS CHRIST, THE ETERNAL WISDOM, THROUGH THE HANDS OF MARY

 Wisdom, Eternal and Incarnate! O most beloved and adorable Jesus, true God and true Man, only Son of the eternal Father and of Mary ever Virgin! I adore Thee profoundly in the bosom and splendors of Thy Father in all eternity; and I adore Thee also in the Virginal bosom of Mary, Thy most worthy Mother, in the time of Thine Incarnation.

I give Thee thanks that Thou hast emptied Thyself, in taking the form of a slave, in order to rescue me from the cruel slavery of the devil. I praise and glorify Thee that Thou hast been pleased to submit Thyself to Mary, Thy holy Mother, in all things, in order to make me, through her, Thy faithful slave.

But, alas! ungrateful and faithless that I am, I have not kept the promises which I made so solemnly to Thee in my Baptism; I have not fulfilled my obligations; I do not deserve to be called Thy son, nor yet Thy slave; and as there is not a thing in me that merits not Thine anger and Thy rebuff, no more dare I come by myself before Thy most holy and august Majesty. On this account, I have recourse to the intercession of Thy most holy Mother, whom Thou hast given me for a mediatrix with Thee. It is through her that I hope to obtain of Thee contrition, and the pardon of my sins, the acquisition and the preservation of wisdom.

I salute thee, then, O immaculate Mary, living tabernacle of the Divinity, where the Eternal Wisdom willed to be hidden and adored by Angels and by men. I hail thee, O Queen of Heaven and earth, to whose dominion everything is subject which is under God.

I salute thee, O sure refuge of sinners, whose mercy fails no one. Hear the desires which I have of the Divine Wisdom; and for that end receive the vows and offerings which my lowliness presents to thee.

I, *N.*, a faithless sinner, renew and ratify today in thy hands the vows of my Baptism; I renounce forever Satan, his pomps and works; and I give myself entirely to Jesus Christ, the Incarnate Wisdom, to carry my cross after Him all the days of my life, and to be more faithful to Him than I have ever been till now.

In the presence of all the heavenly court, I choose thee this day for my Mother and Lady. I deliver and consecrate to thee, as thy slave, my body and soul, my goods, both interior and exterior, and even the value of all my good actions, past, present, and future; leaving to thee the entire and full right to dispose of me, and all that belongs to me, without exception, according to thy good pleasure, for the greater glory of God, in time and in eternity.

Receive, O benign Virgin, this little offering of my slavery, in honor of, and in union with, that subjection which the Eternal Wisdom deigned to have to thy Maternity, in homage to the power which both of you have over this little worm and wretched sinner, and in thanksgiving for the privileges with which the Holy Trinity hath favored thee. I protest that I wish, henceforth, as thy true slave, to seek thy honor and to obey thee in all things.

O admirable Mother, present me to thy dear Son as His eternal slave, so that as He hath redeemed me through thee, through thee He may receive me. O Mother of Mercy, grant me the grace to obtain the true wisdom of God; and for that end, count me among the number of those whom thou lovest, whom thou teachest, whom thou leadest, and whom thou nourishest and protectest, as thy children and thy slaves. O Virgin most faithful, make me in all things so perfect a disciple, imitator, and slave of the Incarnate Wisdom, Jesus Christ thy Son, that I may attain, through thy intercession and example, to the fulness of His age on earth, and of His glory in Heaven. AMEN.

Qui potest capere, capiat.
Quis sapiens, et intelliget hæc?

He that can take, let him take it (Mt 19.12).
Who is wise that he shall understand these things? (Hos 14.10).

THE SPIRITUAL LIFE

IN THE SCHOOL OF ST. LOUIS-MARIE GRIGNION DE MONTFORT:
A DOGMATIC EXPOSITION

AUTHOR'S PREFACE

Many have written on the devotion to the Blessed Virgin called the Holy Slavery to Mary; but we believe that none has yet shown with consistency and to a great extent, that it is, according to the teachings of St. Louis-Marie Grignion de Montfort, a system of spirituality, a special form of interior life, and not merely a collection of pious practices. By this present work, we hope to fill the gap in the understanding of the devotion, for our object is to demonstrate its dogmatic foundations and to shed light on its application to spiritual life.

Did St. Louis-Marie really found a school of devotion? No one who has combed through his *Treatise on the True Devotion to the Blessed Virgin* would doubt it, although St. Louis-Marie did not conceive the book, along with the short work entitled *The Secret of Mary*, as any representation of a methodical and complete treatment of spirituality. Even if we found that the various parts of his teaching are not well developed in these two works, or that we might not read in them a complete set of practical applications, we would be mistaken if we thought that they only allude to, or are merely the seeds of, the doctrine that we hope to unveil; for they amply treat of many questions, and we find in them a ready supply of relevant arguments, even if some are presented in summary form. We hope that this volume not only will have drawn its inspiration from the principles formulated by St. Louis-Marie, but that it may also serve as a commentary on the two books, while remaining ever true to their letter and spirit. In our exposition, we also hope to show that the spirituality of St. Louis-Marie stands out as a particular form of which he is truly the author.

In the sciences and the arts, it is the different points of view and processes that give rise to different schools. The devotion outlined by

3

St. Louis-Marie presents us with an end, a means, processes, and effects, that have a special character and constitute a distinct spirituality.

The end to which the spiritual doctrine of St. Louis-Marie leads us is divine union. True, it is the end common to all schools of spirituality, but here we touch upon a narrower and closer kind, if we consider the union with God under one aspect: that of Christ living in us. We shall arrive at the proximate and special end of this devotion when we propose to make Jesus live in us by the total and absolute dependence which we call "Holy Slavery."

The means chosen to reach this end is none other than the Blessed Virgin Mary. While she plays a role in other devotions and methods of leading the interior life in which there is an emphasis on the importance of the veneration rendered her, and the aid asked of her, she is present in them only incidentally and stands as if on the outside, at a distance; but in the spirituality of St. Louis-Marie, our Blessed Mother plays an essential part, because she is the one who gives it its specific form and distinctive properties. Indeed, the *formal* object[1] of this devotion is the mediation and sovereignty of Mary; its proper act, the consecration to Holy Slavery, also referred to as the "Holy Slavery to Mary," which is its true name, as that name expresses its true nature.

This devotion has its own processes. They consist of two practices, one exterior and the other interior, both of which we shall explain at length and whose particular effects we shall see in the course of this volume.

How far can we assert that St. Louis-Marie is the master of this particular school of spirituality? There are those who will object by saying that his doctrine is not new; others, who wonder how it differs from what many have taught before him.

No, by the grace of God, this devotion is indeed *not* new! If it were, the Church would consider it an error; and the novelty, its irreversible

---

[1] *Formal*, as in giving a "form" or "shape" to an object, not a description of it as being "official" or "customary." It is contrasted to the *material*; that is, its content. See St. Thomas, *Summa*, 2-2.1.1c.

condemnation. We point out that the teaching of St. Louis-Marie is rooted in the foundations of Christianity. Its current flows from the oldest and purest springs of tradition. The very thing that distinguishes it commends itself to what dogma or asceticism have sanctioned. Indeed, what St. Louis-Marie does is to unite certain points of view in a consistent whole, on some of which he sheds light, while in others, develops them to the end and provides their practical results.

He follows the Fathers and the Doctors of the Church even to their farthest considerations concerning the mediation of Mary; and, rejoicing in this rich treasure, he spreads it profusely in his writings. In *True Devotion*, we also find that treasure shared by several schools of asceticism in the seventeenth century, namely the life in union with Jesus through Mary, but emphasizing a singular submission to Holy Slavery.[2] Indeed, *True Devotion* reflects the various nuances of such schools.

The French Oratory[3] is distinguished by its devotion to the Incarnate Word and by a tenor of profound adoration, which blossoms into a special sense of belonging to the Person of Christ, as well as to His divine Mother. St. Louis-Marie was most obviously inspired by these insights in his devotion to the mystery of the Annunciation, in his practice of humbly going to Jesus through Mary, and in the consecration to Holy Slavery. In Fr. Jean-Jacques Olier, devout slave of the Virgin, what is most emphasized, and held in the utmost importance, is the interior life with Jesus and Mary (for their two lives, so to speak, make but one whole). Is it not the aim of St. Louis-Marie, that, through the union of thought and will, we should enter into this interior, and remain there by our dependence, when he speaks to us of abiding *in Mary*, or when he proposes the process of *molding* our spiritual formation? St. Jean Eudes, too, practices and teaches the Holy Slavery to Jesus and Mary[4]; but the principal object of his devotion is

---

[2] ♦We find these same views and practices in several figures of the 17th and 18th century renowned for their piety: B. Jeanne de Lestonnac and Mother Mechtilde of the Blessed Sacrament, née Catherine de Bar, St. Jean Eudes, Fr. Boudon, and so on.

[3] The Congregation of the Oratory of Jesus and Mary Immaculate, founded 1611; not the Oratory of St. Philip Neri founded 1575.

[4] ♦We read in his prayer: "Te laudamus: Tibi cor nostrum donamus. Accipe et posside illud totum," which Le Doré explains is a total and absolute donation. (*Les Sacrés*

their blessed hearts; and, on this account, it retains a more pronounced affective character. We find this nuance also in the thought
of St. Louis-Marie; for Mary's motherhood is ever present in it, so
much so, that it imbues everything with the gentle character of spiritual childhood, and reveals that our dependence is a slavery to
charity.

Now, if he who has made a bouquet with flowers picked here and
there is regarded as its "author," then we can certainly attribute the
authorship of this doctrine to St. Louis-Marie, wherein he forms a
marvelous bouquet out of truths and practices borrowed from various
schools. All the more so, since he limits himself not to gathering them,
but sheds light on them, develops or perfects them in several aspects.
Many in the sciences or the arts have become masters of schools by
this very same process.[5] As we proceed in this volume, we shall see
that our assertions stand on firm ground.

Let us now compare *True Devotion* to the book by Fr. Henri-Marie
Boudon, *God Alone, or the Holy Slavery to the Mother of God*.[6] Besides
a series of dogmatic insights which presents us with a remarkable
vista, we find in the former certain currents in asceticism that exist
neither in the latter nor in other similar works. Recall the master for-
mulation in *True Devotion*, "through Mary, with Mary, in Mary, and
for Mary"; the comparison to the mold; the explanation of the story of
Rebecca; and the exposition of the motives and the effects of perfect
consecration.

Let us not forget that good Father de Montfort is the principal
character in this school, not only for having practiced this devotion to
a rare degree of perfection, but for having disseminated it more than
any other person. History records with what zeal he preached it in his
lifetime. In our day, we see how, through an admirable movement

---

Cœurs, 356). ¦¦ Cf. St. Thomas, *Summa*, 2-2.85, 86. ¦

[5] ◆St. Teresa of Avila has a school of spirituality, because she makes the recollection of
the soul and prayer that all teachers recommend into the principal means by which to
attain union with God, and also because she sheds light on this spiritual path by the
superiority of her teaching. The Roman School of sacred music is called the Palestrina,
because the great artist who lent it his name knew how to bring to an eminent perfection an art that had existed long before him.

[6] This and certain other books cited by Fr. Lhoumeau are not available in translation,
but their titles are given in English for ease of reading. See the bibliography for the titles
in their original languages.

that draws souls to him, the influence of his works continues to rise.[7]
This path of perfection—this Holy Slavery to Mary—previously too
little known, is open to us all. Were it that we but follow up the trails
St. Louis-Marie has marked for us, and use his two immensely popular
books as our guides!

We thus assert that the title, *Spiritual Life in the School of St.
Louis-Marie de Montfort*, is fully justified.

There are some who will ask if this spiritual devotion has had any
impact. In answer, we defer to the testimony of Fr. Frederick William
Faber, who says that St. Louis-Marie, "wrote some spiritual treatises,
which have already had a remarkable influence on the Church during
the few years they have been known, and bid fair to have a much wider
influence in years to come."[8] We see all around how this prediction
has come true in the marvelous growth in the devotion to the Blessed
Virgin. To explain how this came about, we need to compare the times
of St. Louis-Marie with ours.

First, let us observe that neither the dissemination of noted works
nor the strength of character of this or that Saint is sufficient reason
for the appearance of ascetic schools; but, whether apparent or hidden, there does exist a relation between their emergence and certain
epochs in which new perils, new struggles, and new needs arise out of
fresh aspirations. The conditions of social and even material life also
play their part. Nonetheless, we should assign the strongest impulse
to the development of dogma, which, in the life of the Church,
contains the things most intimate and most fruitful, but often the
least known. There is, in fact, a necessary relation between dogma and
spirituality, for *the just man liveth by faith* (Rom 1.17, Gal 3.11), and supernatural life gains strength or weakens in proportion to the brightening
or dimming of this divine light.

Let us now cast a glance at the major ascetic schools and the situation in the Church during the period when they emerged. Consider

---

[7] ♦See, *Règne de Jésus par Marie*, a journal of the Company of Mary, or Montfortian
Missionaries, Jan 1900, 4 ff. ¦ Note that by 1990 there were more than 400 editions in 30
languages for *True Devotion*; 350 editions in various languages for *Secret of Mary*. |

[8] ♦*TD*, Preface, vi. ¦¦ The untitled manuscript published as *Vraie Dévotion*, was only
discovered in 1842, some 125 years after St. Louis-Marie died. (Pauvert, *Vie*, 582). |

in turn the Fathers of the Desert; the old school of the Benedictines with St. Gertrude and St. Mechtilde, who later faithfully reflected its tenor; the Dominican school with St. Thomas Aquinas and his constellation of illustrious masters; the seraphic order of St. Francis of Assisi with the mellifluous St. Bonaventure; then St. Ignatius of Loyola, on the threshold of what is commonly called "modern times"; the school of Carmel with the admirable St. Teresa of Avila and St. John of the Cross; St. Francis de Sales, who today inspires so many books; finally, the French Oratory and the Society of Saint-Sulpice represented especially by Pierre Cardinal de Bérulle, Fr. Charles de Condren, Fr. François Bourgoing and Fr. Olier—everywhere you will see teachings and methods taking different colors according to the needs and the character of the times. We come now to St. Louis-Marie.

One thing first strikes us is that St. Louis-Marie is a man of his times and is ahead of ours. He is man of his times, for he proceeds undoubtedly from the school of the French Oratory and the Society of Saint-Sulpice, to whose most illustrious masters we have just referred. It was that school which, in the first half of the seventeenth century, guided piety to lively and abundant springs through profound insights on the Incarnation, on the life of Christ in us, and on the role of the Blessed Virgin in this two-fold mystery. If now we set aside our inquiry into the spring of St. Louis-Marie's teaching on spirituality, but ask what it has produced, we will find that it was certainly appropriate to the needs of his age. The constant and prodigious success of his preaching, no less than the incessant and hysterical persecutions that inevitably followed, prove how much this valiant apostle got it just right, when, faced with the narrowmindedness and spiritual desiccation that is the error of Jansenism, he proudly flies high the banner of his devotion to Mary. St. Louis-Marie was indeed a man for his times.

But his teaching goes further. His gaze is fixed beyond the horizon, as we may see in his *True Devotion*. It is a work full of wisdom, and sheds light on the times to come; for this great servant of Mary was a prophet as well as a miracle worker. When we read of his life, we may think it a small thing that he predicted a number of specific outcomes, especially in the destiny of his "small work," which, he says, the rage of Hell would hold captive for ages, shrouded in the darkness and silence of a casket.[9] He announced for all to hear that the devotion of Holy Slavery would spread far and wide, and that manifold persecutions would come, and fury would flare to rage against those who would embrace it. He said more. Like St. John, the Apostle and Evangelist, to whom he was so devoted, St. Louis-Marie was able to realize in his life that perfect intimacy with Mary which may be gleaned from these words so full of meaning: *Et accepit eam discipulus in sua,* "and the disciple took her to his own" (Jn 19.27). In another striking similarity, he too, like St. John, had prophetic insights on the last ages of the Church. The Apostle bequeaths us the Book of Revelation, where the Mother of God has her place; St. Louis-Marie gave us his treatise, in which he announces that in the last days Mary will range great Saints in battle array, arm them for the supreme struggle, and prepare them for the final reign of Christ.[10] Is it rash to think that this Queen of the Prophets was no stranger to the revelations partly concerning her and given to her beloved sons?

Be that as it may, the expansion and influence of the devotion of Holy Slavery, by the grace of God, are now clear for all to see. The prophecy has entered history, and what we see today gives us hope for tomorrow.

We may explain the growing influence of the devotion preached by St. Louis-Marie by its being better understood today than during his lifetime, and that it fills the needs of the faithful in the present state of Catholic piety. We are right to hope that it will spread even further, as the transmission of dogma and growth of the Catholic faith reaches parts both known and unknown, paving the way for its full understanding in times to come.

---

[9] *TD*, 74-75: "I clearly foresee that raging beasts shall come in fury to tear with their diabolical teeth this little writing and him of whom the Holy Ghost has made use to write it, or at least to shroud it in the darkness and silence of a casket, that it may not appear. They shall even attack and persecute those who shall read it and carry it out in practice. But it matters not!"

[10] *TD*, 26-36; Cant 6.3, 9. Also, *La Vierge Marie et les apôtres des derniers temps* (1919)

Indeed, what an astonishing contrast exists between the ideas
that spread in France since the latter half of the seventeenth century
and the preaching of St. Louis-Marie! The same year that he was born,
in 1673, there appeared in Cologne a pamphlet which Dom Prosper
Guéranger rightly describes as "despicable." It was written by Adam
Wiedenfeldt, who gave it the provocative title, *Monita salutaria B.V.
Mariæ ad cultores suos indiscretos*.[11] Twenty years later, Fr. Adrien
Baillet, librarian to ¦¦ Chrétien-François de Lamoignon, the advocate
general of the Parliament in Paris,[12] | applied its ideas to his *Devotion
to the Blessed Virgin and the Worship Due Her*, in which the Jansenist
dish is concocted and carefully doled out in a series of accursed,
equivocal, venomous propositions, with the intention to popularize
it. The circumstances of the intrigues and persecutions inflicted on St.
Louis-Marie by the members of the heretical sect remains too little
understood, but we may say that the advent of *True Devotion* was, in
its own way, spurred by Baillet,[13] in whose book we find, sometimes
word for word, the errors that St. Louis-Marie had the occasion to
refute with so much verve and precision, especially when he mocked
the reviews penned by its fastidious partisans.

We have no better comparison for the condition of the Faith
during the period in question than that of the sun in a fog, having
neither radiance not splendor, neither warmth nor life. The night is
not ended, and the sun is there, but lackluster in aspect and reduced
to the contours of its disk, no longer shining, and the day is

---

[11] ¦¦ A pamphlet, some 20 pages long, translated into French and Flemish, that ignited
a firestorm in Europe, and in 1674, was put on the Index of Prohibited Books. The English translation appeared in 1687, with the title "Wholesome Advices from the Blessed
Virgin, to Her Indiscreet Worshippers." | ♦It is summarized in Terrien, *Mère de Dieu*,
11.5, 4:478, along with a list of the large number of writings it aroused.

[12] "Baillet, Adrien," Pérennès, *Biog. Chrétienne*, 1:371-372; *TCE*, 2:206-207.

[13] ♦ ¦ On this question, see Dom Guéranger, *Marie d'Agreda*, Art. 15, part of 28 articles
published in May 23, 1858–Nov 7, 1859 in *L'Universe* about the book, *Mystical City of
God*, by the venerable mystic. At the risk of painting too clear a picture on the history,
it is fair to note that Jansenism, even in France, was not so pervasive. In that period, the
Church boasted a constellation of influential theologians who were clearly in line with
Tradition in their writings. It was the time when Gonet wrote his *Clypeus*; when Contenson published his *Theologia*, including the treatise *Marialogia* (Lib. 9, Dissert. 6,
3:259-302); when Massoulié, besides his other works, rebutted the Quietists in his treatises *de l'Oraison* and *de l'Amour de Dieu*; it was the time when the University of
Salamanca flourished, where lived Lugo, Thomassin, and Bossuet whose sermons on
the Blessed Virgin are renowned, and so on. |

overshadowed by gloom and doubt. Such is the effect that Jansenism had on the central mystery which is the Incarnation, the true sun around which the other dogmas of Christianity gravitate. From the times of the Apostles, through the Fathers, and under the rule of the theology of the great Scholastic school, this dogma freely shone and radiated with outstanding results for the motherhood of Mary, her role, and her prerogatives, which the insignificant contrivance of a mere creature had presumed to constrain. This *Marian* theology may be summarized in this axiom: "God cannot exalt a creature greater than by making Mary the Mother of God."[14] Mary is also the Mother of the Church, the Mystical Body of Christ, and in explaining this mystery, which is an extension of the Incarnation, theology splendidly illuminated the constitution and the life of the Church.

Later, Gallican Jansenism arose. Hypocritical, vague, and almost like a surreptitious, thick, malodorous fog, its mists penetrated everywhere and smothered souls with a filthy atmosphere, leaving them cold and breathing painfully.[15] Faith was not denied, but it was obscured. The enthusiasts of the heresy still believed in the Incarnation, but this dogma, pared down to the mere fact of a God-Man Who redeems the world, was stripped of its effects, like a star made destitute of its rays. The Jansenists no longer desired the Christianity that Louis-Édouard Cardinal Pie described as "the religion of the Son of Mary"[16]; and if any of them accepted the Son of God, born of woman, it was by honoring the Son, and rejecting the woman who gave birth to Him. Baillet's book makes it clear how these so-called "Catholics" had become Protestantized, and how much Satan had breathed into them the hatred towards her who is his personal enemy. They twisted

---

[14] Holtnicker, *Speculum B.V.M.*, 10, 134: "God could make a greater world, God could make a greater Heaven, but a greater mother than the Mother of God He could not make." The work, once attributed to St. Bonaventure, still retains an intrinsic value not unworthy of the holy doctor. Cf. Bonaventure, *Opera*, 14:260.2. See also St. Thomas, *Summa*, 1.25.6 ad 4; St. Albert the Great, "Mariale," 46.4, *Opera*, 37:91.1, and others.

[15] To the rigorist dogmatic stance concerning the relationship of free will to the grace of God in the original error of Jansenism, the Gallican version added the assertion that a general council superseded the sovereign authority of the Pope. (Bachelier, "Le Père de Montfort"). What Fr. Lhoumeau describes applies to the fog, rife with pollution and sulfurous odor, in Victorian and later times.

[16] Pie, *La Vierge*, 290: "The Christian religion is the religion of the Son of Mary. To separate the Son from the Mother, is to divide what God has united. We find Jesus only with Mary, and through Mary; we are sure to reach the Son only through His Mother."

and peeled off the prerogatives of Mary, and the practices of her veneration, one after another. They disputed her Immaculate Conception
and her Assumption. They mutilated the devotions and divine offices
in her honor—those that had been born in centuries of practice; for
in the eyes of these sectarians, it was thought far too extravagant to
sing her praises. In the end, we see that their so-called Gallican
missals and breviaries are fabricated novelties, which, thankfully, now
lay buried in ridicule and oblivion. Logical in their error and hatred,
the heretics, as we well know, even took aim at the divine constitution
of the Church and the prerogatives of her Head.

St. Louis-Marie appeared amidst these oppressive shadows and
faced a diminished Christianity. He quarreled openly with the
heretics, flooded them with the light of understanding, and communicated to souls his ardent love for Jesus and Mary, for the Church,
and for the authority of the Pope.[17]

Placed in the historical context of its time, *True Devotion* shows
that its author held a vigorous faith and possessed the strength of
character which preserved him, unlike others in the same milieu,
some of whom even pious and learned, from being infected with ideas
most unwholesome. By itself, this book may be regarded as the fruit
of a mature man, who was of a rare breed in being so imbued with the
science of the Saints and uncommon in his holiness. If we find that,
in a few pages, the words that flowed freely from his pen summarizes,
as best he could, and concisely, and in a way easily understood, what
theology and the Fathers most profoundly and most importantly have
conveyed about the teaching on the Blessed Virgin. We must recognize, at least in light of the devotion he espouses, that in St. Louis-
Marie there was indeed not only an erudition, but, even rarer, a remarkable theological sensibility. He probably drew much from his
study of many writers, patristic or otherwise, as well as from those
lights of a different order which are given to Saints in contemplation.

When reading *True Devotion*, one wonders what power must
have made the zealous missionary set down the living word, for even
after the passage of centuries and manifold readings, the dead letter

---

[17] ♦ ¦ See *Hymns*, 6.50, "Lights of Faith"; 147, "In Honor of St. Pius V." ¦

of his writings still palpably burns with that fire, and gives off the sweet odor of that unction, which appear never to fade. Prodigious has been its influence, as we have said, and history proves us right; for even in the worst times, there are always souls standing at the ready for the reign of God.

By the time of St. Louis-Marie came on the scene, error had crept into teaching as well as practice, and the conditions had become unfavorable for the understanding and diffusion of the devotion to the Blessed Virgin. The situation is better today and we breathe a purer air. Jansenism and Gallicanism no longer pollute our air, and, they effectively having vanished from the firmament of souls, what is left is but a whisper of a breeze in the far distance.

Faith is like the sun that rises towards the noonday; it shines a bright light on new understandings, allowing dogmas to flourish. Try calculating, if you will, how much the Immaculate Conception, papal infallibility, and doctrinal definitions against Naturalism in all its forms, have brought about in clarity, spiritual consolations, and vibrant supernatural life; then, add to it the increase of devotion to the Sacred Heart, the apparitions and pilgrimages of La Salette and Lourdes, the Encyclicals of Leo XIII on the Rosary,[18] and so on, and you will see how, along with *True Devotion*, we now have a better framework for our spiritual life, and how much better prepared we can be to accept its teachings.

This devotion also is better suited to our present needs; for in our daily trials and battles—a prelude to those of the last days—it shows us with an ever-increasing clarity the leading role of her whose task it is to crush the head of that infernal serpent. The devotion to Mary

---

[18] There were twelve: *Supremi apostolatus*, Sep 1, 1883, on the Rosary devotion; *Superiore anno*, Aug 30, 1884, on the recitation of the Rosary; *Quod auctoritate*, Dec 22, 1885, on the extraordinary jubilee; *Vi è ben noto*, Sep 20, 1887, on the Rosary and public life; *Octobri mense*, Sep 22, 1891, on the power and efficacy of the Rosary; *Magnæ Dei Matris*, Sep 8, 1892, on the relation of the Rosary to the Faith; *Lætitiæ sanctæ*, Sep 8, 1893, on commending the devotion to the Rosary; *Jucunda semper expectatione*, Sep 8, 1894, on the Rosary as witness to Mary's intercession; *Adjutricem populi*, Sep 5, 1895, on the Rosary as the way to unity; *Fidentem piumque animum*, Sep 20, 1896, on the Rosary and the Catholic Faith and life; *Augustissimæ Virgini Mariæ*, Sep 12, 1897, on the Confraternity of the Holy Rosary; *Diuturni temporis*, Sep 5, 1898, a summary of teaching on the Rosary.

affirms piety (far too often superficial), and sets it on the fundamental truths of religion; through the holy and beloved slavery, it deals a fatal blow to the lust for independence which, in our day, inspires public and private life, as well as events and ideas. In the end, not by a harsh and austere method, but by the appeals of our Mother, by her love and her tenderness, does the devotion place the entire man under the action of grace and the dependence on Jesus Christ, in such a manner that it comes into harmony with the inclinations that the devotion to the Sacred Heart and the Blessed Virgin have developed in the spiritual temperament of our time.

It is thus understandable how the small work of St. Louis-Marie, a real grain of mustard seed, tiny and long buried, nowadays yields a magnificent harvest. We spoke just now of the remarkable movement which, by the inspiration of the Holy Ghost, brings souls to the perfect devotion to Mary. This movement is far from slowing down; it is still growing, powerfully assisted by the lively encouragement of the Bishops, and by the indulgences which the Sovereign Pontiff has seen fit to concede, either to the Confraternity of Mary Queen of Hearts, or to the consecration formulated by St. Louis-Marie.

We came to write this book upon reflecting on the foregoing. We also thought it necessary to preserve the true meaning of the teaching of our good Father de Montfort which some recent publications have been inclined to alter. We shall also point out that *True Devotion*, and to a greater extent, *Secret of Mary*, condenses down to a few pages a voluminous amount of dogmatic truths and spiritual advice. If the mouth has ever spoken of the abundance of the heart, surely it would produce these works, in which St. Louis-Marie draws things old and new from the riches of his treasure. Whether they be ideas and intentions that ripened long ago in his soul or newly-born of the breath of the divine Spirit, everything flows most abundantly from his quick-moving quill; it is the *calamus scribæ velociter scribentis* (Ps 45.2), put in the service of an ardent love, but also one that hastens, because time is short.[19] Hence, it is useful to explain this teaching that St.

---

[19] ♦*TD*, 73: "I have now said many things about the most holy Virgin; but I have many more to say, and there are infinitely more which I shall omit, whether from ignorance,

Louis-Marie has summed up in his short works, and that touches on what is most important in religion. Lastly, we had another motive for undertaking this work: it is that we are now better prepared, as we said above, to understand the nature of this devotion and its importance to Christian asceticism.

A word of explanation about the outline of this volume. A large part is made of the dogmatic truths underpinning the perfect devotion to Mary. Surprising as it may be, we had serious reasons for doing so; for to proceed otherwise would have been, first of all, to part company with our good Father de Montfort. It bears noting that, in what he calls his "little treatise," the first and notable part is devoted to the exposition of dogma. And, lest we beat a retreat, we had to enter the fray to react against Separatism which, in prior centuries, isolated morality and spirituality from dogma. The works of Dom Guéranger, of Msgr. Charles Louis Gay, and of Fr. Frederick William Faber,[20] have contributed greatly to this logical and fruitful reform. They place spirituality under the warm and brilliant light of dogma, giving the splendor and life it deserves. What a contrast their books present against so many others that, being born in the ambiance of Cartesianism, more or less tinged with Quietism, Baïanism or Jansenism, sets spirituality down in Winter—cold and impersonal! We cannot read them without getting the impression of some undefinable tedium that never fails to remind us of their analyses of minutiae, oh-so-accurate portraits, or obsessions with certain practical details.[21] Needless to say, this separation of morality from spirituality is laden with implications particularly opposed to the insights and methods of St. Louis-Marie.

Ignorance is what proceeds from a systematic omission of dogma, followed by the weakening of faith and Christian life in all its forms;

---

inability, or want of time." ¦ St. Louis-Marie died in 1716 at the age of 43. ¦

[20] ◆In their wake, there has been a veritable blossoming of good works. We should give a place of honor to those of Sauvé, wherein dogma and spirituality are combined for the greater good of the faithful, and received with great satisfaction, judging by the success of *Élévations dogmatiques*, his multi-volume work.

[21] ◆Compare the treatment of spirituality in the work of Msgr. Gay with those of some rather fashionable authors. They often contain the same considerations; but in the former there is a warmth of sunlight that is lacking in the latter.

notwithstanding the exterior activity so salubrious to our customs and habits, so favorable to our works of zeal and charity. In times past, heresy stressed faith at the expense of works; now we seem to emphasize works far too much and pay faith not enough attention. And while some Christians are content with religious opinions, still far too many are satisfied with mere impressions, sentimentality, nuances, and capriciousness!

It is true that one may object placing undue importance in practice. Well, without doubt, we must not confine ourselves to speculation, or profess a dead faith, or turn intellectualism into piety. But this reproach, most assuredly, we cannot level against St. Louis-Marie; for he believed (and we, with him) that we love as we see,[22] and that we act as we love; that if knowledge is not the measure of holiness, it is its first principle and a powerful means of sanctification, and that a certain degree of acquired or infused knowledge is necessary to progress towards divine union.

We believe that the truly practical formation of souls is in strengthening the interior life in them, by means of an enlightened faith, through which they gain the knowledge and taste for things supernatural. None would contest the idea that a well-developed form of Christian instruction is most helpful in this regard. Now then, this interior life will produce actions, aspirations, virtues, and various practices, sometimes spontaneously, sometimes after some short or prolonged cultivation. Such is how the sap in a tree makes buds bloom and nourishes fruits. But what is the making of paper flowers compared to this natural blossoming, which is true and fertile because it is derived from a vital principle? It is but an external adornment, an ephemeral illusion; for these flowers, exposed to the open air, will piteously disappear into the fog or be blown away by the least whiff of a breeze. This is the image of what happens, if, in the formation of souls, we see fit only to provide them with insignificant rules, exercises, and practices. Absent enlightened faith, absent deep conviction, there can be no interior life, and all our effort will be like artificial flowering: they will last briefer than paper roses and will most certainly not bear

---

[22] ¦¦ St. Thomas, *Summa*, 1.19.5c: | ◆*Voluntas sequitur intellectum*, "the will proceeds from the intellect."

fruit. And when these souls are out of the special and peaceful elements provided by a residence or college, seminary or novitiate, such state of life and such direction, practices, and regulations either will disappear under the fog of tedium and the slightest sign of trouble or they will be carried away by the sudden waft of trials and temptations.

In wishing us to be reinvigorated in the grace of Baptism and to have our souls fortified through his devotion, St. Louis-Marie asks of us that we make it an interior exercise and that it should go so far as to involve the will, to which end, he begins by shining a light on our faith in summing up the theology of the Blessed Virgin.

We indicated what is the outline for this book at the beginning of the preface. We shall study in succession the end, the means, the practices, and the application of the devotion to the Blessed Virgin.

This book is intended, first of all, for ecclesiastics, who, by their state of life, are dedicated to the study of theology; then for all those who, in monasteries, convents, and houses of instruction, are entrusted with the spiritual formation of souls and wish to inculcate in them the devotion to the Blessed Virgin; finally, to the faithful who, in their religious life or in the world, love to read and wish to learn about works on piety.

We hesitated to undertake this volume for a long time; but the encouragements of our Superiors, the obligations inherent in our ministry, and the prayers of those who expressed an interest in the work, have finally made us decide to proceed and complete it. By the grace of God, we were given the opportunity to benefit from the advice of several eminent theologians and renowned spiritual directors. It would only be just to express here our gratitude to them.

In conclusion, we express one hope. However much it be for us the utmost assurance to submit this book to the judgment of the Holy See, and be it ever our concern to remain faithful to the mind of our good Father de Montfort, we pray to the Blessed Virgin most holy, that, through the merits of St. Louis-Marie, her devoted servant, she may concede us the joy of knowing that by this commentary on his writings we have neither weakened their force nor diminished their unction.

Saint-Laurent-sur-Sèvre.
On the Feast of the Annunciation, 1901.

PART I:

OUR END, OR JESUS CHRIST LIVING IN US

CHAPTER 1:

JESUS CHRIST

> Et vidimus gloriam ejus, gloriam quasi
> Unigeniti a Patre, plenum gratiæ et Veritatis.
>
> And we saw His glory, the glory as it were
> of the Only-Begotten of the Father, full of
> grace and truth (Jn 1.14).

esus Christ living in us through grace, according to the word of St. Paul: *Vivit vero in me Christus* (Gal 2:20): This is the fundamental principle underpinning the devotion taught by St. Louis-Marie Grignion de Montfort, and the end to which it aims. The Holy See so states officially in the examination of his writings that preceded his Beatification,[1] and the reader of *True Devotion* will have no doubt in this regard; for St. Louis-Marie writes: "All our perfection consists in being conformed to Jesus Christ,"[2] and states that the devotion to Our Blessed Lady was established "surely to provide more perfectly the devotion to Jesus Christ, and to put forward an easy and secure means for finding Him."[3]

Although he repeatedly stresses this truth, it is mainly of Mary's Motherhood, her prerogatives, and her role in the formation of Christ in us, that St. Louis-Marie wants to speak. He says that his aim is not to write a methodical and complete work on the supernatural life, but

---

[1] "Œuvres," c. 2, in Church, S.C.P., *Analecta juris pontificii*, 1855, 1 (4):742: "The impression we get from the writings of ... Louis de Montfort is very different from that of ordinary works. We sense an interior unction, a peace, and a consolation found uniquely in the writings of souls whom God has favored with particular inspirations. The principal foundation of his teaching is the life of Jesus Christ in the soul regenerated by Baptism."

[2] ✦*TD*, 82.

[3] ✦*TD*, 38.

to teach us a special form of devotion to the Blessed Virgin, where we may find a means to unite ourselves to Christ Jesus, illustrating why he is particularly concerned with truths that refer more specifically to this proximate end.

But we cannot discuss his teaching, without first examining what it means to have "Christ living in us." We are driven to do so, given the ignorance of a multitude of the faithful on the nature of this doctrine, and the errors which sometimes creeps into the exposition of the truth.

Let us first show who Jesus Christ is, before seeking the answer to how He lives in us. The subject certainly is vast, but we can narrow it down to a certain specificity, according to the particular point of view that concerns us. What is this life of Christ in us? It is the life of the divine in our souls, here below by grace and, afterwards, in glory. We take as our theme St. Paul's words: *Gratia autem Dei vita æterna in Christo*, "the grace of God is eternal life in Christ" (Rom 6.23). We shall explain that eternal life, divine life, is in Christ, before we go on to study our participation in it. In this first chapter, our topics will be Jesus Christ, and His three-fold fulness of grace: the grace of union, grace sanctifying, and capital grace.

ARTICLE 1: THE GRACE OF UNION

Who is Jesus Christ? He is the Son of God made Man. Down through the centuries, the lips of children have repeated this answer from the *Catechism of Trent*, simple in its assertion, teaching them a mystery before which the Angels themselves bow down in adoration.[4] Now, how can they unite the two ends contained in the Gospel verse: *Et Verbum caro factum est*, "and the Word was made flesh" (Jn 1.14). The Logos, or Word, that is, the Only-Begotten Son of God, is His splendor and the figure of His substance. He is equal to the Father and, like Him, is God, since the Father and the Son have one and the same divine nature. *Omnia per ipsum facta sunt*, "all things were made by Him" (Jn 1.3), says St. John in the prologue to his Gospel which ought to be read in its entirety. We contemplate on the Word with Him in the bosom of the Divinity; but our human nature, being that we are

---

[4] Ps 97.7.

made of a soul and a body of flesh united, makes us focus on the word "flesh," as if we belonged to that extreme end, where creatures have no rational soul at all. It is by design and with a certain emphasis that St. John, instead of saying, "the Word *became* man," writes, "the Word *was made* flesh," in order that we may understand better how far the Son of God humbled Himself, and how, by being incarnated, the Logos, in the words of St. Paul, *semetipsum exinanivit*, "emptied Him self" (Phil 2.7).

The two ends, God and Man, are come together, and not only united and linked, but also without confusion; for in Jesus, born of the Virgin Mary, the divine and human natures are united in one Person. What does it mean to say "one Person"? It means that in Jesus Christ there was no other "I" than that of the Word, the eternal Son of the Father. It is the same divine Word Who possessed the Body and Soul; He Who, without ever separating His Divinity from His Humanity, acted at times as Man, other times as God. As Man, He prayed, He suffered, He died; but it was the prayer, the sufferings, and the death of God. Consequently, all His acts carry infinite value. As God, He multiplied the loaves, raised the dead. These are the work of the divine Word, acting with the help of the human nature that is united in Him, the very same Whom St. John says, *that we have heard, that we have seen with our eyes, that we have looked upon, and our hands have handled, that was the word of life from the beginning* (1 Jn 1.1). These words affirm the truth of the human nature, visible and sensible, that the Word had taken; but the glory of His Divinity burst out in a thousand ways for all to see. It was said that none of the Prophets had spoken like Him, nor had any done such wonders as He did; and for all *who are born, not of blood, nor of the will of the flesh, His glory was of the Only-Begotten of the Father* (Jn 1.13, 14).

But we, O Jesus, who have come in the latter days, long after Your earthly life had ended, although our ears have not heard You, nor our eyes seen You in the flesh, nor our hands touched You, O living Word, divine life has been manifested in us, since we know You and we gaze on You with the eyes of a soul illuminated by faith. You tell us: *Beati qui non viderunt et crediderunt*, "blessed are they that have not seen, and have believed." (Jn 20.29). Indeed, to us, 'tis a joy to believe without having seen. Increase this our faith, O Lord, so that we may triumph over the world by believing more firmly and more effectively that You are the Son of God.[5]

It is important for us to consider especially in the mystery that, in Jesus, is grace all excelling, meaning that grace is in Him to the degree most eminent; in its exemplar, most perfect, in the most absolute sense of the word.

"Grace," *gratum faciens*, means what is rendered pleasing to God.[6] Now, is it not of Christ that the Father testifies, saying: *This is My beloved Son, in Whom I am well pleased* (Mt 3.17)? Christ is unrivaled in the eyes of God because He is the Only-Begotten Son.

But if by "grace" we understand a gift freely given, *donum gratuitum*, it, too, is grace all excelling, that is, the supreme and absolutely gratuitous gift, as is the Incarnation; for in it, God gives Himself to the creature and nowhere else does He so act. No Angel, indeed, no man, no being created or able to be created by Almighty God, since he is a creature, can, by his natural powers know God in Himself and see Him face to face, possess Him and unite with Him through charity. Thus, if it pleases God to communicate Himself to the creature, by faith here below or by the Beatific Vision, in glory—if He were to render the creature, to the extent that he is capable of being, a partaker of His divine nature, that would be a grace, a supreme and gratuitous gift which he cannot deserve, and of which he would not know naturally even to have the thought or the desire. A plant would sooner rise to the sensitive life, the animal to the intellectual and affective of the highest and most intense, or man to the angelic of the most richly endowed, than some creature, his natural excellence be ever so great, would possess divine life. Properly speaking, that is what is meant by the supernatural; that is, that it surpasses the powers and aspirations of every created nature.

What can we say about the incomparable gift of the Incarnation? O what grace it is for human nature to be united with God to the point that it becomes in Him one divine Person! It is truly a gratuitous gift

---

[5] ◆1 Jn 5.5.

[6] Rom 13.1: *Quæ a Deo sunt, ordinata sunt,* "those things that are of God are well ordered," as rendered by St. Thomas, *Summa,* 1-2.111.1c.

that even the Soul of Christ herself could not have merited,
right, because she is a creature, nor in fact, because she posse
union from the first moment of her existence. Once again, the Incarnation belongs to the supernatural absolute; it is grace at its highest
expression; for here the gift is the *fullness of the Divinity*.

O Jesus, God is indeed in You in a singular way! Not only do You
participate in divine life, as all the righteous do, but You also possess
it entirely. Not only are You deified—are like God, but also You are a
Person in God. And though it may be said of the Prophets, the Apostles, the Saints in general, that they are "men of God," and because
they are consecrated and subject to Him, they act as His representatives and sometimes are His instruments, You alone, O Christ, are the
God-Man.

It is the fullness of this grace of divine union that St. Paul
proclaims when he says: *Quia in ipso inhabitat omnis plenitudo divi-
nitatis corporaliter,* "for in Christ dwelleth all the fulness of the
Godhead *corporeally*" (Col 2.9), on which St. Thomas has much to say.[7]

God is in all beings, and every creature is, in certain ways, an
image of His perfections; but none has His divine nature. We also
know that, by the effects of His grace, God dwells in the righteous in
a supernatural way; but the fullness of Divinity is not in them. Why?
Because the soul acquires not through grace the same substance as
God; neither does she and He form one person, as in the case of the
Word and the human nature of Christ. Lastly, God dwells not corporeally in the righteous. In a certain way the body of the righteous may
participate in the effects of grace, but grace itself acts on the soul; for
it is the soul that knows and loves God, in Whom is eternal life.[8] In
Jesus, on the contrary, the Body itself, as well as the Soul, is united to
the Person of the Word.

Such is how we understand the grace of union in Christ, and what
elevates Him above all rank, to an order that He alone may fulfill, to
that righthand side of the Father where He sits, for He is God. Every
knee bends before Him, on the earth, in Heaven, and even in Hell; but

---

[7] ♦ ¦ St. Thomas, *ad Colossenses,* c. 2, §§96-97, *Opera,* 21:395-396. ¦
[8] 1 Jn 5.20.

those who adore Him repeat this praise: *Gratias agimus tibi propter magnam gloriam tuam*, "we give Thee thanks for Thy great glory"; for we know this glory, and it is none other than that of the only Son of the Father: *Et vidimus gloriam ejus, gloriam quasi Unigeniti a Patre* (Jn 1.14). Such is the first fullness of grace in Jesus Christ.

ARTICLE 2: THE HABITUAL GRACE OF CHRIST

Along with the grace of hypostatic union, there is in Jesus Christ another profound article of faith, another fullness, the fullness of habitual or sanctifying grace. In the Incarnation, the divine and human natures are united in one Person, but they remain distinct; for in this union (the greatest that can ever exist between God and a created nature), Jesus Christ, the Son of God and our Mediator, must have a special and supereminent holiness. His Soul must be, to the highest degree possible, holy in herself and in her powers; but since, by nature, she is a human soul, it was necessary that she be divine by participation; that is, by means of sanctifying or habitual grace.[9]

Grace was thus given to the Soul of Christ; the same grace that we receive, that quality, or manner of being supernatural which unites us to God and makes us like unto Him. For Jesus, as for us, this gift is grace, as we said above, either because it makes us pleasing to God, or because it exceeds all created nature. We hasten to point out that between Jesus and us there is, among many others, this difference: that we possess this sanctifying grace only in part and He, the fullness thereof. *And we saw His glory*, says St. John, *plenum gratiæ et veritatis*, "full of grace and truth" (Jn 1.14).

Full of grace! Scripture tells us that certain righteous people are full of grace or full of the Holy Ghost, meaning that they are filled according to their capacity, be it more or less ample, and according to their special vocation, without any of them exhausting the measure of what a human soul may receive.

Mary, the most blessed, was greeted by the Angel with the salutation "full of grace." It was the fullness of her capacity, which,

---

[9] ♦St. Thomas, *Summa*, 3.7.1 ad 1.

because of her divine motherhood, was unique and incomparably beyond the capacity of other creatures. "She is full of grace," said St. Antoninus of Florence, "in the sense that, in an excellent manner, she possesses all the general and special graces which God has ever endowed, be it to men or Angels; she has graces that no creature other than she has ever received; she receives all the gifts of God to the greatest extent, and in all their perfection, which a simple creature is capable of receiving; and above all, she carries within her the Uncreated Grace, that is God, full and complete"[10] in Jesus Christ, Whom she gives birth for the benefit of the world entire. In sum, "the plenitude of grace in Mary is such that its effects overflow upon all of mankind."[11]

The fullness of grace in Christ is of a different order. He was not only filled with grace to a surpassing degree, but He also had every grace, that is to say the fullness of its perfection and its effects, as befitting the God-Man, Redeemer of all mankind, and principle of all sanctification.[12] Of grace, He lacked nothing, not even that final perfection which is glory, since, from the first moment of her existence, the Soul of Jesus saw God face to face. How wonderful it was! She was both at the end and on the way; in her, coexisted the fullness of grace and of glory. Thus, in Mary's womb, as during her mortal life and even

---

[10] ¦¦ The four-fold fullness of grace in St. Antoninus, *Summa*, 4.15.15, 16, 4:1008-1013: "(1) Invenisti gratiam specialem et generalem quidem, quia gratia, quæ fuit et est in omnibus electis in ipsa fuit, scilicet gratum faciens. ... (2) Invenit gratiam, ut sit apud Deum, idest excellentiori gloria quam aliæ creaturæ. (3) Sola autem Virgo Maria plena gratia fuit inter puras creaturas quia majorem gratiam habere non potuit. ... Est plena omni gratia cujus particeps potest esse omnis pura creatura. (4) Invenisti gratiam increatam idest Deum, et in illa et cum illa omnem creaturam." | ♦Let us also cite the remarkable words of St. Thomas, "Super Joannem," Lect. 10.1, *Opera*, 19:722.1: "Now one fullness is that of sufficiency, by which one is able to perform acts that are meritorious and excellent, as in the case of Stephen. Again, there is a fullness of superabundance, by which the Blessed Virgin excels all the Saints because of the eminence and abundance of her merits. Further, there is a fullness of efficiency and overflow, which belongs only to the Man Christ as the author of grace."

[11] S. Thomas, Exp. de Ave Maria, *Opera*, 27:200.2: "Beata Virgo plena gratia ... quantum ad refusionem in omnes homines."

[12] ♦Sanctifying grace is a created gift, a supernatural quality and, as such, is not infinite because its existence is limited by the subject in which it is found. This subject here is the Soul of Christ who, though very excellent, is nevertheless a creature. But, as a grace, we can say that sanctifying grace in Jesus is infinite, because it is all that grace may ever be; that is, that in the actual order established by God, it is without measure as to its perfection, without limits as to its effects.

in the horror, torments, and agony of His Passion, Jesus Christ possessed the Beatific Vision. Nevertheless, by a particular disposition of His Will (in one of the most profound mysteries of the Incarnation), He retained the effects of this glory in what we call the upper part of the soul; and it did not radiate freely into His body until after His Resurrection, and more completely at His Ascension. For one brief moment at Tabor,[13] Jesus let slip some part of His glory; and what the three favored Apostles saw was enough to make them drunk with gladness.

We, too, O good Master, *satiabitur cum apparuerit gloria tua*, "shall be satisfied when Thy glory shall appear" (Ps 16.15). But here below, meditating on the incomparable holiness of Your Humanity, with our whole heart, we repeat this acclamation of the Church: *Quoniam Tu solus Sanctus*, "for Thou only art holy." In You, there is the exemplary perfection of which every Saint is but a partial copy, more or less complete. You are the principle of all justice, and it is in living in You that souls are sanctified. — Now we turn to the third fullness that Jesus possesses.

ARTICLE 3: CAPITAL GRACE OF CHRIST

There is in Christ another plenitude, visible to our eyes when we consider Him as Head of the Church,[14] His Mystical Body. As Head, says St. Thomas, we must observe ¦¦ three aspects: | His situation, His perfection, and the virtue or power of His personal action.[15]

In the human body, the head is the highest part. Whence what ranks first in action or superior in situation we call "head," as when we say, "the heads of trees," "head of the movement," "head of the line." Now in Christ, by reason of the union with the Word, His grace precedes all others, towering above them. In this sense, He is our Chief, our Leader, our Head.

The head is even more perfect than the other members of the body, for it brings together in itself all the internal and external

---

[13] Mt 17.1-8, Lk 9.1-8.

[14] Christ's own personal sanctifying grace is the source of grace for all men. It is called capital grace, as He is the *caput Ecclesiæ*. See, St. Thomas, *Summa*, 3.8.5, 3.48.1-6, and his source, St. Anselm, *Cur Deus Homo*, PL 158.359-432. For a historical perspective, see Siemering, "Capital Grace."

[15] ◆St. Thomas, *Summa*, 3.8.1c.

senses, sight, hearing, smell, taste, and touch, and touch alone is common to the other members. If then we add the vital functions that depend on the brain, it is evident that in the head resides a fullness, a perfection of life that is not found in the rest of the body.

By reason of this eminent perfection, the work in which a man has assembled and brought to the highest degree the qualities of all his prior works, is called *chef d'œuvre*, a masterpiece, a capital work. We mortals proceed by graduated trials to produce a "masterpiece." Not God. He conceived and made Christ His perfect type, the Masterpiece of Grace, the realized ideal of all Saints. In Him is the fullness of sanctifying grace, of all the gifts, and of all the virtues that we have but the least part. In this sense also is Jesus Christ our Head.

To the head belongs the vital and dominant influence by which it communicates power, sensibility, and movement to the other members it governs. It was for the purpose of signifying this effective power and this dominant role, and of its establishment and ensuring its proper functioning, that God placed our head in a high position, atop our body, and gave it that fullness of life of which we just spoke.

He who governs, communicates movement, maintains order, manages the functioning of a moral body or society, is extended and receives the name "head." So does Christ, Who (as we shall see shortly) exerts a supernatural influence on all the members of His Mystical Body in order to communicate grace and govern them.

Jesus Christ, therefore, is our Head according to the three-fold aspect. In the Church, others may also receive this appellation, including the Pope, bishops, prelates and priests, but only because they participate in the authority of Christ, and even that, only for a certain time and place. Jesus Christ alone is Head of the whole Church by His own power and authority, for which reason we say that capital grace dwells in Him in its fullness.

Now the discussion on the grace of Christ leads us to the consideration of how we have eternal life in Him: *Gratia autem Dei vita æterna in Christo*–Rom 6.23. After meditating on who Jesus Christ is, let us now see how He lives in us.

CHAPTER 2:

CHRIST LIVING IN US

Per ipsum et cum ipso et in ipso.
(Canon of the Mass)

he mystery of grace is not exclusive to Christ, for God
has predestined Him to be *the firstborn of many brethren*
(Rom 8.29). His fullness should flow down to us; His life, or
rather, Himself, should become our supernatural life, that we may
rightly call ourselves Christian; meaning, the life of Christ.

To explain how Christ lives in us, let us take three simple and profound words that end the Canon of the Mass: *Per ipsum, et cum ipso,
et in ipso*, "through Him, and with Him, and in Him." These sacred
words say the nature, the source, and the effects of grace in our souls.
If by Jesus Christ, with Him, and in Him, in the unity of the Holy
Ghost, all honor and glory is to the Father Almighty, world without
end, the reason is that, just as the three divine Persons are united in
one and the same nature, so also are we one with Christ in the unity
of the same Spirit[1]; that through Christ, with Him, and in Him, we
become children of God, redeemed, sanctified, and ultimately, glorified. This is the honor and glory rendered to God in the Incarnation
and Redemption, as well as in the Eucharistic sacrifice, to which virtue
applies without end.

This outline serves a purpose most useful to us. In the exposition
of the mystery that comprehends the whole economy of grace, we
may first limit our considerations to the ones particularly appropriate

---

[1] ◆Jn 17.22: Et ego claritatem, quam dedisti Mihi, Pater, dedi eis, ut sint unum sicut et
Nos unum sumus, "And the glory which Thou, Father, hast given Me, I have given to
them; that they may be one, as We also are One."

to our goal; then approach the point of view expressed by St. Louis-Marie, in order to be of one mind with him, by becoming acquainted with the essential ideas and formulas characteristic of the spiritual doctrine he set down. The importance of these formulas, already so great by reason of the things they express, is further increased by the fact that, between the dogmatic and the ascetic parts of the devotion he teaches, there exists an intimate correspondence. The formula | "through Him, and with Him, and in Him" | appears in the teaching of St. Louis-Marie as the guiding thread, or the masterpiece of his whole system. If we neglect to explain its dogmatic meaning, keeping it vague, we shall have an insufficient understanding of its ascetic range and we would practically benefit only from mediocre results. Let us quote, among many other similar passages, the few words that give us an overview of the perfect devotion to Mary. Speaking of the interior practice that makes us live in the heart of this devotion, St. Louis-Marie says that it consists in doing "all actions *through* Mary, *with* Mary, *in* Mary, and *for* Mary, so that we may do them all more perfectly *through* Jesus, *with* Jesus, *in* Jesus, and *for* Jesus."[2] Further on, we shall study how Mary is a means towards the union with Jesus; but here, we shall consider the union itself, which is intended to be our end. We first show that we have grace *through Christ, with Christ, and in Christ*, and consequently what it means to act *through Him, with Him, and in Him.*

ARTICLE 1: THROUGH HIM

§1. THE MEANING OF THE PREPOSITIONS "BY" OR "THROUGH"

Ordinarily, *"by"* || or *"through"* | denotes a cause or principle of an intermediary action, that is, the means.[3] The agent may find the means in himself, as he would a perfection, a faculty, or a property inherent in his nature. Thus, we say, "God created the world *by* His power," "man thinks *by* his intellect," "the sun makes plants grow

---

[2] *TD*, 178.

[3] ♦See, St. Thomas, *Summa*, 1.36.3c. || In English we say "by" if describing the action of an agent; and "through," if the cause or inducement for the action; whence, for the latter, the idiomatically more correct "by reason of"; or, in the language of Common Law, "in right of." Unfortunately, Latin and French use the same word for both: *per* and *par*, respectively, causing some confusion in certain translations. |

through its light." But the means also may be exterior to the agent; for example, an instrument, a mediator, as in the following expressions: "to talk *by* telephone," "to justify *by* grace," "to issue an order *through* his minister."

The word "*by*" ¦¦ or "*through*" | also denotes the cause of an act, be it physical or moral, as in these propositions: "The ball rolls *by* reason of the impulse received," "I act *through* the command of," "he is motivated *by* the love of gain."

We shall soon see the application of the various meanings of the words "*by*" ¦¦ and "*through*." | Now, let us see how grace comes to us *through* Christ. So as to better understand the divine realities, we shall avoid baby-talks or explaining them unsatisfyingly, by resorting to the two simple and profound images in sacred Scripture: the vine and the body.

§2. THE GRACE OF JESUS CHRIST

Grace comes to us through Jesus Christ. *Ego sum vitis, vos palmites,* "I am the vine; you, the branches." (Jn 15.5).

Just as the vine or the trunk has a visible part above ground, and its hidden parts, the roots, burrowing in the earth to draw the sap it needs to be sustained; so also Jesus Christ, by His human nature, manifests Himself to our senses, and by what is in Him more profound and intimate, that is to say His personality, He plunges into God, is God; and in this hypostatic union, He in His Humanity draws the divine sap, that is, sanctifying grace, of which, as we have seen, He has the fullness.[4]

But the trunk exists not in isolation. There are branches: *Et vos palmites.* Branches draw not sap directly from the earth. The trunk communicates it to them. It acts as a conduit, or intermediary, between them and the earth. Similarly, all grace comes from God through Christ, Who merits it by His Passion and death: *Et de plenitudine ejus nos omnes accepimus,* "and of His fulness we all have

---

[4] ✦Do not take from the above that the Soul of Christ was sanctified by the hypostatic union alone. We see in the previous chapter how the grace of union and the habitual grace are distinct in Christ. We merely wish to say that the latter is the consequence of the former, as St. Thomas, *Summa,* 3.7.13c, writes: *Gratia habitualis Christi intelligitur ut consequens hanc unionem, sicut splendor solem,* "the habitual grace of Christ is understood to follow this union, as light follows the sun."

received" (Jn 1.16). He alone is the Mediator by nature, since being both God and Man, He unites man to God. In truth, we may call others, such as pontiffs of the Old or New Law, or the Blessed Virgin, "mediators," but only secondarily; that is, in union with Christ and under His dependence. Save for Mary's, their delegation is not universal.

Let us observe, however, that the words, "grace comes to us through Christ," mean not merely that grace passes first through Him, then comes to us; rather, that they serve to indicate the order followed for its communication, for they express (and note this well) that this communication is effected by the action of Christ. In other words, that He is the efficient cause; that is to say, He is the producer of grace, as follows:

1. As God, Christ is the primary cause. When we say, "grace is given to us *by* Jesus Christ," we take it to mean that He produces it in us, that He is the principle of our supernatural life. This is the second meaning of the preposition we explained above;

2. As Man, Christ is not the primary cause of grace, for only God, says St. Thomas, can deify a creature, just as only fire can set a body on fire.[5] But the Word communicates grace to us by His Humanity, inseparable from His Divinity, as if by a most perfect organ or instrument. To receive grace "through Christ" as Man, is also to receive it through an intermediary, a means, a mediator;

3. This mediator gives not only grace as from an instrument, but that He merits grace by His Passion, and we know that in Heaven He ceases not to pray that we should obtain it.[6]

This idea of the influence of Christ in the communication of divine life is well expressed in the image of the vine, for the vital principle dwelling in the trunk passes the sap to the branches; but the operation is even more pronounced in the Mystical Body. We begin by quoting the Epistle of St. Paul to the Ephesians: *Doing the truth* (of faith) *in charity, we may in all things grow up in Him Who is the head,*

---

[5] St. Thomas, *Summa*, 1-2.112.1c.

[6] ◆In the language of the Scholastics, as God, Christ is the principal efficacious cause of grace; as Man, its instrumental cause; as God-Man, its moral or meritorious cause.

even Christ, from Whom the whole body (of the faithful), *being compacted and fitly joined together, by what every joint supplieth, according to the operation in the measure of every part, maketh increase of the body, unto the edifying of itself in charity.*[7]

This Mystical Body of Christ, which the Apostle dissects like an organic body to show us the bones and sinews, is the Church with the different ministries instituted by the Savior Himself, along with all the graces, Sacraments, and means of sanctification that flow from them. It is Christ Himself Who acts in an invisible way by His visible ministers, by their action and by the mysteries they re-present in a manner discernible by the senses. He acts, not only because He merits them and unendingly prays in Heaven, offering God the Father His glorious wounds, but also because He is our efficacious inflowing cause. Though it be full of mystery, this influence of Christ in His Church is certainly real. It reaches its highest degree in the Eucharist, where He is present substantially and whose proper effect is to unite us to Christ, to preserve and increase divine life in our souls. There is more. Besides the Sacraments, it is through the Humanity of Jesus Christ, the instrumental cause of grace, that all supernatural life comes to us. Whether it be things of the earth or of Heaven, it is Jesus Who is the Sun over the City of God; it is He Who shines on us here below with grace, and up there with glory; it is He, Who is the Head of all mankind and also the Head of Angels.

"Now," says Hugh of St. Victor, "just as the spirit of man, through the medium of the head, descends to quicken the members, so the Holy Ghost comes to Christians by Christ ... and there is but one body in one Spirit."[8] And, commenting on the words of St. Paul: *Vivit vero in me Christus*–Gal 2.20, Fr. Domenico Palmieri sums up the teaching of the Fathers by saying: "*Christ liveth in me*, that is to say, by the Holy Ghost, the internal principle of my thoughts and my actions."[9]

---

[7] ✦Eph 4.15-16: Veritatem autem facientes in charitate, crescamus in illo per omnia, qui est caput, Christus. Ex quo totum corpus com pactum, et connexum per omnem juncturam subministrationis, secundum operationem in mensuram uniuscujusque membri augmentum corporis facit in ædificationem sui in caritate.

[8] ✦Hugh of St. Victor, *De Sacramentis*, 2.2.1, ¦¦ PL 176.415D: "Sicut spiritus hominis mediante capite ad membra vivificanda descendit sic Spiritus sanctus per Christum venit ad Christianos. ... Et constat unum corpus ex capite et membris et in uno corpore Spiritus unus." ¦

[9] ✦Palmieri, *In ad Galatas*, ¦¦ 2.20, 89-90: "Vivit enim in me Christus, Christus

Something happens to the Christian similar to what the Gospel shows us in Christ. In the unity of Person, it was the Word alone that possessed the human nature He took, but He governed it and made it act by His Spirit. And it is also through His divine Spirit that Christ quickens us and governs us. As God, He sends us the Holy Ghost of authority; as Man, He gives Him to us, as we said above, in the manner of an instrument and as an organ of the Word.[10]

How true and full of meaning is this image of the body which St. Paul uses and St. Louis-Marie often recalls in his writings! No, the Church of Christ is not a body of flesh, neither is she a moral body like some association, but a society of the supernatural order. Besides the external bonds that unite her members, she has an interior, spiritual, and hidden life that binds the faithful one to the other, and unites them to their Head. To express this *intimate and secret* union the Church is called, not a moral body, but the *Mystical* Body of Christ.

§3. TO ACT THROUGH CHRIST

Here begins this ebb and flow, this reciprocity of relationships which forms the basis of the system espoused by St. Louis-Marie. God comes to us by Christ, and through Him we go to God. It is through Christ that grace comes to us; we will live and act through Him, in order to do so in accordance with grace.

How do we act through Christ? In the sense that it is He Who makes us act, Who moves us, and governs us, every time we follow the movement of His Spirit, the impulse of grace. In contrast, if we are moved by ¦ our own selfish mind, or what in the French school of spirituality is called *"l'esprit propre"*[11]; ¦ if we yield to the impulse of our disordered passions, be they great or small, or to the insinuations of the evil spirit, then we act on our own or by the spirit of evil.

Secondly, to act through Christ is to do so by His virtue, that is to say by that supernatural power that He communicates to us along

---

principium est interius, per Spiritum suum, mearum cogitationum et actionum." ¦

[10] ♦When we say that Jesus governs us, quickens us, gives us grace through the Holy Ghost, we must not believe that this divine Spirit is an instrument; for He is God, and as such, the first and foremost cause of grace; but the word "by" indicates that He is intermediate, in the sense that He is a principle proceeding from a principle *principium de principio*, and that He proceeds from the Father and the Son. (St. Thomas, *Summa*, 1.45.6 ad 2).

[11] Cf. Ribet, *L'Ascetique*, 7, 359.

with grace, either by means of the infused virtues and the gifts of the Holy Ghost, or even by a transitory movement, if we be in the state of sin.

Thirdly, we act through Christ, our Mediator, our *way* (Jn 14.6), when we go to God the Father through Him, when we seek His mediation by relying on His merits, when we listen to His doctrine and follow His precepts. In short, the phrase "to act through Christ" may be understood, as we have explained, as the efficient cause or the means.

O Jesus, our Divine Mediator, who is there besides You? What can we do without You? All grace comes through You; and whosoever departs from You, finds neither lasting beauty, nor wholesome good, nor true, full, and fortifying joy. When You are not the principle of our life and our actions, when we ascribe not all to You that we may retrace the way to God, we slip off the path, we go astray, and then comes failure, followed by excesses and disorders, and finally sin itself.

ARTICLE 2: WITH HIM

§1. CO-OPERATIVE GRACE

"Through Him," we said, is the efficient cause or, more often, the means; "with Him" is the association and continuity of action. Let us go into detail on the meanings of this locution.

"Through Him" is the grace that excites the mind[12] or motor impulse to which I obey; but "with Him" is co-operative grace which

---

[12] "Grâce," *EC*, 12:552.1: "In general, grace may be classified as external and interior. The first includes all external help that may make man do good, such as the law of God, the teaching and examples of Jesus Christ, the preaching of the Gospel, etc.; the second, touches man interiorly, inspiring him to good thoughts, holy desires, pious resolutions, etc. Interior grace is divided into habitual grace and actual grace. ... Habitual grace, also called justifying and sanctifying grace, is a supernatural quality that resides in our soul, making us pleasing in the sight of God and worthy of eternal blessedness. We retain it so long as we do not commit mortal sin, which alone can strip us of it. Actual grace is every temporary inspiration that calls us to do good. It is an operation of God by which He enlightens our mind and moves our will, e.g., to do a good deed, to resolve to fulfill a precept, to overcome a temptation, etc. Actual grace is further divided into (i) prevenient grace, which excites the mind, and whose effect, says the Council of Trent [Sess., 6, Justification, c. 5, 32], is to make us long for the good; (ii) operative or concomitant grace, which, according to the same Council, helps us to achieve the desired good; and (iii) subsequent grace, which makes us persevere in the good accomplished." Cf. St. Thomas, *Summa*, 1-2.111.2c, 3c; Pohle, "Grace," *TCE*, 6:689-710; Meinert, *Love of God*, c. 1, n.p.

helps me to do what God inspires me to do, and my action must accord with it.

"Through Him" is sanctifying grace, which comes into my soul, justifies and deifies her; "with Him" is the permanence of this grace; it is God Who dwells in me.

"Through Him" is the path that the Mediator opens before me; "with Him" is His company during the journey, because He leaves me not, after having acted in me.

Thus "with" continues "by" ¦¦ or "through" | and completes it; and that explains why "with" often replaces "through," when it refers to a means. Indeed, we say: "To look with a telescope," "carve with a knife," "with his great intelligence, he will quickly grasp this question," and so on.

§2. ACTUAL GRACE

We may see the purpose of this expression *cum ipso*, "with Him," which is added to *per ipsum*, "through Him." Let us consider more carefully the facts on which the different interpretations set out above are based.

In the vineyard, branches live through the trunk, but also with it. If they be separated from it, they would wither and die.[13] Now, let us turn our attention to the body. Should not the head stay with the members? If the head, even for one brief moment, interrupts all communication with them, life will soon depart.

This continuity of action, this permanent association, which here the word "with" expresses, is found in causes in which the effect lasts only as long as they act.[14] I build a house, I paint a picture, and though I walk away or die, the house or painting still exists outside of me. The child receives life from his ¦¦ father and | mother and can live, after birth, outside her womb and without her. The Mediator can depart when His mission is over; His work is done and it remains. When the sun goes down, the sky is no longer lit. When the soul leaves, the body has no more life, having lost the thing that animates it. It is to these

---

[13] ♦Jn 15.4, 6: As the branch cannot bear fruit of itself, unless it abide in the vine, so neither can you, unless you abide in Me. If anyone abide not in Me, he shall be cast forth as a branch.

[14] ♦In philosophy they are called *formæ assistentes*, ¦¦ or "attendant forms." See, Suárez, *Disp.* 15.5.1, *Opera*, 25:517.2 |

kinds of causes that we attribute God's action in Creation. God creates by an act of His Will, and He continues to create; for if He no longer sustains creatures, they would fall back into nothingness.

The same goes for the supernatural life of the soul. Sanctifying grace is a form, a permanent quality made by God Who that endures. Should He depart from us, no longer dwelling in us; should sin separate us from our divine Head, supernatural life would be extinguished at once, and our soul would be dead to grace.

To be with Christ, therefore, is not only to be at His side where He is; it is to be in the communion of life and action with Him, to participate in His grace and, and, afterwards, in His glory. "A blind man in the sunshine," says St. Augustine, "has the sun present to him, but is himself absent from the sun,"[15] for his eyes are shut and he knows not what joy there is in light. He who receives the sacred Host, but participates not in the life of Christ and opens not to His grace, is he "with Jesus," in the fullest sense of the word? No, he surely is not.

Need we consider more than just habitual grace, that is, look to those aids that we call actual graces? In truth, they do not flow without end and Jesus Christ does not influence our souls continuously. Even so, since without Jesus we can do nothing,[16] He must be with us in all our actions and we must abide by Him through our faithful cooperation. Jesus promises us this permanent help, when He says: *And behold, I am with you all days, even to the consummation of the world* (Mt 28.20). He is there in the Eucharist. He is there in the sanctifying grace by which He lives with us and in us. He is there through the influence that He exercises as Head of His members.[17]

---

[15] ✦St. Augustin, *In Joannis*, Tr. 3.5, ¦¦ PL 35.1398 : "Lux non est absens, sed vos absentes estis a luce. Cæcus in sole præsentem habet solem, sed absens est ipse soli." |

[16] Jn 15.5.

[17] ✦Franzelin, *De Verbo incarnato*, Th. 41, 4.2, 415-416: "Christ is not a Head separate, but is present to His body and by His Divinity, and by His Humanity. This is just as true for the Church Triumphant in Heaven, as for the Church Militant on earth. No doubt, the conditions of this presence are not the same there and here; but they are in accord with the various states of the Church. In Heaven, Christ is in His glory, for it is the state that befits the Church Triumphant; the Church Militant possesses Him as a perpetual and universal Victim on every altar. There He offers Himself, as the Head united to His Mystical Body; there He makes himself our food, in order to produce the internal union of the members among themselves and with Him."

❖

"With him," is the expression denoting Christian life where Jesus, the Emmanuel, that is to say God with us, is both our way and our companion: *Se nascens dedit socium*, "by birth, He was our kin."[18] What power and consolation it is to be able to say "with Him" in our every state, be it joy or sorrow, hale or infirm, or even death! He passes not by. He goes not away. He is the Christ Who was yesterday, Who is today, and Who remains forever more. He repents not of His gifts, especially the gift of Himself. He abides in us, for He says as much; but He also presses us to be with Him: *Abide in me. ... Abide in my love* (Jn 15.4, 9). As often as we go astray, our actions accord no more with the actions of Jesus.

O good Savior, suffer not that we should ever be separated from You,[19] so that the will You expressed in Your priestly prayer may be fulfilled: *Father, I will that where I am, they also whom Thou hast given Me may be with Me* (Jn 17.24).

In the discussion above on what it means to be "with Christ," we also touched on "acting with Him." Let us now come to the phrase "in Him" which marks the union completed.

ARTICLE 3: IN HIM

At every turn of our preceding discussions, we referred to the union, the perfect union of two beings becoming one; of two lives, one flowing into the other, because union is the culmination of mediation and association, and without union, the mystery of grace cannot be explained fully. "In" expresses the link between the containing to the contained[20]; but among the manifold ways in which one being may contain another, or conversely be contained in it, we shall only point to those relevant to our topic. We begin with the word of Our Lord: *Abide in me, and I in you* (Jn 15.4), then we explain how we are in Christ and how He is in us.

---

[18] St. Thomas, "Verbum supernum," in *Opera*, 29:340. Hymn in honor of Jesus in the Blessed Sacrament written at the request of Pope Urban IV, when he established the Feast of Corpus Christi in 1264. Now sung at Lauds.

[19] *Missale*, §1123, Prayer before Holy Communion: "Fac me tuis semper inhærere mandatis, et a te numquam separari permittas."

[20] ❖St. Thomas, *Summa*, 1.39.8c: "In" denotat proprie habitudinem continentis: "*in* strictly denotes the habitude of one containing."

§1. WE ARE IN CHRIST AS MEMBERS OF HIS MYSTICAL BODY.

These words, *Abide in me, and I in you*, are part of the discourse in which the Savior compares Himself to the vine: *Ego sum vitis vera*, "I am the true vine" (Jn 15.1). He speaks here, say the Fathers, as Man and Head of the Church of which we are members; and we take it that we are in Christ as the branch is in the vine, the member in the body, the part in the whole. It is in this sense that St. Paul says we *are grafted into the good olive tree* (Rom 11.24), which stands for Christ, in the same way we mean when we use the following everyday phrase: "we enter *into* the Church."

What is it that brings us into Christ? Says the Apostle: *One faith, one Baptism* (Eph 4.5). Baptism is the visible and external link; faith, the interior and invisible bond. "But if by faith," says Hugh of St. Victor, "we become members of Christ, it is charity that makes us His living members."[21] Adherence and conjunction are not enough. If the branch is not quickened by the sap, if blood circulates not in the limb, and the vital influence of the head exerts not itself there, it is dead and destined to be cut off.[22]

§2. HE IN US, AND WE IN HIM,
BECAUSE HE IS THE PRINCIPLE OF OUR SUPERNATURAL LIFE

We have seen that Christ produces grace in us, that He extends aid to us and governs us. Now, without excluding the other modes of presence, we can say that Jesus Christ is in us because of His operation and as an efficient cause of our supernatural life.[23] Indeed, a being is

---

[21] Hugh of St. Victor, *De Sacramentis*, 2.2.1, PL 176.416B : "He who has not the Spirit of Christ is not a member of Christ. In body is one spirit. Nothing dead in the body, nothing alive outside the body. Through faith we are made members, through love we are vivified. Through faith we receive union, through charity we receive vivification. Now in the Sacrament, through Baptism we are united; through the Body and Blood of Christ we are vivified. Through Baptism we are made members of the body, but through the Body of Christ we are made participants in vivification."

[22] ♦¦ St. Thomas, Super Joannem, 15.1.3, in *Opera*, 20:256.1 : "*Manete in me ...* per sacramentorum participationem; Ibid. 15.1.5, 20.256.2: *Qui manet in me*, credendo, obediendo, perseverando." Cf. St. Thomas, In Joannis, c. 14 et 15 [Catena aurea], in *Opera*, 17:620.1. |

[23] ♦¦ St. Thomas, In Joannis, 15, *Opera*, 17:620.1 : *Qui manet in me*, credendo, obediendo, perseverando, *et ego in eo*, illuminando, subveniendo, perseverantiam donando, hic, et non alius, fert fructum multum, "*He that abides in Me*, by believing, obeying, persevering, *and I in Him*, by enlightening, assisting, giving perseverance, the same, and none other, brings forth much fruit"; Super Joannem, c. 14, Lect. 5, *Opera*, 20:244.2: *Et ego sum in vobis ...* operando et inhabitando interius per gratiam., "*And I in you, ...* acting

present where his action takes him; if he is not there by his substance, he is at least by his power, for he attains to the place in which he acts, in the same manner as the sun is in a room it lights. For the same reason, and having no regard but for the action of Christ in me, do I understand His word, *and I in you.* His Humanity is not substantially present in me (for His Divinity, as we shall see, does live in our soul in this manner), but it is there by His operation.

This is a first explanation of this word: *Vivit vero in me Christus*, "Christ liveth in me" (Gal 2.20). He lives in me because it is He Who makes me live and act; and in communicating grace to me, it is He Who is the principle of my life and of my supernatural actions.

But if Christ is in me, in the same vein I can say *reciprocally* that I am in Him, insofar as He operates in me. How? In the sense that I am contained by the virtue of His action, *in virtute causæ agentis*,[24] subject to it and as enveloped by it. Many popular phrases have a similar meaning: for example, "having a business in hand," "being in someone's hand," by which we mean not that the person or thing is localized or enclosed in the hand (which is often impossible), but that the physical or moral action, of which the hand is the symbol and the organ, catches, *holds with it*, or contains that person or thing. This is how Christ submits us to Him, contains us (or holds us with Him) by His supernatural action, transforms us by grace, governs us, and

---

and indwelling within you by grace." | This is probably less applicable to the instrumental cause than to the first and principal cause, but let us not forget that the Humanity of Christ is not an ordinary instrument. It is the very perfect organ of the Word: an animated, free instrument, master of its action and inseparably united in the Divinity.

[24] ✦St. Thomas, ad Romanos, 11, Lect. 5, *Opera*, 20:548.1: "In another way 'in' designates a relationship of efficient cause, in whose power it lies to dispose of its effects. In this sense all things are said to be in Him, inasmuch as all things lie under His power and arrangement, according to the Psalm: *In His hand are all the ends of the earth* (Ps 94.4)."— In Joannis, 14, Lect. 5.3, *Opera*, 20:244.2: "The statement, 'and you in me,' means that the disciples are in Christ. For what is protected or shielded by something is said to be in that thing, like something contained in its container. ... And with this meaning it is said that *in Him we live, and move, and are* (Act 17.28). ⁞⁞ Fr. Lhoumeau refers to "In Physic., 4, Lect. 4," and quotes the following text, but it is found nowhere in the works by St. Thomas. Portions of it are found in Paquet's commentary on the *Summa* (*De Deo*, 3.4, 85) |: "Unum dicitur esse in alio sicut mobile aut effectus in primo movente aut in causa; sic res familiæ dicuntur esse in patre familias et creatura in Creatore. — Quod est in loco per applicationem virtutis effectricis aut motivæ, non continetur a loco, sed magis continet et sibi subjicit locum." Cf. "In Physic.," 4, Lect. 4, *Opera*, 22:429-432.

makes us act.[25]

We may also use other everyday expressions, such as: "to be swallowed *in* anger," "to be *in* joy or sorrow," "to enter *into* a space." They
simply express that anger, joy, and movement acting on us; that we
are subject to their action, and that they contain us. But these explanations sufficiently suggest that, except for the time of Holy
Communion,[26] the Humanity of Christ is not substantially present in
us, and that we are not so confined, enclosed, localized in Him. There
is a real and physical link between the Humanity of Christ and us; but
it is a linkage of cause-and-effect. His power or His action reaches us,
and we are in His power, subject to His action.

How can we meditate on this way of being in Jesus, and not recall
his poignant lament: *Jerusalem, Jerusalem, ... how often would I have
gathered together thy children, as the hen doth gather her chickens under her wings, and thou wouldest not?* (Mt 23.37). If it were necessary to
comprehend this, we could do no better than to resort to the words
of St. John, who says that Jesus was about to die in order *to gather
together in one, the children of God that were dispersed* (Jn 11.52)." Ah!
May we never slip out from behind those divine wings so often spoken
by Scripture![27] They are the expressive image of the action that spans
far and wide, gathers and contains all the children of the Church, the
new Jerusalem, with Christ, in the unity of the same Mystical Body.

§3. HE IN US AND WE IN HIM,
AS HE IS THE EXEMPLAR OF OUR STATE OF GRACE.

Jesus Christ not only gives me grace, He is also the exemplary
cause of my supernatural state, and in this respect, I can say that He
is in me by His likeness. When you see a perfect and faithful photograph of someone, we recognize him and say, "It is he." Similarly, we
one can say of the soul in a state of grace: "It is Christ!"

Let us now explain how we are in the image of Christ, that we may

---

[25] ◆Here we could again distinguish the same difference between the principal cause
and the instrumental cause as we pointed out in above on p. 40, and note 23 thereto,
and add, in response, the same observation.
[26] Holy Communion is the *reception* of the Eucharist, the consecrated specie, also called
the Holy Sacrament of the Altar. The verb is "to communicate." The terms are not to be
confused with the ones used by our separated brethren. For some, "communion" is the
whole liturgical rite surrounding the species of bread and wine, not just their reception.
[27] Dt 32.11; Rut 2.12; Ps 16.8, 35.8, 56.2, 60.5, 62.8, 90.4.

better understand this truth.

In works treating of grace we often find quoted this classic for-
mulation from writings long attributed to Dionysius the Areopagite:
"Deification [of the creature] is the likening to God, and union with
Him, as far as it is attainable."[28] We speak not of the likening that we
have by our intelligent nature, and of which sin has not robbed us,
but of that supernatural likeness by grace which God gave man when
He created him, according to the words: *Let Us make man to Our image and likeness* (Gn 1.26). "Habitual grace," says the *Catechism of Trent*,
"is a divine quality inherent in the soul, and, as it were, a certain splendor and light that effaces all the stains of our souls, and renders the
souls themselves brighter and more beautiful,"[29] for which we use the
adjective "sanctifying." Made luminous by grace, the soul thus resembles God, the eternal and uncreated Light.

What is this quality, this splendor which puts the divine likeness
in us? It is a participation in the nature of God, in the life of God. Who
can think of these words, *"participate in the divine nature,"* without
having the sensation of a man walking on a narrow and slippery path,
an abyss to each side? Without the hand-guide,[30] without the guard
rail, that is the infallible teaching of the Church, how can we avoid

---

[28] ♦Ps. Dionysius, *De eccl. hier.*, 1.3, PG 3.375A: "Deificatio est ad Deum, quantum fieri
potest, assimulatio et unio."

[29] ♦Let us use the analogy of a window all blackened and impenetrable to the light.
Clean it, it becomes transparent again; as soon as the light penetrates it, unites with it,
it shines. Such is the image of the soul that mortal sin has rendered unclean and dark;
but grace cleanses her and gives her that inner transparency by which God, uncreated
Light, unites with the soul and makes her like unto Him by making her luminous. See
St. Teresa of Avila, *Interior Castle*, 1.2.1-5, 12-16; Gay, *Life and Virtues*, 1:39-40, and so on.
⁞⁞ *Catechism*, 2.2.49, 185, uses the term "grace" and not "habitual grace." Cf. Trent, Sess.
6, Justification, c. 7, 34: When receiving Baptism, catechumens, "immediately on being
born again, are commanded to preserve it pure and spotless, as the first robe, given
unto them through Jesus Christ, ... that they may bear it before the tribunal of our Lord
Jesus Christ, and may have life everlasting." |

[30] The *chiroplast* (French *guide-main*), invented in 1814 by Johann Logier, and perfected
by Friedrich Kalkbrenner, the foremost pianist in Europe of his time (*Meyers Lexikon*,
10:871; Weitzman, *History*, 150-152). It consists of a sliding wooden frame that guides
the hands and fingers to overcome the difficulty of beginners in retaining the proper
position when playing the piano forte.

falling on one side or the other? Either we believe in God, or the real-ities of grace be nothing but vain chimeras. Let us now explain, as best we can, our participation in the divine nature.[31]

Grace changes not our nature to God's nature, which is incom-municable, and we remain truly men; but God gives us a perfection modeled on His nature,[32] in a manner enabling us, as far as a creature is capable of doing, to execute the operations proper to the Divinity. What is the operation proper to God? It is to know Himself, as He is in Himself, and to love Himself with a love that corresponds to this knowledge. When, therefore, God, by His grace, elevates me above all created nature, and suffers me to know Him and to love Him in Him-self, here below in the order of faith, up there, in the Beatific Vision, then I participate in the divine nature, I have in me the life of God; for *eternal life*, says Our Lord, *is that they may know Thee, the only true God, and Jesus Christ, Whom Thou hast sent*–Jn 17.3.[33] And as a crystal becomes luminous, that is to say, like light, by participating in its na-ture (which makes it shine and illuminate); so do we participate in divine life, when grace allows us to know and love God supernaturally, without us being God, or becoming like God.[34] This is what St. Peter

---

[31] ✦In general, we who participate in the nature of a being receive in ourselves, as much as we have the capacity, something of its nature. At times, this something will be the substance of the being, as in a child who participates in the nature of his parents, re-ceiving from them the substance of his body; or it will be a perfection (e.g., a quality, a faculty) peculiar to the nature of the being, and which will enable us to act like it. In fact, the nature of a being is the principle of the operations which are proper to it; by participating in the nature, I participate in the operations. Thus, the proper nature of man is not to grow up, nor to sense, for those he shares with plants and animals; but to think in the manner that befits a rational soul. If I could communicate to a charming little bird the faculty of thinking, I would make it participate in human nature, without ever making it a man; it would receive nothing from human substance, but only a per-fection, a faculty of my nature. Consider light and fire. The natural action of light is to shine, to illuminate, and that of fire to burn. When, therefore, light comes into a crystal, it makes the crystal participate in its nature, by communicating to it a perfection, a way of being, making the crystal luminous as *it* is; however, the nature of the glass is not changed, it does not become light in substance. The same consideration can be applied to fire and charcoal.

[32] ✦Franzelin characterized this participation by these two words: *formalis et analogica*. Participation is a form or way of being divine. But in God it is His essence; in us, it is an accident. ¦¦ (*De Deo uno*, Th. 16, 195; n. 3, 203). |

[33] ✦Notice that Our Lord says: Eternal life is "to *know* Thee" and not "to *see* Thee": for it begins here below by faith which makes us know God, although we have yet to see it.

[34] ✦To express this participation in the divine nature and this supernatural resem-blance, the Scholastics use the words "deified" and "deiformed."

means when he says that by the promises of Christ, we are made *divinæ consortes naturæ*, "partakers of the divine nature" (2 Pet 1.4). My God, how divine munificence surpasses even our natural aspirations! What ought we to render Jesus for having revealed to us, promised, merited, and so widely dispensed this most precious gift of grace?

Two remarks will complete our summary explanation. First, we speak no more of a moral likeness; that is, a certain conformity of will and action between God and us, but of a physical likeness, since grace truly transforms our soul. Second, grace conforms us to the image of the divine nature. Therefore, we do not bear a likeness to this or that person, but to the whole Trinity, and to Jesus Christ in His Divinity. This image will reach its perfection and will reveal itself in glory. *When He shall appear* (and we come face to face), *we shall be like to Him: because we shall see Him as He is.* (1 Jn 3.2).

If now I no longer look solely to the divine nature in Jesus Christ, but to His divine Person, His quality as Son of the Father, may I attribute to Him being the divine exemplar to which grace makes me conform, the model of which I bear a likeness? Yes, certainly. For if He is the image and likeness and Son of the Father *by nature*, we become children of God and are made in His image *by grace*. Due to His personal character, His quality as Son of God, there are between Him and us particular aspects and bonds of likeness, as St. Paul teaches when he says: *Whom God foreknew, He also predestinated to be made conformable to the image of His Son* (Rom 8.29).

How far does this likeness go? Theology allows us to make it clear, as much as the mutterings of a mere creature can express divine realities. No doubt, there are differences between the filiation of the Word and ours; but there are also analogies that fashion the archetype from the divine, the supreme model for our profane sonship. The *Catechism* summarizes them by saying that Baptism makes us children of God *through adoption and grace*.[35] Let us try to understand what these words mean.

---

[35] *Catechism*, 4.9.9-10, 506.

"By adoption" tells us that there is a difference between our son-ship and the filiation of Jesus Christ. He is the Son by nature, that is to say that He has the one and same nature as the Father; while I, a child of God by grace, preserve my human nature, and am a being distinct and separate from God.[36] "By adoption," means that God takes me as a child by the free choice of His love, which is different from the Father generating His eternal Son by way of an emanation of the intellect.[37]

But if we are children *by adoption*, we are children also *by grace*: which means, no doubt, by the gratuitous mercy of God, but also by participation in His nature. And this is what puts our divine adoption in such pellucid contrast to human adoptions. Among men, adoption changes not the nature of the adopted; it infuses him not with the blood of his new family, but only changes his situation, his external relations. Grace, on the contrary, confers something divine in us. This is why our sonship has the eternal generation of the Son of God as the exemplar, even if it is only an echo by profound analogies, so different in order from the filiation of the Word, and imperfect, ¦¦ as with all things temporal. |[38]

Behold what manner of charity the Father hath bestowed upon us, ut filii Dei nominemur et simus, *that we should be called, and should be the sons of God*, says St. John (1 Jn 3.1); and that by our Christian vocation, He predestined us to be made conformable to the image of His Son.[39]

Let us delve deeper. As Man, that is, according to His human

---

[36] St. Thomas, *Summa*, 1.33.3c.

[37] Ibid. 1.34.1c, 2c.

[38] ◆We will only mention a few aspects: (1) We may participate in the divine nature; but Christ, the Son of God, receives it from the Father, is identical to Him as to being and perfection. (2) The divine Word leaves not the bosom, full of mystery, of the Father, who generates the Word in Him; but when God makes us His children by grace, He comes to dwell in us, and our spiritual generation does not separate us from Him but makes us abide in Him, in contrast to human generation where the seeds separate from the parents. (3) Finally, the Son of God *is the image of the invisible Father* (Col 1.15), *the figure of His substance* (Heb 1.3), says St. Paul. We ought to take this to mean that the Son is a perfect and fitting image, since He is consubstantial with the Father. By grace, we may be made in the image of God, and may become like Him, but our likeness, though real, is in truth imperfect and merely accidental.

[39] Rom 8.29.

nature and in His human life, is Jesus Christ our exemplar? Yes, certainly, but not in the same way; for grace likens us to God in His divine nature, and not to a creature, however perfect it may be. Also, as we said above, our supernatural likeness is physical and not just moral. But because Jesus, as Man, has the fullness of grace and, with it, all the gifts and all the virtues, we find in the acts and the states of His human life the most complete model for the grace given us; and it is towards perfecting this *moral* likeness that the work of Christian life is aimed.

Though it be in a different manner, Jesus Christ, as God, as Son of God and as Man, is still our exemplar.

Jesus Christ is in me. He is in me, a little like I am in a photograph of me. He is in me by the supernatural likeness that grace grants me, with His Divinity and His quality as the Son of God. He is in me by the moral likeness produced in the imitation of the virtues, the actions, and the states of His human life.

Conversely, we are in Jesus our exemplar, as every copy is in its original. We are in Jesus in a way that is important to keep in mind. Between a painting and its copy, there is a bond of likeness, but the painting itself makes not the copy; the artist does. In contrast, if you stamp a seal on wax, it forms an image of itself. The wax is our soul; the seal, the Holy Ghost Who imprints on us the image of Christ; and Christ Himself, the divine artist who works in us. By this do we have a complete understanding of the expression, "Jesus is the exemplary cause[40] of our supernatural state," that is to say, He is the model that produces His own likeness. In this quality, therefore, He is in us, as in His imprinting His likeness on us; and we are in Him, as in the cause that submits us to His action, contains us, and transforms us into His image.

St. Thomas, the great Doctor, in his commentary on the words of St. Paul, *Christum induistis*, "you have put on Christ" (Gal 3.27), writes: "When a man puts on clothing, he is protected and covered by it and his appearance is that of the color of the clothing instead of his own. In the same way, he who puts on Christ is protected and covered by

---

[40] St. Thomas, *Summa*, 1.15.1c,

Christ against attack and against heat; and in him nothing appears except the works of Christ." But still, it is not enough to gain moral likeness through works and by the agreement of the will. We must also follow up with seeking physical likeness through grace. St. Thomas goes on: "Just as burning wood takes on fire and shares in the activity of fire, so he who receives the virtues of Christ has put on Christ. .... This applies to those who are *inwardly* clothed with the virtue of Christ. ... And note that some put on Christ outwardly by good works and inwardly by a renewal of the spirit" (the Holy Ghost Who brings us to a new life), and that with respect to both we are configured to Christ.[41]

§4. WE IN CHRIST, AS IN OUR FINAL CAUSE.

After we speak of Jesus as an exemplary cause, we now show that we are in Him as in our final cause.[42] Let us see how this other meaning of "in Him" can be explained. We are familiar with the saying: "He who wills the end, wills the means,"[43] in that the means to attain the end is in the end itself, and is desired because of it. The end is thus not only the cause or the *raison d'être* of what we do to obtain it, but implies the idea and the execution. For example, within the will to obtain a favor is the will to take the necessary steps.

God made us for the sake of Christ. God looks at Christ and sees with Him, and because of Him, every faithful who are subordinate to Christ as to their Head and King; and each one, according to his vocation and the measure of the grace he receives, having the purpose of reproducing Christ in his supernatural life and glorifying God. St. Paul expresses this truth when he says that all things are made for Christ, and that we are His.[44] Thus, according to the thought of God and the plan of His providence, we are in Christ and joined to Him.[45] It behooves us to live and act in accordance with this plan by conforming ourselves completely to Jesus Who is our end.

---

[41] ◆Cf. Rom 13.14. St. Thomas, *Super Galatas*, ⫫ 9 [Gal 3.27], *Opera*, 21:217.2. |

[42] ◆St. Thomas, *in Joannis* 11.36: "*In* designat habitudinem causæ finalis."

[43] "Qui veut la *fin*, veut les *moyens*," usually rendered, "Where there is a will, there is a way." (Jones, *Dictionary*, 327).

[44] ◆Heb 2.10: For Whom are all things; 1 Cor 3.23: And you are Christ's.

[45] ◆"Intentionaliter et in ordine ad eum." It is in this sense that one says of someone: "He is entirely in his studies."

Our end is where we come to rest and rejoice in eternity. When a moving body stops at that place which is the end of its run, it is said to enter it. Using the analogy of this local movement of a body, we say every act, every state, that is the final goal of our desires or of our labors, is like a place we enter, wherein we stop and come to stay, to rest, and to rejoice.[46] Hence these expressions: "To enter into repose," "rejoicing in," "to be at peace," "to lay his happiness on."

Jesus *is the way, and the truth, and the life* (Jn 14.6). As He is the way, so through Him we have access to the Father; but as He is also the truth and the life, He is at the same time the way and the end; that is, as Man, He is the way; as God, the end.[47] This is why He urges us to abide in Him, because in Him we will attain our end and find our rest, in union with God. Such is the thought expressed in a liturgical hymn:

> Be Thou the aim of all our hearts.[48]

Be You, O Jesus, the supreme end of our yearnings. Let them abide in You, and rest in You, as much as they might here below, until finally they attain You in glory.[49] Then shall our union with You be consummated; then shall we enter into the rest of eternal bliss: *Intra in gaudium Domini tui*, "enter thou into the joy of thy Lord" (Mt 25.21, 23).

§5. HE IN US AND WE IN HIM BY FAITH AND CHARITY.

Up to this point, we have discussed the links of causality, likeness, and order between Christ and us. These ideas allow us to say "we in Him" and "Him in us," in their different senses; but we have yet to see that He truly is present in us by the substance of His Divinity or of His Humanity,[50] nor have we seen that, body and soul, we may be in Him. Let me explain. I am on the telephone talking to someone. In one sense, I am present there, to where my word has been carried. On

---

[46] ♦St. Thomas, *Summa*, Suppl. 93.2.

[47] ♦St. Thomas, Super Joannem, 14.2.2, *Opera*, 20:231.1.

[48] ♦ ¦ Vespers, Ascensione, *Brev. Rom.*, 351: ¦ "Sis meta nostris cordibus."

[49] ♦Kempis, *Imitatione*, 2.1, 79: "If thou knowest not how to meditate on high and heavenly things, rest on the Passion of Christ and willingly dwell in His sacred wounds."

[50] ♦We may, indeed, deduce from the likeness to Him imprinted in our souls through grace, that He dwells therein substantially as God, since this likeness is the effect of His supernatural presence in the soul of the righteous; but it is not that this likeness makes Him dwell in us; rather it is that His indwelling causes us to have a likeness to Him.

hearing it faithfully reproduced, my interlocutor says: "It is he. It is his voice." However, I am not present body and soul over there; and the reproduction of my voice is not my voice itself. Similarly, the Divinity and Humanity of Christ are not really present in me by their action and likeness. Still, we must take the words, "You in me and I in you" to mean a presence through substance.

We hasten to state that there can be no presence in us of Christ's Humanity, except through Eucharistic communion. The Body and Soul of Christ are in Heaven in their glory; and in the Sacrament, according to the ineffable mode proper to it. Christ's divine Humanity has nothing to do with us outside of Holy Communion, other than the relations we explained above. We do not go so far as to place Christ's Humanity substantially in us and we in it, although we ought to observe that these relations find their complement and attain their perfection in Holy Communion. The sacramental union with the Body and Soul of the Savior is to signify, produce, or increase spiritual union through charity, which tightly connects the Head to His members; and the members, one to the other. It is this union that makes us *dwell* in Christ and Christ in us, even after the Eucharistic species are altered. Jesus teaches this when He says: *He that eateth My flesh, and drinketh My blood, abideth in Me, and I in him* (Jn 6.57).

It remains for us to explain how, through grace, Christ is really present in us according to His divine nature.

First, let us observe that not only the Son of God but all three divine Persons come to dwell in our souls[51]: *If anyone love Me, he will keep My word, and My Father will love him, and We will come to him, and will make Our abode with him* (Jn 14.26). This stipulated, we say that, by grace, the three divine Persons are truly present in us as the aim or end of our knowledge and love.

St. Thomas writes: "Above and beyond this common mode, however, there is one special mode belonging to the rational nature

---

[51] ♦All works of God outside Himself are common to the three divine Persons, since they have only one and the same nature. All that the Son does, the Father does with him (Jn 5.19); if the Son comes, the Father comes too. The Holy Ghost that the Son promised us (Jn 14.16) must also abide in us, dwell in our hearts and, there, spread charity.

wherein God is said to be present *sicut cognitum in cognoscente et amatum in amante,* as the object known is in the knower, and the beloved in the lover. And since by his operation of knowledge [through faith] and love [through charity] the rational creature attains to God Himself, according to this special mode, God is said not only to exist in the rational creature but also to dwell therein as in His own temple."[52] These words of the Angelic Doctor brings clarity to the topic of our discussion.

We now explain, how, in the natural order, it follows that the object of our knowledge and our love is in us. The idea or image of the things that exist is, in fact, in our intellect; that is why we say: "It occurred to me," "it escaped my memory," "he is present in my thoughts." Let love be added to this idea, and we say of the true object of our love that "we bear him in our heart," for we are as pleased in him as if he were now present before us; we act for him as we would for ourselves, and we regard him as another we; in sum, what is his, appears to us as ours. This is how the beloved is in us who love him. But by a natural reciprocity, in loving, we go out of ourselves in a certain sense, in mind and heart, to be carried to our beloved. We long to pierce through him and enter into his very soul, that we may rejoice in him most *intimately,*[53] adhering to his ideas, partaking of his affections and joys, and enduring his trials; that we may identify with him as much we can, by conforming our will and habits to his. This is how the one who loves is in the one who is loved, according the words of Our Lord: *Where thy treasure is, there thy heart is also* (Mt 6.21).

But this union is a union of thought and affection; that is, a *moral* union. He whom we love in such a union is present in our spirit, and we can live for him, even if he may be absent from us.

By faith and charity, it is no longer just the idea of God that is in my mind, no longer just a bond of affection that unites me to Him; rather, it is He Himself, in His essence, that I attain; He Himself Who is present in my soul. Indeed, faith lets me know God only imperfectly, and I see Him, St. Paul says, *as through a glass, darkly* (1 Cor 13.12); but faith will finally blossom like the light at daybreak in that vision of

---

[52] ◆St. Thomas, *Summa,* 1.43.3c.

[53] ◆*Intus in anima, intima,* "charity tends to union and intimacy."

glory where I shall see Him face to face; where, not a representation of Him, but His very essence will unite with my intellect. Charity, which always accompanies grace, on the other hand, has the same nature in this life as it does in Heaven. It is a love of friendship through which God and the soul give to each other. In one of those profound words of which it has the secret, a word which sums up grace and glory, a word in which we find the seed of all the delights of divine union, a word from which radiates all the joys of Heaven, theology tells us: *Possideo Deum ad fruendum*,[54] "I possess God to take joy of Him." Now, how can I possess Him if He is absent or even if He is at some distance? There may be differences in condition between our temporal and eternal lives, but this possession and this rejoicing here below as it does on high, require that He be present to me through His substance, that I attain to Him and remain united to Him. This is how Jesus Christ, according to His divine nature, actually dwells in our souls in a special way as the end to which our knowledge and our love aim.

We see that this singular and supernatural presence of God in the soul by grace differs, as St. Thomas observes, from the presence in the natural order, by which God is in all creatures, giving them their being and their life. That is why we reserve for Him the term "indwelling," which evokes the idea of full possession, of rejoicing and affection, of an intimate and familial sojourn, which we find not in the simple word "presence."

This distinction of the two modes of presence also explains how one can say that, by grace, God comes to the soul where He is already present. In daytime, when the rays of the sun break through the clouds, do we not say: "The sun is back"? It was always there; but this time, its light shines in another way, more directly and more perfectly. So, too, in our soul, where He is already as He is in all things, giving them their being and their power to act, God *comes*,[55] not only

---

[54] Franzelin, *Deo Trino*, Th. 44, 570: "Præter unionem hypostaticam, proprie dicta unio cum Deo ex parte creaturæ, est solum *possessio Dei ad fruendum*, Deo tamquam ultimo fine."

[55] ♦See, Froget, *Indwelling of the Holy Ghost*, a very clear exposition of the doctrine of St. Thomas on the mode in which God, by grace, is present in us.

because He operates there supernaturally (which He can, even with sinners whom He inspires to acts of faith and hope), but because He also makes Himself present in essence, in this new and supernatural manner which we call *indwelling*.[56]

This final explanation of the term "in Him" gives us its most perfect meaning and places us at the heart of the mystery of grace; it shows us a closer and more sublime union; it makes us understand St. Paul when he says: *Vivo autem, jam non ego: vivit vero in me Christus*, "It is no longer I who livest, but Christ Who liveth in me" (Gal 2.20). He lives in me, since His Divinity dwells in me. He lives in me, since He makes me live and act supernaturally. He lives in me, since grace imprints His likeness in me.

ARTICLE 4: OUR SPIRITUAL GROWTH IN CHRIST

We do not intend to discuss the conditions of the life of Christ in us. It is a hidden life, which will appear only in glory; and here below, we cannot know with the certainty of faith if we have it in us, although we are certain that such life may increase or decrease, and also may be lost entirely by mortal sin. We deem it useful, however, after having explained how Christ abides in us, to say something on how He grows to the fullness of His perfect age. St. Louis-Marie often calls the growth in Christ to mind. Is that not the aim of his devotion? He declares it so when, after asking: "Who is he that will practice this devotion perfectly?" He replies: "The faultlessly faithful ... whom the Spirit of Jesus Christ shall ... lead to the devotion, to advance from virtue to virtue, from grace to grace, from light to light, until he arrives at the transformation of himself into Jesus Christ, and to the plenitude of His age on earth, and of His glory in Heaven."[57] The Epistles of the Apostles speak in fact, on several occasions, of the Mystical Body of Christ, which grows like the human body, or which, like a building under construction, rises and is completed.[58] These texts speak of the entire Church, the Mystical Body of Christ. The Church

---

[56] ♦Satanic possession is only the caricature of this divine possession. God alone enters the soul. The devil can occupy only the outside, acts only on the organs, he reaches the soul only indirectly through the senses. His action is external, superficial, violent, and remote. In sum, true intimacy only exists with God.

[57] ♦Cf. *TD*, 81.

[58] ♦Eph 2 et 4; 1 Pet 2.5, etc.

is developed and perfected over the centuries by the accession of the pagan nations, or the return of the heretics, the schismatics, and the Jewish people, and by the increase of faith and charity in each of the faithful; and, at the end of time, when God will have had the last of His chosen ones, the last stone of His temple, every last member of His Church—when Christ universally will be all and in all, then shall it be the consummation of the world. Following the example of His human Body, which at the age of thirty-three reached the fullness of its growth and perfection, so will the Mystical Body of Christ reach her full development. Even if she already has a certain perfection on earth, above all, she will surely have it in glory, where no spot or wrinkle or blemish will spoil her beauty.[59]

This growth of Christ can be understood not only in the context of the Church in general, but also in each member in particular, since to each of us is said: "Let us grow in Christ in every way,[60] by every kind of good works, and being hallowed in all things." If we recall the explanation given above on the formulas: "Christ is in us," "He abides in us," "He is formed in us," we shall understand how He grows in us and achieves His fullness.

He abides in us, because He abides in us by faith and charity; and as they increase, this abode of Christ in us, this union with Him, will become more intimate, more perfect.

He abides in us, because He works in us, He communicates grace to us through His divine Spirit, through Whom He governs us. Now, when the purifications of the ascetic life will have diminished and will have mortified life itself—the life which hinders so much the action of Christ and His divine Spirit, such action will become freer, more extensive, more profound, and the life of Christ will develop in us.

Lastly, we know that this divine operation conforms us to Christ. Jesus will grow in us in proportion to how the form or idea of Christ, or the likeness to Him, will have been perfected by grace and virtue. Thus, to the extent we attain in this life that degree of holiness which realizes the divine plan for each of us, we shall attain that fullness of

---

[59] Eph 5.27.
[60] Eph 4.15.

which the perfect age of Christ here below is the model. Then, nothing is left for us to do, but partake of the fullness of His glory in Heaven.

It was important for us to develop certain themes in this chapter, for they stand for the foundation of Christian life; that is, the life of Christ in us. How are we to lead this life and progress in it, if we know not what it is? Many have only the vaguest idea, and their piety suffers as a result. There is no shortage of those who oppose it, saying that not all the faithful are obliged to know, or are even capable of understanding, the detailed and in-depth explanations we present above. But they whose mission it is to teach, as well as the faithful who desire the perfect life, have no business being content with a mere acquaintance with the life of Christ in us. Teachers ought to have a firm grasp and acquire a profound understanding, which they will disseminate to others in a suitable form.

It is fitting that we clarify and delve deeper into the doctrine contained in the words: "Jesus living in us," since some works have incurred either a condemnation or just criticism. As a result, if their authors have not discredited the formula, they have at least incited defiance to its subject. Lastly, for our purposes, it was also necessary to explain at length what we mean by "the life of Christ in us," for such is the end of the perfect devotion to the Blessed Virgin.

We should particularly delve deeper into the meaning of the formula: "Through Him, with Him, and in Him," which is the principal part of our system of spirituality. What we said above will allow us, in the pages that follow, to provide the explanations and facilitate our understanding of its applications.

CHAPTER 3:

THE LIFE AND THE WAY OF UNION

he union with Jesus Christ is the end to which our spiritual life is aimed, and, truth be told, this union is contained in the teaching of every school of theology. Notwithstanding the diversity of their points of view and their methods, we see no doctrinal divergence among them, and we wish, first of all, to bring this important point to light and assert that the fact is beyond dispute. Nevertheless, when we examine the works of spirituality, we note that in many of them, certain ideas and particular methods predominate to the degree that they characterize the teaching put forward by the authors, and set pronounced differences one from the other, even though they have a treasure in common as the basis of their doctrine. By grouping writers whose thoughts exhibit this distinctive note, we may consider them as forming a special school. Some may find it excessive to speak of "school" here. To us it seems justified, and we hope, that they would at least grant us that we are indeed presented with a certain system or method. We shall describe the basic idea, outline the history, and highlight certain distinctive notes.

If anyone questions this purpose, we answer that it is to determine of what kind is the spirituality of St. Louis-Marie. We continue and complement the theme of "Christ living in us," the formula for the supernatural life, from the preceding chapter, in order to explain how it and the processes flowing from it constitute the genus or *kind* of his spirituality.

ARTICLE 1: THE FUNDAMENTAL IDEA

To repeat, the idea underpinning our spirituality is expressed by the words: "Christ living in us," which is used as the basis of a whole system, as the hub from which everything radiates and where everything is joined. Let us begin with some details:

Dom Guéranger, speaking of the representatives of this school in the seventeenth century, says that they did not separate the Person of Christ from His doctrine, and that they derived from Him and reduced the entirety of religion to Him.[1] What the illustrious Benedictine states on doctrine, we ought to apply to interior life; for just as Jesus said, *I am the truth*, He also said, *I am the life* (Jn 14.6). On this basis, we consider that in spiritual life, in its admirably diverse forms and manifold acts, the principle from which everything emanates, and where all things unify, is Christ living in the soul. For example, when we consider virtue, no doubt we see the infused or acquired habit adorning the soul; and in the practice of virtue, conformity to moral law; but, above all, we see mainly something of Jesus that we allow to take hold in us, the effects of His grace, the traits of our likeness to Him. "Christ," says Eriguena, "is the substance of all virtues,"[2] the very same, *Who of God is made unto us wisdom, and justice, and sanctification, and redemption* (1 Cor 1.30); meaning, as St. Thomas explains, that all these gifts come to us by our union with Christ and by our participating in His grace, such that to progress in grace and in virtue is to form Jesus in us, and to grow in Him.[3]

In short, in this conception of the supernatural life, we separate not the acts and states from the Person of Christ; and this life is, in

---

[1] ◆We must not take this to mean that in religion there is nothing apart from Christ. The existence of God and the unity of God, the Trinity, Creation, and so on, is deducible from the Incarnation. See Guéranger, ¦ *Marie d'Agreda*, a collection of 28 articles published in *l'Univers* (May 23, 1858 to Nov 7 1859) on the republication of French translation of *Mística ciudad de Dios*. ¦

[2] John Scotus Eriugena, *Periphyseon*, 1:77, PL 122.449C: "As Maximus states, 'Divine Wisdom descends through mercy as far as the human intellect ascends through charity.' Such Wisdom *is the cause and substance of all virtues*. Every theophany, therefore, that is, every virtue, both in this life in which it begins to be formed in the worthy, and in the future life of the man who will receive divine bliss, is produced not outside a man himself but in himself, and arises both from God and from men themselves." [Emphasis added]. Fr. Lhoumeau cites "Origen [sic], *In Canticum*, Hom. 1"; but there is not the slightest trace of this discussion there.

[3] ◆¦¦ St. Thomas, Super 1 Cor 1, Lect. 4, *Opera*, 20:617. ¦ ◆As for the spiritual infirmities of the soul, her failings, the obstacles by which sin sets her at odds with the reign of God, I refer them to the life of Jesus in me, as did Msgr. Gay ¦¦ in *Élévations*, 118, 2:395-398. ¦

the final analysis, a union with Jesus.

But what of the way to reach Christ and of leading this life of union? It is none other than Christ Himself, Christ Who is life, but also the way: *Ego sum via* (Jn 14.6). St. Thomas writes: "Christ referred to Himself as 'the way,' united to its destination: because He is the destination, containing in Himself whatever can be desired, that is, existing truth and life. If then, you ask which way to go, accept Christ, for He *is* the way."[4] In this contemplation, the union with Christ is not only the *end* but also the *means* to attain it. Faithful to this way thinking and without excluding considerations of another order (which would be a mistake and peril), I shall focus mainly on finding in Christ the model for my life, the motive for virtues, the rule of my action, the help for my frailty, the cure of my infirmities: *Learn from* Me, *because I am meek, and humble of heart* (Mt 11.29). Hence, I will be humble, following the example of Christ, and because He was humble, and because I wish to be like Him and to love Him.

O how many reasons press me to accept my sufferings! For St. Paul, the sorrows here below and, in general, the renunciation, the sacrifice, the mortification in spiritual life, appear to him as *bearing about in our body the mortification of Jesus, that the life also of Jesus may be made manifest in our bodies* (2 Cor 4.10).

If we recall how earnestly the Apostle, having been incorporated into Christ, exhorted Christians to chastity and called them to modesty, because Our Lord is near them and in them by grace,[5] we soon will realize how far apart, truly, we are from Him. In short, in this aspect, religion is no longer just some*thing*, it is some*one*; and just as the Church is the living Christ in His Mystical Body, growing and maturing through her, so in every soul (which, according to Dom Guéranger, is the Church in miniature[6]), we shall see Christ living and

---

[4] St. Thomas, Super Joannem, 14, lect. 2, *Opera*, 20:232.1: "Christus seipsum designavit viam, et conjunctam termino: quia ipse est terminus habens in se quidquid desiderari potest, scilicet existens veritas et vita. Si ergo quæras, qua transeas, accipe Christum, quia ipse est via."

[5] Gal 5.1, 13-26.

[6] Rom 16.5: κατ' οἶκον ἐκκλησίαν, *domesticam ecclesiam eorum*, "the church which is in their house," which St. John Chrysostom applied to the family. (*In Eph.*, 20.6, PG 62.143: "Domus est parva ecclesia"; *Serm. 8, in Gen.*, 6.2, PG 54.607: "Domum tuam effice

growing in her until she attains perfection.

Some will perhaps protest that we find these insights and processes just about everywhere. We dispute it not; but we observe that some masters propose them, so to speak, in the foreground; that they assign to them a predominant, habitual, and methodical role in the conduct of souls.

We see now why we have given this chapter the title, "The life and the way of union." Indeed, the characteristic note of the teaching or the school in question is to envisage a union with Christ, both as an end and a means. To us, it is clear that St. Louis-Marie had this thought. What is the purpose of his devotion? Of forming Christ in us, enabling us to attain the fullness of his age, and so on. These and similar terms clearly formulate the basic idea which we have just explained. And the way to reach this union is to live and act in union with Mary, that is to say, "through her, with her, in her, and for her, so as to do it better through Christ, with Christ, in Christ, and for Christ."

ARTICLE 2: A BRIEF HISTORICAL REVIEW

All things considered, this way of looking at things goes to the foundation of the supernatural order of which Christ is the sum, the source, the exemplar, the substance, and the end; that is, *Omnia et in omnibus Christus*, "Christ is all, and in all" (Col 3.11), *ut impleret omnia*, "that He might fill all things" (Eph 4.10). This teaching is found in the Gospel, and many parables, figures, and sentences can be easily adduced to it. It is asserted particularly by St. Paul in his Epistles, from which it takes its characteristics. It is there that we find this capital formula: *Vivit vero in me Christus*, "Christ liveth in me" (Gal 2.20), *mihi*

---

ecclesiam"; and on the responsibilities of the members, *In Ps 41.2*, PG 55.158). Separately, the entirety of St. Benedict's *Rules* may be taken as a description of the monastery as a church in miniature. We read in St. Peter Damian, Opusc. 11, *Dominus vobiscum*, 11, PL 149.239D: "Just as man is called a 'little world,' because in his material essence he is made up of the same four elements as the universe; so also, may each faithful be seen as *minor Ecclesia*, a Church in miniature, when he receives all the sacraments of man's redemption that God conferred on the universal Church." Fr. Lhoumeau's reference to the application of the term to the soul cannot be found in the works of Dom Guéranger.

vivere Christus est, "for to me, to live is Christ" (Phil 1.21); there also is discussed the image of the Mystical Body, whose effects are laid out in a whole host of texts that are so well known and the subject of so numerous a commentary that it truly would not be useful for us to elaborate on the quotations we just made.

If we look to the first centuries of the Church, the language of the martyrs, the inscriptions of the catacombs and baptisteries, the writings of the ancient Fathers (among whom St. Cyril of Alexandria deserves mention), and how many other witnesses of tradition, they tell us that the dependence on Christ was the dominant point of view in dogmatic and spiritual teaching.

These phrases: "Christ lives in me," "I am one with Christ by grace," "I am a Christ-bearer," "temple of the Holy Ghost," had a practical meaning for Christians in those times and were familiar to them. Read the offices of St. Andrew,[7] St. Agnes, St. Cecilia, St. Agatha, the writings of St. Ignatius of Antioch, and so on, and observe how the subject of Christ pervades them all, how nothing is separated from Him; how life, the cross, death, virginity, love, the service of God, all are viewed through Him.

We need not to draw up a complete list of writers who have followed this path of total dependence on Christ. Some thought it particularly permeated the Benedictines and the Franciscans; but it is only by the seventeenth century that we find a constellation of ascetic writers, among whom are Fathers de Condren, Olier, Bourgoing, and Bérulle. The mystery of the life of Christ in us is wonderfully developed in their works, at least in some of them, although we need to take adequate precautions, and to have an excellent understanding of theology, before reading them. In our day, we see other representatives of this school emerge, who have put their considerable talent and knowledge of theology at the service of the devotion, among whom we would be remiss if we did not name Dom Guéranger, Fr. Faber, Cardinal Pie, Msgr. Gay, the pious and learned Bishop of

---

[7] ♦The authenticity of the lessons, responses and legends of many of these offices has been questioned. Be that as it may, they still carry some weight. We also have enough testimonies of the first ages of the Church to support our assertions.

Anthédon, who, as regards our current topic, is the master of masters. His multi-volume *Christian Life and Virtues*, as well as his later *Elevations*, make up a splendid, thorough, and profound exposition of the doctrine.

As we have said, St. Louis-Marie came to take his place among them. To the core idea of their teaching, he adds the union with the Blessed Virgin as a means of uniting with Jesus. We believe that there is no need other than to read his works for us to be persuaded on the usefulness of his teaching. Our task here, therefore, if indeed it is not already superfluous, is to lend credence to how simple and self-evident is his idea.

Let us now speak of the methods and benefits that characterize the spirituality of St. Louis, both of which are abundant in the devotion that he says is "an easy, short, perfect, and secure path."[8]

ARTICLE 3: CHARACTERISTIC NOTES

§1. EASY

The first note is that such a method makes the work of our sanctification easier and more appealing. When speaking of virtue, of God's law, of moral obligation and rule; when preaching humility, obedience; when exalting the Cross and suffering, with firm assurances, we are able to say precisely what we need to say and what ought not to be ignored. When these abstractions are divorced from their application to actual, living persons (as they are in the writings of some authors), exhortations risk suffering the fate of mathematical solutions or geometric proofs. We may remark, "That's right," but they will not touch our heart or move our soul.

Msgr. Gay wrote somewhere: "We put souls face to face with abstractions and will that they be riveted by them!"[9] And in his beautiful

---

[8] Pauvert, *Vie*, 389: "Those who wish not to follow me go by another way, less thorny, and I approve of it; for just as there are many mansions in the house of the Father in Heaven, so also are there many paths that lead to Him. I let them walk on theirs, so let me walk on mine, especially as you cannot deny them their advantages; but mine is the way that Jesus Christ taught by His example and by His counsels. It is, therefore, the shortest, the safest, and the most perfect that leads to Him."

[9] Gay, *Life and Virtues*, 1:205: In the punishment for sin, "there exists such a beauty, and so much goodness in the moral order, that those who are divinely enlightened are enamored with it. From the moment they feel themselves culpable, they are most eager for punishment and they yield themselves with ardor to a justice which they provoke,

treatise *On Christian Suffering*, he makes this remark important for the direction of souls: "If the Cross were nothing else but a cross, these souls [who say they are incapable of loving it] would be right; failure is certain, and the enterprise, foolish. The Blessed Virgin herself would not have succeeded. But let the cross come alive, let it become the crucified One, then all of a sudden love has its reason for being and place. ... Whether it be in a soul to a lesser or greater degree, the love of the cross is always, and can only be always, the holy and fervent love of Jesus nailed upon the Cross."[10]

We must recognize that in preaching virtue, continence, sacrifice, and so on, we ought often to raise our eyes to God, to Jesus in person, or to speak as do the Psalms: *Legem tuam, Domine ... mandata tua*, "Thy law, O Lord, ... Thy commandments."[11]

For those who, in spiritual life, above all, look to the union with Christ and walk on the path of this devotion, the thought of Jesus will be not only the complement and the end of other considerations, but also foremost and dominant in their minds, such as: Who teaches me humility? Jesus, meek and humble of heart. What makes me obedient? The thought of belonging to Him, of doing His Will as faithfully transmitted by Church hierarchy. I shall aspire to become a soul of sacrifice that I may be in communion, by will and state, with Jesus in the Eucharist, and so on.

No longer do I face some*thing*, but some*one*. I have some One to hold on to; I, who am a rational creature and able to love. Before me is God made Man, living a life like mine and is entirely in my likeness, save for sin. Before me, I behold He Who is my Creator and Savior, my Lord and my King, my heavenly Spouse, beloved of my soul, my nourishment and my life. After this life, He will be my Judge. Will He be my eternal crown?

I should be made to contemplate and know Him, because the more I know Him, the more I may love Him. If I love him, I will naturally strive to be like Him, to do all according to His Will, to share in His states, to unite more perfectly with Him. Have I need of the way of fear? No, I will not have fear be my motive for striving to be good.

---

by calling it down upon themselves."
[10] Gay, *Life and Virtues*, 3:133-134.
[11] Together with *testimonia tua*, repeated 88 times in Ps 118.

I need only contemplate Jesus, my God and my Judge—only meditate again and again on the sufferings and humiliations of His Passion; for it is indeed true that the sight of the Savior, the sanctified victim of holy justice, is for us the most frightening and the most profound revelation of divine perfections.[12]

Some would say that all this is pure theory. No, of course not, because it is common practice. Many are the souls that resist the most convincing of reasons to urge them to favor making a sacrifice, who, when put before Jesus, relent, give themselves to Him, and thereafter want nothing but to love and serve Him. The thought of pleasing Him and honoring Him, and, by the grace of these affections, of sensing that they live ever more with Him, makes them accept what they have sometimes tried to haggle with God for far too long.[13]

§2. POSITIVE

A second characteristic note of this spirituality is to put before our eyes the positive before the negative side, the end before the means, the destination before the route.

By all means, let this positive be placed in such light and recalled with so much insistence, that it ranks higher than all things and fixes our gaze, as the leading character does in a scene on stage. Says Jesus: *If any man will come after Me, let him deny himself, and take up his cross, and follow Me* (Mt 16.24). The positive (the end), is to follow Jesus, to unite with Him, to share His states; the negative (the means), is to renounce, to disengage from those things which prevent us from following Him and which hinder our union with Him, be it by abnegation, by mortification, or by sacrifice and humility. In the exercise of our devotion, we must begin there, but let us resolve our intention, before aiming for our destination.

---

[12] ◆Rigoleu, "L'Homme d'oraison," in Champion, *Vie Rigoleu*, 179: "To contemplate Jesus Christ, His perfections, and His virtues, a simple look suffices. This sight, by itself, is able to operate marvelous effects in the soul, just as a mere glance at the brass serpent, which Moses caused to be raised on a cross in the desert, was enough to heal snakebites; for all that is in Jesus Christ is not only holy, but also sanctifying, and is imprinted on souls that appeal to Him, if they have the disposition. His humility makes us humble. His purity cleanses us. His poverty, patience, gentleness, and other virtues, are impressed upon those who contemplate Him. We need not reflect on ourselves, but simply look at Him with esteem, admiration, respect, love, and wanting to oblige Him."

[13] Cf. Gn 18.23-32.

Now, who is blind to the thought of supernatural joys, to the hope of a less imperfect life, to the presentiment of our love being purified and increased? Who sees that all this only leads to sacrifice, that it offers recompense for renunciation, makes the Cross resplendent, calms the repugnance of nature, and gilds life more than the sun in Springtime?

We can explain why we find the spirituality of some authors dry and repulsive, obstinately stuck as they are on the negative side. Reading them, we are tempted to take the means for the end, the scaffold for the temple, the diet for the health, and we are left with the impression that we ought "to love the diet for its own sake, and to find that this scaffold is beautiful, and to relish these means, as if it were a thing most sweet in itself."[14] Thanks be to God, good authors (and they are many in number) are careful to neglect neither one nor the other aspect of spiritual life; but it is clear that the less we isolate the negative from the positive side, the more we regard the former in light of the latter, and the more we have of the true opinion of things, the more apt we are to win hearts.

My God! Why do we not conform ourselves to you, O Lord, Who are life itself? Is there anything more positive than "He Who Is"?[15] And when it has to do with Your life in our souls, why do we not offer You this our life first and foremost? Must we grow old in our spiritual life and all the while hear utterances such as these: "Perfection frightens me." "If such a bond is forbidden, what I must yearn for?" "If it needs be that I sacrifice this or that joy, what am I left with, if not sorrow?" Pity the souls to whom devotion only comes in the garb of mourning! No doubt, no one says explicitly to them that they will no longer love, that they will no longer have anyone to lean on; but why not say to them first and as did God: "*Thou shalt love*; and because you love, you will serve, until you suffer travails and even have to sacrifice."

Note well that we do not here propose acting with love as our sole motive, especially not for those who are just beginning their journey to perfection; but we do say that there is a benefit for all, especially beginners, to be initiated in this positive note of Christian life. Indeed,

---

[14] ◆Gay, *Life and Virtues*, 1:108-109.
[15] Ex 3.4: I Am Who Am.

we raise a child not by privations and corrections only. They may be useful and even necessary to keep him hale, but they are not the things that keep him alive. Forbid him from eating at such a time, or from doing such a thing, though we may, he must nevertheless eat and have something to do. Similarly, souls need to love some*one*, to lean on some*body*, to rejoice in some*thing*. Let us show them that they need mortify only that which hinders supernatural life; that by re nouncing certain joys or certain affections, they will come to enjoy them deeper and, in a sense, more truly. After making modifications to suit their present circumstances, tell them the words of St. Paul, who, after his tribulations, his mortifications, and his sacrifices, ex- claims: *I live*. He feels alive! No longer according to the flesh, but according to Christ: *Vivo, jam non ego, vivit vero in me Christus*, "It is no longer I who livest, but Christ Who liveth in me" (Gal 2.20). Tell them, just as Jesus says: *Blessed are the poor in spirit, for theirs is the King- dom of Heaven* (Mt 5.3); but preach not poverty without the joys that, even here below, go along with it. And when the time is ripe, show them that the vows of religion are a deliverance and a satisfaction of love, far more than it is an austerity and a restraint.

Was not the Gospel first preached by Angels bringing *good tidings of joy* (Lk 2.12), even though it was the Cross, the death to oneself, the renunciation of the world and of all men that Jesus came to teach us? Yes, but these things lead us back to God, to the joy of God—to the spring and beauty of Christian life, whereas the struggle and the suf- fering are their accidentals and transients. Joy: this is the first thing that had to be announced to the simple souls of shepherds. And so, too, it ever should be to the world entire.

In the life of union no longer envisaged only as an end, but also as a method, I look to Jesus and will that He live in me, and, in doing so, I spare neither sacrifice nor labor; rather, I pave the way for them, first and foremost, by fixing my eyes on the goal, or on what I gain by my renunciation. I listen to the Divine Master teaching me that I must carry my cross, but so that I may follow Him.[16] He tells me that I must hate my life in this world and that I ought to lead a life of poverty[17];

---

[16] Lk 14.27.
[17] Jn 12.25, Mt 19.21, Lc 12.22.

but I know that He also says: *These things I have spoken to you, that My joy may be in you, and your joy may be filled* (Jn 15.11).

§3. UNIVERSAL

The third and last characteristic note we wish to point out is that this method of putting ourselves directly and principally before Jesus, in order to live through Him, with Him, and in Him, is universal, which we take it to mean that the process benefits everyone, but we adapt it to suit our individual life.

In the first place, the paths of perfection and the acts of virtue cannot be offered to everyone without due regard. There are those whom we ought to admire more than imitate.

In the mountains, we see isolated peaks, rocks fantastic to behold, summits inaccessible and of some strange beauty, but which the foot of man will never tread nor but few hardy climbers will ever approach. Now, in the world of grace, elevated souls (whom Scripture compares to mountains) perform surprising and seemingly bizarre actions, though are inspired by the Spirit of God. According to divine plan, such actions contribute to the sum beauty of the supernatural world, but are not intended to be reproduced or, at the very least, these souls comprise not a model that everyone should emulate. The lives of St. Simeon Stylites, St. Alexis, St. Rosalie of Palermo and St. Benedict Labre, are examples. Their lives, each by itself is not the life of Our Lord, nor that of the Blessed Virgin. *Quoniam Tu solus sanctus*, "for Thou only art holy," sings the Church; meaning that He is the universal Saint, and that all holiness flows from Him, and in Him is the exemplar of holiness fulfilled. In Him are the summits of perfection to which no creature may presume to rise; still, just as majestic mountains, by their tiered plateaus and gentle slopes, descend and merge with the plains, so also does God, by His condescension, comes down to us in His Incarnation, and lowers Himself even to our level that He can say to all: *I am the way* (Jn 14.6).

Now, setting aside the extraordinary ways, and taking into consideration only the well-beaten paths, we know that we must not be indifferent when directing souls to all kinds of good deeds—to this process of sanctification, or that method of spirituality. We ought to take into account the character, the temperament, the conditions of life of the particular individual, and especially God's plan for him. Still, everywhere and anytime, we can safely practice the life of union as we understand it; because we walk on the way common to all creature, which is Jesus Himself. There is no form of holiness that is not a copy of this divine model; no vocation, at least in principle and idea, that is not in imitation of His life.

In the second place, if Jesus is the way *for all*, He is also the truth *to all*. We mean that in Him Who is God made Man, we find the type of true holiness for all the acts and all the states of our life. What must this life be, if not a Christian one; that is to say, in the image of Christ?

The process of union is common to all as regards the things to which it is applied. Whatever I do, whatever my situation, living for me is summed up in "being Jesus."[18] I need not multiply the rules of conduct according to the multiplicity of acts and circumstances; but, to live in truth and holiness, I must always face this divine model and be conformed to Him.

Too little room is given to Jesus Christ in the spirituality of some people, causing them to speak, sometimes, in a strange tongue. Their tendency is to speak of troubles and difficulties, and when they are asked: "Have you turned your eyes to Our Lord, and sought in His life a state analogous, or a circumstance similar to yours, that you might obtain light and draw strength from it?" we sometimes hear in response: "I knew it not," or, stranger still: "I believed it not that I could unite with Jesus in such a circumstance," or, strangest of all: "Yes, but He is God." Such responses tell us that these people know not how to make certain acts or states of human life conform to the Christian faith. They think that Jesus, being God, lived not truly and sincerely a life like ours ¦¦ (save for sin), | and that, in His life on earth, He knew not miseries, nor infirmities, nor sufferings consonant with His infinite holiness.

---

[18] ✦To be Jesus, to live Jesus, in the sense that we explained, where we spoke of leading our life "by Him, with Him, and in Him." (Part 1.2.1-3, pp. 31-53 above).

Lastly, the life of this God-Man, true Man and true God, teaches me to discern what I must understand by *nature*, in the language of the ascetics, inasmuch as it is opposed to grace. O what practical errors we do commit when we construe notions incompletely or poorly! In studying Jesus Christ, I should not aim to see in Him what of the vicious I have in my nature that I must mortify, but that I also seek to find in mine the infirmities and constraints of human nature, which I must bear and sanctify. Indeed, I learn to recognize what in nature is the work of God. These are the things I must preserve, strengthen, and purify. Here, truth is important in practice, and we must not forget the prayer of Our Lord: *Father, sanctify them in truth* (Jn 17.17).

Msgr. Gay aptly summarizes these considerations, when he says: "To be like Jesus, to live like Jesus, enlightens all things, makes all things easier, puts our existence in orderly relations to everything, to creatures, and to God; but, most of all, it is a radical way of dying to oneself."[19]

Still many more are the particulars to be observed in the method of spiritual formation espoused by St. Louis-Marie, but we shall discuss them fully when we explain how the Blessed Virgin is an easy, short, perfect, and secure path that leads to Jesus.[20]

Before closing this chapter, let us note that the life of union with Jesus was, for Mary, the form of her spirituality, the essential practice of her interior life. When St. Paul's admirable exclamation, *For to me, to live is Christ* (Phil 1.21), resounds in our soul, it awakens in her harmonious reverberations of endless admiration and holy ambitions that make us dream of Heaven. But, O what fullness of resonance we do find in Him, and what visions do pass before our eyes, when we apply such living to Mary! For her, religion was indeed Jesus in person before her. Whence was she going to draw grace, if not in Him, in

---

[19] ◆Gay, *Élévations*, 123, 2:439: "Être Jésus, vivre Jésus, éclaire tout, facilite tout, met l'être dans des rapports réguliers avec tout, avec Dieu et les créatures; et c'est aussi et premièrement un moyen radical de mourir à soi-même."

[20] ◆Note that the devotion to the Sacred Heart, justly given the latitude in spiritual life, bolsters what we have said about the fundamental idea and the characteristic notes said above. See also, Boussac, *Cœur de Jésus*; and Sauvé, *Jésus intime*.

union with Him? Can we think of her prayer, of the veneration due her, of her love, of the service she rendered to Our Lord, without seeing clearly that these things lead, above all, to Jesus, to her God, to God Who had made Himself hers—*Deus, Deus tuus*[21]—and that through Him, she reached the Father? Day by day, the life of Jesus, at every stage, unfolded before the eyes of the Blessed Virgin. It was the theme of her constant contemplations. *Mary*, says St. Luke, *kept all these words, pondering them in her heart* (Lc 2.19). Mary grew in faith and her love for her divine Son, following Him in the growing manifestations of His divine wisdom. The form of Mary's interior life, the law of her external life, was everywhere and always to be linked to Christ, to unite with Him in His states and in His actions, to participate in His mysteries, as only His mother, His only one, and ¦¦ the Spouse of the Holy Ghost | could. God had predestined and created her for Jesus. Faithful to her vocation, she lived more in Jesus than in herself. He was her joy, her sorrow, and the soul of her soul. Mary understood the vanity of earthly goods, the necessity of virtue, the fruits of sacrifice, and the joys of purity. There is none that does not see at first glance that Jesus was the first and the main reason for her actions. He it was that she regarded above all; for Him that she wished to live. When, in obedience to the Law, she went to the Temple for her purification, and, lost in the crowd, she made the offering of the poor, she did it, above all, to follow Jesus.

The school of Mary is, therefore, the school of a life in union. We have no better teacher than she for our formation in it. O how we shall benefit from her lessons and our dependence on her!

---

[21] Ps 44.8, 49.7 ; Heb 1.9.

CHAPTER 4:

ON HOLY SLAVERY

Our Lord Jesus Christ.

The union with Jesus Christ may be practically viewed from different standpoints, among which are the habitual recollection of the soul or the heart of prayer, the purity of intention, the liturgical life, the special communion in our intentions, our actions and our states as regards the mysteries in the life of Our Lord, taken at random. Many of such aspects characterize the spirituality of particular religious Orders.

In our union with Jesus Christ, St. Louis-Marie envisioned our absolute belonging to Him and our practical dependence on Him, which he calls "Holy Slavery." To strengthen us in that devotion, he bids us surrender ourselves unreservedly to Mary. But note that we speak not of two different affiliations: one to God by Jesus, the other to the Blessed Virgin, for the latter is the extension, the consequence, of the first, and the means of attaining it.

> Depend all I on her, my Mother,
> To better lean on Him, my Savior.[1]

In Part II of this volume, we shall speak about said means. Here, we say that, as regards the union with God, Who is the *final end* of our devotion, belonging to Christ is itself only a means, but belonging to Mary is the end. "This devotion to the Blessed Virgin," says St. Louis-Marie, "consists in giving ourselves entirely to her, that, through her,

---

[1] *Cantiques*, 77.8, 132: "Je suis tout sous sa dépendance, / Pour mieux dépendre du Sauveur."

70

we may entirely belong to Jesus Christ."[2]

Continuing our study of the end to which the perfect devotion to Mary is ordered, in this chapter we shall examine three things: (1) What St. Louis-Marie means by "slavery." (2) The basis for this particular manner of considering the life of grace in us. (3) The qualities of this divine servitude.

ARTICLE 1: WHAT SHOULD BE UNDERSTOOD BY "SLAVERY"

What constitutes "slavery" under our consideration is neither the degraded condition of the slave nor the tyranny of the master. It is true that such circumstances often accompany servitude; but they are its accidental, not essential, properties. In general, slavery is the total and absolute submission to a master, in such manner that the slave no longer belongs to himself, but is kept under the dominion of his master, who uses the slave at will and for his gain. St. Louis-Marie clarifies this notion by comparing the condition of the slave with that of the simple servant. The latter gives up only part of his time and labor, and for a predetermined compensation, which is due him ¦¦ by the operation of law and | in justice; while the slave always lives and works for his master.

St. Louis-Marie distinguishes three kinds of slavery, or at least three notions of it, for which one may be in servitude: "The first," he says, "is the slavery of nature. All creatures are slaves of God in the first sense."[3] We shall soon delve deeper into this. The second, is the slavery of constraint, which reduces one to servitude, either by violence or by law, just or unjust. "The demons and the damned are slaves in the second sense."[4] The third, is the slavery of love and of the will, by which "we choose God and His service above all things, even when nature does not oblige us to do so."[5] We deal not with the slavery of constraint in this volume. Instead, we limit our discussion to the slavery of nature and the slavery of the will, the latter of which we treat further on when we set out its conditions. We begin with why St. Louis-Marie gives his devotion the name of "slavery."

---

[2] *Secret*, 20-21.
[3] *TD*, 47.
[4] Ibid.
[5] •Cf. Ibid.

ARTICLE 2: THE FOUNDATION OF HOLY SLAVERY

We are mistaken if we regard the terms, "Slavery to Jesus" or "Slave to Mary," as a formula new, suspect, and inspired by exalted piety; or if we believe that we may substitute the latter, for example, for "Child of Mary," without altering the true idea of this devotion. St. Louis-Marie used the word precisely because he meant what it means. His point of view on our life of grace, and on the practice of the devotion, through this form of union with Jesus Christ, may not be original, but it certainly is secondary, accessory or partial. He took into consideration what is most radical in us, as men and as Christians. He thus imbues his devotion with the very vitality of Baptism, and base it on the fundamental truths of Christianity.

We shall delve into the titles comprising the sovereign dominion that God and, in particular, Jesus Christ has over us: (1) that which God the Creator has over every creature; (2) those that Jesus Christ acquires over us by our Baptism; (3) those which we add by the exercise of our free will in the ways of perfection, be it in a religious or another state of life.

§1. OUR CONDITION AS CREATURE.

Among men, slavery rests not on the difference in nature, for all men are of the one and same human nature, and, in this respect, they are equal. Dependence between them is established through relations external or accidental. Dependence on God is an entirely different matter, it being the most radical, the most absolute that we can imagine, because it is based on our nature and the nature of God Himself.

O Domine, cries the Psalmist, *quia ego servus tuus et filius ancillæ tuæ*, "O Lord, I am Thy servant [lit. slave] the son of Thy handmaid [lit. slave]" (Ps 115.16). You are the absolute, eternal, necessary Being, Creator of all. Would, my God, that I see You face-to-face for all eternity, never exhausting the infinite variety of this contemplation, for I believe that You are one and infinite, that You live and subsist in Yourself, receive nothing from another, comprehend in You all the fullness of perfection of all being,[6] and that *with you there is no change, nor*

---

[6] St. Thomas, *Summa*, 1.3.2 ad 3; Super Joannem, 14, Lect. 8.1, *Opera*, 20:252.2; *Summa*,

shadow of alteration (Jas 1.17), nor of failure. You reveal all this to us when You say: *I Am Who Am* (Ex 3.14).

As for me, I am he who is not, who exists not in himself, but receives everything from God, starting with my existence. It is He Who created me; for I was not, and behold, at the moment appointed in His eternal decrees, [out of nothing] He called me to existence.

O God, why have You chosen me, when there are so many others whom You know and who would have adored You and served You far better?

I presume not to know; for His preference is the mystery of His wisdom and charity, before which I need but be silent, while I worship Him and render Him thanks.

God created me not as the worker fashions an object or builds a machine that exists and works independently. He is in me (as He is in every creature), more intimately than anything created. He sustains my existence by His power. If He withholds His hand but for an instant, I will fall back into nothingness.

Nowhere among men shall I find a like possession, a dominion equal, and, consequently, a dependence such as I have on God. He possesses me, not in my externalities, but in the depths of my being, at every moment, now and ever more; at death, and even afterwards.[7] In a word, I am under His dominion by the mere fact that I exist. I depend on Him completely, always, and in every way. There is no way for me to escape His sovereign dominion. If I flee His charity, I will fall into the hands of His justice.[8] Yes, He truly is my Lord and Master: *O Domine, quia ego servus tuus.* I am Yours, and exist only to serve You; for You are my end and my joy.

Every creature, by the very fact of being a creature, is thus in a relation with God that is necessarily of absolute dependence. This is what St. Louis-Marie calls "slavery of nature." The worship rendered God is entirely founded on the recognition by rational beings of His sovereign dominion and on the practical dependence which is its

---

1.9.1c.
[7] ✦Rom 14.8: Whether we live, or whether we die, we are the Lord's.
[8] Cf. Ps 138.8-13.

consequence. We find that in all religions, adoration is the capital act, and the service of God is the sum of all obligations. Our Lord reminds Satan of authority, saying: *Thou shalt adore the Lord thy God, and Him only shalt thou serve* (Lc 4.8).

The absolute dependence on God, and the obligation to serve Him, are so essentially tied to the condition of being a creature, that we read in the Gospel, concerning the Son of God: *Et Verbum caro factum est*, "and the Word was *made* flesh" (Jn 1.14), and *factus est obediens*, "He was *made* obedient" (Phil 2.8). What does this mean, if not that obedience is not for the Word, since He has the same nature as the Father and is equal in all things; but that in becoming Man, He took a created nature, according to which He became subject and obedient?

The same thought emerges again from the words of St. Paul on the Incarnation: *Exinanivit semetipsum, formam servi accipiens*, "He emptied Himself, taking the form of a servant" (Phil 2.7). The Apostle did not say, remarks St. Thomas,[9] "He became a servant," because this expression would touch the Person. Now, in Jesus Christ, there is only one Person, that of the Word, Who, being by nature the Son of God, cannot be a slave, nor can He be inferior in any way. The Apostle does say, "Taking the form of the servant," referring to that human nature according to which He was subject to the Father.[10]

Henceforth, we may see that the devotion of St. Louis-Marie is an essential one, and that the aspect under which he considers Christian life is far from secondary. Our Saint would that we be established perfectly in this slavery, in this divine service, the same in which Christ Himself was constituted by the Incarnation and which became ingrained like unto a law governing His entire life.

§2. OUR STATE OF GRACE.

Grace erases not our natural dependence, but perfects it, since by our dependence, God takes possession of our being in a more

---

[9] St. Thomas, *Super Philippenses*, 2-2, *Opera*, 21:356.1: "But why is it more fitting to say 'the form of a servant,' rather than 'servant'? Because 'servant' is the name of a hypostasis, which was not assumed, but the nature was; for that which is assumed is distinct from the one assuming it."
[10] ♦Cf. ¦ Franzelin, *De Verbo incarnato*, Th. 38, Schol 2, 366-371; Pétau, *Dogmata theologica*, 7.6, 3:306-307. ¦

excellent way and under new titles. We may understand this point when we recall that grace establishes new relations between us and God, and more particularly between us and Christ.

The divine Guest. God dwells in us by grace. We saw that this word "indwelling" means more than mere presence[11]: it denotes that one visits and stays in a place as in one's home, in other words, as master and to take joy of it. In any event, God indwells not in us without acting on us; and He is master to the extent He acts. The indwelling by grace, therefore, entails the possession of our soul by our divine Guest, in a particular title and in a more elevated manner, since it raises her to the supernatural order.

Divine likeness. Our supernatural likeness to God and to Christ is imprinted in our souls by the Holy Ghost, Who is compared to a seal, or signet: *In quo et credentes signati estis Spiritu promissionis Sancto,* "believing, in Christ you were signed with the holy Spirit of promise," as with a seal. (Eph 1.13). Now, just as a seal is a mark of possession by him whose engraved initials or figure it bears, so also the supernatural image that the Holy Ghost imprints in our soul mark us as belonging to the divine, and attests that the most Holy Trinity has taken possession of us. And since such image is also that of the Son, to Whom we are bound in a special manner by virtue of our sonship of grace, the seal of the Holy Ghost marks us as especially belonging to Christ.

We shall examine other titles (Redeemer, Head and Divine Spouse) to explain why, in Christian vocabulary, "Our Lord" is a proper name of Jesus Christ.

The Redeemer. The Son of God became Man to redeem us; and if grace cleanses us by sanctifying us, it also snatches us away from the slavery to the devil, and makes us children of God.

St. Louis-Marie calls to mind the title of our divine servitude, which is perhaps the best known, and the most popular among the faithful. He writes: "Before his Baptism, every Christian was the slave of the devil, seeing as he belonged to him; but in his Baptism, he

---

[11] Cf. "Indwelling," in Part 1.2.3.5, pp. 52-53.

solemnly renounces Satan ... takes Jesus Christ for his Master and Sovereign Lord, to depend on Him in the quality of a slave of love."[12] Let us say a few words about this belonging, in which, as regards Christ, we find our condition of being the redeemed. That such belonging is fundamental to our Christian religion we clearly see in its being the object of our promises in Baptism, and in the need for us to confess it before the Church confers the Sacrament on us. The *Catechism of Trent* insists on priests reminding the faithful of it, declaring that it is only just that the faithful see themselves perpetually attached and consecrated as slaves to their Redeemer and Master.[13]

Jesus Christ redeems us from the bondage into which sin has cast us. *Whosoever committeth sin, is the slave of sin*, says Our Lord (Jn 8.34). The sinner may be so blinded for a time that he thinks himself free, alive, active, and independent; still, not long after, he feels the double chain shackling him tug at his neck. First, he is bound to divine justice by the debt of punishment, and made a prisoner because of it: *Thou shalt not go out from prison till thou repay the last farthing* (Mt 5.26). Alas, the poor man has nothing. He is helpless whilst yet needing to make satisfaction, but is never to be delivered, unless the Master forgives him. He is bound, secondly, because he is in the grip of the demon who vanquishes him and to whom God has abandoned him, for the sake of justice. *By whom a man is overcome, of the same also he is the slave* (2 Pet 2.19).

What we know about the tyrannical rule of Satan in the pagan world, we see it replicated somehow in the sinner. If sometimes temptation violently seizes and grips us, imagine what happens to the vanquished soul, despoiled and debased, especially when Satan, who punishes the body and torments the soul, blows his spirit into the sinner and slaps on him the fetters of evil habits. We cannot help but dread when we think of what becomes of such all-consuming bondage in the other life, for we already have glimpses of it in the hellish reality

---

[12] ♦*TD*, 86.
[13] *Catechism*, 1.3.12, 39: "It remains, therefore, that the pastor exhort the faithful people, that we, who derive our name from Him, and are called Christians, and who cannot be ignorant of the extent of His favors, particularly in that, by His gift, we are enabled to understand all these things by faith, may know the very strict obligation we, above all other men, are under, of devoting and consecrating ourselves forever, even as *mancipia*, bondservants, to our Redeemer and our Lord."

of diabolical possessions here below.

O my Savior, You merited the remission of our sins and superabundantly satisfied our debt through Your blessed Passion. It is to God that You paid the price for our redemption. You are Lord of all, including Satan, and have no need of settling with him; for he is merely the executor of Your divine justice. Having made satisfaction for our sake, You were free to exercise Your power; yet, by virtue of the name above all names, You, before Whom every knee bends in Heaven, on earth, and in Hell, snatched us away from this tyranny of the devil and delivered the children of God unto liberty. From this day forward, we are Yours, as a thing bought and paid is to the one who buys it. You paid a high price for us, for You paid not *with corruptible things as gold or silver, but with your precious Blood* (1 Pet 1.18, 19). In Heaven the elect, whom You have *redeemed from the hand of the enemy* (Ps 106.2), sing this canticle of thanksgiving: *Thou hast redeemed us, O Lord, in Thy Blood, and made us to our God, a kingdom* (Rev 5.9, 10). This is the song of triumph achieved; and we, who here below yet walk in the line of fire in combats spiritual, we echo their gratitude; for it is also the cry of our faith triumphant over the world and its prince.

Jesus Christ, Our Lord. You are Our Lord under every right: of justice, of gratitude, and of charity; rights of obligations freely contracted at Baptism. The other, that is to say, Satan, is a mere usurper and cursed tyrant. He has no rights, gives nothing good, and *cometh not, but to steal, and to kill, and to destroy* (Jn 10.10). Therefore, "I renounce Satan, and all his works, and all his pomps, and give myself over to Jesus Christ forever."

The Head and Spouse. Grace washes away Original Sin by tearing us away from the bondage of Satan; more importantly, it gives us a divine life and makes us children of God by incorporating us into Christ.

Jesus Christ is our Head, and, as such, He is *our Lord*; for when we say, "head," we mean pre-eminence, direction without and vital influence within; and for the members, intimate and perfect subjection.

The Apostle teaches this dependence that is derived from our incorporation into Christ, when he explains the unity of His Mystical Body: *Unus Dominus, una Fides, unum Baptisma,* "one Lord, one Faith, one Baptism" (Eph 4.5). There is only one Lord and Master, because there is only one Head; one Faith, the one Christ teaches; one Baptism, the one He instituted to make us partakers of His grace.

We take it for granted that our dependence on Christ, as members of His Mystical Body, is voluntary and full of love, and we shall come back to the subject later; but it is, nonetheless, true that this dependence is more perfect than a servitude of constraint, because it is just as greater as it is more intimate. And what an intimacy it is that results from the communication of life and the functioning of the organism!

To this capacity of Head is joined that of Spouse, wherein Christ commands us, has power over us, and we owe Him our subjection and service. Let us recall the words of St. Paul: *Let women be subject to their husbands, as to the Lord: because the husband is the head of the wife, as Christ is the Head of the Church. As the Church is subject to Christ, so also let the wives be to their husbands in all things* (Eph 5.22-24). The wife, therefore, serves the husband, says St. Thomas, as the servant his master, but with this difference: The master uses his servants for his personal good, while the husband uses his power over his wife and children only for the common good of the family.[14] Even so, this explanation diminishes not the rights of Christ over us, nor our duties towards Him; for the good of the Church is also His, since she is His body and He, her Savior: *Ipse est Salvator corporis ejus* (Eph 5.23).

We speak here only of the reality of our subjection to Christ, our Head and our Spouse; further on we shall treat of the qualities of this dependence to show its excellence and the fruits it bears.

The ways of perfection. In Baptism, every Christian acknowledges Jesus Christ for his Lord, and promises his dependence and service to Him, Who is his Redeemer, Head, and Spouse. Just as there are degrees in belonging and self-giving, so also there are degrees of union with Jesus Christ, and between one and the other, there exists a perfect correspondence.

---

[14] St. Thomas, Super Ephesos, 5, Lect. 8, *Opera*, 21:331.2.

Holiness, the intimate union with God cannot exist unless He exercises more freely and fully His rights over us; neither can it be without us serving His holy will more docilely.[15] Here we have the condition and the means of perfection, either in the world or in the eminent states in the Church, namely the priesthood and the religious life. The latter is qualified by two words, which express the idea of holiness. We say the "religious state" and the "consecrated states." "Religious," because one is formally linked to God by a closer bond; and "consecrated," in order to show that one belongs to Him exclusively, and that one is avowed entirely to Him.

What is consecration, if not a ceremony by which a creature is purified, sanctified, and dedicated solely to the service of God? Now, through the vows of religion, a creature gives himself up entirely and forever: his body, his soul, his will, his powers, his life, everything belongs to Jesus, our Lord and Spouse.

It is the honor of God and the joy of those who love Him, that there are on this earth souls in whom is realized with the perfection of an admirable degree which Jesus Christ asks of us in these words: *Adveniat regnum tuum*, "Thy Kingdom come." Hungering for this reign, impassioned for the rights of Our Lord, in love with His sovereign dominion, these souls, neither the least elevated nor the least enlightened, believe rightly that the necessary and common dependence that is to say, the subjection solely to the commandments of God, neither honors Him as much as He deserves to be, nor satisfies their love. To satisfy the hunger and thirst for justice, they ought to give without reserve what they have and, above all, themselves; they ought

---

[15] ✦As with holiness, so it ought to be with our devotion. Msgr. Gay, *Élévations*, 105, 2:322: "Holiness for us is to adhere to God in such a way that we are but *one and the same spirit* with Him (1 Cor 12.11). It is to be so steeped in His grace, filled with His life, enlightened by His light, loving of His Will, *dependent on His conduct*, in accordance with His thoughts, matched to His tastes, loving His loves, *given over to His rights*, open to His gifts, devoted to His interests, *docile to all that pleases Him*, that we are as if *possessed* by Him, and that, henceforth, we no longer have our own and independent life. ... The more this adherence to God, this dependence on God, this union with God, this locating our being in God, are perfect, the holier we creatures become. ... Holiness is but a plenary and perpetual 'yes' that we creatures say to God; a living 'yes' in which we submit our entire being; a fervent, active, practical, effective 'yes'; a 'yes' that tears us away from all that is low and elevates us to devote ourselves, to consecrate ourselves, to surrender ourselves as *a thing, a victim, and prey* to Him Who is above: that is to say, ultimately, to the Most High, to Christ, Son of God and true God." [Emphases added].

to deliver entirely that which far too many people give *in words*, albeit with a certain goodwill, but so few sacrifice completely *in fact*, and of which many of these two groups do not even possess full knowledge. To that end, these souls will surrender themselves to the free exercise of divine rights, they will push for the practice of vows and virtues to their very end, they will seek ever more intimate and closer bonds, to become to God, "His thing, His victim, and His prey," three words which, in the ways of holiness, mark a sublime gradation, formidable to nature, desirable to love.

Such is the ideal of these souls; and it was also that of St. Teresa, when she exclaimed:

> Better to be, is better to Thee:
> In Thy grace do Thou dispose of me.[16]

Such sentiments lie at the bottom of every longing for a perfect life, and especially for religious life, though to varying degrees and in multiple shades; but when, by the breath of the Holy Ghost, this yearning for the reign of God lights up in a soul, it is to elevate her to heights of self-denial, to make her a powerful and docile instrument of works divine.

Glory is the bloom of grace. In consuming our union with God, it will also render perfect the divine possession begun here below. Indeed, in Heaven, God will be most generous with us. Our walls torn down and resistance gone, He will shed His grace on our soul to overflowing, flooding her with glory and sanctifying her. This is the perfect image of the reign of God, and it is what we long for when we say: *Thy Kingdom come: Thy will be done earth as it is in Heaven*; for inasmuch as divine Will is fulfilled here below, wherein God exercises His sovereign dominion over us, His reign is come and Heaven has begun.

Can we consider in this aspect our state of grace without lifting up our eyes to Jesus Christ? Just as we have contemplated in Him the

---

[16] The French, "Le mieux, c'est d'être mieux à Toi. / À ton gré dispose de moi" (Alet, *L'esprit*, 355), of the poem "En las manos de Dios," by St. Teresa of Avila, "Poesía," 27.8.6-7, in *Escritos*, 1:518.1: "Revolvedme aquí o allí / Qué queréis hacer de mí? — Toss me here, throw me there / What wilt Thou that I be?" The French is a curious rendering, given the clear theme of the poem, expressed in its French title, "Hymne de la Sainte Indifférence"; i.e, the indifference to externalities born of the complete surrender to the Will of God that runs through the entire original in Spanish, which begins with "Vuestra soy, para Vos nací — Thine I am, through Thee I came to be."

fullness of grace and its exemplar fulfilled, so also can we see in Him the noblest type of our divine belonging.

The union of the two natures into one Person is the grace of all graces, the summit of the supernatural, the *summum* or pinnacle of divine union; but in which state does it place the Humanity of Christ with respect to the Word, if not in one of absolute belonging and marvelous dependence? Among men, does slavery leave the personality to subsist? Always. We note that the phenomena of diabolical possession or hypnotism are only accidental, morbid, and intermittent, and not natural, states. Now, in Christ Jesus, human nature, without losing anything of its integrity of state and its truth, is possessed by the Word so that it has no distinct personality; the Word is His "Me"; He governs it by His Spirit according to the will of His Father and for the sake of His glory.

The highest state of belonging to God is the most sublime exemplar of dependence, and we should strive to imitate it as much as we can. It goes without saying that, here, we speak not of the unity of person.

ARTICLE 3: QUALITIES OF THIS HOLY SLAVERY

From this total and absolute belonging, under any title, we must exclude all the lamentable conditions inherent in servitude that make it odious. As St. Louis-Marie remarked, Christians do not force men into a slavery of constraint; only Turks and idolaters do.[17] He further notes that it is abhorrent for a creature to have an absolute dependence on anyone other than his Creator, and frequently reminds us that our belonging to Jesus Christ and His Mother is a holy, glorious, voluntary, and loving servitude. By the tongue of St. Louis-Marie's, these qualifiers are not spoken as some pious lip service, nor are they simple artifices of style to soften the word "slavery" (for the odium attached to the practice is as great yesterday as it is today); but they bespeak the principle of our servitude, which is the virtue of charity; its condition, voluntary; its fruits, the holiness, honor, and holy liberty of the

---

[17] *Secret*, 24. ♦ ¦ St. Louis-Marie often mentions the piteous Turks and idolaters, especially in his hymns. See, e.g., "Amende honorable au cœur de Jésus," *Cantiques*, 47.17: "Si le cœur d'un Turc infidèle / T'avait aimé jusqu'à ce point, / Tu l'aimerais, ô cœur rebelle; / Pour ce Cœur, tu ne l'aimes point." ¦

children of God.

Ineffably sweet it is to contemplate these truths; but if we wish to take joy of one of the remarkable spiritual vistas offered by the world of grace, in the same blink of an eye we must embrace the advancement that charity, dependence, glory, and holy liberty offer us in our devotion. In other words, the more charity there is in a soul and the more she becomes a slave, the more her servitude is voluntary, holy, glorious, and free.

§1. THE DOMINION OF GOD

The tyranny of Satan in no way resembles the sovereign dominion of God over His creatures. Creation is a great act of charity, in which God grants us the first and vital gift: our very being, our existence. As such, the obligation to serve God as our Creator is, by definition, infused with the gratitude and love we owe Him, and the honor and freedom we find in our natural dependence on Him. Scripture reminds us of honor in bold terms: *Homo cum in honore esset non intellexit*, "man when he was in honor did not understand" (Ps 48.13).[18] We are guaranteed our liberty, for *God made man from the beginning, and left him in the hand of his own counsel* (Sir 15.14); that is, man is free to act by the intellect and will endowed by God. These two testimonies are brought together in the Book of Wisdom, with the touching words: *Cum magna reverentia, Domine, disponis nos*, "with great forbearance, O Lord, dost Thou govern us"[19] (Wis 12.18).

§2. THE DEPENDENCE ON GOD

To its precepts and manifold prescriptions, the Old Law added that the Israelites should have a dependence on God and especially bound them to His service, that they may become *His* people, *His* inheritance, *His* chosen dominion. They may have been obedient for fear of divine retribution; that is, they were governed by the law of

---

[18] St. Augustine, *Enarr. in Psalmos*, 48.1.16, 2.11, PL 36.554, 563: "What is, 'being in honor'? Being made after the image and likeness of God, man is preferred to beasts. For God made not man as He did a beast. God made Man, that beasts should minister him. ... Wherein is the intellect, wherein is the mind, wherein the power of discovering truth, wherein is faith, wherein is your hope, wherein your charity, there God has His Image. ... [Therefore], be *not like horse and mule, which have not understanding* (Ps 31.9)."

[19] RSV; cf. DR: "With great favor, O Lord, Thou disposest of us."

fear, but their servitude had charity as its foundation. Its aim, no doubt, was of forming and governing "servants," but servants of a Lord who, at every turn and even in the reproaches of His anger, failed not to reiterate His beneficence and His tenderness: *Ego sum Dominus Deus tuus*, "I am the Lord thy God" (Ex 20.2). He reminded this forgetful and ungrateful people, whom He pardoned so often and sustained so patiently, that He never ceased to shower them with gifts. O how many times the Prophets and Psalmists did try to win their hearts until promises too great for words, appeals, and counsels were ringing in their ears! Fear may have prevailed over their love of God, but it was still love that bound them to Him—love, more or less perfect, that moved the true children of Abraham to serve Him; for the Law says not only, "Thou shalt adore" and "Thou shalt serve,"[20] but also, "Thou shalt love."[21]

For this reason, the service to God was, in a sense, done out of free consent. God had deigned to make this chosen people His own, binding them to Him in a pact and covenant, so that they might serve Him by keeping His Law.

By accepting this divine servitude, the Israelites were kept free from the tyranny of Egypt, and, for as long as they remained faithful to their God, they had no fear of strangers having dominion over them. Such was their liberty.

It was a signal honor indeed for the Hebrews to be the only people that possessed the pure truth and the divine promises, that lived free from the corruption of the Gentiles and bound to their God in a manner the likes of which all the other nations, what with their idols, could never even have imagined.[22]

§3. A BONDAGE OF LOVE

In the law of grace, love takes the place of fear, for the first and greatest commandment is this: "Thou shalt love."[23] For God, as well as for us, the names, the tenderness, the relations of intimacy and ineffable love, announced, prepared, and outlined in the Old Law, have

---

[20] Ex 20.5, rendered into the positive, "Thou shalt adore and serve Me, not idols."
[21] Dt 6.5.
[22] Cf. Dt 33.29.
[23] Mt 22.37, Mk 12.30, Lk 10.27.

their full meaning and their full realization in the New. God calls us to be His children and His friends,[24] and by grace we truly are that. Jesus is our Redeemer, our Brother, our Head and our Spouse. On the one hand, charity leads to a more complete self-giving; and on the other, it makes the dependence nobler, more affectionate, and sweeter. Imagine how far apart is the submission and service of a child to his father, from the obedience of even the most devoted servant to his master! We see now why our subjection to Christ, as our Head and Spouse, is more perfect and is of a more excellent order than could have existed under the Old Law.

As our servitude, above all, is a bondage of love and not of fear, we must freely give it our consent. We require the one adopted or the one who enters a society to show his acceptance. Think how much more the free assent is necessary to contract a conjugal union, lest we exclude love from it and deprive the bride of her dignity! In His loving and compassionate wisdom, it has pleased God to act with similar care with us. To redeem us and make us His sons by adoption, to incorporate us in Christ, and to become the Spouse of our souls, He asks us for our consent in Baptism, and we, in turn, through the exercise of our will, freely choose to renounce Satan and take Jesus Christ for our Lord.

We said above that the possession of the Humanity of Christ by the Word is the ideal, the type of our belonging to Our Lord. We now point out how, in this union of the two natures in Jesus Christ, in the tightest dependence ever, there also exists the greatest love that could ever have united God to a created nature.

Contemplate the incomparable dignity granted to human nature, since the Word deemed it worthy of Him to take and possess it. Cardinal Franzelin, in his usual manner of bringing a breath of fresh air to theology, carefully choosing the subjects of his theses, and never failing to elucidate in his expositions, explains in his treatise *De Verbo Incarnato*, that for the human nature of Christ not to have a distinct personality, does not mean that it lacks any perfection, nor that it should descend to a state of inferiority; rather that it rises to a more

---

[24] Jn 15.15.

perfect state,[25] thereby becoming the human nature of the Word. As for us, the principle of our present dignity and of our future glory lies in the union with Christ and belonging to Him. In theology, we use the term *natura assumpta*, nature taken by the Word and raised up to Him in the unity of Person, to express the majesty to which the Incarnation raised the human nature of the Savior; and *natura elevata*, nature elevated to supernatural order, to describe the nobility of our state of grace.

In sum, along with honor, this dependence brings us holy liberty or emancipation. Dare we say that it is also a form of kingship? Christ is King. All power is given to Him, and His name is above all names.[26] If we acknowledge Him as our Lord, first we will be redeemed from the slavery to sin, restored to the liberty of the children of God,[27] and, by the anointing of His Spirit, made holy kings and priests; then, we shall judge the world and reign with Him.[28]

Commenting on the words of the Apostle, *Paul, a servant of* Jesus *Christ* (Rom 1.1), St. Thomas says: "Without doubt, servitude is in itself a vile condition, but it is made commendable by reason of what is added, namely, 'of Jesus Christ.' For 'Jesus' means 'Savior' and 'Christ'

---

[25] ◆Franzelin, Th. 31, II, Corollarium 1, in *De Verbo Incarnato*, 278: "Humana natura si non esset assumpta a Verbo, eo ipso, si existeret, per se subsisteret et esset persona; quia vero assumpta est a Verbo, jam non subsistit in se sed est natura Verbi; assumptio ergo impedivit imperfectum humanitatis in se subsistentis, elevando eam ad perfectionem longe excellentiorem, ut sit natura Verbi seu subsistat in Verbo, hæcque exclusio subsistentiæ in se *improprie* appellatur consumptio."

[26] Mt 28.18, Phil 2.9.

[27] ◆Objections to the devotion of Holy Slavery stems from its seeming opposition to the spirit of childhood, liberty, and charity that animates Christianity. St. Paul says: *You have not received the spirit of bondage in fear; but you have received the spirit of adoption of sons* (Rom 8.15). Also: *Therefore, now he* [the faithful] *is not a servant, but a son. And if a son, an heir also through God* (Gal 4.7). And this, the word of Our Lord: *I will not now call you servants, but friends* (Jn 15.15). However, the elevation to the supernatural order or the adoption, and the right to the heavenly inheritance, do not remove absolutely the servitude essentially attached to the creature; for the adopted sons are themselves servants, by nature, in comparison to the Son; but by our divine adoption, we cease to be slaves, in the sense that we no longer are strangers who have no right to inheritance. (Franzelin, Th. 38, Schol. 2, *De Verbo Incarnato*, 367). On the other hand, the servitude which St. Paul compares to the condition of the son refers to the servitude to sin, corruption, and servile fear, from which Jesus Christ delivers us; and not to the servitude to justice and charity that befits Saints and the spiritually perfect. The latter servitude is not opposed to liberty, for St. Paul says: *Delivered from the servitude of corruption, we begin to delight in the firstfruits of this glorious liberty of the children of God* (Rom 8.21). On the slavery to the B.V.M., see Lépicier, *Tr. de B.V.M.*, 3.2.1.9, 423.

[28] 1 Cor 6.2, Rev 5.10.

means 'anointed.'" The more we are subject to Him, the more we participate in the salvation and anointing of which He is the source. "Furthermore, it is praiseworthy for a person to be subjected to the spiritual anointing of grace, because a thing is perfect to the extent that it is subjected to its perfection, as the body to the soul, and air to light."[29]

§4. A BONDAGE TO CHARITY

When we consider the more profound bond to God created by the religious and certain states of perfection, what do we see in them? First, the donation and dependence that grow along with charity. Charity, in fact, from God as well as from the creature, is the reason for these higher vocations, which are truly the triumph and the flower of Christianity. The Church has a canticle that consecrated virgins sing on the day of their profession. From their lips come these words of affirming their donation: "The empire of the world and all grandeur of this earth I have despised for love of Our Lord Jesus Christ."[30] In general, in all the ways of perfection, seen from both sides, that of God and the soul, it is a higher gift, a mutual possession, a reciprocal enjoyment, as these words of the Canticle express so very well: *My beloved to me, and I to him* (Cant 2.16).

But if true love exists in consecrated life, how can it not in Holy Slavery? Who loves without becoming a slave to the beloved? Use we not words such as "bond" and "captivity," "belong," and even "idol" and "adoration" in the language of love? If the lover goes astray and enters into illicit love, he profanes these words, as he does profane the very name of love, but he would still be right to call it love ¦¦ albeit in a sense totally devoid of morality. | But since the love of creatures may hold a soul captive, notwithstanding that it is a mere shadow of truth, eternal beauty, and infinite good, are we wrong to say that we are

---

[29] St. Thomas, ad Romanos, 1, Lect. 1, *Opera*, 20:382.1: "Videtur autem esse abjecta conditio servitutis si absolute consideretur. ... Sed redditur commendabilis ex eo quod additur Iesu Christi. Jesus enim interpretatur salvator. ... Christus interpretatur unctus. ... Quod autem aliquid subjiciatur suæ saluti et spirituali unctioni gratiæ, laudabile est, quia tanto aliquid est perfectius quanto magis suæ perfectioni subjicitur, sicut corpus animæ et aër luci."

[30] ◆*Pontificale*, 195: "Regnum mundi, et omnem ornatum sæculi contempsi, propter amorem Domini nostri Jesu Christi: Quem vidi, quem amavi, in quem credidi, quem dilexi." ¦¦ See also, England, *Works*, 4:213.1. |

slaves of charity to Him Who, by the essence truth, is the supreme beauty, and joy, and bliss infinite?

Also, when this supernatural light shines in the eyes of a soul, making her despise the earth, Jesus is illumined in her, she becomes a voluntary captive of His charity, and she herself forges the chains to satisfy her longing to belong, to surrender, and to serve. Vows religious or private, or even the usual practice of evangelical counsels—everything serves to give herself as much as she can. She becomes the prey of God, Who is for her an *ignis consumens*, "consuming fire" (Heb 12.29), and surrenders herself to His rights. She sacrifices to His holy jealousies, to His divine good pleasures, to the minutest tenderness of His charity, her very life, her judgment, her will, her affections—all that no profane slavery could even pretend to win over. In the lives of Saints, we see to what great extent charity delivers souls to God.[31]

To an eminent degree, such is the servitude to charity, which is the same as saying that it is open to constraint. Always respectful, reserved, and gentle with us, God asks for our consent in Baptism. He makes the religious state and certain abnegations purely the object of careful consideration and good counsel; for "such acts," says Msgr. Gay, "surpasses our nature to give, ... and, above all, they carry [in the eyes of the Lord] such a heavy price that He wills to accept them from none but the freest and most spontaneous generosity of our hearts."[32]

Let us now discuss *holy liberty*, the fruit of this loving slavery. O how souls are indeed emancipated, those that are released from their attachments to the world and to themselves! They are done with the seductions of here below; they admirably dominate the servitudes inherent in our present condition. Their lives reflect, as faithfully as possible, the resurrected life of Christ, and their state borders on this

---

[31] ◆Msgr. Gay has an unpublished poem entitled, *À Jésus Pontife*. An excerpt: "Fifty years gone by have I given all to Thee, / And never Thou tookest of me that is not Thine. / I will to please Thy love, 'tis that enliveth me. / When cometh time, ... Jesus, consumest this soul, mine." Let us also mention the ecstatic canticles of St. Francis of Assisi, *Works*, 152-162, in particular, Canticle III, Amor *de Caritate*, from which we extract the following lines that recall what we just read: "My heart is rent in twain, / And burns with love of Thee. / It burns and burns again, / All restless with desire. / 'Tis bound it cannot break its chain; / ... I've given all for Love alone, / Barter'd the world and self away; / ... The soul thus bound by sweetest ties / Is yearning for her Lord's embrace; ... But since thy Love hath dealt the blow, / I've bartered self away to be / Chang'd into Thee anew, and so / Lead a new life and utterly. (Italian text, *Opera*, 166-194).

[32] Gay, *Rosarie*, 246.

fulsome liberty of Heaven, the fruit of the perfect fulfillment of divine Will.

St. Louis-Marie agreed, because for him, the slavery of charity and liberty stand not in opposition. We see this in the exclamation in his Prayer for Missionaries: *Da matri tuæ liberos, alioquin moriar,* "Give children and servants to Thy Mother, otherwise it would be better that I were dead."[33] And making light, as he liked to do, of the depths of the grammatical or mystical meaning of words, he declares that he wants "children," free souls (*liberos*), free from all things, but nevertheless are *slaves*, and solely to God's charity and will.[34]

It will be remembered that on several occasions he points out that, among the fruits of the faithful practice of Holy Slavery, is the ease of approaching Our Lord without servile or scrupulous fear. And, if we must give substance to this assertion, we need only cite, by way of examples, the acts of holy familiarity, and the astonishing boldness that the Saints have with God. Their complete abandonment to His Will affords them to be entirely at filial liberty with Him.

We turn now to speak of the honor, the dignity of the creature so completely and so lovingly delivered to Our Lord. To serve God, though in a common and ordinary manner, is already to reign; but how reigns he who serves Him only so far? The holy honor by which the Church surrounds the religious state speaks volumes about its interior and hidden nobility; so much so, that the world itself pays tribute and falls under its influence. Msgr. Gays calls consecrated lives

---

[33] *Prayer for Missionaries*, §§6, 14, VD, 252. French title, "Prière Embrasée," composed by St. Louis-Marie at the end of his life, pleading God to send him men for his missions. See VD, 249-265. Cf. Gn 30.1 : Da mihi liberos, alioquin moriar.

[34] Ibid., §§7, 8, 11, VD, 253-254: "What, then, do I ask of you? *Liberos*: Priests who are free with the liberty that comes from You, detached from everything, having no father, mother, brothers, sisters or relatives according to the flesh, nor friends according to the world, nor worldly possessions, riches, cares, nor even their own will, to encumber or distract them. *Liberos*: Men who are free but still in bondage to Your charity and Your will; men after Your own heart who, without the taint or impediment of self-love, will carry out Your will to the fullest. ... *Liberos*: True children of Mary, whom she has conceived and begotten by her charity, carried in her womb, suckled at her breast, nourished with her milk, raised by her cares, sustained in her arms, and enriched with her graces." The Company of Mary has its own, less literal English translation at www.montfortian.info.

"the eminent states in the Church"?[35] Do the gifts, the favors of every kind, with which God adorns Saints, not testify how much He honors them? Indeed, He does so honor them that the Psalmist could not restrain this cry of grateful admiration: *Thy friends, O God, are made exceedingly honorable* (Ps 138.17). We need not go far into divine intimacy, before we are also seized by the same sentiment. Every soul advancing in the way of self-sacrifice and self-giving, by the light of faith sees clearly that to belong to God so totally, to serve Him so unreservedly, is an honor that knows no price, and a signal grace of which she is unworthy. Then, as mad with love and as she is with gratitude, she senses the need to humble and empty herself. "It is too much honor to be a slave to the Son and the Mother," cried St. Bernard[36]; and St. Louis-Marie echoed him when in his letters he appends to his signature the appellation, "Slave unworthy of Jesus and Mary."

Before concluding this wide vista of our holy devotion, let us cast a last glance in order to sum up its spiritual delights and emblazon in our minds its living image. In one quick look, let us take in the various phases and aspects of belonging to God. We have indeed travelled a great distance, in all respects, from the *Ego sum Dominus Deus tuus*, "I am the Lord thy God" (Ex 20.2), by which God marked the precepts of the Old Law, to the cry of the Christian who, conquered and overcome, surrenders himself without reserve to charity and falls at the feet of his divine Master, saying: *Dominus meus et Deus meus*, "My Lord and my God"! (Jn 20.28).

Even so, this is a mere prelude of things to come. Let grace radiate ever so gently, and bind us to You ever so tightly, O Lord Jesus, King of souls, to us greater still will glory be, as it alone is the consummation of all things; for only then will be fully realized this holy belonging, this loving captivity, this mutual possession of the soul and of God; and only then will it be an embrace, an act of love, of union, and of rejoicing.

---

[35] Msgr. Gay, *Life and virtues*, 1:lvi.

[36] St. Bernard, *De gradibus*, 22.53, PL 182.970D, speaking of Martha when she approached Our Lord about her dead brother, Lazarus (Jn 11.20-28): "With what face, then, can I, a common slave, to whom it is a high honor to be in the service at once of the Son and of the Mother, presume to ask for the life of one who has been dead for four days?"

ARTICLE 4: THE VALUE OF THE WORD "SLAVERY"

From all that we said in the preceding discussion, particularly on the difference between a servant and a slave, we believe that the word "slavery" is the right one to use in the context of our devotion. It remains to be seen whether it is fitting in the language of Christians, and whether it is sanctioned by Tradition.[37] In his *True Devotion*, St. Louis-Marie condensed in a few pages a number of documents written, amongst others, by several authors of his time. They demonstrate that the term "slavery" conforms to the language of Scripture and Tradition. Let us summarize them, by adding to them other notes that we may easily multiply.

§1. THE EXAMPLE OF CHRIST

We begin with Christ Himself, He Who *emptied Himself, taking the form of a servant* (Phil 2.7). His first word on commencing His public life was: *Behold, I come to do Thy will* (Heb 10.5). He also said: *My meat is to do the will of Him that sent Me, that I may perfect His work* (Jn 4.34). We are justified in using the title "servant," the very same which the Prophets used when they foretold of Him,[38] a title which, by reason of His divine Person, diminishes Him not but affects His Humanity through which He renders His Father reverence, love, submission, and service.

The Most Blessed Virgin acknowledges herself to be *ancilla Domini*, "handmaid of the Lord" (Lc 1.38). Following the example of the Divine Master, the Apostles proclaim themselves slaves of Christ, as did St. Paul when he writes: "Paul, slave of Christ" (Rom 1.1). And it is in this same apostolic spirit that the successors of St. Peter sign: *Servus servorum Dei*, "Servant [lit. slave] of the servants of God." When St. Louis-Marie wrote: "Before Baptism we belonged to the devil, as his slaves; but Baptism has made us true slaves of Jesus Christ,"[39] he almost literally translates these words of St. Paul: *Nunc vero liberati a peccato, servi autem facti Deo*, "now being made free from sin, you are become servants to God" (Rom 6.22).

---

[37] ◆On this point, see de Montfort, *Life and Select Writings*, c. 11, "The Bondservant of Christ"; and, "Éclaircissements," in *Le Règne de Jésus par Marie*, July 1900.

[38] Ps 115.16; Is 42.1, 49.3, 50.10, 52.13, 53.11; Jer 30.10, 33.21; Ez 34.23, 37.24; Zec 3.8.

[39] *TD*, 45.

It is true that in modern languages we render the Latin *servus*, "servant." The abolition of slavery in civilized societies, and the longing for liberty spreading around the world, have succeeded in making the condition of human bondage odious, leaving its reputation in tatters, and pegging an evil to the word. For this reason, the word "servant" has been chosen to stand for the noun *servus*, papering over its proper meaning, weakening its force, and translating it only imperfectly. Whatever lurks in the background of its usage in everyday language, let us keep the words "servitude" and "slavery," but on the condition that in our mind they should retain the ideas of the sovereign dominion of God and of our absolute dependence on Him; for we ought not to jettison the words—the very words used by St. Louis-Marie—that express our thoughts with precision. He spoke the language of the authors of his time, the same one used in Christian Tradition. The word "slavery," for instance, accurately renders the *mancipia Christi* used in the *Catechism of Trent*.[40] It is also this word which expresses exactly the *servitude* to Christ of which the first Christians boasted. We read, in fact, in the office of St. Agatha: "I am free born," she answers the judge. "One becomes sovereignly free, when one becomes enslaved to Christ. ... I am a slave to Christ, and as such, I declare myself a person of servile condition."[41]

§2. THE SAINTS AND THE WORD "SLAVERY"

This language has been passed on from the first Christians to the masters of spiritual life down through the ages. Whatever the import of the flux in social life, however language varies from one age to another, Christianity changes not! Our condition of redeemed and baptized creatures remains set in the foundation of our faith, which prompts us always to declare: "Jesus Christ, Our Lord." We read in the work of St. Ildefonso this declaration: "In order to be a devoted slave

---

[40] Part 1.4.2.2, note 13, p. 76.

[41] ¦¦ "De S. Agatha," 1.5, *AS*, 5 Feb, 4:600C: "Non solum ingenuis ac nobilibus, sed et locupletissimis nata parentibus sum. ... Ancilla certe quidem sum Christi, ideoque, ut recte ais, servæ instar me habeo. ... Nostra ingenuitas et gloria iis in rebus consistit, quibus Christi servitus declaratur." Ant., S. Agathæ, *Brev. Rom.*, 613:"I am well born and of a respectable family, as all my relations testify. The best of my birth is that I was born the slave of Christ. I look like a slave because I am one. I am the slave of Christ." St. Agatha of Sicily, was martyred c. AD 251. ¦

of the Son, I aspire to become the faithful slave of the Mother."⁴² St.
Bernard exclaims: "I am but a vile slave, for whom it is too great an
honor to serve the Son and the Mother."⁴³ In the last chapter of her
Interior Castle, St. Teresa writes these remarkable words: "Know you
what is true spiritual life? It is to make oneself a slave of God and to
bear the mark of this slavery, I mean to be branded with the Cross of
Jesus Christ. It is to belong so much to this crucified God, to give Him
such a gift of our own liberty, that He may, at His pleasure, sell and
sacrifice us for the salvation of the world, as He Himself was sold and
sacrificed."⁴⁴ In addition to St. Peter Damian, Cornelius à Lapide, and
the pious people quoted by St. Louis-Marie, we should mention here
St. Jean Eudes, and Fathers Olier, de Condren and de Bérulle, who use
the term "slavery" to express their absolute dependence on Jesus and
His Mother.

It is still slavery, if it be not in word, at least in the strict sense
which we find in the well-known prayer of Fr. Niccolò Zucchi: "O my
Lady, O my Mother, keep me, defend me as your goods and property."⁴⁵ This is precisely the consecration in the life of Holy Slavery and
in almost identical terms formulated by St. Ignatius of Loyola, when,
after a beautiful contemplation on the love of God, he says: ¦ "Take,
Lord, and receive all my liberty, my memory, my understanding, and
my will entire; all that I have and possess. You have given all to me.
To You, O Lord, I return them. All is Yours: Dispose of it all according
to Your will. Give me Your love and Your grace, for they are sufficient

---

⁴² ◆St. Ildefonso, *De virginitate perpetua SS. Mariæ*, c. 12, PL 96.108A : "Ut sim devotus servus Filii, servitutem fideliter appeto Genitricis."
⁴³ Note 36, p. 89. ¦¦ Cf. St. Bernard, *De laudibus Virginis Matris* [Super *Missus est*], Homilia 3.1, et 4.1, PL 183.71B : "Woe is me, not because I have held my tongue, but because I have spoken; I, whose lips are impure. Alas! What vanities, what lies, what shameful words has this foul mouth vomited! And now it presumes to treat of the things of heaven?" ¦
⁴⁴ St. Teresa of Avila, "Las moradas," 7.12, *Obras*, 2:204: ¦¦ "Know you what it is to be truly spiritual? It is for men to make themselves slaves of God, branded with His iron which is in the form of a cross. Since they surrender their liberty to Him, He can sell them as slaves of the entire world, as He was sold, which would do them no wrong, but rather render them the greatest favor." Cf. *Interior Castle*, 7.4.12, 286. ¦
⁴⁵ Cros, *Le prière du P. Zucchi*, 46: "O my Lady! O my Mother! I offer you all of me, and for proof of my devotion, today I consecrate to you my eyes, my ears, my lips, my heart—all of me. And since I belong to you, O my good Mother, keep me, protect me, as I am your goods and property."

unto me."⁴⁶ | St. Francis de Sales prays in these words: "Let us become slaves of devotion, whose serfs are happier than kings."⁴⁷

We could amass testimonies without much adding to the strength of our already conclusive evidence.⁴⁸ Let us close this first

---

⁴⁶ St. Ignatius of Loyola, *Ejercicios*, 104: "Tomad, Señor, y recibid toda mi libertad, mi memoria, mi entendimiento, y toda mi voluntad, todo mi haber, y mi poseer: vos me lo distes, á vos Señor lo torno, todo es vuestro, disponed a toda vuestra voluntad. Dadme vuestro amor y gracia, que ésta me basta."

⁴⁷ de Sales, *Love of God*, 12.10, 550: "Our freewill is never so free as when it is a slave to the Will of God, nor ever so much a slave as when it serves our own. It never has so much life as when it dies to itself, nor ever so much death, as when it lives to itself. We are at liberty to do good or evil; yet to choose evil, is not to use, but to abuse our liberty. Let us renounce this miserable liberty, and let us forever subject our freewill to the rule of heavenly love: let us become slaves of the devotion (*dilection*) whose serfs are happier than kings." Cf. "Amour de Dieu," 12.10, *Œuvres*, 5:341.

⁴⁸ ♦See the writings of: Mother Mechtilde of the Blessed Sacrament; B. Jeanne de Lestonnac; Mother de Sales Chappuis, and so on. — Canon Didiot has published his annotated and commented *Vraie Dévotion*, (Caillières, 1891), which contains a note concerning Holy Slavery that seems strange to us. Since it came from the hand of such a distinguished theologian as Didiot, we can hardly ignore it; and as, in our opinion, its lies deceive the faithful and tend to deprecate the devotion espoused by St. Louis-Marie, we report here the defects in his argument. This note begins as follows: "What St. Louis-Marie has said many times and what we have said ourselves regarding the slavery of Christians to God and Mary, sufficiently shows that it is a question of the most filial, the most tender, the most amiable, the most opposed to constraints, to violence, to the shame of slavery itself." (p. 272). — True enough. However, these things are accidentals, and holds no water as to the very essence of slavery, for it consists in absolute dependence which, at least with respect to God, is congruent with respect and love. Canon Didiot continues: "This expression of slavery could thus be used as originally intended, or in a metaphorical and tempered sense." (p. 272). It is, however, in the strict sense that St. Paul employs it, as did the martyrs, the *Catechism of Trent*, St. Teresa of Avila, and so on. "However, let us admit that it does not correspond perfectly to the spirit of Catholicism, which is all grace, holy liberty, and filial love." (p. 272). We have shown above that Holy Slavery is reconciled to all these things, witness the testimony of Cardinal Franzelin and other theologians; that it is born of the links between grace and love; that it is, in sum, a cause of liberty and honor. Moreover, Canon Didiot himself writes: "As for his principles, as St. Louis-Marie expounds them, this devotion is not new; it is intimately connected with the very foundations of the Catholic religion." (p. 263). How do we reconcile this affirmation with what Canon Didiot says prior and his following statement: "Rome, guardian of the true theological traditions, no longer wants to tolerate a devotion, or rather a formula of devotion, that ill fits with them." (p. 273). The condemnations of the Holy See to which the Canon Didiot refers are set forth in a special note (pp. 273-274); but it appears that, while certain abuses may condemn the practices, confraternities, and books, the doctrine of the Holy Slavery to Mary, as well as other confraternities and congregations, are approved and enriched with indulgences: Those which the Sovereign Pontiff Leo XIII deigned to grant to the formula of consecration composed by St. Louis-Marie and to the Confraternity of Mary "Queen of Hearts"; those, following his example, which the Bishops have agreed to concede, show that there is no need to cast a shadow on this devotion. It is therefore wrong for Canon Didiot to express this opinion: "We think that individuals, as well as associations and congregations, will do well to give it up, as the Blessed de Montfort will not

part by quoting the consecration set down by St. Marguerite-Marie Alacoque, inspired by Our Lord Himself, as Fr. Croiset reports in his book, *Devotion to the Sacred Heart*. St. Marguerite-Marie did bid what she calls the "Little Consecration"[49] be included in it, saying: "This consecration comes from Him, and He would not be pleased if it were omitted." The Sovereign Pontiff Leo XIII enriched it with 300 days of indulgences, applicable to the souls in Purgatory. The brief act ends with these words: "I desire to place all my happiness and all my glory in living and dying *as Your slave*."[50]

---

hesitate for a moment to tell them!" (p. 273). It is a little bold what he says. — Finally, after having justified the conduct of our Saint, under the pretext that "the memory of [St. Louis-Marie] should not suffer from a subsequent condemnation which aims not at the substance of his teaching," (p. 273), Canon Didiot proposes to change *the form, the expressions* of the devotion and concludes: "Let us replace *the idea and the expression* [it is no longer just the form!] of *slavery* by that of *filiation*: let us substitute the rosary for the chains of times gone by, and everything will be perfect in this *Treatise*." (p. 274). Replacing the chains with the chaplet touches not the nature of the devotion of St. Louis-Marie; for such changes relate to a mere external practice, independent and incidental; but to wish to substitute the idea of filiation for that of slavery is to misunderstand completely the nature of this devotion and to change its purpose. Otherwise, it would be necessary to admit that this perfect consecration adds nothing to the vows of Baptism, and that the kingship of Christ and the queenship of His Mother, whom we honor by absolute dependence, constitute not the proper and distinct viewpoint of this devotion. — We will conclude this long note by citing two facts which confirm singularly what we have said both in this note and throughout this chapter. They relate to two approvals given by the Holy See: one by Urban VIII in 1631 to the *Constitutions of the Regular Canonesses of the Holy Sepulcher*; the other by Leo XIII in 1887 to the *Constituciones de las Esclavas del Sagrado Corazón*, "the Slaves of the Sacred Heart." The first of these institutes has in its Constitutions a consecration as slaves of Jesus and Mary (Chanoinesses, *Règles*, 177-178), which resembles that of St. Louis-Marie. They even wear chains.

[49] There are two formulas for this consecration both signed and both preserved at the Monastery of the Visitation at Nevers; one addressed to Mother Louise-Henriette de Soudeilles, the other to Sister Felice-Madeleine de la Barre, which is the one quoted below. They are almost identical, and their differences may be explained by scribal license in their transcriptions. St. Marguarite-Marie calls this beautiful prayer, the "Little Consecration." (Alacoque, *Vie et œuvres*, 2:111, 129, 313). She believed that the Sacred Heart of Jesus inspired her to set it down. On Aug 21, 1690, less than two months before she died, she wrote to Croiset: "Je vous dirai de mettre [dans votre ouvrage] la petite Consécration laquelle, si je ne me trompe, venant de Lui, Il n'agréerait pas qu'elle y fût omise." On the inspiration, see Croiset, *Devotion*, 1.2, 6-10, in which book we find an act of devotion but not the Little Consecration.

[50] The full text of the Little Consecration (Alacoque, *Vie et œuvres*, 2:135-136): "I, [Name], give and consecrate myself to the Sacred Heart of Our Lord Jesus Christ my person and my life, my actions, my pains and sufferings, that I may no more will to make use of any part of my being save to honor, love, and glorify the Sacred Heart. This is my unchanging purpose, namely, to be all His, and to do all things for love of Him, renouncing with all my heart whatever may displease Him. I therefore take Thee, O Sacred Heart, to be the only object of my love, the guardian of my life, the assurance of my salvation, the

If we succeeded in bringing to light the nature of Holy Slavery as understood by St. Louis-Marie, we also hope that we have fully demonstrated that this portion of the mystery of grace is capital; that this form of devotion is not fanciful, since it rests on the fundamental dogmas of Christianity and summarizes our obligations to them; that, in sum, this word "slavery" is as fair in itself as it is in conformance with the language of Tradition.

---

remedy of my weakness and inconstancy, the atonement for all the faults of my life and my sure refuge at the hour of my death. Be Thou, O Heart of goodness, my justification before God Thy Father, and turn away from me the bolts of His righteous anger. O Heart of love, I place all my confidence in Thee, for I fear all my wickedness and frailty, but hope for all things from Thy goodness and Thy bounty. Do Thou consume in me all that may displease Thee or resist Thy holy will. Let Thy pure love imprint Thee so deeply upon my heart that nevermore shall I forget Thee or be separated from Thee. Grant, I beseech Thee, that in all Thy goodness, my name may be written in Thee, for I desire to place all my happiness and all my glory in living and dying as Thy slave. Amen."

PART II:

OUR MEANS, OR THE UNION WITH JESUS THROUGH MARY

PROLOGUE

he aim of our devotion is to live in perfect dependence on Christ so that He may live in us. The means we choose to establish our dependence and to form Jesus in us is Mary.

> Depend all I on her, my Mother,
> To better lean on Him, my Savior.[1]

One may go to Jesus by various means, all of which are to be recommended; but St. Louis-Marie goes through Mary: *Ad Jesum per Mariam*.[2] The Holy Slavery to Mary is indeed the proper name of this devotion, since it indicates its nature and object.[3]

In a few words, this object[4] is none other than Mary considered as Mediatrix and Sovereign. We see that it has two sides. The formula "To Jesus through Mary" expresses only one side of our devotion, namely the mediation of the Blessed Virgin; but it says nothing about

---

[1] Note 1, p. 70.

[2] St. Bernard, *In Nat. B.V.M.* [de Aquæductu], §6-7, PL 183.440-441: "Learn, O man, the counsel of God, and see it as the design of wisdom and of mercy. Before bedewing the whole earth, He bathed the clouds; desiring to redeem all mankind, He placed the entire ransom in the hands of Mary. ... Let us strive, therefore, to understand with what devout affection God wills us to honor Mary, in whom He placed the fullness of all good. ... Let us venerate Mary with every fiber of our heart, with all the affections and longings of our soul, for so wills He Who arranged that all should come through Mary. This, I say, is His Will, and He wills but for our good." *In Vig. Nat. Domini*, Sermo 3.10, PL 183.100A: "If she were only mother, it sufficed her to be saved by bringing children into the world; if she were only a virgin, she would be sufficient unto herself; but the blessed fruit of her womb would not be [Christ], the ransom price for all mankind. Thus, in the first mixture is the remedy, in the second it is applied to us; for God wanted us to have nothing that did not come to us through the hands of Mary."

[3] ♦Devotions are specified by their object. The word "slavery" indicates the type of devotion; and by adding "to Mary," we designate its proper and *formal* object. It is the specific element that completes its constitution in itself and differentiates it from other devotions of slavery.

[4] ♦We speak here of the object in the *formal* sense. See note 1, p. 4.

her sovereignty, which we honor by a singular dependence. Instead of "Mediatrix and Sovereign," St. Louis-Marie says, "Mother and Lady," for in her spiritual motherhood, he rightly sees the culminating point, the principal function of her mediation founded on her divine motherhood. Mary is therefore a mediatrix, because she is the Mother of God, and, above all, because she is the Mother of Mankind. As for her sovereignty, it is not here joined to her mediation by the free choice of a piety which follows her appeals, but because it is the consequence of her divine motherhood and the means for Mary to exercise her spiritual motherhood. We will soon elaborate on these thoughts; but from now on, we shall observe how this devotion is firmly supported by the foundations of Christianity on all sides. Its end is the same as the purpose of the Incarnation; that is, to unite ourselves to Christ and, through Him, to God. Its means is none other than the means of the Incarnation; namely, Mary, who gave birth to Jesus and who, spiritually, gives birth to Him in our souls. Its practice is the perfect self-giving to the service of Our Lord, the basis and sum of all our religious duties.

At this point, we can already see more clearly the spiritual system of St. Louis-Marie delineated, admire the strict sequence and perfect concordance of its parts.

We have life in God through Christ, with Christ, and in Christ, our first and principal Mediator. Jesus is given to us and we receive grace through Mary, with Mary, and in Mary, our Mother and Mediatrix, secondarily.

What else can we say, other than to unite ourselves to Christ in the same way that He chose to come to us; that is, through Mary, with Mary, and in Mary! Thus, whether one considers the end, the means, or the practice of the perfect devotion, we see everywhere an admirable unity of ideas and formulas. Everything stands together, everything is supported by the great truths of religion; for it is a system with a structure as simple as it is strong.

Our plan is drawn. We have no need of establishing a complete series of theses on the motherhood of the Blessed Virgin, any more than we had to produce a treatise on grace; but, as regards the mediation of the Blessed Virgin in general, and her motherhood in particular, we shall present those truths which have a special bearing on the teaching of St. Louis-Marie: (1) In what sense is Mary our Mother; (2) What is meant by these words: "All graces come to us through her"; (3) What is the nature of her co-operation with the action of the Holy Ghost? We shall follow these considerations with a discussion on the titles and the exercise of her queenship.

CHAPTER 1:

MARY IS OUR MOTHER

any Christians may have a limited idea of the Blessed Virgin Mary. Yes, they acknowledge her to be the Mother of the Word Incarnate. By extension, they recognize her as being a collaborator in the mystery of the Incarnation, and attribute to her a certain power over men, who in gratitude give her the titles of honor, Queen and Mother. Were it so, she would be *like* our Mother, whereas in reality she truly *is*.

St. Louis-Marie returns frequently to the motherhood of the Blessed Virgin, one of the foundational ideas of the devotion he set down. Let us follow his explanation. Like a true theologian that he is, he goes immediately to the very heart of the mystery of grace and takes up the dogma of our incorporation into Christ. And because by reason of this union we abide in Christ and Christ abides in us—*manet in Me, et Ego in eo* (Jn 15.5)—St. Louis-Marie envisages the motherhood of the Blessed Virgin under this two-fold aspect. He explains how she conceives us in Christ and then conceives Christ in us.

St. Antoninus was the one who set down the idea. He writes: "She gave birth not to one, but to a multitude of sons; that is to say, all those who are redeemed by Our Lord. She bore them all at the same time in the sense that, by a single act and in an instant, she gave Him Who is for all the cause of life. She bore them not all at the same time, in the sense that the application of the fruits of the Passion was not made to all at the same time, for this application, which in reality produces life in all souls, is made in each only in due time."[1]

---

[1] ✦St. Antoninus, *Summa*, 4.15.14.2, 4:1002B: ‖ "Parturivit B.V. Maria postea juxta Crucem, ... non unum sed multos filios, qui redemti sunt a Domino, simul quantum ad virtutem causæ, non simul quantum ad esse, sed diversis temporibus, quantum ad

In other words, Mary gives birth to us in Christ, because she wanted to become the Mother of Him Who is the principle of our supernatural life; and she gives birth to Christ in us, in that the fruits of Redemption are applied to us. We cooperate in Redemption for the motherhood of Mary, as we do for the life of Christ in our souls. We now show, according to the considerations and formula of St. Louis-Marie, that, *through Mary, with Mary, and in Mary*: (1) we are conceived in Christ, and (2) that Christ is formed in us.

ARTICLE 1: MARY CONCEIVES US IN CHRIST

"If Jesus Christ, the Head of all mankind," says St. Louis-Marie, "is born in her, the predestinate who are the members of that Head ought also to be born in her by a necessary consequence. One and the same mother brings not forth into the world the head without the members, nor the members without the head; for this would be a freak of nature. So, in like manner, in the order of grace, the Head and the members are born of one and the same Mother."[2]

We hardly need to elaborate on this thought. It states a capital truth and a profound mystery in plain enough language.

In the divine plan, Christ is not only the Word made flesh, He is also the Savior of the world; in fact, it is to be Savior that He became incarnate. The fruit of Redemption is in making each redeemed soul a member of His Mystical Body, which is the Church.

There are two parts in the Humanity of Christ: His natural Body and His Mystical Body. Let us use an analogy to explain what this means: When we look at the sun, we first distinguish its disk or material body, then the splendor which surrounds and completes it by *being one* with it, so that the whole sun is not the disc by itself, nor its splendor alone, but the one and the other forming one whole. In Christ, we distinguish His natural Body and His Soul united to His divine nature in the Person of the Word. Grace radiates from Jesus in the Church, and this Church is His splendor, His complement, that *is one* with Him; so that the whole Christ, as we have said, is not only His physical Humanity united to the Word, nor the Church alone, but

---

applicationem effectus ipsius Passionis." |
[2] ◆Cf. *TD*, 17-18.

Christ *and* the Church forming a single Mystical Body.[3]

Take any one of these three aspects of Christ Jesus, you will dis-figure Him and destroy the plan of God. Remove either His divine or human nature, you no longer have the God-Man and the mystery of the Incarnation ceases to exist. Suppress the quality of Savior and keep Christ, He ceases to be Jesus, and we no longer have Redemp-tion. Cut off His Mystical Body, you no longer have the whole Christ: you separate the Redeemer from the redeemed, the Head from His members. In effect, you have, in line with the remark of St. Louis-Marie, a freak in the order of grace.

Now consider that it is from a human mother that Christ receives His entire Humanity—the mother who, according to the flesh, con-ceives His natural Body, and who, at the same time, spiritually gives birth to His Mystical Body. There is no logic to supposing that there are two mothers: one for the natural Body, the other for the Mystical Body; that is, two mothers for one and the same Christ. Surely, not. Mary is the only Mother of Jesus in the order of nature, as well as in the order of grace. Similarly, when we consider the Mystical Body of Christ, there cannot be one Mother for the Head, and another for the members; for as St. Louis-Marie, says: "One and the same mother brings not forth into the world the head without the members, nor the members without the head; for this would be a freak."[4] Such is the law, and so it came to pass, as the Gospel teaches us.[5]

When Mary assented to the Incarnation, she knew that her divine Son would be the Savior of the world and the Head of the whole Church. Too well-versed in the Scriptures, too steeped in the sublime and special lights of the Holy Ghost, to misconstrue the divine plan, she perfectly understood what the words of the Archangel meant: *And thou shalt call His name Jesus* (Lc 1.31), meaning Savior, as it was ex-plained at greater length to St. Joseph, *for He shall save His people*

---

[3] ◆See Part I, for what we say about this truth. We think it useful to return to it in order to shed some light on the spiritual motherhood of Mary.

[4] Cf. *TD*, 17.

[5] Christ is specifically mentioned as Head of the Church in Eph 1.22, 5.23 and Col 1.18; that He founded her on St. Peter, in Mt 16.18. The Blessed Virgin Mary is given to us as Mother by Christ Himself, when He says on the Cross: *Behold thy Mother* (Jn 19.27).

from their sins (Mt 1.21).[6] When, therefore, Mary consented to become the Mother of the Incarnate Word, Savior and Head of the Church, there was a two-fold conception in her. In her motherhood according to the flesh, she conceived in her immaculate womb the natural Body of Christ; but by the same act of her will, in her spiritual motherhood, she conceived spiritually His Mystical Body, by assenting to beget her Son, Who is the principle of our salvation.[7]

It is true that at the moment of the Incarnation, the Mystical Body of Christ had not been manifested, since the Church had not existed; but she existed in Him, nevertheless. Now, a woman ceases not to be the mother of the child she conceived, because after his birth the child grows up outside of her. Did she not ¦¦ along with her husband | give the child the principle of his entire life and all that he needed to mature?[8] Likewise, although this grain of wheat, which is Christ, sprouted later and is multiplied; although this divine and *true vine* has spread far and wide across many branches, the principle, the seed of all spiritual growth was deposited in Mary.

---

[6] ♦*His* people, that is to say, not only the Israelites, but all who are united to Him by faith and will recognize Him for their Lord; and it is not from an external enemy, but from their sins that He must save them. ¦¦ St. Alphonsus Ligouri, says more on Mary's spiritual motherhood, writing that she became our spiritual Mother on two occasions: First, when she merited to conceive her Son; the second, she "brought us forth to the life of grace, was when she offered to the Eternal Father the life of her beloved Son on Mount Calvary, with such bitter sorrow and suffering." ("Glories of Mary," 1.2, *Works*, 7.49) |

[7] ♦This reasoning is same as the one established on this axiom of philosophy: *Causa causæ est causa causati*; that is to say, an effect produced by a cause which, as such, itself depends on a superior cause, is ultimately attributed to it. In other words: one imputes to a cause not only what it operates by itself, but also what it causes to operate by another. In the order of physical causes, e.g., a wheel moves the hands of a clock; but the spring or the weight which moves the wheels is the primary cause of the march of the needles. In the order of moral causes, observe a man who strikes another, in which the primary cause of the aggression is a third party who advised or ordered it. — Let us now apply this reasoning to the motherhood of the Blessed Virgin. It is Jesus who, becoming Man, became our Savior, and from Him all grace comes to us: He is the proximate and efficient cause of our salvation. But it was through Mary and in Mary that He became Man; it was as Savior and Head that He was conceived and given to the world through her. Mary is, therefore, the mediate and moral cause of our salvation, for in the economy of the divine plan, without her, we would not have our Redeemer, Jesus Christ. As St. Irenaeus, *Adversus hæreses*, 3.22.4, PG 7.959C, says: "Just as Eve's disobedience was for her and all of mankind a cause of death; so also did Mary, through her obedience, become the cause of salvation, both for herself and all of mankind."

[8] Remark added, lest asexual reproduction in humans is understood.

Is the motherhood of Mary a true motherhood? It certainly is, if we mean that a spiritual motherhood gives birth to spiritual life. Consider the role of the mother. It is *through* her and *in* her that life is communicated to the child. Now, it is through Mary, namely through the assent of her will, that the Son of God is incarnated to be our Savior and our Head. However, this by itself is not sufficient to explain the entirety of the Blessed Virgin's motherhood, because one may be the cause of life without being a mother.[9] Just as Christ was conceived in her immaculate womb, so is it also in the thought and the will of Mary that we were spiritually conceived in union with Christ.

These two aspects of Mary's motherhood, one that looks at the natural Body of Christ, and the other, His Mystical Body, give a deeper meaning to the words of the Church Fathers, who teach us that the conception in Mary was first a moral act before being a physical one. "She conceived in the mind," says St. Leo, "before conceiving in her body."[10] She conceived Jesus Christ by faith before conceiving Him according to the flesh.[11] St. Thomas writes: "Without doubt, it was in order that the Blessed Virgin should believe in this mystery before it was fulfilled in her, and that she received Christ spiritually in her heart before she carried Him in her womb,"[12] that the Annunciation occurred before the Incarnation of the Son of God took place. However,

---

[9] ◆Paternity and motherhood, as well as creation and generation, are of a different order.

[10] St. Leo the Great, *Sermones*, 21.1, In Nat. Domini, 1, PL 54.191B.

[11] ◆A Sequence from the Middle Ages says in a picturesque and significant simile: *Gaude, Virgo Mater Christi / Quæ per aurem concepisti / Gabriele nuntio* ¦¦ —"Glad us, maiden, mother mild; through thine hearing thou wert with child; Gabriel to thee be told," for which Josquin des Prez, the Renaissance musician, composed a motet. |

[12] ◆St. Thomas, *Summa*, 3.30.1c: ¦¦ "It was reasonable that it should be announced to the Blessed Virgin that she was to conceive Christ. First, in order to maintain a becoming order in the union of the Son of God with the Virgin; namely, that she should be informed in mind concerning Him, before conceiving Him in the flesh. ... Secondly, that she might be a more certain witness of this mystery, being instructed therein by God. Thirdly, that she might offer to God the free gift of her obedience: which she proved herself right and ready to do, saying: "Behold the handmaid of the Lord." Fourthly, in order to show that there is a certain spiritual wedlock between the Son of God and human nature. Wherefore, in the Annunciation, the Virgin's consent was besought in lieu of that of the entire human nature." |

this spiritual conception by an act of faith seems particularly necessary, when one thinks that Mary was to conceive the Mystical Body of Christ, inseparable from His human nature.

ARTICLE 2: MARY CONCEIVES CHRIST IN US

This is the second way of looking at Mary's spiritual motherhood. We said above that through her and in her is the principle of our redemption produced. Let us now to see how through her and in her the fruit is applied to us; for through her and in her are we born to the life of grace. In sum, she forms Christ in us.

St. Louis-Marie took pains not to neglect this aspect of the spiritual motherhood of the Blessed Virgin, for he says: "It is certain that for each man in particular who possesses Him, Jesus Christ is as truly the fruit of the womb of Mary, as He is for the whole world in general; so that if any one of the faithful has Jesus Christ formed in his heart, he can say boldly, 'All thanks be to Mary! What I possess is her effect and her fruit, and without her, I would never have had Him.'"[13]

For an explanation of this mystery and to show that Mary acts truly as mother, we have only to follow the thought of St. Louis-Marie: "The Holy Ghost," he says, "having espoused Mary, and having produced Jesus Christ, the Masterpiece that is the Word Incarnate, in her, and by her, and from her, and having never repudiated her, so does He continue every day to produce His predestined in her, and by her, in a manner hidden but true."[14] The pious author thus puts the generation of Christ according to the flesh side-by-side with His spiritual generation in our souls, in order to illustrate their analogies.

It is *through* Mary, that is, through her consent and cooperation, that the Word became incarnate; it is from *her* also, that is, from her substance, that He took flesh, since she provided the blood most pure from which the body of her divine Son was formed. In sum, it is in *her*, in her virginal womb, that this mystery was made manifest.[15] Thus, in every sense is Mary truly the Mother of Jesus Christ.

Mary has an analogous role in our spiritual generation. It is through her that we receive grace because our grace presupposes the

---

[13] ♦Cf. *TD*, 18.
[14] ♦Cf. *Secret*, §7, 12.
[15] St. John Damascene, *De fide orthodoxa*, PG 94.986B.

assent of her will and her prayer.[16] We can even say that this grace, this divine life, somehow comes from *her*; for if grace is not assuredly a portion of her substance, at the very least, it is something that belongs to her and comes from her. The source of grace, indeed, is Jesus, of Whom she is the Mother; and in that capacity she also has a kind of right over all graces.[17]

Let us listen to what St. Louis-Marie has to say on this subject: "Whoever wishes to be a member of Jesus Christ, full of grace and truth, must be formed in Mary by means of the grace of Jesus Christ, Who dwells in her in His fullness, in order to be communicated in fulness to her children, the true members of Jesus Christ."[18]

Finally, St. Louis-Marie says: "It is *through* her, *in* her, and *of* her, that the Holy Ghost forms the predestined every day."[19] We shall come back to the idea of "in her" when we explain what it is to live and act in Mary.[20]

ARTICLE 3: PHASES OF THE SPIRITUAL MOTHERHOOD OF THE BLESSED VIRGIN MARY

We are now able to reconcile the apparent divergences among authors, some of whom say that Mary gave birth to us at Calvary; others, that she became Mother of the Church at Pentecost; yet others, that her motherhood dates from the Incarnation. To aid us in our discussion, let us distinguish the three phases of motherhood: conception, gestation, and birth, ⫶ the emergence of the child from the womb, otherwise known as the mother | giving birth ⫶ to him. |

We said above how, at the Annunciation, Mary conceived the

---

[16] ♦We reserve the explanation of "*with* her" for when we discuss her cooperation with the Holy Ghost. (Part 2.2.3, p. 121). We will then say what it is "to act with it."

[17] ♦⸠ Part 2.2, p. 112 ff. and note 22, p. 120. |

[18] ♦*Secret*, §6, 12.

[19] *TD*, 10.

[20] ♦Provided that we do not set aside the analogy or propose approximations, we can observe a curious concordance between this explanation of spiritual motherhood and the definition of the physical generation: *origo viventis* (if not the production of a new person or a new nature, it is the communication of a new life); *a vivente* (through Mary and of Mary, in the sense that we explained); *principio conjuncto* (with her and in her), in *similitudinem naturæ*, we become like Mary and by the state of grace and the imitation of her virtues.

natural Body of Christ according to the flesh, and His Mystical Body, spiritually. By uniting the Head and the members in the same act of will, she became our Mother by right and in principle. For nine months she carried her divine Son in her immaculate womb, then brought Him into this world the night of Christmas Day. By this birth, she gave us the Word made flesh. At that same instant, He was our Savior, because He had had the mission, the power, and the plan to redeem us; but this Redemption was chiefly to be accomplished by the Passion; and in the plan of His charity, all the rest of His mortal life had no value to save us, except in union with that blessed Passion. We thus can say that after having conceived us spiritually with Jesus, our divine Mother carried us in her heart for thirty-three years, during which, in union with Jesus, she prepared our spiritual birth and our Redemption.

It was at the foot of the Cross that this Redemption came to term, so to speak; it is there that our divine Mother gave birth to us spiritually. The Doctors are unanimous in proclaiming it,[21] and they contrast the sorrows and trials at Calvary to the pure joys at Bethlehem.

And so, in union with Jesus, Who called that hour, His *hour* (Jn 2.4), Mary could very well apply to herself His words: *A woman, when she is in labor, hath sorrow, because her hour is come* (Jn 16.21). Truly, at that instant, amidst untold sufferings, she let go of her Son from the bottom of her heart by a sheer act of her will, that He might become the sacrificial victim. She procured His immolation, and hence secured our salvation, of which His Passion is the meritorious cause.

It is thus that "she gave birth," says St. Antoninus, "not to one, but to a multitude of sons, that is to say, all those who are redeemed by Our Lord. She bore them all at the same time in the sense that, by a single act and in an instant, she gave Him Who is, for all, the cause of life."[22] And just as the mother is presented with the child she brings into the world, so also does Jesus present to Mary all Christians, in the person of St. John, to whom she becomes Mother, saying: *Woman, behold thy son* (Jn 19.26).[23]

---

[21] Summarized in St. Alphonsus Liguori, "Glories of Mary," 1.1.2, *Works*, 7:22-28.

[22] ◆Note 1, p. 102.

[23] ◆It is remarkable that the name "woman" is the same under which Mary is prophesied in Eden, the earthly paradise, she who was to be the Mother of Christ the Redeemer,

❖

St. Antoninus said that at Calvary, Mary gives birth to a multitude of sons *quantum ad virtutem causæ*, in the sense of giving us He Who is the cause of our life, and adds, "but She bore them not all at the same time, in the sense that the application of the fruits of the Passion was not made to all at the same time, for this application, which in reality produces life in all souls, is made in each only in due time."[24] At Pentecost, Mary began this function officially and publicly. At the Incarnation, the Holy Ghost came upon her to form the Head of the predestined. At Pentecost, He came to form the members. It was the confirmation and fulfillment of her motherhood as proclaimed by Jesus from the Cross. In the course of time, an interior Pentecost occurs each instance the Spirit of God enters or reenters a soul to form and to make Jesus grow the more, all through Mary of whom shall always be born Jesus, called the Christ.[25]

The day of our Baptism is the day of our birth into the life of grace. Let us remember that in the Church *dies natalis*, stands for the day of a triumphant entry into Heaven[26]; for then, in effect, the supernatural life of souls attains its end or its perfection. Seen from such end, all of the present life is only a means, and with respect to that *dies natalis*, the years spent here below are but a period of long gestation. This thought, so true and so noble, escaped not the attention of St. Louis-Marie, and we read in *True Devotion*: "St. Augustine, surpassing himself, ... affirms that in this world, in order to be conformed to the *image* of the Son of God, all the predestinate are hidden in the womb

---

and the enemy of Satan (Gn 3.15). Now, in the instances she is called "woman" in the Scriptures, we may note that she appears and acts as the new Eve, Mother of the living and opponent of the serpent, in fulfillment of the ancient prophecy to which this name harkens. As it was at Calvary (Jn 19.26), so also at the Annunciation where the Angel salutes her a woman blessed among all women (Lk 1.28); at the wedding at Cana (Jn 2.4); in the Book of Revelation, where she is the woman clothed with the sun and pursued by the dragon after she gave birth (Rev 12.1-17).

[24] ◆Note 1, p. 102.

[25] Cf. Lk 1.35.

[26] St. Paulinus, *Poemata*, 21.170-174, PL 61.578-579: "Et merito sanctis iste natalis dies / Notatur, in quo lege functi carnea / Mortalitatis exuuntur vinculis, / Et in superna regna nascuntur Deo, / Secumque lætam spem resurgendi ferunt"; cf. *Poemata*, 14.1-4, PL 61.464-465. Beleth, *Div. officiorum*, 4, PL 202.17C: "Natalis vel natale et natalitium vocatur sanctorum ex hoc sæculo commigratio, quia ut sæculo et mundo moriuntur, ita tunc cælo nascuntur." The Church celebrates only three birthdays: those of Our Lord, of Our Lady and of St. John the Baptist.

of the Blessed Virgin, where they are protected, nourished, nurtured, and reared by that good Mother until after death she delivers them unto glory."[27] How sweet it is for us to imagine that if grace is given to us through Mary, it is through her also that we attain glory; and there is no doubt that while God sheds grace upon grace,[28] directing them through the heart and hands of a woman and a mother, He still reserves for us a surfeit of sweetness by giving us still greater glory through her.

Such is also the thought of St. Louis-Marie, who tells us that Jesus is born of Mary in all three orders: of nature, of grace, and of glory.[29]

---

[27] *VD*, 21; cf. *TD*, 18-19. The source is hard to determine. The closest is Ps. Augustine (most likely Quodvultdeus, a disciple of Augustine), *De symbolo*, Sermo alius, 1.1, PL 40.659-660: "It is by the most sacred sign of the cross that Holy Mother Church conceives you ... in her womb that, with the utmost joy, she may give birth to you spiritually, and that you may become the future begetting of a Mother ever so glorious, waiting for the day when she may regenerate you with the salvific laver, and restore you to the Light; and those whom she carries in her womb, she nourishes with proper sustenance, that she may deliver them on the blessed day of their joyful rebirth."

[28] ♦Sir 26.19 : *Gratiam super gratiam mulier sancta et pudorata*, "a holy and shamefaced woman is grace upon grace."

[29] Found neither *TD* nor *Secret*. The closest is, *TD*, 90: "It is towards that fervent and generous soul ... that Our Lord and His holy Mother are most generous in this world and in the next, in the orders of nature, grace, and glory"; which may be taken to suggest that we will have all these benefits by reason of Jesus being born in us through Mary.

CHAPTER 2:

MARY, TREASURER AND DISPENSER OF GRACE

ary is not only constituted our Mother that we may be born into the life of grace, but also that we may grow up in it until fully mature. After a child is born, does all that serves to rear him not fall within the scope of the duties of motherhood? Of course, it does. St. Louis-Marie often reminds us that Jesus is born in us; that He is formed in us, that He grows up in us, through Mary unto the measure of that perfection which we call the *fullness of the age of Christ*[1]: "Mary has received from God a special dominion over souls, in order to nourish them and to make them grow up in God."[2]

Let us now take up the consideration of Mary as treasurer and universal dispenser of all graces.[3] What is meant by those terms, and how do we explain that all graces come to us through her? St. Louis-Marie discusses this truth at length, and relies on ancient texts to flesh out his arguments.

ARTICLE 1: TREASURER

Mary is the treasurer of graces, for she found grace, as the Archangel said to her, and she found it in its fullness: *Ave Maria, gratia plena,* "Hail Mary, full of grace." It bears repeating what we said above[4]

---

[1] Cf. Eph 4.13: *ætatis plenitudinis Christi*, "the age of the *fullness of Christ*," a subtle distinction, with the stress on Him completing at Calvary the purpose of His life, and becoming, as St. Thomas says, the exemplar of the perfection of human nature ("Super Ephesos," 4, Lect. 4, *Opera*, 21:311.2), and, to a lesser extent, on attaining the age of 33 when He died on the Cross.

[2] ◆*Secret*, §8, 12.

[3] *TD*, 145.

[4] Part 1.1.2, p. 26.

what this fullness is: Before distributing the fruits of Redemption to all of mankind, God "placed the entire ransom in the hands of Mary."[5] Msgr. Gay adds: "All natural gifts that pours to overflowing into all other creatures, God first amassed in her according to His good pleasure. ... Into a nature already perfect, He pours forthwith an entire ocean of supernatural gifts. Apart from the grace of the hypostatic union reserved for the holy Humanity of Christ, of which Mary receives but faint echoes, she has all, for God grants her all. ... Whether it be theological, moral, or intellectual virtues; or gifts of the Holy Ghost; or fruits He produces in the souls of the just; or beatitudes He creates in them; or multiple forms, varied shades, diverse strengths of union with Jesus, or powers and operations resulting therefrom; or graces for all states of life, or those underlying or attendant upon missions, nothing is wanting in Mary; nay, nothing is wanting, for everything abounds in her."[6] The Blessed Virgin has all this in a measure of which she alone is capable. She has the fullness of capacity from the very beginning, and, in order that grace might increase, her soul did expand to contain it. Moreover, Mary has Jesus as does no other creature possesses Him Who is the fullness of grace personified.

Let us note here that a treasurer receives nothing in his own right, nor does he keep anything for himself. A treasurer receives and stores in the name of another, and is given to administer and distribute. Mary is thus treasurer of all graces, not only because she is full of grace, but also because she must give it to us from her fullness.[7]

> Glory be thine, treasurer of grace:
> The bounty to thee Our Lord did give,
> Let, in part, be ours that we may live. [8]

Nothing in the works of God is incomplete or contradictory. His wisdom conceives and realizes them in the magnificent unity of a plan

---

[5] St. Bernard, *In Vig. Nat. Domini*, Sermo 3.10, PL 183.100A, at note 2, p. 99.

[6] ◆Gay, *Conférences*, 27, 1:450.

[7] ◆St. Bernard, *de Aquœductu*, §5, PL 183.440C: "She deserved to find what she sought who was not satisfied with her own plenitude nor content with her own abundance, but according to that which is written, *They that drink me, shall yet thirst* (Sir 24.29), solicited a superabundance that might suffice for the salvation of all."

[8] ◆de Montfort, "Petite Couronne," Denis, *Le règne*, 321: "Gloire à vous, trésorière des grâces du Seigneur; / Donnez-nous part à votre trésor."

whose every part is in harmony from start to completion: *Sapientia attingens a fine usque ad finem,* "Wisdom reacheth from end to end mightily" (Wis 8.1). He thus wanted Mary, Mother of God, to be also Mother of Mankind, and after having given birth to the Redeemer, she was associated to our Redemption. In the entire series of mysteries concerning Christ, nowhere is the new Man, the celestial Adam, without the Woman; nor the Woman without the Man. ¦¦ In the words of Fr. de la Broise: "The Word incarnate saved us and He alone could save us. He could also have left His Mother in background, and be shown that He achieved His mission Himself; but God willed that His Son would always appear accompanied by the blessed woman with whom the prophets had associated Him since the beginning of the world. The flower came out of the root of Jesse through its stem, and the stem and the flower were always together, never separated. By a decree, unnecessary but befitting His wisdom, God ordained that Mary would assist in every work of Jesus. This cooperation is necessarily secondary, since the substance of the work belongs entirely to Christ; but, in this lower order, it has been as much as a pure creature could give."[9] |

Mary is not an instrument God used for the Incarnation of His Son, to be cast aside, leaving Him to act without her. This false and narrow conception, which admits of the Son of God being born of woman, but rejects the woman of whom He is born, is a pet theory of heretics; but the Catholic Church, guardian of the Truth, proclaims Mary, Mediatrix, Mother of Men, Co-Redemptrix, Treasurer and Dispenser of all graces: *In me is all grace of the way and of the truth, in me is all hope of life and of virtue* (Sir 24.25).

Innumerable are the testimonies of the Fathers and Doctors on this important point.[10] St. Louis-Marie cites a certain number, and he summarizes the principal ideas as follows:

"God the Father made an assemblage of all the waters, and He named it *mare,* 'sea.' He made an assemblage of all His graces, and He has called it *Maria,* 'Mary.' This great God has a treasury or storehouse most rich in which He has laid up all there is of beauty, of splendor,

---

[9] ¦¦ de La Broise, "Toutes les grâces," *Études,* May 1896, 68 (5):9–10, citing, Gn 3.15, Is 7.14, Jer 31.22, Mic 5.3. | Cf. ♦1 Cor 11.11.

[10] ♦See, Terrien, *Mère de Dieu,* the entire vol. 3 [Tome 2, Part 1].

of rarity, and of preciousness, even His own Son; and this immense treasure is none other than Mary, whom the Saints have named the Treasure of the Lord,[11] out of whose plenitude all men are made rich.

"God the Son has communicated to His Mother all that He has acquired by His life and by His death, His infinite merits and His admirable virtues; and He has made her the treasurer of all that His Father has given Him for His inheritance. It is by her that He applies His merits to His members, and that He communicates His virtues, and distributes His graces. She is His canal full of mystery; she is His aqueduct, through which He makes His mercies flow gently and abundantly.

"To Mary, His faithful Spouse, God the Holy Ghost has communicated His ineffable gifts; and He has chosen her to be the dispenser of all that He possesses."[12]

We add to these testimonies the remarkable words of the Angelic Doctor, in his commentary on the *Ave Maria*: "Mary is so full of grace that it overflows to all of mankind. It is fitting that a Saint should have so abundant a grace that he may save a great number of souls; but to have enough to save all men would be the supreme privilege, and it is found *in Christ and in the Blessed Virgin*."[13]

We said above why grace is "in Christ"; but why do we now say that it is "in Mary"? Because her grace is the one that befits the Mother of Mankind. In her quality as Mother, she receives in order to give. The purpose and function of motherhood is first to give life, then to give what is needed to nurture and rear the child. But because she is the Mother of Mankind, Mary obtains and dispenses grace to every one of them. This is why Jesus and Mary have grace in its fullness which should flow to all of mankind.

There is a difference between the two, however. The fullness of

---

[11] Origen applies the title *Thesaurus Domini* to the Church (*In Jeremiam*, Sermo 3, PL 25.611); Denis the Carthusian, to the B.V.M., ("De præc. Mariæ," 1.10, *Opera*, 35:485.1C); Jordan repeats and adds, *et thesauraria gratiarum ipsius* ("De B.V.M.," *Opera*, 116).

[12] *TD*, 11-12.

[13] St. Thomas, Exp. de Ave Maria, *Opera*, 27:200.2: "Plena fuit gratia ... quantum ad refusionem in omnes homines. Magnum enim est in quolibet sancto, quando habet tantum de gratia quod sufficit sibi 'ad salutem,' sed majus quando habet tantum quod sufficit sibi ad salutem multorum; sed quando haberet tantum quod sufficeret sibi ad salutem omnium hominum de mundo, hoc esset maximum: et hoc est in Christo, et in Beata Virgine."

grace in Christ is that of the source, the fullness in Mary is that of the channel. In Jesus Christ, it is the fullness of life that suits the head, whence come the vital impulses that course through the whole body; in Mary, it is the fullness of the neck, the organ that transmits them.[14] Even in the Mystical Body of Christ there exists a symbol for the Blessed Virgin: Christ is the head, she is the neck. How fitting! The neck is lower than the head, but it is closely united to it and sits atop the rest of the body. Thus Mary, pure creature, is below Christ, Who is God; but she is inseparably united to Him, and is raised above Angels and men. Her grace, too, in a way, is capital, since it has the excellence and fullness befitting the Mother and universal Mediatrix of all men.

Here as everywhere, the new Eve is with the new Adam; she remains *adjutorium simile sibi,* "a help like unto himself" (Gn 2.18), associated with His mysteries and, by grace, participates in the prerogatives that He possesses by nature.

We should now understand why all the heresies that recognize Christ as Head, but cut off the neck of His Mystical Body by rejecting Mary, have killed off churches, left their cadavers on the wayside, and never could survive as living bodies. Beheading kills, for blood is spilt, and the mobility, the vital influences, coming from the head and passing through the neck, are lost to the members. Suppress the mediation and the spiritual motherhood of the Blessed Virgin, the faithful no longer can communicate with Christ, and grace no longer reaches them. And if, as some heretics persists in pressing, they presume to unite with Christ without Mary, the result will be a monstrous body, much like one with the head resting on the shoulders without the neck in between. Such a thing may possibly turn out, but it would not be a man, as man is fashioned by the hands of God and intended

---

[14] ¦¦ Ubertino da Casale. *Arbor vitæ,* 1.8, [30?]: "Plenitudo gratiæ fuit ... in Christo ut in capite influente. In Maria ut in collo quasi toti corpori et ecclesiæ transfundente." St. Bernardine, "Fest. B.V.M.," 3.3.2, 5.1.8, 13.1.10, in *Opera,* 4:81.1, 92.2, 128.2: "Plenitudo gratiæ fuit in Christo sicut in capite influente, in Maria vero, sicut in collo transfundente," and credits St. Jerome; but Ps. Jerome, Epistola 9 [Ad Paulam et Eustochium], sometimes referred to as "Sermone in Assumptione B.V.M.," PL 30.127D: "In Mariam vero totius gratiæ, quæ in Christo est plenitudo venit, quamquam aliter." ¦

to be, complete with the beautiful form and organic function of the neck. Such a thing is the image of those heretical sects that repudiate the veneration of Mary. They | are cut off from the Church, for their conception of her is not the one intended and made by Christ. Put their "churches" and the Mystical Body of Christ side by side, we see that they | have no life, and have none of the proportion, the beauty, the perfection of *the* Church. In fact, they are monstrous things that should scare us.[15]

This symbol of the neck should inspire us to tender reflections. A child struck by fear or moved by love runs to cast his arms around his mother's neck; and the neck he grabs to make her lean her head forward that she may give him a kiss or he to give her one. What a true and touching symbol of devotion to Jesus through Mary! It is to Mary that we must throw ourselves to hold onto Jesus, and ask Him to incline towards us, that we may receive His divine caresses, and that holy kiss, after which the chaste soul will sigh: *Osculetur me osculo oris sui*, let Him kiss me with the kiss of His mouth (Cant 1.1).

ARTICLE 2: DISPENSER OF GRACE
AND COOPERATOR OF THE HOLY GHOST

Let us first explain what is meant by these words: "All graces come to us through Mary."

The graces. We need not take away from the mediation of our Mother the favors of the natural order relating to salvation; much less exclude, as explained above, the sanctifying or habitual grace that

---

[15] ♦In a commentary on the Savior's promise to our first parents, Billot explains Mary's cooperation in Redemption and her universal mediation by her intercession. The learned professor says that the new Eve is indissolubly linked to the new Adam in the Christian religion, since, from the revelation God first made in Eden regarding the Mediator and Redeemer—the revelation that contains the seed of Christianity—Christ is not shown alone, but is with the woman who will give birth to Him. With Him, she is, therefore, the hope and promise of the world before the Incarnation, and since then the object of veneration and love of the Church. Billot ends with this remarkable conclusion: "Ubicumque non est [ille cultus Mariæ], ibi eo ipso ... abest et genuina Christiana religio. Non enim genuina illa Christianitas esse potest, quæ truncat rationem religationis nostræ per Christum a Deo institutam, separando benedictum mulieris semen a muliere ipsa cujus est semen, et abjiciendo ordinem quo solo solvitur antiqua innodatio qua per diabolum fuimus colligati." (*De Verbo Incarnato*, 347). To which we add the reflection of St. Louis-Marie: "If anyone glories in having God for his Father, without at the same time having a tender filial love for Mary, he is a deceiver, who has only the devil for father." (*Secret*, 11)

comes to us through her. Our concern here lies with actual graces; that is, supernatural help, whatever its form or purpose. We insist on saying, "*all graces* that God gives to men." As Fr. de la Broise rightly observes, all my prayers pass through Christ, the principal and necessary universal Mediator, whether I say *per Dominum Nostrum Jesum Christum*, "through Our Lord Jesus Christ," out loud or in my heart. Likewise, though I may not invoke Mary explicitly, the grace that I obtain comes to me through her, the secondary but universal Mediatrix.[16] This is what differentiates her mediation from the mediation of other Saints, for the latter is restricted to such cases, such places, such persons, as when they are invoked, and that God grants them the dispensation for the graces. St. Anthony of Padua, for instance, has nothing to do with the grace bestowed on me when I pray to St. Bernard; but, to whichever Saint I address myself, the Blessed Virgin does intercede in the concession of favors requested.

The words of the Saints quoted by St. Louis-Marie are texts that are, in a sense, classic and known to all; we can thus dispense with reproducing them. Let us say rather that we rest this universal mediation of Mary on her quality as Mother of God and Spouse of the Holy Ghost. Because she is Mother of God and Mother of Mankind, we may agree to conclude that she has the solicitude of every single one of them in all his needs. But she is also the Spouse of the Holy Ghost; and, on this account, her intervention is universal in the dispensing of graces. Allow us to follow | our good Father de Montfort | and be a little insistent on the latter privilege.

"God the Holy Ghost ... is become fruitful by Mary whom He has espoused. It is with her, in her, and of her that He has produced His

---

[16] de La Broise, "Toutes les grâces," *Études*, May 1896, !! 68 (5):7, 18: "In the present order of Providence, we receive not ... grace, if the Blessed Virgin existed not and interceded not for us. Just as Our Lord is always invoked implicitly, even when we do not say *per Dominum Nostrum Jesum Christum*, for He is the necessary Mediator without Whom neither Angels nor Saints can do anything for us; so also does the Blessed Virgin exercise a universal mediation in the dispensing of graces. ... It is, first of all, the Will of God that grants all graces; then the will of Our Lord, the Mediator, who merits and obtains them by Himself in all righteousness; finally, the will of Mary, a secondary mediator, who deserves and obtains them, fittingly, through Our Lord." | See also, Terrien, *Mère de Dieu*, Part 2.5, 3:341-432.

Masterpiece: God made Man."[17] In this we see Mary's cooperation in the Incarnation; and, as regards her spiritual motherhood wherein she spiritually bears us unto divine life, St. Louis-Marie adds: "It is with her, in her, and of her, that every day the Holy Ghost produces the predestined, the members of the Body of that adorable Head, and will produce until the end of the world."[18]

In stout language full of truth, St. Louis-Marie calls Mary the "cherished and indissoluble Spouse" of the Holy Ghost, whom He "never repudiated."[19] Grace forms Christ and makes Him grow in us. And if in the order of grace, as well as in the order of nature, Jesus were not the fruit of the Holy Ghost and of Mary, it is because she would have been repudiated or divorced. Can we imagine such a thing in the case of the *faithful* Virgin? God, Who in Scripture fiercely proclaims Himself *strong and faithful* (Dt 7.9), *faithful in all His words* (Ps 144.13), how could He not be faithful to this blessed Virgin, after He said through the Angel, "The Lord is with thee"? If it is the characteristic of divine wisdom to secure the end from the outset, to pursue and complete His works in the unity of the same plan, why would He interrupt His primordial designs for the Incarnation and Redemption? Will He forsake her whom He *possessed in the beginning of His ways* (Prv 8.22), and with whom He has partnered in such an intimate collaboration? The great law of marriage, set down by God Himself, is that *a man will cleave to his wife* (Gn 2.24). What supereminent union it must be, then, between the Holy Ghost and Mary, where the two are united in spirit! *Qui adhæret Deo unus spiritus est*, "he who is joined to the Lord, is one spirit" with Him (1 Cor 6.17).

¦ God, in His mercy and condescension is pleased to reward the just, among whom are the most humble and lowly, in which may be counted those who are chaste in their conjugal unions,[20] inasmuch as God has ordained, according to St. Paul, that a spouse be the holder

---

[17] ♦*TD*, 10. – His Masterpiece: This must be understood in the Catholic sense that in the Incarnation the Holy Ghost did not intervene as father, but as the active principle, the divine agent to miraculously form the Body of Christ of the blood of Mary most pure.

[18] Cf. *TD*, 10-11.

[19] *TD*, 11, 20.

[20] St. Bernardine, *Conciones de Tempore*, Sermo 8.1.2, *Opera*, 4:165.1.

of the other.[21] And who is so chaste, so pure; aye, ever virgin and immaculate, if not the Spouse of the Holy Ghost, our Blessed Mother, that St. Bernardine ventures to say: "Since the Incarnation, Mary has acquired a sort of jurisdiction over all temporal missions of the Holy Ghost"[22]; to which St. Bernard adds, "so that no creature receives graces except through the hands of the Virgin Mother."[23] |

We now may see how, as the Spouse of the Holy Ghost and the Mother of Christ, the Blessed Virgin has the universal stewardship of graces. It is in light of these beautiful truths that St. Louis-Marie, after invoking Mary as the "treasure house of the Lord's graces," at end of the prayer that closes the devotion called the "Little Crown," he says: "Grant that for love of you I may despise all earthly consolations and ever cling to those of Heaven until, through you, faithful Spouse of the Holy Ghost, Jesus Christ your Son may be formed in me for the glory of the Father." [24]

Let us conclude with the words of St. Bernardine of Siena: "All the gifts, virtues and graces of this same Holy Ghost are dispensed through the hand of Mary to whom she wills, when she wills, in the manner and as much as she so wills."[25]

---

[21] 1 Cor 7.4: The wife hath not power of her own body, but the husband. And, in like manner, the husband also hath not power of his own body, but the wife.

[22] ♦St. Bernardine, *De Annunt. B.V.M*, Sermo 6.1.2, *Opera*, 4:95.2: "From the time that she conceived the Son of God in her womb, she had, *ut sic dicam* (I might say), a certain authority or jurisdiction in every temporal procession of the Holy Ghost, ..." We take the restrictive qualifier, *ut sic dicam*, used by St. Bernardine as a recognition that a divine Person cannot be sent by another but by reason of His procession.

[23] St. Bernard, *In Vig. Nat. Domini*, Sermo 3.10, PL 183.100A, for which see note 2, p. 99. — The above paragraph has been rewritten. In the writings of St. Bernardine, there is no explicit link between his use of 1 Cor 7.4 and the prerogatives of the B.V.M. The original text of Fr. Lhomeau's reads as follows: "Une autre loi du mariage apparaît encore ici: celle-là même que saint Paul énonce, quand il parle des droits réciproques des époux [here footnoting 1 Cor 7.4]. S. Bernardin en montre l'application, en disant que 'depuis l'Incarnation, Marie a acquis, etc.'" Note that on the three-fold process of communicating grace, St. Bernardine, cited in note 22, above, relies on the authority of Scripture: (1) Grace flowing from the Eternal Father to His Only-Begotten Son, on Jas 1.17: *Every best gift, and every perfect gift, is from above, coming down from the Father of lights*; (2) from the Son to His Mother, on Jn 1.16: *And of His fulness we all have received, and grace for grace*; and (3) from the B.V.M. to all mankind, on Cant 7.4: *Thy neck is like a tower of ivory*. On the reference to "hands," see St. Bernard, ibid.

[24] "Petite Couronne," in Denis, *Le règne*, 324.

[25] ¦¦ S. Bernardine, loc cit.: ... *ita quod nulla creatura a Deo recepit gratiam virtutis, nisi secundum dispensationem Virginis Matris*, "that no creature receives any grace of virtue from God except according to the dispensation of the Virgin Mother herself." | ♦We read in the *Secret*, 19: "God, being absolute Master, can communicate by Himself that

ARTICLE 3: HOW THE BLESSED VIRGIN COOPERATES OR BY WHICH ACTS SHE EXERCISES HER MEDIATION

The motherhood of Mary, her universal mediation, and her constant cooperation with the action of the Holy Ghost in us, are fundamental truths in the spirituality of St. Louis-Marie. We find in them the reason for his devotion to the Blessed Virgin, the love he affirms for her, and the dependence on her that he professes. Let us dig deeper and discover how Mary co-operates with the Holy Ghost in dispensing graces; that is, to answer the question "By which acts is her mediation exercised?" Our Saint is pleased so often to call on the good offices of our divine Mother, to repeat that she leads us to the light of Truth, bears us, supports us, protects us, and nourishes us, that it is useful for us to determine the meaning of these expressions, and to understand how far they may represent the imagery and boldness of a pious language.

§1. HOW THE BLESSED VIRGIN DISPENSES GRACE AND COOPERATES WITH THE HOLY GHOST

We must not imagine Mary dispensing graces in the manner of a servant distributing money in the name of his master. The coins subsist in themselves, regardless of who gives and who receives; not so

---

which ordinarily He communicates only by Mary; and, lest we be rash, we cannot even deny that at times He does so; nevertheless, according to the order established by divine Wisdom, He ordinarily communicates Himself to men only through Mary." None can argue against God acting, in the orders of grace and of nature, outside of the laws He establishes; still, the assertions of St. Louis-Marie's may be awkward. Terrien, in *Mère de Dieu*, Part 2.1, 7.4.2, note (13), 3:585-586, gives a satisfying explanation of whether or not God acts directly at times or through Mary every time; that is, on the assertions of St. Louis-Marie with regards to her universal mediation. He says that St. Louis-Marie is referring to the obligation to pray to the Blessed Virgin to obtain grace, and not to the expanse of her mediation. In other words, to the question: "Do all the graces come to us through Mary?" St. Louis-Marie would say, "Yes, absolutely all." And on: "Are we always obliged to pray to her every time we needed something?" He would reply: "In the ordinary course established by God, we should go through Mary; but we would be rash if we denied that God may communicate, and sometimes does communicate, His grace without her." In this manner is the first grace freely given us without any request on our part; that is, even without our having prayed to Mary for it. ‖ Trent, Sess. 6, Justification, c. 5, 32: "In adults, the beginning of ... justification is to be taken from the *prevenient grace* of God, by Jesus Christ; that is to say, from His vocation, by which they are called, and without the existence of any merits on their part" ‖. This most precious Mother intercedes for us in the concession of favors, even if we asked them not of her, so that, in the ordinary course, we ought to be devoted to her and should pray to her, as does the Church, in reciting the *Ave Maria* at every *Incipit* of the Divine Office. Cf. Le Rohellec, *Marie*, 23-38.

with grace. Grace is an *accident*, a quality,[26] and exists not outside the soul that receives it; just as whiteness, beauty, and life are found only in a living being, or in a white or beautiful object.[27] As for actual graces, they are a supernatural operation of God to make us act supernaturally, or acts of His providence disposing of things in order that we may obtain grace and, in the end, salvation.

Another truth that we should keep in mind is that all graces originate in God and He is their principal agent, the first Who dispenses them. All creatures, the Blessed Virgin included, may be but ministers or instruments of grace, and it is in this manner that the Humanity of Christ, the organ of His Divinity, produces grace and works miracles. Just as the Blessed Virgin did not make the union of the Eternal Word to human nature in the Incarnation, so, too, she cannot produce grace through her own virtue, nor be its principal cause, in the justification of souls.

These truths allow us to understand more precisely how the Blessed Virgin cooperates with the Holy Ghost in the dispensing of grace. Let us turn to the mysteries of the Incarnation and of Pentecost.

When the Word was made flesh, it was the Holy Ghost Who formed His body, and after she gave her consent to the mystery, it was Mary who gave the matter of the purest blood.

Her cooperation principally consists of these: assistance and consent.

On the day of Pentecost, the same Holy Ghost descends to form the Mystical Body of Christ, which is the Church, and to pour charity along with His gifts into souls. What was Mary doing? The Acts of the Apostles say that she was in the holy assembly, but with a particular title and in a rank that distinguish her from everyone else. There, as everywhere, she is and she acts as Mother of the Savior. *Hi omnes erant perseverantes unanimiter in oratione cum mulieribus, et Maria matre Jesu, et fratribus ejus*, "all these were persevering with one mind

---

[26] ¦¦ St. Thomas, *Summa*, 1-2.110.2 ad 3: | "Sicut dicit Boetius: *Accidentis esse est inesse*, the being of an accident is to inhere." ¦¦ Cf. Boethius, *In Categ. Aristotelis*, PL 64.170D-171A. |

[27] St. Thomas, *Summa*, 1.90.2c.

in prayer with the women, and Mary the Mother of Jesus, and with His brethren" (Act 1.14). Under the title Mother of Jesus Christ, along with Spouse of the Holy Ghost, she prayed, and all prayed with her; for if her prayer and consent had been necessary for the Son of God to be incarnate, in the Upper Room they were required so that Jesus might send the Paraclete. And when He came, He came first to her, then from her into the souls of the disciples to sanctify them and there make Christ grow.[28]

Let us now see how Mary co-operates in the dispensing of graces. Whether it be in regards to the habitual grace received or increased, or the supernatural help we call *actual graces*, it is always the Holy Ghost Who comes, and comes upon us, in all the ways that He acts.[29]

What does He do? What is His role? He enters and dwells in our souls, as do the other two Persons of the Holy Trinity. But because He personally is the Gift of God, we call Him, Uncreated Grace; because He is the *nexus*, the living bond that unites the Father and the Son,[30] the end and fruit of their embrace, we attribute to Him the union of our soul with God; because He is the substantial love of the Father and the Son, the Holy and Sanctifying Spirit, we regard Him as the engine of our supernatural life. Between His action and that of Jesus we notice this difference: Our Lord, by His Humanity, is visible and functions in the Church as her Head; and the Holy Ghost, by His hidden role and as Love is assimilated into the heart. From Him come, let us say, the good thoughts, the good movements, and all those streams of grace in our souls that are necessary for our salvation, just as the circulation of blood in our bodies is for our life.[31]

---

[28] Acts 2.2-4, say only that there came a sound from Heaven, that tongues of fire sat on *every one*, and that they were *all* filled with the Holy Ghost at Pentecost. Bourassé, in the entire "Historia Mariana" and "Theologia Mariana" in *Summa B.V.M.*, 1:1-2:916 and 7:755-8:612; and Terrien, *Mère de Dieu*, all 4 vols., are silent on the order of the descent. But both are in agreement on the Blessed Virgin's fullness of grace beginning from the Incarnation. See also the three plenitudes according St. Thomas, in note 10, p. 27.

[29] ◆Some theologians admit not that there is a mission of the Holy Ghost in a simple increase of grace; they only grant it for a change of state in the soul.

[30] St. Thomas, *Summa*, 1.37.1 ad 3: "The Holy Ghost is said to be the bond (*nexus*) of the Father and Son, inasmuch as He is Love (*amor*); because, since the Father loves Himself and the Son with one Love (*dilectione*), and conversely, there is expressed in the Holy Ghost, as Love (*amor*), the relation of the Father to the Son, and conversely, as that of the lover to the beloved."

[31] ◆And if, in the assistance He gives by actual grace, He acts upon a soul deprived of habitual grace due to mortal sin, then, without altering the substance of the soul, He

Such is the role of the Holy Ghost in the sanctification of souls. He produces grace because God alone has the power to do so; the creature can only participate in it as a minister or instrument, or to predispose us to receive it: *ministerialiter et dispositive*.[32] Confined within these limits, we say that Mary's cooperation consists in her intercession (which, naturally, implies her consent) and in her influence. Under what conditions does her intercession take place and by what acts is her influence exerted? These, we shall see in the following sections.

§2. HER INTERCESSION.

The prayer of Mary whilst she yet lived her mortal and pilgrim life is a subject of sweet and deep contemplation. To enter into this spiritual paradise, we ¦¦ mere mortals | must vault above the choirs of Angels, though their love and adoration be for us already a lofty enough ideal of the ascension to God; but when it comes to Mary, saying that she "prayed like an Angel" is not nearly enough. Her prayer is the loftiest as her holiness is the most perfect; that is, the Blessed Virgin surpasses all the Angels in the knowledge of the divine—more than they, she has passed into God,[33] entered into His Will, is filled with His power, and inflamed with His love. Oh, what would we know or could say of her prayer, whether at the moment of the Incarnation, or in the cave at Bethlehem when she gave birth to her divine Son, or at Calvary, or in the Upper Room? With this Daughter of the Most High, we live always in the heights spiritual; and though we may attain some peaks, we have yet to reach the summit, for we need to climb higher, much higher, if we are ever to presume to pray like Mary, for she is now in the glory of Heaven, where she prays to intercede and mediate for us before her Son. We know that, in Heaven,

---

communicates to her faculties the power to do certain supernatural acts.

[32] St. Thomas, *Summa*, 3.26.1c, 1 ad 1: "Nothing hinders certain others than Christ from being called, in some respect, mediators between God and man; that is, insofar as they cooperate by predisposing or ministering (*dispositive vel ministerialiter*) in the union of man with God."

[33] St. Irenæus, *Adversus hæreses*, 4.33.4, PG 7.1074-1075: "How can men be saved unless it was God who wrought out their salvation upon earth? How shall man *transiet in Deum*, 'pass into God,' unless God has first passed into man? How was mankind to escape this birth into death, unless he were born again through faith, by that new birth from the Virgin, the sign of salvation that is God's wonderful and unmistakable gift?"

everything flourishes, is fulfilled, and gestates to term in conditions of perfection, of which we have yet to see and cannot understand. We ought, therefore, to speak of the holiness and intercession of our Mother. The set of truths we presently will call to mind are, to her, a crown of glory, of power, and of goodness. Could we contemplate her, ever so great and merciful, without loving her all the more, without entrusting ourselves ever more to her prayer and maternal solicitude? Let us raise our eyes to the throne of Mary, and finally realize how remarkable are the conditions in which her mediation of intercession takes place.[34]

On high,[35] in that place reserved for Him and fitting only for Him, Christ "sitteth at the right hand of the Father," as we chant in the *Credo*. These words express that kingship and judgeship which, even as Man, He possesses by virtue of Himself and by nature. Mary, being only a creature, though pure, sits not at the right hand of God; but after Christ and with Him, she does have dominion over all Creation. This is why it is not only said that she stands before God, as do Angels,[36] but that she, and she alone, *stands* as Queen at the right hand of Christ the King.[37] We even say that she *sits* there; for she is not there only to serve Him, but also to participate in His kingship and in His other prerogatives to a degree that is not given to any other creature.

Here is another truth: In the vision of the divine essence that no created intellect can fully embrace, what is Mary's participation? Angels and Saints draw eternal life from such vision; some to a greater extent, others lesser, but each to his full capacity. As she exceeds them

---

[34] *TD*, 59. For a good account of Mary's aid through her prayers, her mediation of intercession, see Journet, *l'Église*, 2:651-758.

[35] The Greek ἄνω is the specific, "in Heaven." But note that St. Augustine says in, *Sermones*, 123.4, PL 38.686: "He is on high, and here below; on high in Himself, here below in His people; on high with the Father, below in us."

[36] ‖ Gabriel, Lk 1.19; Raphael, Tob 12.15; in general, Zec 6.5. *Missale*, §4464, Graduale, Dedic. Eccl.: | ♦ "Deus, cui adstat Angelorum chorus, exaudi preces servorum tuorum— O God, on Whom choirs of Angels do attend, hear the prayers of Thy servants."

[37] ‖ *Missale*, §3138, Grad., Com. Virginum, Ps 44.10: | ♦The queen stood on Thy right hand.

all in grace, the Blessed Virgin surpasses them in glory, and none of them may fathom the depth and intensity of the vision whose manifold layers their Queen pierces open by her mere gaze. But as regards this vision, only one point interests us: Angels and blessed souls in glory gain insight into things of this world that even the separation by distance cannot cloud.[38] For example in the Gospel account of Lazarus and the rich man, Abraham sees from Heaven into Hell, where the rich man suffers; and earth, where Lazarus' brothers yet live.[39] Such knowledge is not all-encompassing, however; particularly in our case. Angels and blessed souls know our future, the secret of our thoughts, and the divine plan of our life only to the extent that God reveals them, which He does in respect of their roles in our lives and their links to us, either in prayer or in the functions of their ministration.

For Mary, it is an entirely different matter. As Mother of God and ¦¦ Mother | of Mankind (titles that are exclusively her own), in her role of universal Mediatrix, she extends her solicitude to all in all things. Her knowledge rises to the level of her functions, and here again, she is unique. When her gaze turns to God, immediately, without searching, without effort or doubt,[40] she sees each and every man, their actions, their situations, their needs, and God's plan for them; even penetrating down to their thoughts, for she sees all of these things.

As great as this last prerogative of Mary's may appear, it stands lesser to her Immaculate Conception, and most certainly lower than the Divine Maternity, as the knowledge of mortals is a mere consequence of and an accessory to her perfection. Perhaps now we may

---

[38] ✦St. Thomas, *Summa*, 1.2, 1.89, Suppl. 92.3; 2-2.83.4, 4 ad 2. ¦¦ It is useful to read the entirety of the foregoing references. Some highlights: 1.2.2 ad 3: "We can demonstrate the existence of God from His effects; though from them we cannot perfectly know God as He is in His essence." 1.89.1c: "If inferior substances [men] received species in the same degree of universality as the superior substances [say, Angels or separated souls], since they are not so strong in understanding, the knowledge which they would derive through them would be imperfect, and of a general and confused nature." 2-2.83.4c, 4 ad 2: "We pray to the blessed souls, whether Angels or Saints, not that God may, through them, know our petitions, but that our prayers may be effective through their prayers and merits," for "whatever it is fitting for them to know about what happens to us, even as regards the interior movements of the heart, is made known to them in the Word." |

[39] Lk 13.23-31.

[40] ✦St. Thomas, *Summa*, 2-2.52.3.

come to understand what St. Bonaventure means when he says: "God could make a greater world, a greater Heaven, but He cannot exalt a creature greater than by making her the Mother of God."[41] With these words, we may take in what St. Thomas writes: "The Blessed Virgin, from the fact that she is the Mother of God, has a *certain* infinite dignity from the infinite good, which is God. And on this account, she cannot be any better than she already is; just as there cannot be anything better than God."[42]

This prerogative to know all that is, has been, or will be, exceeds not the condition of the creature. The Soul of Our Lord possessed it, from the first moment of His Incarnation, and St. Thomas admits it is possible that the elect may have this knowledge *of vision* after the Last Judgment.[43] All learned men agree, however, that the Blessed Virgin possesses it now in glory; although a good number think that she had it during her mortal life, that is, since the Incarnation.[44]

In any event, we are now under her gaze and we may say that we are thus present before her.[45] When, therefore, St. Louis-Marie exhorts us to exercise all our actions in union with the Blessed Virgin, to remain interiorly and exteriorly on her dependence, we know that for our every renunciation, our every commitment to her care, every aspiration of our soul towards her, there is on her part a corresponding gaze or prayer that often engulfs us, makes up for our weak efforts, and fills our emptiness to overflowing.[46]

Now let us turn to the third truth: Mary, who sees all, intercedes

---

[41] Note 14, p. 11.

[42] St. Thomas, *Summa*, 1.25.6 ad 4.

[43] Ibid. Suppl. 92.3c: "The knowledge of the Angels and of the souls of the Saints can go on increasing until the Day of Judgment. ... But afterwards, it will increase no more, because, then, will be the final state of things, and it may be possible therein that, by the knowledge of vision, all will know what God knows."

[44] ♦Fr. Jeanjacquot, in *Simples Explications*, ¦ 159, cites Georges de Rhodes, St. Albert the Great, St. Antoninus, St. Bernardine of Sienna, and Hugh of Saint-Cher. See also Terrien, *Mère de Dieu*, 1.1, 7.3-4, 1:365-392. |

[45] Richard of St. Laurence, "De laudibus B.V.M.," 5.2.10, St. Albert, *Opera*, 36:285.1: "As *the eyes of the Lord are upon the just* (Ps 33.16), so also are the eyes of Our Lady upon her children, as a mother watches lest they fall; and if they did, that she may lift them up."

[46] ♦*Missale*, §1543, Oratio, Dom. IX post Pent.: Deus, qui abundantia pietatis tuæ et merita supplicum exedis et vota: effunde super nos misericordiam tuam; ut ... adjicias quod oratio non præsumit, "God, Who in the abundance of Thy kindness are wont to beyond our merits and our prayers: pour down Thy mercy on us, ... and grant us all that we dare not ask in prayer."

for us without end. She prays not only upon presenting herself before God, so that, at the sight of her, He grants us graces in consideration of her merits and of the love she bears us; she prays also with an actual, explicit, formal, and particular request for each one of us. *Sancta Maria, ... ora pro nobis, nunc et in ora mortis nostræ,* "Holy Mary, ... pray for us, now and at the hour of death." In her liturgy, the Church often addresses those words of petition to Mary. Is it not in view of the actual, formal, and particularized prayer that the Mother of God is given the sight of all that concerns us and all that is done in the Church? If that is not the only office of her mediation, it is at least the principal one.

How does the Blessed Virgin pray? *Per Dominum Nostrum Jesum Christum,* "through Jesus Christ Our Lord"; for she is our mediatrix, under Him Who is the necessary mediator for all with God. She therefore prays, by offering the Christ given to us, Who was first given to her like to no other, for the Son of God is also the Son of Mary. She prays by offering the merits of Jesus to which she unites hers. Now, since the will of the Mother never differs from the will of the Son, as they always act together in the unity of the same spirit, Mary, in the most exact and perfect sense, really prays in the name of Christ.

Mary's prayer is all-powerful. Let us delve deeper into this truth to rekindle our hope. The prayer of Jesus Christ, being the prayer of God, by itself has an infinite value. That Mary's prayer is all-powerful is a prerogative of her divine motherhood, as St. Thomas explains: "Since prayers offered for others proceed from charity, the greater the charity of the Saints in Heaven, the more they pray for wayfarers, since the latter can be helped by prayers: and the more closely they are united to God, the more are their prayers efficacious."[47] But who is nearer to God than the august Virgin? Did the Angel not say to her, *Dominus tecum,* "the Lord is with thee"? We shall never know anything greater than this, and it affirms how she excels above all Angels and men, who are but servants and adoptive children. Mary alone is

---

[47] ✦St. Thomas, *Summa,* 2-2.83.11. ¦¦ Cf. Richard of St. Laurence, *De laudibus B.V.M.,* 4.29.1, 307E: "She is Queen of that City, of which her Son is King, and as King and Queen they enjoy the same privileges according to the law. And as the Mother shares, through His grace, in the power of the Son, she is made omnipotent through His omnipotence." And, St. Albert the Great, "Laudibus B.V.M.," 4.30.1, *Opera,* 36:254-255. ¦

Mother of God and Spouse of the Holy Ghost; she alone is related by blood to Christ and, in a certain sense, has a kinship with God; she alone has passed into the singular bonds of intimacy, of love, and even of authority with her divine Son, all of which is reason enough for Our Lord to give her all for the asking.[48]

Contemplate for a moment the Church in prayer. She is like an ocean of an infinite number of waves, undulating across the vast surface; they peak and swell in harmony, then crest and spill over, churning the waters, and rise again. We see waves of supplications rising from all sides, from where we stand to the far distance; and there, at the very edge of the horizon, just as it would be no mirage if we thought the water blends into the sky, so also do the prayers of the Church Militant unite with the prayers of the Church Triumphant, and come to be laid down at the feet of Our Lord in Heaven. Who will ever know of the power of these countless waves, each standing for a prayer in the name of Christ, each with its own divine virtue? In Heaven, she who in Scripture is likened to the moon,[49] has dominion over this vast ocean. She regulates ¦ the rise and fall of its tide, and the ebb and flow its waves. | Through her, our supplications rise to God; through her, are our prayers answered and graces showered upon us.

The Fathers of the Church are clear and resolute when they speak of the power of intercession conferred on Mary. They say that her prayer has more credit than all the prayers of Angels and Saints put together[50]; that if all Heaven prayed contrary to the Blessed Virgin,

---

[48] Quod Deus imperio, tu prece, Virgo, potes, "What God does by command, thou, O Virgin, by a prayer canst effect," or poetically: "God can all things by behest— / Thou by prayer, O Virgin blest!" The pentameter is found in many books, always without an indication of the source; cf. Pinamonti, *Il Sacro Cuore*, in *Opere*, 328; Pepe, *Grandezze di Gesù Cristo*, 7:601. Also, Ps. Bernard, *Ad B.V.M.*, 7, PL 184.1014B: "Speak, O Lady, for your Son hears you, and whatever you ask, you will obtain."

[49] St. Thomas, explicitly compares Mary to the moon in "Exp. de Ave Maria," in *Opera*, 27:200.1: "Sic ergo plena est gratia, et excedit Angelos in plenitudine gratiæ; et propter hoc convenienter vocatur Maria quæ interpretatur illuminata in se; ... et illuminatrix in alios, quantum ad totum mundum; et ideo assimilatur soli et lunæ." Holtnicker, *Speculum B.V.M.*, 96, interprets Cant 6.9: *Who is she that cometh forth as the morning rising, fair as the moon, bright as the sun, terrible as an army set in array?* as alluding to her. In Rev 12.1, we have: "And a great sign appeared in heaven: A woman clothed with the sun, and the moon *under* her feet, and on her head a crown of twelve stars."

[50] Holtnicker, *Speculum B.V.M.*, 6, 84: "It is a great privilege that before God she is more powerful than all the Saints."

she would prevail despite it all; that God cannot turn His face away from His Mother; and that if the prayers of a multitude were not heard (which is impossible to imagine), the Son of God would nonetheless listen if they came from His Mother.[51]

In his treatise on the Sacrifice of the Mass, Cardinal Franzelin says that God, seeing the reverence, holiness, and love of His beloved Bride, the Church, accepts the divine sacrifice that she publicly offers Him in His name as a holocaust of the most sweet odor.[52] ¦ Now, if the prayers in any particular Mass are public prayers, that is, they are the prayers of the entire Church as a whole, and as such there is attached to them a special, efficacious, impetratory character, independent of the disposition of the priest celebrating (*valor ex opere operato*), imagine how much greater is the character of Mary's prayer—she, who is greater than all the other members of the entire Church put together. Let us have confidence, then, that when our Mother prays for us, God answers her without fail. |

This very point did St. Louis-Marie put forward, when he speaks of what should excite our confidence: ¦¦ "Mary ... does nothing contrary to the eternal and immutable Will of God. When we read ... that in Heaven and on earth everything, even God Himself, is subject to the Blessed Virgin, they mean to say that the authority which God is well pleased to give her is so great, that it *seems* as if she had the same power as God, and that her prayers and petitions are so powerful with God, that they always pass for commandments with His Majesty, Who never resists the prayer of the beloved Mother of God, because she is

---

[51] Eadmer of Canterbury, *De excell. B.V.M.*, c. 6, PL 159.570B: "If he who prays does not merit to be heard, the merits of the Mother to whom he recommends himself will intercede effectually." The work was once attributed to St. Anselm.

[52] Franzelin, *SS. Eucharistiæ*, Th. 13.1, 370-371. ¦¦ The rest of this paragraph has been completely revised. Lhomeau jumps to: "Il suit de là que les oraisons de la Messe, en tant qu'oraisons de l'Église, valent *ex opere operato*," without giving the basis of Franzelin's assertion. His next sentence is problematic: "Aux yeux de Dieu, Marie est à elle seule *plus que* toute l'Église." But St. Augustine says in *De Evangelii*, Sermo 25.7, PL 38.938: "Mary is holy, Mary is blessed, but the Church is something better than the Virgin Mary. Why? Because Mary *is part of* the Church." Elsewhere, St. Augustine adds that, in spirit, Mary is Mother of the members, but not of the Head, for it is she who is spiritually born of Him. (*De virginitate*, 6, PL 40.399: "Et mater quidem spiritu non capitis nostri, quod est ipse Salvator, ex quo magis illa spiritaliter nata est"). Cf. Gihr, *Mass*, 119. In Fr. Lhoumeau's defense, below in Part 5.3.2, we read: "Marie ... indépendamment *du reste de* l'Église," from which we say that the phrase in question, here and elsewhere, was unintentionally dubious. |

always humble and conformed to His Will."[53] |

How beautiful and fruitful are the thoughts that flourish in the soul, when we meditate on the unending prayer of Mary! The Blessed Virgin is there still inseparably united to Christ. He stands at the right hand of the Father, always fervent for our cause and importuning on our behalf, and Mary is at the right hand of Christ, praying with Him and through Him. On earth, her prayer and contemplation were endless (the paintings in the catacombs portray her as the Orant[54]); in Heaven she continues her sublime function. This is a vital lesson that she gives us, and how brilliant is her example! Absorb it well, and by and by, we will embody the precept Jesus gave us, that is, *we ought always to pray* (Lk 18.1); for, above all, Mary intercedes in the great work of dispensing graces. It is her main office, and if her prayer were not united to the intercession of the Savior, nothing would be done for the salvation of the world. This is a lesson directed at those who wish to work for the salvation of souls. Now, it should be clear that the spirit of Mary is the essence of prayer, and in that respect, she is indeed the faithful Spouse of that divine Spirit which Scripture calls *Spiritum gratia et precum*, "the Spirit of grace and of prayers." (Zac 12.10). Let us implore the blessed Virgin that all who wish to strictly belong to her may be sharers of her holy fervor. Whether it be the religious state, the priesthood, or the perfect devotion, let us remember that prayer is the great office of consecrated life and of souls devoted to the apostolate.

§3. HER INFLUENCE.

Mary not only cooperated spiritually in the Redemption of all mankind, hastening by her prayers the coming of the Messiah and

---

[53] ◆*TD*, 14.

[54] In Christian art, the Orant is a figure in a posture of prayer, usually standing upright, elbows close to the side, hands stretched out, palms Heaven-ward. If not identified with a particular person, the Orant may be a symbol of the Faith or of the Church herself. In Byzantine painting, Παναγία Βλαχερνιώτισσα, Our Lady of Blacherniotissa or the Madonna orant, is a major type in the depictions of the Blessed Virgin. Used to decorate the main apse of a churches, she stood symbolically as interceding with Christ on behalf of the faithful. Fr. Lhoumeau refers to the Orant of the catacombs of St. Agnes, Rome, below in Part 5.4.2, p. 363.

consenting to the Incarnation, she also contributed to it by providing Jesus with the substance of His body; and after giving birth, she nourished Him, brought Him up, and blanketed Him with a thousand cares; at Calvary, she offered Him on the Cross; and, finally, in all the mysteries of her life, she was linked to Him as the Eve of the new Adam, as His mother, His only one, and the Spouse ¦¦ of the Holy Ghost. |

In the application of the fruits of the Redemption, is her cooperation limited to her praying for us? The answer is, No. We spoke above of her influence. What is it? To which acts does it refer?

Aside from her *fiat* and her intercession of which we have just spoken, we shall see that the object of Mary's influence is to illuminate our intellect with good counsels, to incline our will towards good movements, to lead or govern us in our external actions, and to defend us against our spiritual enemies.

Let us now turn to each of these offices.

SHE ILLUMINATES OUR INTELLECT

In commenting on these words, *Fili mi, acquiesce consiliis meis*, "my son, follow my counsels" (Gn 27.8), which Rebecca said to her son Jacob, St. Louis-Marie says that the Blessed Virgin inspires us with good counsels.[55] Further on, he mentions that the living faith and the lights that she communicates to us are among the fruits of a perfect devotion to her.[56] Indeed, if the Angels, being the fair mirrors of divinity, can illuminate our intellect by making it stronger and clearer in presenting images to our mind's eye,[57] what shall we say about the Virgin, the spotless mirror of eternal Light with its brilliance and splendor?[58] In one of his hymns, St. Louis-Marie sings:

> ¦ She is more brilliant
>   Than all the Cherubim;
> She is more afire

---

[55] *TD*, 141.

[56] *TD*, 150.

[57] On intellectual and imaginary visions, see St. Teresa of Avila, *Interior Castle*, 6.8-10, 215-241; mental and corporeal images and the forming of the soul, especially in the theology of St. John Chrysostom, see Rylaarsdam, *Divine Pedagogy*, 56-74.

[58] ◆Wis 7.26: For she is the brightness of eternal Light, and the unspotted mirror of God's majesty, and the image of His goodness.

Than all the Seraphim.[59] |

The sun that is her garment, the twelve stars that make her crown, tell us that this woman, as if engulfed by the Divinity and lost in His splendor, gathers in her all the gifts of light that God has invested in His creatures by participation. It is right, then, that we should turn to Mary for good counsels and the lights of faith.

SHE INCLINES OUR WILL TO GOOD MOTIONS

To the good thoughts that illuminate our mind with which the Blessed Virgin helps us, we should add the right movements that would excite our will and help it to act accordingly. It is true that no creature can have any direct action on our will or change it, for the power belongs to God alone; but man, or Angel, can push it to one direction or the other, either by persuasion or by exciting holy or disordered passions. The holy Angels persuade us by making our soul shine with the truth to which she is drawn; the evil ones, alas! lead her by the seduction of false goods. Men, and even more, Angels, can act on our senses and our imagination in a thousand different ways for the purpose of soliciting our will. It is also within the power of spirits to upset the body, to trick the sight, to change the taste, to act on the moods and the sensations, of which we know frightening examples in diabolical possessions.

Now, whether it is to excite or aid our will to move towards the good through appeal and persuasion, to act on our passions to rule, purify and, if necessary, calm them, there is none better to turn to other than Mary. Who will render unto us the truth in all its splendor, if not she who, in giving us the Son of God made Man, made real what the Prophet had foretold: *In funiculis Adam traham eos, in vinculis caritatis*, "I will draw them with the cords of Adam, with the bands of love" (Hos 11.4)? She is the Mother of grace, since she is the Mother of Jesus, and it is to her that the Church sings: ¦¦ *Trahe nos, Virgo immaculata, post te curremus in odorem unguentorum tuorum,* | "Draw us, Virgin undefiled, we shall run after thee in the odor of thy perfumes."[60] We also read in the hymns of St. Louis-Marie:

---

[59] *Cantiques*, 76.11, 128.
[60] ◆Ant., Vespers, Assumptione, and Conceptione Immaculata, *Brev. Rom.*, 762; *Officium parvum B.V.M*, 101.

It is through Mary
That Heaven draws us.[61]

Further on, he sings of the *raptrix cordium*,[62] ravisher of hearts,
that the Fathers of the Church had occasion to use:

> She rains down favors from her hand,
> So bathe her faithful servants all;
> She steals our hearts; O Lady, band,
> Sweet joy e'er new, we in thy thrall.[63]

Who can say by how many means she does also calm our passions,
act on our senses, on our sensitive tastes, and, above all, give us the
supernatural taste for things divine which we call Divine Wisdom!
Who has not felt internal turmoil abate, infatuations vanish into thin
air, anger or impatience retreat, when praying to her with confidence,
when looking at her image, when touching or kissing the rosary,
medal or scapular?

SHE PROTECTS US

She keeps us, defends from our enemies, and guards us against all
peril! We often petition Mary for these things in prayers, a beautiful
example of which is the antiphon, *Sub tuum præsidium*: ¦¦ "We take
refuge under thy protection, O holy Mother of God! Despise not our
supplications in our need, but deliver us always from all dangers, O
Virgin, glorious and blessed!"[64] |

Angels are entrusted with the care of a soul, a city, a kingdom; but
Mary, Mother of all mankind, must protect them all. St. Louis-Marie

---

[61] *Cantiques*, 155.1: "C'est par Marie / Que le Ciel veut nous charmer."

[62] In the expanded version of Giacomo da Milano, *Stimulus amoris*, found among the works of St. Bernard, *Med. in Salve Regina*, §2, PL 184.1077D, and of St. Bonaventure, *Opera*, 12:699-700: "O Domina, quæ rapis corda hominum dulcore, nonne cor meum, Domina, rapuisti? ... O *raptrix cordium*, quando mihi restitues cor meum? ... Guberna illud cum tuo, et in sanguine Agni conserva, et in latere Filii colloca. Tunc assequar quod intendo, et possidebo quod spero, quia tu es spes nostra." "O Lady, who by your sweetness do ravish the hearts of men, have you not ravished mine? O *raptrix cordium*, ravisher of hearts, when will you restore me mine? Rule and govern it like your own; preserve it in the Blood of the Lamb, and place it in your Son's side. Then shall I obtain what I desire, and possess that for which I hope; for you, O Mother, are our hope."

[63] *Cantiques*, 80.9: "Elle prodigue ses faveurs / À tous ses serviteurs fidèles; / Elle sait enlever les cœurs / Par des douceurs toujours nouvelles."

[64] Compl., *Officium parvum B.V.M.*, 100: "Sub tuum præsidium confugimus, sancta Dei Genetrix: nostras deprecationes ne despicias in necessitatibus, sed a periculis cunctis libera nos semper, Virgo gloriosa et benedicta. Amen."

enumerates this defense and protection of the Blessed Virgin among the good offices she renders to her servants. "She hides them," said he, "under the wings of her protection, as a hen hides her chicks. She speaks, she humbles herself, she condescends to all their frailties, to safeguard them from the hawk and the vulture."[65] He reminds us that Mary, the adversary of Satan, "must be terrible to him and his crew, *as an army set in array* (Cant 6.9)."[66]

HER PROVIDENCE

Sis pia nostra gubernatrix,[67] "be thou our loving guide" and govern us in thy mercy! We now examine the last object of Mary's influence; that is, her care for us or, if you will, Mary's cooperation with Divine Providence. But first, let us understand how this life of continual dependence and total abandonment in the perfect devotion is fully justified.

¦ Divine Providence is God Himself in that act of ordering and governing all events in the universe to realize the end of Creation; that is, all creatures should manifest His glory, and man should glorify Him, recognizing the work of His hand in nature, serving Him in obedience and love, and thereby attaining to the full development of his nature and to eternal blessedness in Him.[68] | This plan and ordination of the universe are in the mind and Will of God; but for the execution of His designs He makes use of creatures ordained to be in a hierarchy, so that the superiors rule the inferior, and the most perfect rule the least perfect,[69] to which we trace the origin of power and the reason for obedience.

Now, in a singular measure, Mary is initiated in the *counsels* of Providence; that is, to God's foresight and the ordination of His plan, and, more than any other creature, she is also associated with the *execution* of His Will.

God reveals to his Angels and his Prophets certain of His designs,

---

[65] Cf. *TD*, 147.

[66] ♦*TD*, 30.

[67] "Petite Couronne," Denis, *Le règne*, 321.

[68] Pohle, "Divine Providence," *TCE*, 12:590.

[69] St. Thomas, *Summa*, 1.22.3c, 1..110.1c.

and sometimes gives them the task of executing them; but to the
Virgin most holy, it is His general plan that He uncovers. In fact, she
herself enters into the plan and plays a prominent part; because with
Christ and because of Him, she is ¦¦ *in initio viarum suarum,* | "in the
beginning of His ways" (Prv 8.22). That is why the Fathers say that the
world was made for her.[70] And by saying "her," we understand all that
it means and all derived from it: beginning with her people, that *semen illius,* "her seed," of Scripture,[71] of which first and personally is
her only Son, Jesus Christ; then all who, in Him and through Him, are
His brethren in grace, and children of Mary. It is from this understanding of Mary's providence that St. Louis-Marie often repeats: All
to Mary, all through Mary to Christ, and through Christ to God. Thus,
we may apply to her these words from Proverbs: *Cum eo eram, cuncta
componens,* "I was with Him forming all things" (Prv 8.30).[72]

But this very prudent Virgin is not only initiated into the ways of
God and enters not only into His plan, she is also all-powerful to procure its execution. Her royal power, of which we speak below, subjects
the whole of Creation to her and enables her to govern us according
to the desires of her maternal heart. "She conducts and directs them
according to the will of her Son. .... She shows them the paths of eternal life. She makes them avoid the dangerous places. She conducts
them by her hand along the paths of justice. She steadies them when
they are about to fall; she lifts them up when they have fallen. She
reproves them like a charitable mother when they fail; and sometimes
she even chastises them lovingly."[73] St. Louis-Marie had previously

---

[70] Ps. Bernard, *In Salve Regina,* Sermo 3.2, PL 184.1069: "Propter hanc totus mundus
factus est"; St. John Damascene, *Sermo,* 6.1, In Nat. B.V.M., PG 96.662: "Illa quippe
mundo bonorum peperit thesaurum, quem vis nulla auferre possit. Per eum siquidem
Creator naturam universam media humanitate in melius commutavit"; Eadmer of Canterbury, *De excell. B.V.M.,* c. 1, PL 159.550B: Per "quem cæli cælorum, quem omnes
rerum creatarum machinæ capere nequeunt, virginalis uterus beatæ Mariæ cepit,
quando eumdem ipsum de se verum et perfectum Deum et hominem in una persona
concepit et generavit"; St. Bonaventure, "Psalterium B.V.M.," Ps 118, *Opera,* 14:216.1:
"Dispositione tua perseverat mundus: quem et tu cum Deo fundasti ab initio."
[71] Gn 3.15.
[72] ♦These words, like many others in the wisdom books, in the literal sense, are said of
Eternal Wisdom or the Word; but the Church applies them to the Blessed Virgin.
[73] ♦*TD,* 146.

compared Mary to Rebecca, whose loving skill obtained Isaac's blessing for her favorite son. Then he adds: "As she sees clearly through
God every good and evil, all good and ill fortunes, His blessings and
curses; she so disposes things from afar, that she may exempt her servants from all sorts of evils, and shower them with all sorts of goods;
so that if a creature may strike it rich in God's ¦¦ endeavors, so to
speak, | by his fidelity to some high office, it is certain that Mary will
procure that good fortune for any one of her true children and servants, and will give them all the grace to faithfully bring it to fruition.
Ipsa procurat negotia nostra, says a Saint."[74]

Those sweet thoughts give us a sense of the following words:

> Depend all I on her, my Mother,
> To better lean on Him, my Savior.
> Body and soul and my welfare all,
> On her good graces mayest they fall.[75]

Who among those who practice this dependence and live according to this abandonment, even if a little, has not experienced the
manifest power and providence of Mary? Histories bearing witness to
her maternal care for us fill many books. Still, what better story helps
us to understand and touches us than our own? In this world, we cannot know the divine plan for our entire life, yet what glimpses of it we
already have fills us with awe and gratitude. Clearly, Mary is the
sweetness of life, *vitæ dulcedo.*[76] Ours seems bathed in the mercy of
which she is the mother.[77] To us, she is worth more than a thousand
lives[78]; but without her, what would any one of them be worth? It is
thus the duty and necessity of our love to abandon ourselves ever
more to the Blessed Virgin.

---

[74] *TD,* 140-141. Perhaps alluding to St. Albert the Great, "Laudibus B.V.M.," 2.1.18, *Opera,*
36:68.2: Mary, as "our advocate before the Son, just as the Son is before the Father,
procurat negotia et petitiones nostras, ceases not to take an interest in the business of
our salvation before both Father and Son." Cf. Jordan, "De B.V.M.," Prol., §2, *Opera,* 116:
"Apud Patrem et Filium, Maria ~, et sæpe quos Justitia Filii potest damnare, matris mi-
sericordia liberat."
[75] *Cantiques,* 77.8, 132: "Je suis tout sous sa dépendance, / Pour mieux dépendre du Sauveur, / Laissant tout à sa providence, / Mon corps, mon âme et mon bonheur."
[76] ✦From an older text. Afterwards it was changed to *vita, dulcedo,* "our sweetness and
our life."
[77] ✦Ps 32.5: The earth is full of the mercy of the Lord.
[78] ✦Ps 62.4: For thy mercy is better than lives."

ANGELS IN THE SERVICE OF THEIR QUEEN

We come now to the acts implicit in the word "influence." It remains for us to say how Mary exercises them. Does she affect us directly or through intermediaries?

The answer is, in general, they come through the ministry of Angels, according the hierarchical order instituted by God for the governance of creatures.

God, the Author and principle of all things, is atop the heavenly hierarchy; then comes Christ, the principal, necessary, and universal Mediator. After Christ, and ever inseparable from Him, is His Mother most holy, mediatrix between Him and us. But the hierarchy does not end there; it spreads, stretches, and branches out. The Blessed Virgin is like the neck to the Head of the Mystical Body, says St. Bernardine, and adds: "Here follows the hierarchical order and the flow of celestial gifts: From God in the blessed Soul of Christ, then from Christ in the soul of the Virgin, spreading on to the Seraphim, the Cherubim, and successively to the different choirs of Angels and Saints; finally to the Church Militant, where a choice portion is given to the friends of God and the glorious Virgin."[79]

Hence, whether it be the light of glory or gifts of grace, all go through Mary,[80] the universal and supreme intermediary between

---

[79] ◆St. Bernardine, | "Fest. B.V.M.," 3.3.2, *Opera*, 4:81. | ¦¦ "Nam sicut per collum spiritus vitales a capite diffunduntur per corpus: sic per Virginem a capite Christo vitales gratiæ in ejus mysticum corpus, et specialius in amicos, atque devotos continue transfunduntur. Unde iste hierarchicus ordo, et defluxus cælestium gratiarum, ut prius a Deo defluat in Christi animam benedictam. ... Deinde defluat in animam Virginis, inde in Seraphim, deinde in Cherubim; et sic successive in alios ordines Angelorum, atque Sanctorum: demum in Ecclesiam Militantem, et maxime in amicos Dei, et Virginis gloriosæ." |

[80] ◆We can say this, even admitting with St. Thomas that the grace and glory of Angels (*Summa*, 1.62.3c), as well as the grace given to our first parents at the moment of their creation (*Summa*, 1.95.1c), neither came from Christ nor passed through Mary. The reason is that the Incarnation was to take place for the salvation of man. Hence, what we say must be understood in the following sense: If the Angels receive not from Christ their essential glory, at least they are hierarchically subordinate to Him. As Head, Christ has influence over them, He purifies them, says St. Dionysius, and illuminates them touching the mysteries of faith and the divine things ¦¦ (*Cælesti hierarchia*, 3.2, PG 3.166B). | That is why the Angels eager for these lights seek them in Christ: *In quem desiderant Angeli prospicere*. (1 Pet 1.12). On the other hand, says St. Thomas, in "Exp. de Ave Maria," *Opera*, 27:200.2: "Mary is full of grace [and, consequently, also of glory], exceeding the Angels in this fullness [and, consequently, of her glory]; and on this account, she is fittingly called Mary, which is interpreted "she who is illumined in herself"; ¦¦ whence, *The Lord will fill thy soul with brightness* (Is 58.11). And she will illumine

Christ and every creature. She belongs to no angelic hierarchy; she is alone in her rank.

The nine choirs of Heaven are divided into two main groups: The first are the Seraphim, the Cherubim, and the Thrones, the Angels who stand before the throne of God, who serve Him and draw the knowledge of the mysteries from the clarity of the divine essence itself. The second are the Dominions, Virtues, Powers, Archangels, and Angels, who are ministers, that is to say, those who prepare the fulfillment of the divine decrees or who execute them.

Mary is Queen of them all. She stands at the right hand of Christ, above the Angels who attend before the throne of God. None is like unto her in relationship with the three divine Persons. She surpasses the Angels in her closeness to God.[81]

But the Blessed Virgin is not only a *helper*, she is also a *cooperator* of God in the government of the world. The former has contemplation as its end; the latter, action, and the two exist side-by-side in Mary. We read of them in the Gospel regarding Martha and Mary,[82] which the Church chants on the Feast of the Assumption[83] as a reminder that our Mother continues in Heaven the double role she fulfilled on earth.

More illumined than all the Angels, even those of the first hierarchy, she illumines them in turn.[84] *I made that in the heavens there should rise light that never faileth* (Sir 24.6). It is Mary who imparts to the Angels the knowledge for the execution of God's aims; it is from her also that all things go forth. The *Dominations* arrange the plan of execution, so to speak; but they do so with authority and lights that she, who is *Domina*, the Sovereign most excellent, sends them, because the Lord is with her: *Dominus tecum*. Placing their power in the service of their Queen, the Virtues and the Powers act, the former on physical bodies in the working of miracles; the latter, against the evil

---

others throughout the world, | for which reason she is compared to the sun and to the moon."

[81] ♦St. Thomas, in "Exp. de Ave Maria," *Opera*, 27:200.2: "Maria ... excellit Angelos in familiaritate divina."

[82] Lk 10.41-42.

[83] Matins, Lect. 8, *Brev. Rom.*, 764.

[84] ♦Note 80, p. 138.

spirits they must fight. Finally, the Archangels and Angels (especially our guardian Angel) carry out the orders.

Now we may comprehend the influence or action of Mary on us. In sum, when we pray to her or if she spontaneously wills to grant us some grace, she intercedes through Christ and obtains from God that such grace be granted us. The charity that comes or grows in our souls, and the good movements of our will, we attribute to our blessed Mother, because the Holy Ghost operates on the prayer and with the consent of His faithful Spouse. Be it for good influence, support in temptation, a temporal favor, the graces may come to us through the ministry of Angels, but they all submit to her command.

There are several passages where St. Louis-Marie alludes to the action of Mary through the heavenly spirits. Let us quote only the following two: "If it is not by herself that she gives these counsels, it is by the ministry of the Angels, who have no greater honor or pleasure than to descend to earth to obey any of her commandments, and to succor any of her servants."[85] And further on: "This good Mother and powerful Princess of the Heavens would rather dispatch battalions of millions of Angels to succor one of her servants than that it should ever be said that a faithful servant of Mary, who trusted in her, had had to succumb to the malice, the number, and the vehemence of his enemies."[86]

> Let us crown the Queen of Angels
> Here on earth and there in Heaven
> ...
>
> Under God, she reigns supreme
> O'er yon celestial city.
> O most Holy Trinity,
> Didst place on her a diadem.
>
> Her light doth shine ever brighter
> More blinding than Cherubim's;
> Yon flare of the Seraphim,
> Snuffs the flames of lesser fire.

---

[85] ◆TD, 141.
[86] TD, 147.

All Heaven's radiance around,
All Thrones there in glory be,
And Virtues we do not see,
Are but jewels that adorn her crown.

She holds in her dependence,
Manifold battalions
Of Thrones and Dominations,
Principalities and Powers.[87]

Steeped in this truth, St. Louis-Marie had a constant devotion to the holy Angels. It was the logical consequence and complement to his devotion to the Blessed Virgin. He could not honor the Queen, without honoring her envoys and the ministers of her wishes.[88]

---

[87] ◆*Cantiques* (1758), "En l'honneur de Notre Dame des Anges," 486-487.

[88] ◆Does the Blessed Virgin sometimes act directly and immediately on us, outside the ministry of Angels? We may say she does, in cases of visible manifestations, such as apparitions that occur under certain conditions (cf. as applied to Christ, in St. Thomas, *Summa*, 3.57.6 ad 3). But what of the influence she exerts on our soul? Though it be incontestable that the Blessed Virgin can act immediately and without the participation of the Angels, it is difficult to establish that she does so and to specify for what purpose there would be such an exception to the hierarchical order of divine government.

CHAPTER 3:

THE QUEENSHIP OF MARY

Mother and Lady.

Mary, Mediatrix and Queen, is the object of the devotion taught by St. Louis-Marie. We spoke above of her mediation, and particularly her motherhood, which is the foundation and her principal role. Let us now speak of her sovereignty. We shall briefly summarize her titles and the extent of her sovereignty, with particular emphasis on the one she exercises in our souls. This is the point that concerns the perfect devotion to Mary the most, and it justifies her title of "Queen of Hearts."

ARTICLE 1: THE TITLES OF HER QUEENSHIP

The title of Queen means not only that Mary excels in some sort of quality, in the sense that a rich man is said to be the king of millionaires; a woman, a queen of beauty; a writer, the king of poets, and so on. By "Queen," we say that the Blessed Virgin has a right of true possession, a real dominion, a royal power.

This queenship, like all the other prerogatives of Mary, is a consequence of her divine motherhood. In fact, her kinship with Christ, her offices as Co-Redemptrix, Treasurer, and Dispenser of all Graces, and so many other titles on which her sovereignty is based, are all derived from her motherhood.

§1. MOTHER OF CHRIST.

The mother of a king is the queen mother, the wife of a king is also a queen, for kinship creates a participation in the same goods. For this reason, Mary has a share in the prerogatives of Christ. He is

King, she is Queen; He is Our Lord, *Dominus*; she is Our Lady, *Domina*. "In dominion and power," says Arnauld de Chartres, "you cannot separate the Mother from the Son, for they are of the same flesh, spirit, and charity; and from the time it was said to Mary, 'The Lord is with thee,' they are inseparably preserved in that divine promise and grace."[1] Along with many other authorities,[2] St. John Damascene said as much: "Mary became truly the sovereign of all created things in becoming the Mother of the Creator."[3]

It is thus in the proper sense of royal power that, in the Psalms, Mary is called the Queen that stands at the right hand of the King,[4] and that the Church, in her prayers, so often hail the Blessed Virgin with this glorious title, and also applies to her these words from the Wisdom books: *By me kings reign, and lawgivers decree just things; by me princes rule, and the mighty decree justice* (Prv 8.15-16).[5]

§2. CO-REDEMPTRIX.

We call Jesus Christ not only King and Lord, but "Our Lord," because He is ours in many ways, especially as Redeemer. Now, Mary cooperates in this Redemption.[6] That is why we call her "Our Lady," that is, our Queen and Sovereign. The quality of Co-Redemptrix is the second title of her queenship. As with all her other titles, it is derived from her divine motherhood, since the Mother of Christ is Mother of

---

[1] Arnauld de Chartres, *De laudibus B.V.M.*, PL 189.1729B: "Nec a dominatione vel potentia filii mater potest esse sejuncta. Una est Mariæ et Christi caro, unus spiritus, una caritas, et ex quo dictum est ei: 'Dominus tecum,' inseparabiliter perseveravit promissum et donum."

[2] Concisely summarized by Pope Pius XII, Radio message to Fatima, May 13, 1946, *AAS*, 38:266; tr., *Am. Eccles. Rev.*, July 1949, 121 (1):358: "He, the Son of God, reflects on His heavenly Mother the glory, the majesty and the dominion of His kingship, for, having been associated to the King of Martyrs in the ineffable work of Redemption as Mother and co-operatrix, she remains forever associated to Him, with an almost unlimited power, in the distribution of the graces which flow from the Redemption. Jesus is King throughout all eternity by nature, and by right of conquest: by Him, with Him, and subordinate to Him, Mary is Queen by grace, by divine relationship, by right of conquest, and by singular election. And her kingdom is as vast as that of her Son and God, since nothing is excluded from her dominion." See also, Roschini, "Royauté de Marie," in du Manoir, ed., *Maria*, 3.3, 1:601-618; and Pius XII, *Ad Cœli Reginam*. For an extensive study on Mary's queenship as seen throughout history, see the six articles in *Marian Studies*, 4 (1953): 13-169.

[3] •St. John Damascene, *De fide orthodoxa*, 4.14, PG 94.1158-1159.

[4] Ps 44.10.

[5] Matins, Lect. 1, In Festis B.V.M. per annum, *Brev. Rom.*, 88*.

[6] Part 2.1, p. 102 ff.

the Redeemer and also, in the order of grace, Mother of all the redeemed.

It is worth recalling here the words of St. Anselm: "Just as God,
Who does all things by His power, is the Father and Lord of all creatures, so is the Blessed Virgin, the Mother of God, who redoes [or
restores] all by her merits, is Mother and Mistress of all things."[7]

§3. DISPENSER OF ALL GRACES AND SPOUSE OF THE HOLY GHOST.

Mary's third title to sovereignty deserves our special attention.
How could the Blessed Virgin govern us and dispense graces to us, if
we were not subject to her? St. Louis-Marie answers at great length.
"Mary," says he, "received from God the dominion over the souls of
the elect; for she cannot make her dwelling in them, as God the Father
ordains, and form them in Jesus Christ, or Jesus Christ in them, and
plant the roots of her virtues in their hearts, and be the indissoluble
companion of the Holy Ghost in all His works of grace—she cannot, I
say, do all these things unless she has a right and dominion over their
souls by a singular grace of the Most High, Who, having given her
power over His only and Natural Son, gave her also the power over
His adopted children, not only as to their body, which would be a
small matter, but also as to their soul."[8]

Let us now turn to the intimate link between the two titles St.
Louis-Marie often repeats: "O my Mother and Lady!"[9] She is Lady or
Queen, we said above, for she is the Mother ¦¦ of God. | She is Lady or
Queen for the aim of fulfilling her functions. She is Lady, not only in
the sense of *Domina*, sovereign Lady, but also *Magistra*, teacher or
educator, as every mother ought to be. Here again, Mary is always
with Our Lord and participates in His prerogatives, because He is
Master in the two senses which the Apostles knew of Him. They called
Him, *Magister*, and Jesus Himself tells us that they also called Him,
Dominus, for in the Gospel we read: *You call me* Master, *and* Lord; *and*

---

[7] ¦¦ Not St. Anselm, but Eadmer of Canterbury, his companion and biographer. | ✦*De
excell. B.V.M.*, c. 11,¦¦ PL 159.578B : "Sicut ergo Deus sua potentia parando cuncta Pater
est et Dominus omnium, ita beata Maria suis meritis cuncta reparando mater est et
domina rerum; Deus enim est Dominus omnium, singula in sua natura propria jussione
constituendo; et Maria est domina rerum, singula congenitæ dignitati per illam quam
meruit gratiam restituendo." |

[8] ✦Cf. *TD*, 20-21.

[9] *TD*, passim.

you say well, for so I am (Jn 13.13).

Mary as Spouse of the Holy Ghost cooperates with Him in the dispensing of graces. This is another title of Mary's sovereignty. We chant in the Creed that this Divine Spirit is *Dominum et vivificantem*, "Lord and Giver of life." Why? Because, by virtue of the law of appropriation which attributes power to the Father, wisdom to the Son, we appropriate goodness and the giving of life to the Holy Ghost.[10] Now all the goods, all the rights and privileges of the husband are the portion of the wife, all the more legitimately in this case inasmuch as the Spouse, that is to say Mary, cooperates in the action of the Holy Ghost. If, therefore, in order to govern and quicken souls, He has the right of dominion over them, likewise, Mary must participate in His kingship. So did St. Louis-Marie assert above.

We may also affirm the queenship of the Blessed Virgin based on the state of original justice where it was established by right of the Immaculate Conception. *Let us make man to Our image and likeness: and let him have dominion over the fishes of the sea, and the fowls of the air, and the beasts, and the whole earth, and every creeping creature that moveth upon the earth* (Gn 1.26). When he sinned, Adam lost this dominion over all Creation given to him by God. Saints have recovered a small measure of it with their innocence and holiness, as may be seen in the wonders of their lives. But the Blessed Virgin did not have to regain a queenship of which sin might have deprived her; for she was immaculate from the moment she was conceived, and she put on the mantle of queenship from the time she entered this world. Since her righteousness surpasses that of our first parents' at the moment they came forth from the hands of the Creator, and since the splendor of her grace eclipses the lights of the Angels and Saints, her sovereignty, in order to be in accord with the excellence of her state, must exalt her above all, save God.

ARTICLE 2: THE EXTENT OF HER QUEENSHIP

In the name of Jesus, every knee should bow, of those that are in Heaven, on earth, and under the earth (Phil 2.10). The kingship of Christ is universal, as also is the sovereignty of Mary, to which point Arnauld

---

[10] ◆St. Thomas, *Summa*, 1.45.6 ad 2.

de Chartres says: "In my opinion, she has not only a glory akin to the glory of her Son; rather, it is the same glory that she shares."[11] Let us now take a brief look at the different provinces in the realm of Mary.

First, it comprises all that is on earth, even creatures that have not the faculty of reason. In Holy Scripture, inanimate things, including vegetation and animals, are represented to us as being subject to the most Blessed Virgin and dedicated to her service. The sun is her garment, the moon is under her feet, the stars form her crown[12]; her throne is in a column of clouds[13]; she passes over the seas[14]; the earth rescues this woman pursued by the dragon,[15] and so on. It can be summarized in the words of St. Bernardine: "There are as many creatures in the service of the Blessed Mary as there are in the service of the Creator."[16]

We now delve deeper into the dominion of Mary over men and nations.

If we could go down to Hell even for a short time, what we see would make us believe and fill us with dread. The power of Christ holds down in Hell those who have entirely rejected the yoke of His love. Mary is appointed by God to triumph over Satan, the adversary. To him she is *terrible as an army set in array* (Cant 6.9). She is the rod of Aaron, who devours the other rods changed into snakes.[17] The Fathers expressly mention her power over Hell. In the *Speculum* attributed to St. Bonaventure, she is said to be sovereign over demons.[18] St. Bernardine, commenting on these words of Ben Sirach: *Et profundum abyssi penetravi*, "I have penetrated into the bottom of the deep" (Sir

---

[11] Arnauld de Chartres, *De laudibus B.V.M.*, PL 189.1729B: "Unitas divisionem non recipit, nec secatur in partes, et si ex duobus factum sit unum, illud tamen ultra scindi non potest, et filii gloriam cum matre non tam communem judico quam eamdem."
[12] Rev 12.1.
[13] Sir 24.7.
[14] Perhaps, Bar 3.30.
[15] Rev 1.16.
[16] ◆St. Bernardine, "Fest. B.V.M.," ¦¦ 13.6, *Opera*, 4:92.1: "Tot creaturæ serviunt B. Mariæ Virgini, quot serviunt toti Trinitati." |
[17] Ex 7.10-12.
[18] ◆Holtnicker, *Speculum B.V.M.*, 3, 38: "After all we have said, we must consider how Mary is interpreted as 'Lady.' Such a title well becometh so great an empress, who is in very deed the sovereign Lady of the inhabitants of Heaven, of the dwellers upon earth and in Hell. She is, I say, the Lady of Angels, the Lady of all mankind, the Lady Sovereign in Heaven, on earth, and in Hell."

24.8), says that the dominion of the Blessed Virgin extends to Hell.[19] How does she exercise her power there? It has the effect of restraining the pride and malice of evil spirits and the damned associated with them. It is also exercised in the sense that she who is the "Gate of Heaven"[20] closes the gates of Hell, or at least keeps it firmly shut. Great is the number of souls she saves from the mouth of the pit and prevent from being swallowed up in the deep![21]

Thus far only will we shall go, lest we venture into suspect speculations.

From Hell our eyes go to Purgatory. It, too, is part of the realm of Mary, and there we find her children in a painful phase, waiting to be reborn into eternal glory. St. Vincent Ferrer, St. Bernardine of Siena, Louis de Blois and others explicitly proclaim Mary to be Sovereign of Purgatory,[22] and St. Louis-Marie urges us to think and act in accordance with this belief. He teaches us to entrust the merit of our prayers and satisfactions into the hands of Mary; and promises us that, in return for this offering, the souls of those dear to us will obtain greater relief than if we directly apply our suffrages to their benefit.[23] Through her prayers, the Mother of God can procure that they be given a greater measure of the infinite satisfactions of Christ. She can also let them take a portion of hers, which is a rich treasure indeed for the Church. Also, it is within her power to relieve those souls indirectly, for example, by stirring the faithful on earth to pray for them.[24] If the

---

[19] St. Bernardine, "Fest. B.V.M.," 3.2.2, *Opera*, 4:80.1.

[20] Litany of Loreto: "Janua Cæli"; Ps 117.20: "Porta Domini."

[21] ◆Ps 68.16: *Non me absorbeat profundum, neque urgeat super me puteus os suum*, "Let not ... the deep swallow me up: and let not the pit shut her mouth upon me."

[22] ◆St. Vincent Ferrer, "De Nat. B.V.M.," Sermo 2, in *Sermones*, 3:259.2: "Maria bona existentibus in purgatorio, quia per eam habent suffragium." St. Bernardine, "Fest. B.V.M.," 3.2.3, *Opera*, 4:80.2: B. Virgo "in regno Purgatorii dominium tenet; propterea inquit: *Et in fluctibus, maris ambulavi*. ... Et ab iis tormentis liberat, maxime devotos suos, ... scilicet visitans, et subveniens in necessitatibus [suis]."

[23] Cf. St. Thomas, *Summa*, Suppl. 71.1, 2 and 6.

[24] 2 Mac 12.46: It is a holy and wholesome thought to pray for the dead, that they may be loosed from sins. — Trent, Sess. 25, 212, affirmed the existence of Purgatory, saying that it is where souls "are helped by the suffrages of the faithful, but principally by the Sacrifice of the Altar, so worthy of being acceptable to God." St. Thomas, *Summa*, 2-2.83.11 ad 3, 4 ad 2, says that souls in Purgatory "are not in a condition to pray, but rather in a condition that requires us to pray for them," and although "the dead ... do not know what takes place in this world, especially the interior movements of the heart," and thus, our prayers, St. Alphonsus Liguori, "Great Means," 1.1.3.2, *Works*, 3:36, says that "we may piously believe that God makes our prayers known to them," and that it is our

Saints, in the general opinion of the Doctors, come to the aid of the souls of Purgatory, think how much more would the Virgin Mary!

We speak now of Heaven, of the blessed souls, and of the Angels. We, Christians, are familiar with Mary's titles of "Queen of Heaven," "Queen of Angels," "Empress of Heaven." Indeed, the Church venerates her above all, save God, chanting on the Feast of the Assumption: "The holy Mother of God hath been exalted, over choirs of Angels, into the heavenly kingdom,"[25] and of the celestial realm of the Blessed Virgin we may glimpse from what we said above regarding her beatitude, vision, and mediation.

Let us set our eyes even higher. We need not dwell here on Christ being subject to Mary, for He Who is her Son is above her. As we said,[26] St. Louis-Marie submits this fact as the reason and model of our submission to Mary. In Heaven, the Mother of Jesus has a kind of authority, and we might even venture to say, a sovereignty, over her Son. It is evident that this influence belongs to her by a singular grace, and not by nature; that it is always exercised with the concurrence of Him Who is subject to her; and that in the presence of Christ it is become a most mighty form of supplication. Having stipulated these reservations, let us say with St. Peter Damian: "How can He, the Christ-King born of your flesh, resist your power? You approach the golden altar of propitiation, not only to pray for the souls of man, but also to command, as Sovereign and not mere handmaid."[27]

Let us sing with St. Louis-Marie:

> She is the Sovereign
> O'er the entire universe,
> She has in her domain
> Heaven and that infernal place,
>
> She holds in dependence
> Goods of Jesus Christ, only Son,

---

duty to pray for them.

[25] Ant., Assumptione, *Brev. Rom.*, 761, 762, 764: "Exaltata est sancta Dei Genetrix super choros Angelorum ad cælestia regna."

[26] Part 2.2.3.2, p. 130.

[27] ◆St. Peter Damian, *Sermones*, 44, In Nat. B.V.M., 1, ¦¦ PL 144.740B : "Quomodo enim illa potestas tuæ potentiæ poterit obviare, quæ de carne tua carnis suscepit originem? Accedis enim ante illud aureum humanæ reconciliationis altare, non solum rogans, sed imperans, domina, non ancilla." ¦

> She doth give and dispense
> Gifts of the Holy Ghost, her Spouse.[28]

¦ Holy Scripture speaks of Ahasuerus the King of Persia who, in his colossal pomp and pride, made a great feast which lasted a hundred and fourscore days, to boast of the astonishing luxuries, riches, and power at his command. Now, to cap off the festivities, and further flaunt the ostentations of his court, he required of Vashti, his queen, who was exceedingly fair, to come before him with but a crown set upon her head. ¦ She refused, and the king had her deposed. Then came Esther, most beautiful and kind, to take her place.[29]

It is the destiny of certain empires, despite their vice and repugnant corruption, to serve the designs of God in the preparation for the Kingdom of His Christ, and, in a certain sense, even to be an image of it. But this royal Persian feast bore only a vulgar likeness to the celestial kingdom.

When, on the day of Ascension, Christ entered into His glory and flung open the Gates of Heaven to His elect, it was into a banquet hall that He brought them, since, according to the Gospel, the eternal life is like a banquet where God Himself passes among His guests to minister unto them.[30] But it was not enough for the divine King to show His elect the splendors of His Kingdom and the radiance of His own glory. At the heavenly feast, He hastened to call the Queen, and on the day of her Assumption she came to be crowned. Imagine what must have been the thrills of joy, and the acclamations of the heavenly court; what must also have been the triumph of Jesus when, to His right, above the Angels and men, appeared in unparalleled glory, that Queen who, ¦ to a much greater degree than Esther, is to her very core full of unction, and of compassion, and of beauty.[31] ¦ The celestial feast

---

[28] *Cantiques*, 76.6, 126: "Elle est la Souveraine / De tout cet univers, / Elle a, dans son domaine, / Le ciel et les enfers, / Elle a dans sa puissance / Les biens de Jésus-Christ, / Elle donne et dispense / Les dons du Saint-Esprit."

[29] Est 1.9-11, 2.15-17.

[30] Lc 12.37.

[31] Fr. Lhoumeau: "cette Reine qui méritait pleinement le nom de Vashti, c'est-à-dire 'd'excellente.'" The etymology may be correct, but in Rabbinic literature, Vashti is regarded as a vain woman, who was cruel to her Jewish handmaids, and had indeed appeared nude at court, but refused the command of her king and husband for a repeat, because she had contracted a sickness that put a blemish on her skin. (*Jewish Encycl.*,

lasts for all eternity. We hope, by the grace of God, to be invited, and it is the consolation of our exile to know her a little better who is "the radiance of the Lord of lords,"[32] and, whilst we await the day, to lovingly submit to her glorious and maternal dominion.

ARTICLE 3: QUEEN OF HEARTS

Our treatment of the queenship of the Blessed Virgin would be incomplete and insufficient for our purposes, if we did not specifically speak of her as "Queen of Hearts," which was so dear to St. Louis-Marie and under whose patronage the Confraternity dedicated to the Holy Slavery of Mary was recently erected.[33] If we set aside all sentimentality, be it ever so misty, we shall come to see that the title "Queen of Hearts" stands for the object on which the queenship of Mary is exercised in a special way.

In Holy Scripture and in the language of the Church, the word "heart" carries multiple meanings. It is the fleshy organ that circulates blood in us. But it is also used to designate the whole interior of a man, all his thoughts, his desires, and his passions. In this latter sense, we read in Scripture: *Man seeth those things that appear, but the Lord beholdeth the heart* (1 Sam 16.7); and later: *Rend your hearts, and not your garments* (Joel 2:13). Sometimes "heart" is taken to mean the faculties of the soul: *The meditation of my heart always in Thy sight* (Ps 18.15, 76.9), that is, "I always remember You, Your presence, and Your holy Will." In *My son, attend to my words in thy heart* (Sir 16.24), it refers

---

12:402.1). Rabanus Maurus, one of few Fathers that has commented on the Book of Esther, calls Vashti, *stultissimæ reginæ*. (PL 107.643D). In contrast, Esther's Hebrew name, הֲדַסָּה, *Hadassah* (Est 2.7) is "myrtle," which stands for the righteous of Israel. St. Alphonsus Liguori says that she, not Vashti, was a great type of Mary and "if Ahasuerus, through love for Esther, granted, at her request, salvation to the Jews, how can God refuse the prayers of Mary, loving her immensely as He does, when she prays for poor miserable sinners, who recommend themselves to her." ("Glories of Mary," 1.1, *Works*, 7:15).

[32] *Cantiques*, 76.9, 128: "Elle est ... la magnificence du seigneur des seigneurs." Cf. Christ is the splendor of the glory of God (Heb 1.3), and of eternal Light (Wis 7.26).

[33] The Confraternity of Mary Queen of Hearts was established by Joseph-Thomas Duhamel, Archbishop of Ottawa, on March 25, 1899. (Texier, *Manuel*, 7). In France, the name is "Fraternité Mariale Montfortaine" (in the U.S., "Association of Mary, Queen of *All* Hearts"), committed to cooperating with the mission of the Church through the Fathers and Brothers of the Company of Mary (Montfortians). It should not be confused with the association of the same name established by the Priestly Fraternity of Saint Pius X in 2004. See also, note 48, p. 93.

particularly to memory, ¦¦ of which echo we have in the saying "to learn by heart." | We read also in the Psalms: *Incline my heart into Thy testimonies* (Ps 118.36); that is to say, "my will." ¦| This word "heart" may also designate understanding, or sensibility, or courage[34]; but it *principally* expresses affection: *Let my heart be undefiled in Thy justifications, that I may not be confounded* (Ps 118.80). *Their heart is far from me* (Mt 15.8). We see this in the phrase: "to win someone's heart."

Now, it is by virtue of the varied but precise meanings of the word "heart" that the title "Queen of Hearts" expresses what Mary must be in us who have especially submitted ourselves to her, and what should be the specific motive for our subjection.

§1. MARY, QUEEN OF HEARTS, REIGNING OVER OUR INTERIOR

The reign of Mary is the means to establish the reign of God exercised in the interior: *Regnum Dei intra vos est*, "the Kingdom of God is within you" (Lk 17.21); that is, Jesus must possess and govern us in our soul and over her faculties. Hence, it needs be that the means used is capable of reaching into our interior, so that the desired effect is produced there, which is why St. Louis-Marie is doubly correct in insisting that the devotion to Mary be internal; otherwise it will neither be true nor efficacious. Elsewhere, he says that the essence of this devotion is in the same interior where it must form: ¦¦ "Mary cannot make her residence in the souls of the elect, ... and form them in Jesus Christ, or Jesus Christ in them, and plant the roots of her virtues in their hearts, and be the indissoluble companion of the Holy Ghost in all His works of grace, ... unless she has a right and dominion over their souls by a singular grace of the Most High. ... Now, as the kingdom of Jesus Christ consists principally in the heart and interior of a man, ... in like manner the kingdom of our Blessed Lady is principally in the interior of a man, that is to say, his soul; and it is principally in souls that she is more glorified with her Son than in all visible creatures, and that we can call her, as do the Saints, the *Queen of Hearts*."[35] |

---

[34] ¦¦ Just prior to this sentence, the example of "de grand cœur" for "will" deleted. The locution means "joyfully, gladly, willingly." | ♦Ps 14.1: The fool hath said in his heart; Ps 54.5: My heart is troubled within me; Ps 30.25: Let your heart be strengthened; Ps 94.8: Harden not your hearts.

[35] ♦*TD*, 21.

It bears repeating that the sovereignty of Mary is based on her divine motherhood and is put in the service of her spiritual motherhood. If we abandon not ourselves, neither subject ourselves to her, or if we prevent her from taking possession of us, she cannot fulfill her functions as our Queen. Let us remember that it is our very soul that attains the operations of grace; and, thus, the dominion of the Blessed Virgin extends into our soul inasmuch as we let her maternal mediation into our interior.

Note also that the acts by which Mary exercises in us, as part of her mediation, reach into the most intimate part of our soul. Some have contested this view by saying that her influence over us is not direct; for example, because she prays to the Holy Ghost to act upon us, or that she ordains our guardian Angel to light our way, and so on. Be that as it may, at the very least these very same acts presuppose that she does indeed see into our interior, as we affirmed above, where we relied on the teachings of Doctors of the Church. She alone among creatures is privy to this sight, and it is an act of ¦ transcendent ¦ dominion,[36] which appertains to God alone; and if Mary participates in it, it is but by the grace of the prerogatives of her motherhood.

Let us pause here for a moment and savor this thought so useful in our devotion.

He who says "home" evokes the idea of a dwelling that he owns and of which he is master. If a hateful, and nettlesome, stranger barges in uninvited, the "home" ceases to exist, and the man no longer thinks himself master of his domain. More rigorous is the dominion we, rational creatures, have over our acts of thought and will, which generally go by the name of "secrets of the heart." There is nothing that is ever so intimate. It is naturally reserved for God and us alone

---

[36] Theologians of the School of Salamanca use the term *dominium transcendens*, or *excellens*, or *altum*, for the absolute power God has over the entirety of Creation by right of being the Creator; e.g., Suárez, Disp. 48.2, *Opera*, 18:468.1: "Habuisse Christum Dominum per se et directe excellens quoddam dominium, et potestatem in res omnes creatas, et super omnes omnium hominum et Angelorum actiones." For a concise discussion, see à Lapide, "In Proverbia," 8.16, *Commentaria*, 5:212: "Allegorice, per sapientiam incarnatam, etc." The necessary preconditions for such *dominium* to exist are *capacitas*, *potestas*, and *usus*, or *status dominandi*, for which see Suárez, "De opere sex dierum," 3.16.5-18, *Opera*, 3:278.2-283.1. Not to be confused with the derivative concept of *dominium eminens*, formulated by Grotius, which operates under common law, and translated into French as "haut domaine," the same term Fr. Lhoumeau uses.

to know them; otherwise, none of us actually has his individual liberty. Our thoughts and passions will remain secrets between God and us, except when we consent to divulge them to men, Angels, and Saints, either by external actions or by mental prayer.

Now, God in His Providence has given Christ and His Mother to be our mediators, and as such, they must be able to see into our interior in order to act in our hearts. One may act differently from the other, but with them the circle of those who know the operations of our soul is closed. Is our dominion circumscribed in this case? Is our privacy violated? Or is our freedom under assault? Certainly not; for Jesus and Mary are so firmly united to God, and they to us, that it is as if the knowledge of the movements of our hearts were still just between God and us. Mary leads us to Jesus, and Jesus leads us back to God. He does so to return us to intimacy itself, for God Who gave us life is by far the closest to us; and to secure us in our liberty and our possession of ourselves,[37] for it is Divine Wisdom that gave us these things to keep.[38] In addition, Jesus is our Head, and Mary is our Mother. The head must needs intervene in the operations of our being, just as the mother, in the life of her child, but without infringing on our liberty or intimacy. But to us who so long to belong to Mary, and through her, to Jesus, it is a source of joy, of consolation, and of assurance, to know that we are under her gaze, and that we are open that she may see into us. It is a source of joy, since we have surrendered our interior to her. It is a source of consolation, because if our ignorance, our blindness, and our distractions make it difficult for us to know our own heart, at least we know that our sweet Mother is ignorant of nothing. This joy, this consolation, helps us to rest safely in the arms of her maternal providence. All that is left for us to do is to abandon our will entirely to her so that she may complete the reign of Jesus Christ in our soul.

§2. QUEEN OF HEARTS OR QUEENSHIP OF LOVE

By right, the sovereignty of Christ extends over every creature, and a time will come when those who have not submitted to it through love, will perforce bow down and bend their knee under His

---

[37] ♦Sir 15.14: God left man in the hand of his own counsel.
[38] ♦Sir 51.28: I possessed my heart with Wisdom.

might. Similarly, we see that Mary does not let devils escape her formidable power. She crushes their heads underfoot. But this is not the
only way she exercises her influence. She uses it also in the manner of
that other sovereignty for which we ask with the words: *Adveniat regnum Tuum, fiat voluntas Tua, sicut in Cœlo et in terra*, "Thy Kingdom
come, Thy will be done on earth as it is in Heaven"; that is, in all its
fullness and liberty. At Baptism we willingly and lovingly accept the
reign of Jesus, recognizing His sacred rights. We do so more profoundly when we offer the gifts in which we profess a more complete
dependency. It is a belonging by charity, since love is its principle and
purpose, as we explained at length. We surrender ourselves because
we love, and in order to love deeper. This is the Holy Slavery in which
we are committed to Mary by a perfect consecration. Yes, we may even
call it a slavery of love. "Is it not reasonable," says St. Louis-Marie,
"that amongst so many slaves of constraint, there should be some of
love, who of their own goodwill, in the quality of slaves, should choose
Mary for their Lady?"[39] Imbued with these sentiments, he often invoked Mary under her title of Queen of Hearts[40]; and, not content to
give himself fully to her, he hid not the ardent desires of his vocation
which racked his soul. We witness this in the following verses in
which the touching naïveté adds a certain charm to the sentiment that
inspired them:

> Her I love fervently
> Next to God my Savior;
> Give my life willingly
> A heart hers to favor.
>
> O good Lady ours be!
> Seek we not thee to know?
> Bruit abroad, let all see
> Thee we serve and hallow.[41]

St. Louis-Marie draws on texts the Church applies to the Blessed

---

[39] *TD*, 51.

[40] In 1705, at the start of his mission, St. Louis-Marie converted an abandoned barn at
Montbernage, a suburb of Poitiers, into a chapel and dedicated it to "Marie, Reine des
Cœurs." (Pauvert, *Vie*, 175). The chapel sits today within the private Catholic school,
St. Radegund, founded by sisters of the Daughters of Wisdom.

[41] *Cantiques*, 76.1, 125-126: "J'aime ardemment Marie / Après Dieu mon Sauveur; / Je
donnerais ma vie / Pour lui gagner un cœur. / O la bonne Maîtresse ! / Si l'on vous
connaissait, / Chacun ferait la presse / À qui vous servirait."

Virgin to speak of the interior queenship of Mary in our souls, without excluding her dominion over the external. Briefly commenting on them, he paints the three divine Persons giving Mary a three-fold investiture, crowning her with a triple diadem.

It is to Mary that God the Father says: *In Jacob inhabita*, "let thy dwelling be in Jacob." (Sir 24.13). The Old Testament is, in a certain sense, the reign of the Father. Now, time and time again, God is there like the God of Jacob. *O ye seed of Abraham His servant; ye sons of Jacob His chosen* (Ps 104.6). *I will sing to the God of Jacob* (Ps 74.10). *The God of Jacob is our protector* (Ps 45.8, 12). *Jacob the lot of His inheritance* (Dt 32.9). It was Jacob that received the paternal blessing.[42] Should she, the Virgin descendant of the great Patriarch, but especially Daughter of the Father, and blessed among all, not dwell among the children of Jacob? Was she not there, strictly speaking, at home and in the domain of her family? If Jacob was the servant of God,[43] she is most excellently the handmaid of Our Lord. It was prophesied that *a Star shall rise out of Jacob and a scepter shall spring up from Israel* (Nm 24.17); a Star full of mystery, and a figure of the Messiah of Whom Mary is the Mother.

For want of space needed to make a full account, we leave it to the great number of authorities to explain that, in the end, God hated Esau and rejected him, and that Jacob was His beloved. Was it fitting that she who is the Beloved of the Canticle and chosen from among all creatures to be the one and only, should live in the house of Esau and receive him for her portion? Indeed, not. "O Lady, live therefore in Jacob, the figure of the elect whose Mother you are, and who by grace are become, in Jesus, the sons of the eternal Father."

Et in Israël hœreditare, "and let Israel be your inheritance" (Sir 24.13), was said to the Son, Who, as an inheritance, received from His Father all the nations of the earth which He governs by force or by love; but Israel (that other name for Jacob, full of mystery) is His faithful and chosen people. In the testimony of Isaiah, other nations

---

[42] ♦Rom 9.13: Jacob dilexi, Esau autem odio habui, "Jacob I have loved, but Esau I have hated."

[43] ♦Ps 77.70-71: Elegit David ... pascere Jacob servum suum, "He chose David ... to feed Jacob His servant."

receive certain blessings of Our Lord,[44] but Israel is carefully set in contrast to them and set apart to be favored by Him. Thus did Nathanael say to Our Lord, *Thou art the King of Israel* (Jn 1.49); and according to St. John, when He entered Jerusalem in triumph, the crowd acclaimed Jesus with the same title that often recurs in Holy Gospel.[45]

Mary, heiress and Daughter of the Father, co-heir of Christ and sharer of His kingship, surely will make her Son's enemies, deep in the abyss of Hell, shudder at her formidable power. But as co-heir, she will have the faithful, represented by Israel, as her portion; the same people of Christ, *populum suum*, that He purchased with His blood. On the right hand of Christ, she will be enthroned by love, will govern by mercy, and will receive the praise and honor rightly due her; for if Christ the Redeemer is King, Mary participates in His kingship over Israel as Co-Redemptrix.[46]

In sum, the Holy Ghost unites His faithful Spouse to His dominion: *Et in electis Meis mitte radices*, "and take root in My elect" (Sir 24.13). This sovereignty has a particular character, for the action of the Holy Ghost is as full of mystery as it is profound. It pierces into the most intimate parts of the soul, striking root, and fixing the tree of grace in the soil of our soul in a manner hidden and remarkable. Such is the interior dominion of Mary, who cooperates with the Holy Ghost, *Dominum et vivificantem*, the Lord and Giver of life. May this rod of Jesse[47] put down its roots so deep into the heart that, though the ravages of the enemy[48] might have caused it to shrivel and decay, she would inject new life into it, make it bud green again, and, in the verdant expanse, let blossom the divine flower, which is Jesus, the Son of the Virgin Mary!

---

[44] Is 60.3.
[45] ◆Mt 27.42; Mc 15.32, 24.22; Jn 1.49, 12.13.
[46] ◆ ¦ Eadmer of Canterbury, *De excell. B.V.M.*, c. 11, PL 159.578B: "Sicut ergo Deus sua potentia parando cuncta Pater est et Dominus omnium, ita beata Maria suis meritis cuncta reparando mater est et domina rerum; Deus enim est Dominus omnium, singula in sua natura propria jussione constituendo; et Maria est domina rerum, singula congenitæ dignitati per illam quam meruit gratiam restituendo." The work was attributed to St. Anselm. ¦
[47] Is 11.1.
[48] Mt 13.28.

There are many the reasons that bid us live under the dependence of the Blessed Virgin. St. Louis-Marie mentions one example, and that is of Jesus submitting to His Mother, which act we ought to imitate and honor. "The human mind is at a loss,"[49] he says, when it reflects on this subjection, for the Gospel sheds but a single ray of light on the obscurity of the hidden life of Jesus Christ.[50] Our pious author often returns to this consideration. In a hymn, he sings:

> God on her to depend
> Was made Man here below.
> Nay, no more shall I stand
> His steps I will follow.[51]

Still, that was not enough for him. Desirous to drag every heart, tooth and nail, so to speak, for the purpose of laying them down at the feet of Mary, St. Louis-Marie gathers the arguments of an enlightened faith; and intimately familiar with the profound truths of dogma, he speaks to us of the ways of the Holy Trinity, that is, His manner of acting in regards to Mary, summarizing his considerations as follows: "The Father gave not and gives not His Son, but by her; He has no children but by her, and communicates no grace but by her. God the Son was not formed for the entire world, but by her; and He is not daily formed and engendered, but by her, in unity with the Holy Ghost; neither does He communicate His merits and His virtues, but by her. The Holy Ghost formed not Jesus Christ, but by her; neither does He form the members of Our Lord's Mystical Body, but by her; and through her alone does He dispense His favors and His gifts. After so many and such emphatic indications by the Most Holy Trinity, can we, without willful blindness, dispense with Mary, and not consecrate ourselves to her, and not depend on her for attaining to God and for sacrificing ourselves to God?"[52]

Thanks be to God! The time has long passed since St. Louis-Marie

---

[49] Cf. *TD*, 93, which has the non-idiomatic "the human mind loses itself."

[50] Lk 2.51: *Jesus was subject to them*; meaning Mary *and* Joseph.

[51] *Cantiques*, 76.2: "Mon Dieu pour en dépendre / S'est fait homme ici-bas. / Je ne puis me défendre / De marcher sur ses pas."

[52] ♦Cf. *TD*, 94-95.

was obliged before the faithful to insist on these prerogatives of Mary, and to restore them in all their radiance with a jealous care, because heresy endeavored to deny them or to diminish them. This *Stella matutina*, Morning Star, now shines bright in a sky unencumbered by the fog and dark clouds of error.[53] One no longer fears "to dishonor the Son by honoring the Mother, to abase the One in elevating the other."[54] He even satirized with some flair those devotees of scrupulosity who hold on to the baseless fear of exalting Mary too far. In two pages marked by a concise, vigorous, and spirited style, he crushes them with his arguments, corners them in their contradictions, unmasks them with ridicule, and ends up routing them.[55] We who have the full light of faith, let us sing with him of the joy of our love:

> O how she does surpass
> All that is not of God;
> After Him, and by grace,
> She's first where none hath trod.[56]

---

[53] Jordan, "De B.V.M.," 8, 16, *Opera*, 254, 393: "Fuisti insuper in tua beatissima nativitate *Stella matutina*, dirigens in hujus mundi pelago viatores, illos ab erroris semita revocando. ... Semper fuisti in mane oriens, et nunquam tetendisti ad occasum peccati; sed semper splendidat Stella fuisti illuminando populum, qui ambulabat et ambulat in tenebris peccatorum."

[54] *TD*, 64.

[55] *TD*, 64-65.

[56] ♦*Cantiques*, 76.11, 126: "Enfin elle surpasse / Tout ce qui n'est pas Dieu; / Après lui, par la grâce / Elle a le premier lieu."

PART III:

THE PRACTICE OF THE PERFECT DEVOTION TO THE BLESSED VIRGIN

CHAPTER 1:

THE SPIRIT OF MARY

Mary is our mediatrix to go to Jesus, and the means by which He may be formed in us. We should have no doubt that this formation is adaptable to the special sense of our devotion, to that singular sense of belonging and total dependence which characterizes our way of contemplating the union with Jesus. On this point, as with all others, an admirable unity and a perfect correspondence links the different parts of the spirituality of our good Father de Montfort. The spirit of Mary is the spirit of Holy Slavery. Indeed, the means fits most wondrously with the end.

It may strike us that our approach to the main idea of this chapter would have been better set in Part II of this book, where we spoke of the means. We shall not contradict it; but note that the object of this Part III is the two-fold practice of our devotion, internal and external. By studying the spirit of Mary, we understand better the distinguishing mark of her true children. Then follows what St. Louis-Marie bid us do: First, we stand before our model, then enter into the interior of this "handmaid of the Lord" most excellent, and in the same stroke, place in the light of day, under her radiance, those practices we intend to explain and whose meaning she will impart. As such, this chapter may serve as an introduction to the study of the perfect consecration.

Let us see who the Blessed Virgin is with regard to Our Lord, what she is to Satan, and then note the fruits she produces in our souls.

ARTICLE 1: THE HANDMAID OF THE LORD

Ecce ancilla Domini, "Behold the handmaid of the Lord." (Lc 1.38). We ought to see in these words something other than an offhand response, or a mere expression of Mary's reaction to the message of the

161

Archangel. In fact, they reveal the interior of the Blessed Virgin. They convey the habitual disposition of her soul, the depth of her thoughts, and the law of her wishes. Msgr. Gay goes further. He says that Mary did not just say the words, she lived it.[1]

Grant, O Lord, that this our good Mother may impart to us the knowledge and the practice of our devotion to her.

Let us remind ourselves of the circumstances surrounding her speaking the above words. The Archangel Gabriel had told her that the Son of God was to be incarnate in her immaculate womb. On hearing the salutation of the Angel, she first had a moment of confusion and astonishment, but soon she was reassured, and her doubts vanished; and in a divine calm, which suffices to demonstrate how much she had passed into God, this blessed Virgin had a glimpse of the mystery of Christ. The divine plan and her unique part in it unfolded before her eyes, like a splendid horizon with infinite perspectives. How was she going to answer?

First, she looked to God. It was certainly not, as we often do, heedlessly and in an effort to lull the conscience into a semblance of prayer and reflection. Neither was it with a look of powerlessness in trying to understand divine Will, as we so intensely do whilst wading through the murky life of dissipation, bedeviled by passions. With the gaze of a dove, so simple, so tranquil, and so penetrating, Mary saw, above all, that God *is*, that He is absolute, that He exists of Himself, and that He receives nothing from another.[2] He alone creates everything from nothing; and all that exists, exists and lives not but by Him. He is thus the sovereign Master of all things and, without exception, every creature depends on Him. His command cannot exceed His power and His rights, because He possesses them all, and He alone has them all fully. If we possess anything here below, it is only by His leave and on His dependence; and He, on the other hand, possesses us to the very core of our being. The gaze thus fixed on the Absolute and on the

---

[1] Gay, *Conférences*, 46.1, 2:292: "These words leap from her soul, like the air passing through her lips. She does not merely say them, she lives them. They are the breath of her heart and the moral form of her being. Mary lives subject to God; she gives, surrenders, abandons, delivers herself to Him. She offers herself to no end, everywhere and for the sake of everyone. God contains and possesses her."

[2] Αὐτουσία or *aseitas*, the Latin from *a se*, "of Himself." Among many passages in Scripture, Ex 3.14: "I Am Who Am." See also, Wilhelm, *Manual*, 2.1.2.60, 1:175-177.

sovereign dominion of God, the Blessed Virgin did not call Him the Most High, the Almighty, or the Holy of Holies, but *Dominus,* "the Lord."

Second, gazing up at God by that pure light which makes all things shine in their true colors, Mary regards herself. This sight was not superficial, as it is too often the case when we pay ourselves and the things of this world some attention. When we are enamored of ourselves, or seduced by creatures, is such a sight not incomplete and false? O Virgin holy and prudent, *turn away my eyes that they may not behold vanity* (Ps 118.37).

Third, Mary saw herself to the depths of her being. Even though she is the most blessed and full of grace, she did receive everything, starting with her existence, from God. Her Immaculate Conception, no doubt, set her apart, and the Divine Maternity was to place her at the summit of Creation; soon she was to enter into the unheard-of bonds with the Father, the Son, and the Holy Ghost, which divine omnipotence alone might realize; her participation in the mysteries of Christ was to be unequaled; and as Mother of Jesus Christ according to the flesh, she was to extend her spiritual motherhood to all men, and, on this account, she would have in the Church as many functions as they are sublime. But all this is the gift of God Who *hath regarded the humility of His handmaid* (Lc 1.48), because, at bottom and in spite of everything, she is still a creature drawn out of nothing. As she exists only by the grace of God, she belongs to Him absolutely and entirely. He, however He deigns to act, is her sovereign Lord; and she, His handmaid who lives only to fulfill His Will. Such were her thoughts and the disposition of her soul from the moment she was created, as we see in her withdrawal into the Temple and her vow of virginity; but now after God reveals His plans to her, He asks for her consent in that ineffable and loving condescendence. The Virgin opens up, surrenders herself to the very core of her being and says, *Ecce ancilla Domini,* "Behold the handmaid of the Lord."

Since that time, Mary has never relented from her perfect submission to God; never has she forgotten her condition of creature and servant of the Lord. At the Visitation, she expressly declares that her happiness comes from the fact that the Lord *hath regarded the humility of His handmaid* (Lc 1.48). Her undergoing the purification rites,[3] her silence and calm on hearing the prophecy of Simeon,[4] or later, the words of Jesus on Calvary,[5] tell us enough how divine Will operated in her, and how fully she was convinced of the sovereignty of God. Examine her entire life, and you will find her conviction is at the root of all her acts, which is why we say that the spirit of Mary is contained in these words: "Behold the handmaid of the Lord."

So now we see that this Virgin, in the favorite expression of St. Louis-Marie, is "the secure means and the straight way to go to Jesus."[6] How perfectly is the Son like the Mother! The *fiat* of Mary scarcely pronounced, the Divine Spirit, the Spirit of Jesus came and overshadowed her.[7] He taught her to think, to love, and to speak as Jesus was soon to do; that is to say, as a handmaid of His Father in Heaven.[8]

¦ In the firmament[9] that is our Holy Church, | Jesus is the Sun of Justice,[10] and you, O Mary, likened to the moon, you reflect His light on us, tempered but unaltered. You truly are "the echo of God."[11] Indeed, "the Lord is with thee," and you are but one spirit with Him. St. Cyril of Alexandria writes: "Hail, Mary, Virgin, Mother, and handmaid: Virgin, because your Son is born of you yet you remained a

---

[3] Lk 2.22.

[4] Lk 2.33.

[5] ♦Jn 19.26, 27: *Mulier, ecce filius tuus. … Ecce Mater tua*, "Woman, behold thy son. … Behold thy Mother."

[6] *TD*, 29.

[7] Lk 2.35.

[8] ♦Is 12.6, 49.5; Zac 3.8; Ps 39.

[9] Fr. Lhoumeau: *cieux vivants*, "living heavens," perhaps taken from Le Maistre de Sacy, *Histoire*, 404. Writers of the Romantic period made florid descriptions of it; e.g. Klopstock, "Messias," 8.433-443, *Werke*, 4:89, on which Goethe comments in "Leben," 2.10, *Werke*, 9:397: "Die *lebendigen Himmel* jauchzen in tausend Engelstimmen um den Thron, und ein Liebesglanz übergießt das Weltall, das seinen Blick kurz vorher auf eine gräuliche Opferstätte gesammelt hielt." As did later French Catholic writers; e.g., Monsabré, "Épiphanie," *Enseign. cath.*, 1867, 17:72, and *Avent*, 262; Billard, *Œuvres*, 3:113; Gay, *Life and Virtues*, 2:290. It even entered into Church documents (Martin, *Conc. Vaticani*, 117: "cælos viventem"). It is an injudicious use of the term. After Smith's *Chaldean*, appeared in 1876, Lawrence popularized the pagan notion of the "living heavens," meaning the sky as a living thing on which man's imagination plugged a deity! (*Apocalypse*, 131-132). In the cosmology of the Bible, the Hebrew רָקִיעַ, *raqia*, is the created *firmamentum* (Gen 1.6), sometimes rendered "vault of Heaven." (Shakespeare, 2 *Henry IV*, 2.3; Milton, *Paradise Lost*, 1.669, 1:33).

[10] Mal 4.2.

[11] *TD*, 159: "She only exists with reference to God. She is the echo of God, who says nothing, repeats nothing, but 'God.' If you say 'Mary,' she says 'God.'"

virgin; Mother, because you carried Him in your arms and nourished Him with your milk; handmaid, because of Him, Who received from you the form of a slave."[12]

Let us not move on from this mystery of the Annunciation without casting a glance at the unfathomable depths of Mary's word. At the same moment when, by divine motherhood, God made her Queen of the world, the Virgin, understanding that all Creation had become her realm, she and all other creatures prostrated at the feet of the Lord to adore and serve Him. In one act, our divine Mother consented to the Incarnation and established the principle of our salvation; and when she proclaimed herself the handmaid of the Lord, she returned Creation to the command of the authority and to the submission, against which it had rebelled through the disobedience of Adam and Eve, our first parents. Note that this first act of Mary's sovereignty prepared the way for the reign of Jesus, before He was to come into this world, and from that moment on, the yearnings of our heart began to be fulfilled: *Ut adveniat regnum tuum, adveniat regnum Mariæ!* "Let the reign of Mary come, that the Kingdom of Christ may come!"[13]

Think you that the soul of Mary was filled with joy when she contemplated, as she alone was capable, the entire world returned to the loving subjection to the Lord, and the Kingdom of Christ brought to *as many as received from Him the power to be made the sons of God* (Jn 1.12)? St. Teresa tells us that upon hearing chanted this article of the Credo: *Cujus regni non erit finis*, "of Whose kingdom there shall be no

---

[12] St. Cyril, *Homiliæ diversæ*, 11, ¦¦ PG 77:1031C: "Salve, Virgo Maria, mater et serva: Virgo quidem propter eum qui natus est ex te Virgine; mater vero, propter eum quem in tuis ulnis gestasti, et lacte tuo nutristi; serva propter eum qui servi formam cepit." | ◆It is a question disputed among theologians whether one can absolutely say that she was a handmaid of Christ (*ancilla*). Many, including St. Albert the Great and Cristóbal de Vega, believe that Mary, though submissive to Jesus Christ as her God, Master and Redeemer, could not serve Him in this capacity, in the strictest sense, because she is His Mother. She is but a handmaid (slave) of God, *ancilla Domini*; and this would accord with that word of the Psalm which is applied to Christ, speaking to God the Father: *Ego filius ancillæ tuæ*, "I am the son of Thy handmaid"–Ps 115.16. — ¦¦ St. Albert the Great, "Mariale," 51, *Opera*, 37.96.2: "Dignitas personæ exhibentis respectu omnium viatorum in summo fuit in beatissima Virgine: ipsa enim mater Dei, alii omnes servi: et improportionabiliter magis est esse matrem Dei, quam esse servum Dei: ergo improportionabiliter major est latria matris Dei, quam servorum Dei." Vega, *Theol. Mariana*, 1671, 2:363-364: "Quæri hic possit, an Deipara aliquo modo dici posset Christi Domini serva. Censeo nullo modo dici posse." |

[13] *TD*, 155.

end," she would be seized by a holy transport.[14] Merely the thought of the kingship of Christ spreading everywhere, eternal and at last unrivaled, would fill this seraphic soul with untold joy. So what was it that filled Mary with trepidation, for she tells us that she was shaken and delighted: *Et exultavit spiritus meus in Deo salutari meo*, "and my spirit hath rejoiced in God my Savior" (Lc 1.47), when she heard the Archangel announce to her the eternal kingdom of her Son, Jesus: *Et regni ejus non erit finis*, "and of His Kingdom there shall be no end" (Luke 1:33), and that she was aware that, by consenting to the Incarnation, she was inaugurating this divine realm?

O sweet Virgin, "may your soul be in me to glorify the Lord, may your spirit be there that I may rejoice in God."[15] I may yet have a better reason than David to cry out: *O Lord, I am Thy servant, and the son of Thy handmaid* (Ps 115.16). ¦¦ I read | the Apostle saying of Jesus Christ, *formam servi accipiens*, that "He took the form of a servant" (Phil 2.7). And from whom did He receive it? From you, O Mary, who gave Him His human nature, and only in this nature may the Son of God be His servant. And when you gave birth to us unto grace, O Mother, did you not but made us the servants of the heavenly Father? ¦¦ I know that | a child naturally resembles his mother; but does he not moreover receive, before and after his birth, all kinds of influences which establish bonds of physical and moral resemblance between the two, as also of temperament and condition? Thus, you who begot us unto grace by an act of humility and proclaiming yourself a handmaid of the Lord, O Mother, fill us with this fire of humility and holy subjection, so that, in following your example, we may live as true servants of the Lord. We consecrate ourselves to you so that the Kingdom of God may enter our souls in its fullness. Let His Will being done in us as perfectly as it is in Heaven be the means for us to do so. And in saying this, O Mary, our thoughts soar to the ¦ firmaments[16] | where the Saints are;

---

[14] St. Teresa of Avila, "Camino," 31, *Obras*, 3:141-142.

[15] ¦¦ Ps. Thomas, De humanitate D.N., 3, *Opera*, 6:179: "Dicit Ambrosius: | Sicut in singulis anima Mariæ Deum magnificat, sic in singulis spiritus Mariæ in Deo exultat." ¦¦ Cf. St. Ambrose, *In Lucam*, 2.27 [Lc 1.44-45], PL 15.1562B: "Magnificat autem anima Mariæ Dominum, et exsultat spiritus ejus in Deo; eo quod et anima et spiritu Patri Filioque devota, unum Deum ex quo omnia, et unum Dominum per quem omnia, pio veneretur affectu." |

[16] Fr. Lhoumeau: "cieux vivants"; see note 9, p. 164.

to that most admirable and superior Heaven of your immaculate soul, the faithful mirror of the Soul of Jesus, and to that Heaven of Heavens where dwells the fullness of the Divinity.

ARTICLE 2: THE ENMITIES

> Inimicitias ponam inter te et mulierem, et semen tuum et semen illius.
> I will put enmities between thee and the woman, and thy seed and her seed (Gn 3.15).

There is a radical opposition, a profound enmity, between Mary and Satan that we ought to understand if we are to live as Christians and true children of the Blessed Virgin.

St. Louis-Marie's commentary in *True Devotion* on the above-quoted passage from Genesis is worth studying. He begins by saying: "God has never made or formed but one enmity; and it is an irreconcilable one, which endures and is ever fiercer until the end."[17] What the word *ponam*, or "I will put," or "I will establish" refers to is the eternal hatred that replaces the passing rapport Eve had with the devil; a hatred that truly targets God, because the object of this hatred is God and His Christ.

¦¦ St. Louis-Marie goes on to say that the enmity is also, "between the children and the servants of the Blessed Virgin, and the children and instruments of Lucifer. ... Ever since the days of the earthly Paradise, though Mary existed then only in His idea, God has inspired her with so much hatred against that accursed enemy, with so much skill in unveiling the malice of that old serpent, with so much power to conquer, to overthrow, and to crush that proud impious rebel, that he fears her not only more than all Angels and men, but in some sense more than God Himself. It is not that the wrath, the hatred, and the power of God are not infinitely greater than those of the Blessed Virgin's, for the perfections of Mary are limited, but it is, firstly, because Satan, being proud, suffers infinitely more from being beaten and punished by a little and humble handmaid of God, and is humiliated by her humility more than by Divine power; and, secondly, because

---

[17] *TD*, 30-31.

God has given Mary such a great power against the devils, that in spite of themselves (as they have often been obliged to confess by the mouths of the possessed), they fear one of her sighs for a soul more than the prayers of all the Saints, and one of her menaces against them more than all other torments."[18] |

The plural *inimicitias*, "enmities," is not only emphatic and solemn, it also foretells a set of acts and attitudes whose secondary causes are various, but which all have, on the one hand, the Spirit of God, and, on the other, the specter of Satan; and from this opposition the struggle arises that will continue until the end of time.

Between thee (the snake) *and the woman.* There is no doubt but that the worldly heart is opposed to the Gospel, as Satan opposes Jesus Christ; but when we contrast the worldly heart to that of Mary's and regard her as the personal adversary of the devil, and victorious over him, we hew to the divine plan and believe that the "woman" in the passage, *between thee and the woman*, to refer to her who has given us Jesus Christ the Redeemer, to Whom she is always bound in promise, in struggle, and in triumph. God made her such a fierce personal enemy of Satan that, though their initial states and circumstances may have been similar, the antagonism between her thoughts and the serpent's, and her deeds and his, cannot be any clearer. Let us explain:

At the time he was created, Lucifer was endowed with excellent prerogatives.[19] At the instant of her conception, the Blessed Virgin received a plenitude of grace which made her the "blessed among women." Thus far only the resemblance. But while Lucifer was prideful of God's gifts, and turned them against Him,[20] the humble Mary instantly paid homage to Him and used His gifts to break the power of Satan, for which reason the Church chants on the Feast of the Immaculate Conception: *Immaculata Conceptio est hodie sanctæ Mariæ Virginis. Quæ serpentis caput virgineo pede contrivit.* "This day is the Holy Virgin Mary conceived without sin. The Virgin's foot hath bruised the serpent's head."[21]

---

[18] Cf. *TD*, 31.

[19] Ez 28.12-15.

[20] Is 14.12-15; St. Thomas, *Summa*, 1.63.2c.

[21] Vespers Hymn, *Brev. Rom.*, Suppl. 41.

¦¦ Though it lies in the area of speculative theology that[22] ¦ the Incarnation was revealed to Satan, it is at least worth considering that, in their trials, God may have given all Angels to see the future fulfillment of the divine mystery, and bid them pay His Son made Man homage by their faith, their obedience, and their love. Satan and his rebellious angels refused and claimed to be like[23] the Most High. Mary, on the other hand, offered herself to the Lord as His humble handmaid for the fulfillment of His plan. It is remarkable that she, as well as the Archangel Gabriel, speak of the Incarnation as a work of power accomplished by the Most High,[24] for the prince of this world was indeed about to be cast out.[25]

Finally, Satan and Mary were to have descendants. The ones beholden to Satan were to be all those who, moved by his specter, become *children of the devil* (Jn 3.10). Those of Mary, first, He Who was to be born of a Virgin and is alone, strictly speaking, the *semen mulieris* "seed of the woman"; then, with Christ, all of us who were to receive Him and, by grace, to become the children of God and Mary, brethren to Jesus Christ.[26] "But," says St. Louis-Marie, "God has set enmities, antipathies, and secret hatreds between the children and slaves of the devil and the true children and servants of Mary."[27] These two lineages are ever at war, which will only end in the final triumph of the Lord.[28]

We should meditate on the enmity separating the children of Mary from the children of Belial, or the slaves of Satan, or the friends of the world, for they all amount to the same thing, says St. Louis-

---

[22] Cf. Suárez, "De angelis," 7.13.5-9, *Opera*, 2:882-884.

[23] Fr. Lhoumeau: *s'égaler au*. St. Thomas, *Summa*, 1.63.3c, distinguishes between wanting to be as God by equality and by likeness. The first is impossible, since nothing can have the nature of God other than He Himself. Satan sinned, "by desiring as his last end of beatitude, something which he could attain by the virtue of his own nature, turning his appetite away from supernatural beatitude, which is attained by God's grace. Or, if he desired as his last end that likeness of God which is bestowed by grace, he sought to have it by the power of his own nature." In sum, he fell by the sin of pride.

[24] Lk 2.35, 49.

[25] Jn 12.31.

[26] Bede, *Hexæmeron*, PL 91.58A: "Semen mulieris totum est genus humanum, ... fructus boni operis"; cf. Gn 3.15.

[27] *TD*, 32.

[28] ♦On which see Billot, *De Verbo Incarnato*, ¦¦ Pars II, Theses 46-54, 329-476. ¦

Marie.[29] Still, how few is the number who do ask of the Blessed Virgin for inspiration, not only to distance themselves from the world (which is not nearly enough for their purposes), but also to despise it with a living contempt that never lets up! Such contempt marks the children of the Blessed Virgin distinctively, as much as the love of Jesus is the necessary consequence and the indispensable guarantee of it. Are we in possession of enough Christian sensibilities, or have we enough knowledge about the promises we made at Baptism, to appeal for the grace of this contempt? We join sodalities, and confraternities; we process in ceremonies wearing white ribbons or white dresses; we burn candles, we offer flowers, we sing songs, but we remain oblivious to the fact that these things, though good in themselves, merely trap us in a fog of self-deceit if we practice not to the core of our heart and live out the contempt of the self, as the Gospel would have us do.[30] We must detest what is sinful in us, what leads us to sin, or what keeps us in the state of sin; we must hate the ideas and allures of the world that glorifies evil, propagates it, and makes it seductively appealing; for such loathing is the characteristic sign of the true devotion to the Blessed Virgin, interiorly and exteriorly. Would to God that the children of Mary never forget it! We are certain that this sweet Mother represents to us the love of God in its tenderest and most generous expression; it is the love of the heavenly Father becoming a *mother* to His children. Sometimes, Mary is also the valiant woman[31] most excellent, and her true devotees, that is, the children she has formed, such as St. Louis-Marie, have become souls that are as much loving as they are steely forged ¦¦ in faith. | The sweetest names, the tenderest expressions of our devotion which, in our filial love, we lavish on her may be truly justified; but if we season them not with the salt of divine wisdom, among which is the hatred of sin, they will amount to nothing but silly and mawkish sentimentality.

St. Louis-Marie long emphasized the antagonism arising out of

---

[29] *TD*, 32.

[30] Jn 12.25: He that loveth his life shall lose it; and he that hateth his life in this world, keepeth it unto life eternal.

[31] Prv 31.10.

the seed of the devil and the seed of the Virgin, inasmuch as the end times approach, which the Apostle points out being as particularly perilous.[32] Why? Three centuries of bloody persecution were about to begin, yet St. Paul speaks not a word of it. The persecution to come was to him not the greatest danger. To Timothy, his disciple, his advice was to avoid the false Christians, who would rise to great numbers and a detailed portrait of whom he summarized in his final treatise: *Erunt homines ... habentes speciem quidem pietatis, virtutem autem ejus abnegantes*, "they shall be men ... having an appearance of godliness, but denying the power thereof" (2 Tim 3.5). This is the monstrous and impossible connection that so many Christians today try to enforce between life in the world and religious practices, between worldly demands and the precepts of the Gospel.

Let us pray to Mary. Let us obtain her protection from Satan and his devils, from the world and its followers. Let us repeat with conviction the invocation: *Da mihi virtutem contra hostes tuos*, "give me strength against thine enemies."[33] And since our enemies are the enemies of Mary, and her cause is our cause, let us stand firm in our confidence in her, and be rest assured that we will triumph in the end.

ARTICLE 3: EFFECTS OF THE SPIRIT OF MARY

To better understand the spirit of Mary contained in the words: *Ecce ancilla Domini*, "behold the handmaid of the Lord," we shall try to show the dispositions that it produces in the soul, the virtues to which it inclines us. We shall see how everywhere and always this spirit of Mary is opposed to the spirit of world; and then, when we explain the scope and meaning of our perfect consecration as St. Louis-Marie would wish for us, it will be clear that the spirit of our Mother is faithfully reflected in it, quickens our practice of it, and that here as in every part of this volume, in essence, Holy Slavery undergirds our special devotion to the Blessed Virgin.

We know that every virtue has humility at its root; but what is

---

[32] 2 Tim 3.1.

[33] R̃. Festis B.V.M., *Brev. Rom.*, 765, 86*, 91*, 92*, 101*: *Dignare me laudare te, Virgo sacrata ~*, "Holy Virgin, my praise by thee accepted be ~."

humility itself, what does it consist of? Many, including the pious, hold on to a mistaken notion. The proof of it is this common phrase: "to make humble," which means to bring low, and sometimes applied to one who has so low an estimation of himself that people scarce would believe it. Mary gives us the correct attitude in the practice of the virtue of humility when she says: "Behold the handmaid of the Lord," for Christian humility is a true knowledge of God and of our-selves, which leads us to abase ourselves before Him. Now it is an unquestionable truth that we, at our core and in our essence, are the creations of God; that is, He created us out of nothing. This Mary did see and confess before God with such clarity of vision and admirable conviction; and, in so doing, she emptied herself, she opened herself down to the depths of her soul, to become a pure vessel of divine gifts.

Unlike the Blessed Virgin, when we undertake to "empty our-selves," all we find are the nothingness out of which we came, along with sin and its consequences. But sin, too, is a nothingness, inas-much as it is a disorder and an evil. If we pierced through the depths of our miseries and our corruption, we would always find everything in us that is purely of us as nothing. There is nothing we may arrogate, nothing from which we may gain glory, because ¦¦ all that we are and all that we have (everything, save sin), | we received ¦¦ from God. | Such is how humility is contained in the words, *Ecce ancilla Domini*. Whoever admits it with all his heart is truly humble.

Adoration goes hand in hand with humility. Adoration is the most important act of divine worship. Let us stand in wonderment at the enlightened faith of Mary, who gives it the highest estimation, and empties herself before the Lord, at the moment when she consents to be bound to Him so nobly and intimately through her motherhood.

We note that the great masters of spiritual life and the Saints, whose love blossomed into ineffable ardor and holy tenderness, were always deeply imbued with the sense of adoration and reverence. St. Ignatius of Loyola in his *Exercises* often refers to God with the honor-ifics and titles of "His Divine Majesty" or "Creator and Lord."[34] St.

---

[34] St. Ignatius of Loyola, *Ejercicios*, 10, etc.: "Su Divina Majestad"; 23, etc.: "Creador y Señor."

Teresa frequently speaks to her sisters of the "Sovereign Majesty," or "Master and Lord."[35] We also read in the *Life* of St. Louis-Marie that he often walked bareheaded, out of respect for the presence of God.[36]

The soul steeped in the understanding of the absolute being of God and of His sovereignty will always lay prostrate before Him, her entire life will be an act of worship, and her actions will be bathed in that piety which the Council of Trent particularly commends to priests: *Nil nisi religione plenum præseferant*, "that they bear nothing about them but what is replete with religiousness."[37] Yet, why is it that we still have priests and religious who do not know how to pierce through to the spirit of Mary, although by their state they are set apart for the purpose of divine worship and are expected to excel in religion? They ought to find in the perfect devotion of Holy Slavery a powerful help in living in a manner conforming to their high calling. The vigor of adoration will hold them responsible for acting as expected, and the fear of God will preserve them falling into dire sloth. Of course, the fear we speak of is ¦¦ *timor Dei,* ¦ the filial and reverential kind, which is a gift of the Holy Ghost,[38] and has nothing in common with that false, servile, infernal, and anti-Christian fear called ¦¦ *pavor Dei,* ¦ the "dread of God." Filial fear is like the guardrail of piety. It does not hinder Him, but focuses our love on Him, giving it strength and security. Filial fear prods away that routine which wears out reverence, that shamelessness which kills intimacy, from our daily actions with respect to the Lord, and from our frequent recourse to holy things. With God and her Son Jesus, Mary's filial fear lets her grow in holiness. Why? Because she never departed from the reverence and the life of adoration that a creature must render unto God.

It goes without saying that humility and adoration lead us to

---

[35] St. Teresa of Avila, "Camino," 6, 54, *Obras*, 3:224, 315: "Maestro y Señor Cristo."

[36] Pauvert, *Vie*, xxi, 247, 461.

[37] Trent, Sess. 22, Reformation, c. 1, 149: They ought "regulate their life and manners, as that in their dress, gesture, gait, discourse, and all things else, they bear *nothing about them but what is* grave, moderate, and *replete with religiousness*; that they avoid even slight faults, which in them would be most grievous; that so their actions may impress all to veneration."

[38] St. Thomas, *Summa*, 2-2.19 and 22.2c, summarized as: "I fear God because He is just; I love Him because He is good; I am lost in Him because He is gentle." (Maucourant, *Pocket Retreat*, 49).

obedience. "I am the handmaid of the Lord," said the Blessed Virgin. Just as the mind of worldlings summed up in the defiant, "I will not serve,"[39] is the principle of all revolt and the root of all sin; so also the spirit of Mary that inspired her response to the Archangel is the principle of all virtue and the basis of the service to God. Of this we did speak above in the part on Holy Slavery.

There is no worship without confidence, explains Fr. Faber in a remarkable chapter of his *Conferences*. ¦¦ "It is worth our while to have lived," he says, "if it were only to have known the delight of trusting in God. But it is not our joy only. It is our absolute necessity, and therefore belongs to the lowest of us. It is our only true perfection, and therefore belongs to the highest of us."[40] | The demons, it is true, believe and tremble, their knees bent forcibly under the hand of God, but they worship not. In any event, devotion or the act of self-giving, as the soul of outward worship, cannot be done without some measure of confidence and love; which measure may grow and thereby render our worship more perfect. We see it in Mary, whose *ecce* and *fiat* not only express her total oblation and ardent desire to fulfill His divine Will, but also her confidence and her love. We cannot doubt, therefore, that this motive of belonging and subjection so wonderfully modeled by our Mother is inspired, especially to this degree, by the most perfect charity. St. Louis-Marie is right to describe his devotion as the "slavery of love."[41]

A number of other virtues may be seen as the fruits of the spirit of Mary. As we said above, in principle, it comprises them all. We have just spoken of the principal ones, and it suffices our purpose to have described them briefly.

---

[39] Jer 2.20: *A sæculo dixisti: Non serviam*, "Of old time thou saidst: I will not serve."
[40] Faber, *Conferences*, 7, 292-293.
[41] *Secret*, 24.

CHAPTER 2.

THE CONSECRATION

> Ut sim devotus servus Filii, servitu-
> tem fideliter appeto Genitricis.
> "In order to be a devoted slave of the
> Son, I aspire to become the faithful
> slave of the Mother."[1]

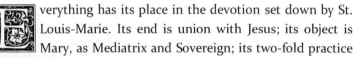verything has its place in the devotion set down by St.
Louis-Marie. Its end is union with Jesus; its object is
Mary, as Mediatrix and Sovereign; its two-fold practice
honors this two-fold prerogative. From the moment we are consecrated to the Blessed Virgin, we live under her dependence and, in all
things, act through her mediation.

St. Louis-Marie teaches us the "two-fold practice," saying: "This
devotion consists in giving ourselves up entirely to the Blessed Virgin,
in the quality of slaves, in order to belong wholly to Jesus Christ; and
in the next place, to do all our actions through Mary, in Mary, with
Mary, and for Mary, in order to do them more perfectly through Jesus,
with Jesus, in Jesus, and for Jesus, our last end."[2]

Here we must distinguish (1) the external practice, or the act of
consecration which is done by the recitation of a formula, from (2) the
interior practice or special direction of our intentions, dispositions,
and actions. We shall examine in this chapter the act of consecration,
as formulated by St. Louis-Marie; then, in the following, the interior
practice or the way of acting through Mary, with her, in her, and for
her, as well as the questions attendant thereon.

---

[1] Note 42, p. 92.
[2] ♦Secret, 20-21.

> I choose thee this day for my Mother and Lady. I deliver
> and consecrate to thee, as thy slave, my body and soul, my
> goods, both interior and exterior, and even the value of all my
> good actions, past, present, and future; leaving to thee the en-
> tire and full right to dispose of me, and all that belongs to me,
> without exception, according to thy good pleasure, for the
> greater glory of God, in time and in eternity.[3]

Such is the content of our act of consecration to Mary, extracted from the great formula composed by St. Louis-Marie. Our task now is to demonstrate its scope and practical consequences, for which purpose we shall study it, first, by itself and in each of its clauses; then, in comparison to other similar acts; lastly, having examined the substance of this consecration, we shall end with the consideration of its advantages.

ARTICLE 1: SCOPE OF THIS CONSECRATION AND ITS PRACTICAL CONSEQUENCES

St. Louis-Marie gives the following details to describe what he means by the perfect consecration: "We must give Mary (1) our body, with all its senses and its members; (2) our soul, with all her powers; (3) the external goods which we call *goods of fortune*, whether present or to come; (4) our interior and spiritual goods, consisting of our merits and our virtues, and our good works, past, present, and future. In a word, we must give her all that we have in the order of nature and in the order of grace, and all that, in the future, may become ours in the orders of nature, grace, and glory; and this we must do without reserving so much as one mite, one hair, or one least-good act; and we must do so also for all eternity, and furthermore, we must do so without pretending to, or hoping for, any other recompense for our offering and service, except the honor of belonging to Jesus Christ through Mary and in Mary, even if that sweet Lady were not, as she always is, the most generous and the most grateful of creatures."[4]

Before considering each of the above points, it is important to fix the orthodox sense of the words: "without pretending to, or hoping

---

[3] "Formula of Consecration," *TD*, 192.
[4] Cf. *TD*, 82-83.

for, any other recompense." Here we must avoid any interpretation that may be subject to censure. To instruct and safeguard the faithful, we shall briefly recall certain well-known concepts of the theologians.

It is false to believe that pure love or perfect charity should exclude all expectation of reward, perfection, eternal bliss, or salvation.[5] What makes charity *perfect* is the motive, or the reason why I love God, that is, for Himself. Thus, my love is perfect, if I desire eternal beatitude for the sake of God, to know Him, glorify Him, and let His Will be done in my soul. On the other hand, it is true that my charity may rise to such heights that I am oblivious to my salvation and bliss being in God, that I then say with St. Teresa, "O Lord, were there no Heaven I would still love you, ¦¦ were there no Hell, I would still fear you, | just as much."[6] It is false, however, to be believe that this act of love can become a *habitual* state of the soul. Moreover, we must note that such acts *rise above* considerations of recompense, but do not necessarily *exclude* them. God trains His gaze on the soul. We may say that He absorbs her attention to the point that she momentarily forgets her own good; but it follows not that the soul becomes *indifferent* to her salvation and happiness. Indeed, she cannot and must not be, because it would be contrary to nature, against the Will of God and the order established by Him.

We bring up above the thought of St. Louis-Marie only to remind us that we give ourselves to the Blessed Virgin as slaves, and not as hired help. Moreover, it is clear for all to see in several parts of *True*

---

[5] ◆Innocent XII, *Cum alias*, §1: "A habitual state of the love of God is possible, which is pure charity, and without any admixture of motive of self-interest. Neither fear of punishments nor desire of rewards has any longer part therein. God is no longer loved on account of meriting, nor on account of the happiness to be found in loving Him." The Bull condemned the semi-Quietism of Fénelon.

[6] From the sonnet, *A Cristo crucificado*, lines 9-11: "Muéveme, al fin, tu amor, y en tal manera, / que aunque no hubiera cielo yo te amara, / y aunque no hubiera infierno te temiera." It was attributed to a number of authors, among which are St. John of the Cross, St. Teresa of Avila, St. Francis-Xavier, and St. Ignatius of Loyola. The idea is found in: (1) St. Anselm, *Medit.*, 10, PL 158.762C: "O my Lord, ... let there be no hell, nor yet no paradise, still for Thy sweet goodness' sake, still for Thine own Self's sake, would I desire to cleave to Thee." (2) St. John of the Cross, who, on the words of Jer 31.33, *Dabo legem meam in visceribus eorum*, writes: "Y de aquí es, que aunque no hubiese infierno que amenazase, ni paraíso que convidase, ni mandamiento que constriñese, obraría el justo por sólo el amor de Dios lo que obra" (Audi filia, c. 50, *Obras*, 2:156). Conradi, in his article, "Santa Teresa," says that the attribution to St. Teresa of Avila cannot stand, because she never wrote in long meters. Today, the sonnet is ascribed simply to an anonymous writer.

Devotion that his thoughts are entirely opposed to the opinions of the false mystics of the seventeenth century. ¦¦ He enumerates the motives for embracing perfect devotion: (1) its excellence, (2) its fittingness and advantages, (3) its marvelous effects, (4) it is an excellent means to work for the greater glory of God, (5) it is a way to arrive at union with Him, (6) it leads to interior liberty, (7) obtains great good for our neighbor, and (8) it is an admirable means of persevering and being faithful in virtue,[7] | the greatest number of which treat with our salvation and our spiritual progress. He devotes an entire chapter to the advantages of faithfully practicing the devotion to Mary.

From the foregoing we may also conclude that the "love" in the formula, "May the pure love of God reign in our hearts,"[8] which St. Louis-Marie used in the salutations of his letters, must only be understood as the love undefiled, free from all aberrant elements, such as the sense of vanity, or the hunt for a disordered pleasure, which might be incidentally mixed in with the good intention.

Let us now examine in detail what it is that we give to the Blessed Virgin by our consecration and the obligations that flow from it.

§1. DONATION OF OUR BODY

1. We give Mary our body, along with all its senses and members. We reserve only the use of them, and only for the service and at the pleasure of God and the Blessed Virgin, at that. We ought not to use them, therefore, with no regard for rules or reverence, or our own satisfaction as the aim. Where does this leave us in regards to modesty, chastity, keeping sensual life at bay, and corporal mortification, generally?

We should also speak of the good and ill that visit the body, those things that we sum up as physical pleasure, health, maladies, and death; for these things, too, we do surrender ourselves to Mary. We shall receive them through her hands, and we shall give them up to her will. Whether it be to pray or to persist in our self-abandon, we have an open path through Mary.

2. We pay homage to Mary with our goods of fortune[9]; we entrust

---

[7] *TD*, 91-122.

[8] Pauvert, *Vie*, 84, etc.: "Le pur amour de Dieu règne en nos cœurs."

[9] St. Thomas, *Summa*, 1-2.2: The are four, namely, wealth, honor, glory, and power,

them to her maternal providence so that she may preserve and manage them as God sees fit, especially when we are powerless amidst difficulties. In order that she may truly be the mistress of these goods, let us make use of them with detachment and under her dependence. As much as it is in our power, let us not forget to dispense a portion for her glory and for the reign of God. If we seriously carry out this consecration, it will be a bulwark against disordered passions, and will make it easier for us to accept a loss of fortune or setbacks in our life; for she would sanctify our use of worldly goods, which is always so perilous.

3. Then comes the gift of our soul and all her powers. Far too many Christians, by their acts if not also by their words, apply the impious words borne by the Psalmist: *Labia nostra a nobis sunt, quis noster Dominus est?* "Our lips are our own, who is Lord over us?" (Ps 11.5), to their thoughts, their desires, their passions, and their affections.

The aim of our homage is to restore to God, through the hands of Mary, the dominion over everything that, in the present order, douses the fire of pride and puts out the flame of the disorderly love of pleasure. And to live out the idea of this consecration, we must use our faculties, but humbly and under the guidance of our Mother. Let us bid her give us light and counsel when racked with doubts. Let us bid her strip us of all prideful self-confidence. We must sacrifice to her the use of our faculties, if it goes against her glory and her will. We shall forego, for example, useless or dangerous thoughts, vain or uncharitable judgments, the unbridled curiosity of seeing and knowing; above all, we will let go of our will, and our heart will emerge from the whirlwind of desires and vain affections, where it likes to be. Humbly contented with the measure of the gifts we received in the order of nature, or in the order of grace, we pray our good Lady that she would relieve our helplessness and make good our ills. May she protect our mind from all error, especially persistent error, and our heart from every seduction. Under her dependence, we shall be able to sanctify the joys of the soul, which are often made feverish by the imagination. The mere presentiment of them is sometimes enough to exhilarate us.

---

which "are due rather to external causes, and in most cases, to fortune; for which reason they are called *goods of fortune.*" (1-2.2.4c).

Imagine how much we need her maternal direction if we wish to savor them without putting our soul at peril, considering our fallen nature. Mary is *Mater pulchræ dilectionis, et timoris, et agnitionis, et sanctæ spei,* "the Mother of fair love, and of fear, and of knowledge, and of holy hope!" (Sir 24.24).

§2. DONATION OF OUR SPIRITUAL GOODS

4. We reserved the renunciation of all our spiritual goods, past, present, and future; that is, our merits, and the satisfactory or impetratory value of our good works, for a separate section, because of the importance of the subject. Before explaining the scope of our donation, its practical consequences and advantages, we shall clarify what is meant by "merit," "impetratory value," and "satisfactory value," terms often poorly defined for the faithful.

Every good work done in a state of grace gives us a real claim to an increase of grace here below and of glory in Heaven.[10] This claim is what is called *meritum de condigno,* condign merit, where the reward is ¦ due us on account of the intrinsic worth of our righteous act. | There is also *meritum de congruo,* congruous merit, by which one renders oneself in a manner worthy of a favor by one's acts or good dispositions, without acquiring a rigorous right. ¦¦ The essential difference between the two merits is this: Other than those works which claim a remuneration under pain of violating strict justice (as in contracts between employer and employee, or in buying and selling), there are also other works deserving of merit which, at most, are entitled to reward or honor for reasons of equity or mere distributive justice, as in the case of an employee who deserves recognition for his industry, or a citizen who makes himself worthy of a post for his efforts and talents. If the reward due to condign merit be withheld, there is a violation of right and justice and the consequent obligation in conscience to make restitution, while, in the case of congruous merit, withholding the reward involves no violation of right and no obligation to restore, it being merely an offense against what is fitting or a matter of personal discrimination. "Hence, the reward of

---

[10] ♦We have no intention of settling the question of whether or not there are indifferent acts in the state of grace, even though we welcome the opinion that holds as natural and deserving any work that is good in itself and made by a righteous soul.

congruous merit always depends in great measure on the kindness and liberality of the giver, though not purely and simply on his good-will."[11] |

By *impetratory value* we mean not only the power of our prayers to obtain what we ask for, but also the merit of convenience which is found in every good work and is the price for which God grants us grace. For example, I give alms: Besides deserving an increase of grace and glory, I can also offer this action to obtain a cure, the knowledge of my vocation, etc. This offering of our actions with special intentions is well known to the faithful.[12]

Consider the suffering, effort, or deprivation one imposes upon oneself in carrying out acts such as almsgiving, fasting, labor, prayer, and so on. One's offering such suffering, effort, or deprivation to God in satisfaction, that is to say in payment of the debt of one's sins, is what is called the *satisfactory value* of one's work.

Strictly speaking, condign merit is a personal and incommunicable good. | The merit of a reward in Heaven in a man's work accrue to his benefit, and no one else's. | Jesus Christ alone, as Head and Savior, could merit the glory of His Humanity, in addition to the salvation of all, to which St. Louis-Marie adds that, if we give up our merits to the Blessed Virgin, it is not that she should communicate them to others, but that she should preserve them and increase them.[13] Thus, when, in everyday language, the faithful sometimes say with their heart, "Grant me a share in your merits," that should be understood solely as referring to the impetratory and satisfactory value of their actions.

Let us now turn to the scope, nature, purpose, and consequences

---

[11] Pohle, "Merit," *TCE*, 10:203.1.

[12] ♦Too often *impetratory* is confused with *impetration*, which is the fruit of prayer and cannot be said deserving of merit in a broad sense. Value, in fact, is the price or merit of an act, to which a reward corresponds; here, justice is more or less in question, as it pertains to merit rigorous or of convenience. As for prayer, it is true that it may be considered *good work*; and, as such, it also has its value or merit, either the rigorous or the convenience kind; but envisaged as a *demand*, it has not, strictly speaking, a *value*; rather, it is a *force* or *virtue* of impetration. I obtain what I ask for, not because my action is meritorious, but because I ask in the name of Jesus Christ whose promise and merits give strength to my prayer. In praying, I speak not to justice of God, but to His goodness. Hence, impetration and merit are separable. For example, Saints in heaven pray, and their prayers are answered, though they can neither merit nor make satisfaction.

[13] *TD*, 84.

of the donation of our spiritual goods.

Scope. "I deliver and consecrate ... my goods, both interior and exterior, and even the value of all my good actions, past, present, and future."[14] And again: "A person who is thus voluntarily consecrated and sacrificed to Jesus Christ by Mary can no longer dispose of the value of any of his good actions. All he suffers, all he thinks, all the good he says or does, belongs to Mary, in order that she may dispose of it according to the will of her Son, and His greatest glory."[15]

It is apparent that in the act of consecration nothing is reserved. Do we, by this part of the formula, renounce the direct[16] application of the prayers and of the satisfactions that we would be given us after our death, in such a manner as we should profit by them only according to the will of Mary? St. Louis-Marie seems to reply in the affirmative. He says that we ought to give the Blessed Virgin "all we have in the order of nature and in the order of grace, and all that may become ours *in the future* in the orders of nature, grace, and glory; and this we must do *without any reserve*."[17] It is as if we were giving up a future inheritance in favor of another that would henceforth take care of our needs.

Nature. This is a donation to Mary, our sovereign Queen and Mediatrix. We pay homage to her as our sovereign with our spiritual goods in recognition of our dependence on her. Henceforth, they belong to her. We cease to be owners of them. We give such goods to her as our mediatrix so that she may offer them to Jesus, and that they may be used through her mediation. We derive several advantages from this mediation that we will discuss them below.

Purpose. For what purpose do we thus give our spiritual goods to the Blessed Virgin? So that she may distribute them and apply them ¦ "according to her good pleasure, and to the greatest glory of God," ¦ says St. Louis-Marie.[18] This free disposition is the consequence of her right as Sovereign which we acknowledge by our consecration.

---

14 ♦"Formula of Consecration," *TD*, 192.
15 *TD*, 85.
16 ♦That is without Mary as intermediary.
17 *TD*, 83. [Emphasis added].
18 "Formula of Consecration," *TD*, 192.

If we have been sufficiently clear in our explanation, the reader will realize that this donation is not a divestment in favor of another person, but rather an act of dispossession; that we do it not principally and directly for the purpose of charity towards our neighbor, but rather as an homage to our Queen, for as we are slaves of love, we and all our goods belong to her.

Consequences. We place all the impetratory and satisfactory value of our good works in the hands of the Blessed Virgin,[19] for her to dispose of them as she pleases. Perish the thought that Mary should be, in any way, capricious. Her will is united always to the will of her Son. She prays that she will always be in harmony with Him, that the fruits of our good works may be applied according to His aims and for His greater glory. If it be the Will of God that she apply these fruits to me for my salvation and sanctification, she will faithfully comply. Thus, I shall receive them from my Sovereign and Mother, appropriating nothing to myself, neither shall I reserve or repudiate my donation.

§3. QUESTIONS AND ANSWERS

In the manner of the distribution of these fruits, can we ask Mary that it be to our benefit or that of others? We always *may*; in some cases, we *ought to*. We *may*, because to pray is to recognize our poverty and our dependence on our Mother, to whom we have given everything. To ask is to resort to her mediation. Instead of we ourselves disposing of our property, we pray that she does it for us. In this way, we are faithful to both the substance and the practice of Holy Slavery.

In some cases, we *ought to* pray for a specific a person and purpose. This duty falls to us as a result of the obligations of our state, of justice or of charity, be it in regards to us or to our neighbor. That is not acting as owners of our goods spiritual; rather, it is in conforming ourselves to the Will of God and the Blessed Virgin. Consequently, we ought to pray for ourselves, because prayer is a necessary means of salvation. | Also, a priest who receives a stipend is bound by state and justice to apply the special fruit of the Mass he says according to the intention sought. By charity, a nun should offer her communions and

---

[19] ♦One may also add, "the fruit of our prayers."

her prayers for the deceased of her Order, as prescribed in its rule, and so on. |

This consecration, therefore, inhibits not our obligations, says St. Louis-Marie; and elsewhere he explains: "If, after having thus consecrated ourselves to the Holy Virgin, we desire to relieve some soul in Purgatory, to save some sinner, to help one of our friends by our prayers, our alms, our mortifications, or our sacrifices, we must ask it of her humbly, and leave everything to her good pleasure and determination, without wanting to know anything about it."[20]

We sometimes hear people say: "When I pray, I ask not for anything in particular, I leave it to the Blessed Virgin." It would be a strange mistake to make this practice a general rule. What motive do they allege? That Mary knows our needs? But we pray to her not to let her know what she knows not; rather, it is to make us recognize our poverty and to excite ourselves to implore the help of God.[21] Would asking for something in particular contradict our renunciation and prevent us from casting all our cares on Mary?[22] No, because the words of the Psalm to which we make allusion, is interpreted as a disapproval of an excessive and disorderly solicitude, and most certainly not just any solicitude.[23] Still, we may be solicitous without risking the loss of confidence in God. Nothing opposes our limiting ourselves to a general demand, either by internal appeal or by special circumstances; but we should ask in particular for things that God wills that we do. For example, light to know our vocation, fortitude in certain occasion, and so on. Our confidence in God is not diminished, since we rely on our Mother for the answers to our prayers.

In sum, this donation is a dispossession, and since we act no longer *cum animo domini*,[24] as owners of our spiritual goods, we are

---

[20] ◆*Secret*, 23.
[21] St. Thomas, *Summa*, 2-2.83.2 ad 1, ad 3: ‖ "We need to pray to God, not in order to make known to Him our needs or desires but that we ourselves may be reminded of the necessity of having recourse to His help in these matters" |; 4 *Sent.* 15.4.4.qc 1 ad 2, *Opera*, 10:427.1: ‖ "In those things that God wishes us to want, we must cast our care on Him so that we may expect His help in obtaining them." |
[22] ◆Ps 54.23: *Jacta super Dominum curam tuam*, "Cast thy care upon the Lord."
[23] Ps 11.5.
[24] In Roman law, and every European law based on it, ownership of a thing is *presumed* by the *animus*, intent, to assert the will to possess, and be *dominus*, master, of that thing. (Sohm, *Institutes*, 332, n. 2). Hence, *cum animo domini* means "to have full ownership of." Ownership at Common Law is *evidenced* by possession (Pollock, *Possession*,

not deviating from the letter or the spirit of our consecration.

ARTICLE 2: THE PERFECT CONSECRATION
COMPARED TO OTHER ACTS

The promises of Baptism. St. Louis-Marie rightly calls this consecration "a perfect renewal of the vows and promises of Holy Baptism"[25] by which the Christian renounces Satan, his works and his pomp, and recognizes Jesus Christ as Lord. We do the same through Mary in our consecration.

This renewal is perfect for two reasons: First, "because in thus consecrating ourselves to Jesus Christ, we make use of the most perfect of all means, namely, the Blessed Virgin"[26]; whereas in the vows of Baptism, we give not ourselves to Jesus Christ through the hands of Mary, or at least in explicit terms.[27] Second, because after Baptism we remain entirely free to apply the value of our good deeds to whomever we choose, or to preserve it for ourselves; whereas this consecration leads us to give the value of all our good works to Our Lord, through the hands of Mary, thereby professing a more complete dependence.

§1. OTHER CONSECRATIONS TO THE BLESSED VIRGIN.

By comparing the perfect consecration to the Blessed Virgin with those made in certain circumstances, for example in the missions, within the enclosure of a retreat, the day of first communion, or when we are enrolled in associations of piety, we shall find:

1. That the other congregations, associations, and confraternities commit us not to a total and unreserved donation; that they make no demands on their members other than certain works and practices, which leave them free to do all the other things in the remaining moments of their lives; but that this devotion makes us "give to Jesus and Mary, without reserve, all our thoughts, words, actions, and

---

25), from which we have the dictum, "possession is 99 per cent. of ownership." See also, Taitslin, "Possession and Ownership," in Moréteau, *Legal History*, 341-378.

[25] *TD*, 112.

[26] ♦*TD*, 88.

[27] ♦For some time now, it is true, one generally uses this formula: "I renounce Satan ... and I give myself to Jesus Christ forever by the hands of Mary"; but to the renewal of the promises of Baptism, these words include not a donation to Mary as complete and as special as in the consecration formulated by St. Louis-Marie.

sufferings, at every moment of our life."[28]

2. That this consecration to the Blessed Virgin has a character which is not inherent to the others of which we speak; it is "that we consecrate ourselves at one and the same time to the most holy Virgin and to Jesus Christ: to the most holy Virgin, as to the perfect *means* which Jesus Christ has chosen, whereby to unite Himself to us, and us to Him; and to Our Lord, as to our *Last End*, to Whom we owe all we are, as our Redeemer and our God."[29] This is expressed in the very title of the formula of St. Louis-Marie: "Consecration *of oneself* to Jesus Christ, the Incarnate Wisdom, by the hands of Mary."

§2. THE HEROIC ACT

If we compare this consecration to the *heroic act* in favor of the souls in Purgatory, we shall note that it is of greater scope.

The heroic act relates only to our making satisfactions, the application of which is limited to the souls in Purgatory, whereas our consecration also places in the hands of the Blessed Virgin all the impetratory value of our good works,[30] so that she may dispose of them at will, without restriction of any kind.

Note again that the heroic act is an act of charity or isolated piety; that is, it does not form a complete whole, a well-coordinated system, with other acts or certain truths. On the contrary, the abandonment of the fruit of our good works to the Blessed Virgin is the consequence of our holy and loving slavery, a fruit infused with the sap of the tree that produces it, full of the vitality of total belonging that we profess to Mary. Finally, if one lives out and acts according to this consecration, it will not be a mere passing act of devotion, an homage to be renewed every now and then; rather, it will become the principle that

---

[28] ◆*TD*, 91-92.

[29] *TD*, 85.

[30] ◆We can give up all our satisfactions in favor of our neighbor, but not the impetratory value of all our good works which, at least in part, are necessary for our salvation and our sanctification according to divine Will. See Lehmkuhl, Tr. 3, De discordia et concordia, 2.2.5, in *Theologia moralis*, 1:168 ¦¦ "Operum bonorum vim impetratoriam et de congruo meritoriam non possumus totam in alios transferre, quoniam ipsi nos divinæ gratiæ auxiliis continuo egemus, eaque implorare nobis tenemur. Aliud autem est de vi satisfactoria quoad pœnas temporales: hanc, si volumus, totam in alios, præcipue in animas sanctas in purgatorio detentas transferre nobis licet; imo id facere, quum sit eximium caritatis exercitium, condignum meritum et impetrationem nobis proficuam multum auget." ¦

rules one's state, the form of one's whole interior life, elevating it above the other consecrations to the Blessed Virgin.

It would be indelicate to opine on the respective merits of the heroic act and the perfect consecration to the Blessed Virgin. However, nothing prevents us from reconciling the two donations with the heroic act through the hands of Mary. Msgr. Gay has a remarkable thing to say about them. He says: "Nothing is less like trifling than this act of renunciation, and the Church does not act heedlessly in accepting that it be called a *heroic* act. Never let it be done from impulse, or from the mania of imitation; but freely following in this matter one's own attractions when they appear to be true, let those of other people be always inviolably respected. ... I know those thus affected, who, full of admiration for these acts of generosity, have absolutely so much relish in leaving in the hands of Jesus, their satisfactions, their merits, their life, and their whole being, as not to be willing to settle with Him beforehand, as to the use He would make of them; equally disposed as they are, that He should use them according to His own will, whether for others, or for themselves, without ever asking an account of Him, nor even the reason why. It may seem probable that the souls in Purgatory feel more gratitude towards the former. I would not like to answer for their not having some additional sympathy for the latter."[31] ¦¦ What he says of the donation to Jesus, is also true of the one made to the Blessed Virgin. |

ARTICLE 3: THE IDEA OF THIS CONSECRATION

We have studied the content or articles, or, if you will, the body and material part, of our donation. Let us now turn to the idea that animates it. Let us seek the motives that inspire it, the dispositions to which it inclines us, the virtues it makes us practice, and, with little effort, we shall see that the idea is none other than Mary, the same as in the substance of Holy Slavery, of which act of consecration seems to be the perfect expression and characteristic act of the devotion to her.

---

[31] ♦Gay, *Life and Virtues*, 3:370.

§1. AN ACT OF RELIGION

First, this consecration is a profound act of religion, by which the soul, plunging into its nothingness, makes the humble homage to God for what she is and what she has received from Him.[32] By the terms of the consecration, this tribute is total, because our dependence to the Blessed Virgin is absolute; and our offering, without reservations. From the most pure heart of Mary, where we deposit our offering in a living censer, it ascends as a sweet odor of incense to God in acknowledgement of His sovereign dominion. It may be said that, of all our acts of religion, of all our sacrifices of the internal and private order, this consecration is the most excellent; that it fully realizes the adoration *in spirit and in truth* (Jn 4.23); and that it is a faithful echo of the *Ecce ancilla Domini.*

§2. A PRACTICE OF HUMILITY

Second, this consecration is a practice of true, gentle, and sure humility. Through it, we answer for that holy jealousy of God, Who Scripture says, will not give His glory to another.[33] Nothing really belongs to us, says Fr. Faber, except sin; and he adds: "God is jealous of anything like a proprietary feeling, even in the gifts of nature; but in respect of the gifts of grace, this jealousy is increased a thousand-fold."[34] This explains certain of God's processes in the intimate life of the Saints, and it is also one of the reasons why, through Mary, we render God the homage of our merits, our virtues, and the graces received, which we cannot otherwise communicate to others. The offering is not some formality. St. Louis-Marie says that, well understood and faithfully observed, "there is no other practice equal to this which rids us of a certain [proclivity towards] proprietorship that has covertly crept into our best actions."[35] Fr. Faber elaborates on that last observation, saying: "Our humility is always in peril, if we detain a gift

---

[32] According to St. Thomas, *Summa*, 2-2.82-91, the eleven acts of religion are, devotion, prayer, adoration, sacrifice (out of reverence for God), oblation, offering of firstfruits, offering of tithes, vow (promises made to God), oath (swearing by the Name of God), adjuration in the Name of God, and vocal praise of God.

[33] Is 42.8: I the Lord, this is my name: I will not give my glory to another, nor my praise to graven things.

[34] ♦Faber, *Foot of the Cross*, 119.

[35] ♦Cf. *TD*, 92.

of God, even if it were for no longer than to look it in the face, and love it, and then think of it with complacency when it is gone. We must refer everything to God. It is the secret of being holy."[36] And that is also why the practice of our devotion is "a secret of holiness."[37]

The same Fr. Faber, who so savored the spiritual doctrine of our good Father de Montfort, says further: "We must make [God] the depositary of His own gifts, because we know not how to use them rightly. We must be like children who bid their father keep the little treasures which he himself has given. So, with the gifts of God. They are more ours, when in His keeping, than in our own. ... Nothing good is meant to stay with us. It would not keep good. It would spoil."[38] In these lines, we hear the clear echo of the affirmations in *True Devotion*, in which St. Louis-Marie says that "this devotion to our Lady is ... an admirable means of persevering and being faithful in virtue"; and instead of relying on himself and believing that he is "capable of guarding the treasure of his graces, of his virtues and merits," a man ought to take the Blessed Virgin "for the universal depositary of all his goods of nature and of grace."[39] In sum, let us listen to Fr. Faber's other reflection: "Everything which increases our feeling of dependence upon [God] is sweet, and safe, and true, and right, and the best thing."[40] Indeed, this is reason for our total consecration, and the summary of its fruits.

§3. AN ACT OF THANKSGIVING

We can hardly speak of humility without speaking also of thanksgiving, which buds forth like a flower from its stem, and, no less than humility itself, wafts through the air like a fragrance of sweetness, truth, assurance, and righteousness. Who but a humble soul, convinced of her nothingness and unworthiness would need to give thanks? ¦ In the life of Mary we see outward signs of her gratitude to God, most vividly in the *Magnificat*, which begins with those memorable words: *My soul doth magnify the Lord* (Lk 1.46). | We can never be

---

[36] Faber, *Foot of the Cross*, 119.

[37] *Cantiques*, 77.19, 133: " Je fais tout en elle et par elle, / *C'est un secret de sainteté* / Pour être à Dieu toujours fidèle, / Pour faire en tout sa volonté."

[38] Faber, *Foot of the Cross*, 119.

[39] *TD*, 120.

[40] Faber, *Foot of the Cross*, 119.

too mindful of giving thanks, as it is a sign of spiritual progress, according to a remark of the aforementioned writer, that one is more inclined to offer thanks to God.[41]

Thanksgiving also solves a knotty problem many have; that is, trying to square humility with the gratitude for the gifts that God grants us. Humility consists not in thinking that one has received no talent, no quality, no grace; rather, it is in ascribing everything that is good in us to the grace of God, and in glorifying Him for what He gives. If we succeed in our work, if we receive some spiritual favor, it is not pride to realize that we indeed did. Who does not recall with what earnest indignation St. Teresa puts down this false humility?[42] In this, too, let us take the Blessed Virgin as our example. Elizabeth praises her saying that she is blessed above all women, after the Angel has said in his greeting that she is "full of grace." Mary denies not the truth of these divine prerogatives and favors, and rejoices in them and attributes them all to the Lord, *quia respexit humilitatem ancillæ suæ, fecit mihi magna,* Who "hath regarded the humility of His handmaid," and "done great things to her" (Lk 1.48, 19). Let us imitate our Mother, and acknowledge God's gifts to us, let us rejoice in them whatever they may be; but let us not claim credit for anything. In the act of thanksgiving, everything is offered up to God, and what we keep for ourselves is only our baseness; that is, our condition as creature and sinner.

Thanksgiving fits in very well with the substance of our perfect consecration in that, according to St. Louis-Marie, it is reputed to be among the motives of this total and absolute donation. He says: "Jesus, our great friend, has given Himself to us without reserve, body and soul, virtues, graces, and merits: *Toto se totum me comparavit,* 'He has bought the whole of me by the whole of Himself,' says St.

---

[41] Faber, *Conferences*, 241-242: "Years of saying the Angelus, with great love, with intense attention to God, with an interior spirit of jubilant thanksgiving for the Incarnation, would take us half way to Heaven"; *All for Jesus*, 8, 273: Thanksgiving leads us "to break more effectually with the world, and not to trail its clouds and mists along with us on our road to Heaven."

[42] ♦St. Teresa of Avila, "Life," 10.4, *Works*, 59: ¦¦ "Some think it humility not to believe that God is bestowing His gifts upon them. Let us clearly understand this, and that it is perfectly clear God bestows His gifts without any merit whatever on our part; and let us be grateful to His Majesty for them; for if we do not recognize the gifts received at His hands, we shall never be moved to love Him." ¦

Bernard.[43] Is it not, then, a simple matter of justice and of gratitude that we should give Jesus all that we can give Him?"[44]

§4. AN ACT OF LOVE

We said above that confidence and love always accompany adoration to some extent; for God's supreme excellence, which we reverence by adoration, is His goodness and love, as well as His power and Majesty. In sacrifice, which is the act of worship most excellent, there is, more or less explicit, the confidence that God will grant us amply what we sacrifice to His glory. Thus, if we give ourselves without reserve, it is because we long to love and entrust ourselves to Him entirely. Whoever lives out the idea of our devotion, lives under the law of pure love; that is, of a love devoid of even a trace of selfishness that would alter charity or render it imperfect. We shall revisit this path of perfection and love further on; but let us emphasize here the character of abandonment in our donation to Mary.

§5. AN ACT OF SELF-ABANDONMENT

Body and soul and my welfare all,
On her good graces mayest they fall.[45]

Thus chants St. Louis-Marie. These words summarize his entire teaching, and leads us to understand that, by our consecration to the Virgin, it is not enough to *give* oneself, but that one must *surrender* oneself.

"To abandon oneself," said Msgr. Gay, "is to renounce oneself, to quit, to alienate, to lose oneself, and all together to yield oneself to Him Who has the right over us, without any measure, without reserve, and almost without noticing what we do."[46] He who only *gives himself* has a calculating mind, reserving more or less according to what he may get in return. Now, *that* is not the abandonment expressly asked of us in the perfect consecration in which we deliver to Mary "all ... without any reserve of so much as one mite, one hair, or one least good action; ... without pretending to, or hoping for, any other

---

[43] St. Bernard, *Sermones de Diversis*, 22.6 [De quadruplici debito], PL 183.598C.

[44] ♦*TD*, 92-93.

[45] Note 75, p. 137.

[46] ♦¦ Gay, *Life and Virtues*, 3:155. In this Treatise, Gay faithfully reflects on the idea and practice of Holy Slavery. See also, de Sales, *Conferences*, 2, 16-28; cf. *Œuvres*, 6:19-30. ¦

recompense for our offering and service, except the honor of belonging to Jesus Christ through Mary and in Mary."[47] "To abandon oneself,"
said Msgr. Gay, "is to flow," to melt away, according to the "Spouse of
the Canticles, who says: *My soul melted when my beloved spoke* (Cant
5.6). What is liquid has no form of its own; it takes its form from the
vessel in which it is held. ... Such is the soul which abandons herself:
She melts into water at the word of God; not the word which thun-
ders, nor even the Word which commands, but at the word of simple
desire and of the least preference."[48] When we read these lines, we recall that St. Louis-Marie compares Mary to a heavenly mold into
which we throw ourselves to be transformed into Jesus. Let us take
care, however, to keep ourselves malleable; for "we only cast in a mold
what is melted and liquid."[49]

St. Francis de Sales tells us that to surrender oneself is to be rid of
one's own will, which passes over and is lost in God.[50] It is the very
thing that St. Louis-Marie recommends. The soul must "lose herself
in Mary,"[51] or to lose herself in the depths of the interior of Mary to
become a living copy of her.[52] We should add that love is the principle
of abandonment, for it is love that inspires it, and that its fruits are
peace and the liberty of the soul.

ARTICLE 4: THE RICHES OF OUR POVERTY

The title above is the same as given by Fr. Faber to a chapter in
his book, *All for Jesus*, and it is not inappropriate to say that we may
find a source of its idea in the following words of St. Louis-Marie: "The
Blessed Virgin is a Mother of sweetness and mercy. She never lets herself be surpassed in love and liberality. Seeing that, to honor and to
serve her, we give ourselves entirely to her in stripping ourselves of all
that is dearest to us in order to adorn her, she gives also her whole

---

[47] ♦*TD*, 83.

[48] Gay, Ibid. 3:155.

[49] ♦*TD*, 157.

[50] de Sales, *Conferences*, 2, 19: "You must know that to practice self-abandonment, and
to forsake ourselves, is nothing else but to yield up and get rid of our own will that we
may give it to God. For ... it would be of no benefit at all to renounce and forsake ourselves, if it were not done in order to unite ourselves perfectly to the divine Goodness."
Cf *Œuvres*, 6:21-22.

[51] *TD*, 180.

[52] *TD*, 155.

self, and gives in an ineffable manner, to him who gives all to her. She causes him to be engulfed in the depths of her graces. She adorns him with her merits; she supports him with her power; she illuminates him with her light; she inflames him with her love; she communicates to him her virtues. ... She makes herself his bail, his supplement,[53] and his dear-all in regards to Jesus. In a word, as that person is consecrated entirely to Mary, so is Mary wholly for him."[54]

Our Saint speaks at length on the return by which Mary rewards our donation, when he explains the motives that commit us to the practice of Holy Slavery, ¦¦ a summary of which we provided above.[55] | It is not our intention here to repeat what he wrote on such motives in *True Devotion*. We urge the reader to consult the book at his leisure.[56] Better, it seems, to insist on certain considerations to show the soundness of these motives and to clarify their meaning.

§1. MARY, THE CUSTODIAN OF OUR TREASURE

Sicut qui thesaurizat, ita et qui honorificat matrem suam, "he that honoreth his mother, is as one that layeth up a treasure" (Sir 3.5), to which St. Louis-Marie adds: "He who honors Mary, his Mother, even unto subjecting himself to her and obeying her in all things, will soon become exceedingly rich."[57]

The first step to enrich oneself is to conserve what one has received or gained. Mary is a faithful custodian and guardian. The Gospel teaches us that she "kept all in her heart"[58] what she drew from the inspiration and graces she obtained from Jesus. She will not fail to keep the deposit of our spiritual treasure. Bear in mind that we render her homage with our merits, gifts received, acquired virtues, and thus put them in a safe place, entrusting them to her who will protect them from ¦¦ devils who are sly thieves,[59] termites that eat away at the foundation of our faith. St. Louis-Marie goes on:

"They watch day and night for the favorable moment. To that end

---

[53] Old French, *supplément*, "make-up for a deficiency," not modern "addition."
[54] ◆Cf. *TD*, 97-98.
[55] Part 3.2.1, p. 178.
[56] *TD*, 91-122.
[57] *TD*, 106.
[58] Lk 2.19, 51.
[59] *TD*, 59.

they roam about us incessantly to devour us, and in one instant, by one sin, to snatch away from us all that we were able to gain in graces and merits over the course of years. Their malice, their experience, their stratagems, and their number, ought to make us fear this misfortune immensely, especially when we see how many persons, fuller of grace, richer in virtues, better founded in experience, and far higher exalted in sanctity than we are, have been surprised, robbed, and unhappily pillaged. Ah! how many of the cedars of Lebanon, how many of the stars of the firmament, have we not seen falling miserably, and in the twinkling of an eye losing all their height and all their brightness! Whence comes that sad and curious change? It has not been for want of grace, which is wanting in no man; but want of humility. ... They trusted in themselves, relied on themselves. They thought their house secure enough, and their coffers strong enough, to keep the precious treasure of their grace. It is because of that scarcely sensible reliance upon themselves, while all the while it seemed to them that they were relying on the grace of God, that the most just Lord has permitted them to be robbed by leaving them to their own devices. Alas! if they had but known the admirable devotion, ... they would have confided their treasure to the Virgin, powerful and faithful, who would have guarded it for them as if it had been her own possession; nay, who would have even taken it as an obligation of justice on herself to preserve it for them."[60] |

Let us continue on to a consideration on perseverance which follows immediately.

To persevere is to remain stable in the state one is in; consequently, it is to be firm in the resolution taken, to endure in the virtue possessed, to preserve the acquired merits, and to continue to do good, in spite of the difficulty of a prolonged effort. He stops persevering who loses what he has already won, and, above all, does not maintain himself in a state of grace.

In the words of St. Louis-Marie, to entrust virtues and merits to the Blessed Virgin by the homage of a perfect consecration, is "an admirable means of persevering and being faithful in virtue."[61] In his

---

[60] Cf. *TD*, 59-60.
[61] *TD*, 120.

opinion, if so many conversions last not; if so many of the righteous are weak and inconstant; if, instead of progressing, they retreat by losing what they have acquired, it is that "they rely too much on their own strength, believing that they are capable of guarding the treasure of their graces on their own."[62] They should entrust everything to Mary, build on her strength, and hope in her goodness.

To persevere in grace requires special help from God. This help consists in a set of actual graces to strengthen our will, to urge us to do right, and to repel temptations. To these movements, directions, and inner help must be added external protection, or providential disposition of events, which separates us from the occasions of sin, and gives us opportunities to do right. This is not, however, the same as final perseverance. In addition to the aforementioned exterior and interior helps, opportunely arranged to lead us to a good end, *in fact* it will be necessary for us to be in the state of grace at the moment of our death.

Now, if we read and re-read what the good Father de Montfort said, especially where he sets out the *eighth motive* of devoting ourselves entirely to Mary ¦¦ ("that it is an admirable means of persevering and being always faithful in virtue"),[63] ¦ and we understand that, given the abundance of help of all kinds, among which is the vigilant and steadfast love of our Mother abundantly filling the hearts of her devout servants and slaves; and given the special providence she exercises over them during the course of their life, and especially at the hour of their death, we shall find in our devotion specific reasons for hope. And if it is indispensable to resort to prayer for the grace of final perseverance, which is a free gift, special and of a supreme importance, imagine how much more effective will be our request, since it relies on the more perfect means and more excellent titles of the mediation of Mary!

Thus far the theory. Need we elaborate on what joy fills the hearts of priests and, in general, of all those who work in the apostolate? The evidence in the practice has so far been beyond all our expectations. Volumes are filled with edifying, and sometimes strange, stories that

[62] *TD*, 120.
[63] *TD*, 120-123

tell the wonders of Mary's kindness to poor sinners. They are not always, at least in some respects, the most implausible.[64] Numerous are the wonders hidden today which will be made known to us tomorrow. Many are the souls saved and preserved who will sing forever the mercies of the Lord,[65] and praise the one who is called the Mother of Mercy!

§2. MARY AUGMENTS OUR MERITS

Mary not only preserves our merits and virtues, she augments them, says St. Louis-Marie.[66] How? Undoubtedly, because the abundant graces she obtains for us, and the external protection with which she surrounds us, fosters the increase of our merits and allows us to advance in virtue.

She also augments the value of our spiritual treasure by the excellent manner she disposes of it. It is a boon to derive the highest return on a fortune, while wasting it or leaving it unproductive is a real loss. From this point of view, it is to our great advantage to entrust the Blessed Virgin, be it so delicate a matter, with the application of the fruits of our works. For the application to be fully efficacious and advantageous would require a knowledge of souls, a science of divine Will—a discernment of times and places, and even a vision of the future that we have not. All of this is the portion of our divine Mother. Let us then be "persuaded that the value of our actions, ... dispensed by the same hand, of which God makes use to distribute to us His graces and His gifts, cannot fail to be applied to His greatest glory."[67]

We ought also to speak of the extrinsic value which our deeds acquire by the working of Mary; that is, in what she makes up for their deficiencies, either by sharing part of her own treasure, or because she makes her own those works she receives in homage and which relies on her mediation.

In the words of St. Louis-Marie, before Jesus, Mary is our beloved

---

[64] For Marian miracles, see index in Bourassé, *Summa B.V.M.*, 13:1163-1164. St. Louis-Marie would have been familiar with the 69 miracles Spinelli cataloged in *Thronus Dei*, 2:596-653.

[65] Ps 88.2: Misericordias Domini in æternum cantabo.

[66] *TD*, 120.

[67] ♦*Secret*, 23.

supplement.[68] She makes up for our frailty, by aiding us and buttressing us in our perseverance. Let us now see how she also makes up for our unworthiness with the power of her good name; and for our poverty, by the abundance of her treasure.

In a delightful analogy, St. Louis-Marie speaks of a poor peasant whose offering is but a fruit of little value. Being shrewd, he had it borne by the hands of the queen, so that her husband the king, giving *her* due consideration, would accept it, though it be trivial and unworthy.[69]

Thus, "when we present Jesus anything by the pure and virginal hands of His well-beloved, we go through His weakness, if our use of such a term is appropriate. He considers not so much the thing that is given Him, as the Mother who gives it. He considers not so much whence the offering comes, as by whom it comes."[70]

We see there the clear explanation of the principle that the value of a work is the sum of its worth and its author, as well as the intermediary who offers it in his own name. We see in the material order manifold examples of the transformation, or the increase in the power, beauty, and goodness derived from a transmission through an effect or force. It suffices for us to mention the enlargement of images by a magnifying glass, the increase of a moving force by a pulley, etc.

But let us return to the supernatural order. The formula: *Per Dominum nostrum Jesum Christum*, "through Jesus Christ, Our Lord," which concludes our prayers, teaches us that, despite our unworthiness, they acquire a power through the mediation of Jesus. Now, Christ is the mediator between us and His Father, and Mary is a mediatrix between us and Christ. Thus, when we pay her homage with our deeds by asking her to offer them to God, *Mary makes such work hers, by right of ownership and in her role as mediatrix.* She prays for us, and our deeds that she offers in her name receives a supplementary value from her good name and her dignity. But in this case, the increase becomes the principal. Our Mother stands ahead of us,

---

[68] *TD*, 98.; see note 53, p. 193.

[69] *TD*, 99-100.

[70] ◆Cf. *TD*, 101. French *faible*, "weakness" as in "special fondness for."

because as an intermediary she is closer to Jesus than we are; but she neither annihilates our work nor absorbs our personal merit. It is she whom He sees first, she to whom He listens first, she who comes forward first. We come behind her, hidden and sheltered under her mantle, so to speak. And being ahead of us, Mary outshines us. Her voice speaks louder than ours; and, like a spark in a blazing hearth, we are lost in the splendor of her glory, which effaces the blemishes in our works that offend infinite holiness. Such is how Mary purifies and makes acceptable what we deliver into her hands.

Let us now see how the Most Blessed Virgin enhances the works we give to the Lord through her hands, when she adorns them with her merits and virtues[71]; in other words, how she supplements, not only our unworthiness with her good name, but also our poverty with the abundance of her treasure.

In the simple and fair analogy cited above, St. Louis-Marie says that the queen, taking the peasant's apple, offers it to the king on a large and beautiful golden platter, and in so doing, she especially supplements its value.[72] Notice the subtle movement from the question of the dignity of she who offers our deeds to God, to the increase she imparts by taking them into her own treasure.

What is this treasure? *Ipsa est thesaurus Domini*, "she herself is the treasure of the Lord," as she is "full of grace," in the sense we explained above,[73] demonstrating to us that she is the masterpiece of God. Not only has she received, but she personally acquired treasures, along the notable words of Proverbs: *Multæ filiæ congregaverunt divitias, tu supergressa es universas*, "many daughters have gathered together riches: thou hast surpassed them all"–Prv 31.29.[74] This treasure touches the infinite. It has an inestimable and inexhaustible value for us. Our feeble faculties cannot fathom the depths of what she merited and obtained, or how she made satisfaction with her acts, whose perfection surpassed the heroism of Saints, and every one of which gave

---

[71] *TD*, 99.
[72] *TD*, 99-100.
[73] Quote form St. Antoninus, on p. 26.
[74] ◆Part 2.2.1, p. 113.

greater glory to God than all the praises of the heavenly hierarchies.

Among the riches of Mary, we find the progress of her holiness. Even if we could imagine a relatively weak starting point and an out-landish mode of growth, by dint of its inadequacy, our attempt at estimation fast collapses and our calculation becomes impossible. Instead of aiming to determine the amount of her accumulated merits, let us just acknowledge that all our effort will come to naught; let us be content to say that they surpass the sum total of all the merits obtained by all the righteous.[75]

Is that all? No, there is more. We should include in the treasure of Mary, in addition to her personal merits, all that she has received for herself and for us. First, she received Jesus and His infinite merits: Jesus is hers, and you will know if she gives Him to us. Listen to the word from the book of Wisdom: *Infinitus est enim thesaurus,* "for she is an infinite treasure to men" (Wis 7.14).

Now, this is the very same treasure that the Blessed Virgin most holy will open to all, begrudging none: ¦¦ *By the means of her I shall have immortality, and shall leave behind me an everlasting memory to them that come after me* (Wis 8.13). | Who has not in mind the insistent and loving invitations of Divine Wisdom, calling all those who wish ¦¦ to empty themselves of the spirit of the world, | and fill themselves up with the fruits Mary bears?[76] When he promises us her generosity, in return for our total consecration, St. Louis-Marie expresses not his own thought but those in the Wisdom books. He says that she is the valiant woman[77] who will clothe us in double garments.[78] As Rebecca did for Jacob, so will she give us the precious garments of our elder brother, Jesus Christ; that is, His merits and His grace that are in her possession, and have us share her own merits.[79]

Let us never fear that our works would be less beneficial to those whom we wish to help, when we give our Mother leave to apply their fruit. St. Louis-Marie assures us, saying that if we ask Mary to aid our

---

[75] ♦Terrien, *Mère de Dieu,* 2.1, 7.1-4, 3:519-606.

[76] *TD,* 160-161: "Those who wish to begin this particular devotion, after having employed twelve days, at least, in emptying themselves of the spirit of the world, should employ three weeks in filling themselves with Jesus Christ by the holy Virgin."

[77] Prv 31.10.

[78] Prv 31.21; *TD,* 145.

[79] *Secret,* 28.

parents, friends or benefactors, she will know how to with our small spiritual income or *by other means*[80]; that is, by drawing from her own treasure and from the wealth of merits and satisfactions of her Son.

Still, we may wonder to what extent our Blessed Mother would do so. None may know precisely, but we should not fail to acknowledge that our hope in the goodness of Mary is grounded on sound reasons.

First, it is her generosity, grateful for those who, in her honor, divest themselves of their goods. Our Saint declared it so in the words quoted at the beginning of this article. He often liked to repeat them. Sometimes he borrows from everyday language, as when he tells us that the Blessed Virgin would let us catch a mackerel if we throw a sprat.[81] Other times he recalls the promise of Jesus for a glass of cold water given in His name.[82] He even asks what God would give to those who would dispossess all that is best in them in honor of His divine Mother. In answer to which we refer to St. Thomas, who says that it is congruous and in harmony with friendship that God should fulfil the desire for the salvation of another, if it is expressed by a man in the state of grace who satisfies His Will.[83]

We may hear it said that it appertains to merit congruous, not condign; that is, to the fitness of things and not to justice. Most assuredly so. But are not such things as meet the fitness of things, friendship, and gratitude, as sacred, and sometimes as urgent as those of righteousness, even if they impose not a rigorous obligation on us? How can we doubt that God would magnanimously reward our donation? Let us remind ourselves that He is God Who is ever merciful and loving; the very same that Scripture declares to have always the first

---

[80] *TD*, 89.

[81] Fr. Lhoumeau: *rend un bœuf à qui lui donne un œuf*, lit. "give and an ox to him who gives an egg." Cf. *VD*, 153; *TD*, 126. The reverse of the French locution, "Donner un œuf pour avoir un bœuf," is comparable to the English, "to throw a sprat to catch a mackerel."

[82] Jn 4.13-14: Whosoever ... shall drink of the water that I will give him, shall not thirst for ever; but the water that I will give him, shall become in him a fountain of water, springing up into life everlasting. *Secret*, 16: "Happy, and a thousand times happy, is the soul here below to whom the Holy Ghost ... gives access to this fountain, by suffering her to draw from it, and to drink deep draughts of the living waters of grace!"

[83] ◆St. Thomas, *Summa*, 1-2.114.6c.

and last word on generosity.[84] And since Mary perfectly conforms to His sensibility and Will,[85] and by her office is the channel of His graces, the instrument of His mercies, is it possible that she would not generously reward the donation made to her in this consecration?[86] How, according to her promise, will she not love those who love her: *Ego diligentes me diligo* (Prv 8.17)? We have nothing to fear but one thing: that our confidence should persist far below the level to which it must boldly rise.

May our good Father de Montfort be right in exclaiming "that to find grace—a powerful grace—we must find Mary"![87] The same thought we find in St. Bernard: *Quæramus gratiam et per Mariam quæramus*, "let us seek grace and seek it through Mary," adding: *quærant alii meritum; nos invenire gratiam studeamus*, "let others seek merits; and we, let us put our efforts to finding grace."[88] Surely meritorious works cannot be useless, and neither ought we to neglect them, but these words show us that, in her hopes and prayers, the soul is predisposed to rely less on her own merits than on divine grace and the mercy of Mary. So also do we when we entrust her with the care of distributing the fruits of our merits and works, by entrusting them all to her.

---

[84] ◆Rom 11.35: Recompense shall be made to him who hath first given to God.

[85] To be sensible is to know, in the sense that the senses exist for a kind of knowing. God may be said to be sensible because He knows, and supremely sensible because He is all-knowing. (St. Anselm, *Proslogion*, 6, PL 158.229-230).

[86] ◆See the section in Lépicier, *Tr. de B.V.M.*, 2.1.4.12, 409-410, bearing the title "B. Virgo non æqualiter apud Deum pro omnibus hominibus intercedit."

[87] *Secret*, 10.

[88] St. Bernard, *de Aquæductu*, §8, PL 183.442A.

CHAPTER 3:

THE INTERIOR EXERCISE

he essence of this devotion is to make a soul *interiorly dependent* and slave to the Blessed Virgin; and, through her, to Jesus.[1] These words leads us to understand that in addition to the external consecration, there is an internal practice described as "essential" by St. Louis-Marie himself. Indeed, without it, our consecration would be a mere act of external and passing piety. In contrast, the interior practice will quicken our every act with the beating heart of our consecration, and set us firmly in the habitual dependence on Mary. On which point St. Louis-Marie made the following important and judicious reflections:

"It is not enough to have given ourselves once to Jesus through Mary, in the quality of a slave; it is not even enough to do it every month, or every week: *this would be a devotion too fleeting, nor would it raise the soul to that perfection to which it is capable of raising her.* There is not much difficulty in enrolling ourselves in a confraternity, or even embracing outwardly the devotion of which I am speaking, in saying a few vocal prayers every day; ... but the great difficulty is to live out the idea of this devotion, which is to make a soul interiorly dependent upon, and a slave of, the most Holy Virgin, and, through her, of Jesus. I have known many, who, with admirable zeal, have entered into this Holy Slavery, outwardly; I have found but few who have acquired its habits, and still fewer who have persevered in it."[2]

This same thought is again expressed in the *True Devotion*, where St. Louis-Marie says: "As the essential of this devotion consists *in the*

---

[1] *Secret,* 32.
[2] ◆Cf. Ibid.

interior which it ought to form, not everyone will equally comprehend it. The greatest number will halt at its exterior, and will go no further. A few will enter into its interior practice."[3]

What is this interior practice? "It may be expressed in four words: to do all our actions *through* Mary, *with* Mary, *in* Mary, and *for* Mary; so that we may do them all the more perfectly *through* Jesus, *with* Jesus, *in* Jesus, and *for* Jesus."[4]

The reader now realizes that this is not a vain formula, or an idle exaggeration. He sees that, from where we stand, the teaching of St. Louis-Marie unfolds as an admirable unity; that he can probe the depth of its formulas and appreciate the vitality of its practices.

"Through Mary, with her, in her, and for her," closes the circle and completes the system. Indeed, since God comes to us by Jesus and Jesus is given to us through Mary, on our return journey to God at the end of time, we shall follow the same path He took when He came down from Heaven. Passing through Mary, we will go on to Christ, and from Christ to God. This is how we apply the formula and see its use compared to the formulas of other devotions.

As to its intrinsic value, what we said above in explaining "through Christ, with Him, and in Him,"[5] shows how much this formula is full of meaning and to what depths the interior exercise is immersed in dogma. How true it is that, in St. Louis-Marie, we should admire the master of spiritual life, no less than the missionary and the founder of religious institutes!

Let us now delve deeper into the meaning of the formula: "To act through Mary, with Mary, in Mary, and for Mary," and compare it to its analogous expression: "To act through Christ, with Christ, in Christ, and for Christ." We should specify how they agree or differ; but let us begin by making a couple of observations in order to avoid any misunderstanding:

First, the reader will no doubt have noticed that St. Louis-Marie does not always keep the same order in the expression of the maxim.[6] Perhaps it was because he wrote his works in haste. In any event, the

---

[3] ◆*TD*, 81. [Emphasis added].

[4] ◆*TD*, 178.

[5] Part 1.2.1-3, pp. 31-53.

[6] ◆*TD*, passim, 77-178; *Secret*, 21, 31.

variations on the terms are insignificant. We shall simply will follow the order adopted in *True Devotion*, where we have the main commentary on them; that is, the order used in the liturgy, which is closer to the sacred text,[7] and the most logical.

Second, it is difficult for us to follow the opinion offered by some regarding the formula: "Through Mary, with Mary, and in Mary." They say that these expressions could mark three successive degrees in the union with Our Lord or with the Blessed Virgin: *through* would be for the beginners in the spiritual path; *with*, for the ones making progress; and *in*, for those who have reached perfection, ¦¦ corresponding to the three degrees of spiritual life: the purgative, illuminative, and contemplative way, respectively. | Such an explanation seems inaccurate to us. The words may indeed express distinct things; and, absolutely speaking, even separable, things. For example, a sinner who prays under the influence of actual grace, in truth, may very well pray through Christ; yet we cannot say absolutely that he prays in Him, because, not being united to Him by charity, he has yet to remain in such grace through love. But since this is a matter of the practice proposed for justified souls in making them grow in grace, these three expressions: "through Christ," "with Christ," and "in Christ" are inseparable. These are three aspects or three phases of a single movement of union: *through*, is its point of departure; *with*, its course; and *in*, its arrival, all of which are found in every act that the righteous soul does in union with Christ. We should say the same of the phrases: "through Mary," "with Mary," and "in Mary." Whether we speak of a soul at the beginning of spiritual life, or advanced in perfection, the entire difference will lie in the various modes of the union; *through, with,* and *in*, more or less will be perfectly practiced, as we shall see anon.

ARTICLE 1: TO ACT THROUGH MARY

To act through Mary is, first of all, to act by the impulse and the virtue of the grace she dispenses to us, which in the popular language St. Louis-Marie uses, means to obey her in all things and to be led by

---

[7] ¦¦ Cf. *Missale*, §1112, Final Doxology, Canon of the Mass: Per Christum Dominum nostrum, ... | ♦Per ipsum, et cum ipso, et in ipso. We read in Rom 11.36: Quoniam ex ipso, per ipsum et in ipso.

her spirit.[8]

To act through Mary is, secondly, to engage her as mediatrix in going to Jesus and uniting us to Him; it is to have our offerings borne in her hands, to rely on her intercession, to have recourse to her help, to be schooled by her, that we may know and love Jesus better.

Now let us turn to how acting through Mary is acting through Christ. St. Louis-Marie tells us that we must "do all our actions through Mary, with Mary, in Mary, and for Mary, so that we may do them all more perfectly through Jesus, with Jesus, in Jesus, and for Jesus."[9]

Any explanation is superfluous, if we mean "through" in the sense of mediation; for we have already shown that Mary leads us to Jesus. But how can one say that to act through Christ (or by the movement of His Spirit) and to act through Mary is all one and the same thing? We may summarize the thought of St. Louis-Marie on this point as follows: To act through Mary is to obey her in everything and to be led by her spirit. Now, as the spirit of Mary is none other than that of Jesus, to be led by Mary, it is therefore to be led by Jesus.[10]

We must not take the said proposition, "the spirit of Mary is that of Jesus," to mean that the Holy Ghost, Who proceeds from the Father and the Son, also proceeds from Mary or is sent by her. Neither ought we to understand that she gives Him to us in the same way Our Lord does. Nevertheless, there is truth in saying that the Spirit of Jesus is the spirit of Mary. First, because she is filled, possessed, and governed by the Spirit of Jesus in certain respects and in a manner more excellent than is any other creature. Secondly, because in her capacity as Mother of God, she may be considered as the Spouse of the Holy

---

[8] *TD*, 192-193, 179: "O Virgin mild, ... I protest that I wish henceforth, as thy true slave, to seek thy honor and to obey thee in all things"; "none are true or faithful but those who are led by her spirit."

[9] *TD*, 178.

[10] *TD*, 178, 179: "Those [of us] whom the Holy Ghost calls to high perfection ... must do our actions through Mary; that is to say, we must obey her in all things, and in all things conduct ourselves by her spirit, which is the holy Spirit of God, ... because she was never led by her own spirit, but always by the Holy Ghost, who has rendered Himself so completely master of her, that He has become her own proper spirit. It is on this account that St. Ambrose says: '*Sit in singulis Mariæ anima, ut magnificet Dominum; sit in singulis spiritus Mariæ, ut exsultet in Deo (In Lucam*, 2.26, Lc 2.44-45, PL 15.1561D) — Let the soul of Mary be in each of us, so that she magnifies the Lord, and the spirit of Mary be in each of us, so that it rejoices in God.'"

Ghost, and she has received a *certain authority* over His missions or His coming into souls.[11] Thus, when the Holy Ghost works in us, it is in concert with Mary; and, consequently, to act through Mary is "not to undertake any kind of interior life, or perform any spiritual action, except in total reliance on her,"[12] rendering us attentive and docile to the direction of this divine Spirit.

Always appreciative of the grand sweep of ideas, St. Louis-Marie then looks to the more distant consequences of this truth. He briefly reminds us of our quality as children of God and those of Mary's, and based on the text of St. Paul: *Quicumque Spiritu Dei aguntur, hi filii Dei sunt*, "whosoever are led by the Spirit of God, they are the sons of God" (Rom 8.14),[13] he makes substantially a similar argument, saying: "Whosoever are led by the spirit of Mary are the children of Mary, and consequently, the children of God,"[14] since we speak of the same Spirit at work!

However, there is a difference between the two formulas: "to act through Christ" and "to act through Mary." The first signifies that Christ produces grace in us, and we perform supernatural acts through the movement of such grace, and by virtue of it. It is He Who leads us by His Spirit, and our action depends on the direct and physical influence He exerts on us. The second formula, on the other hand, expresses only a moral and indirect account, as grace comes to us from Mary in the sense that she obtains it for us by her merits, her prayer, and her will.

Given the foregoing explanation, we should not fear being inaccurate when we say that we act through Mary, or that we obey her, or that we give her leave to lead us by her spirit. Indirect though it may

---

[11] ♦Part 2.2.2, p. 120, and note 25.

[12] *Secret*, 33.

[13] ♦St. Thomas, ad Romanos, 8, Lect. 3, *Opera*, 20:490.1, explains: "We say beings acting under the impulse of a higher instinct, whether they are moved or driven. Thus, animals without reason are driven, pushed, but they act not, they behave not; for in what they do, they obey the instincts of their nature and have no properly deliberate or voluntary movement. Similarly, what inclines the spiritual man to act is not primarily the movement of his own will, but the impulse of the Holy Ghost."

[14] ¦¦ *TD*, 178-179. | ♦With this difference, however, that the Holy Ghost makes us children of God by making us partakers of the divine nature, but our quality as children of Mary puts us not in such a relationship with her.

be, moral causality does indeed contribute to effective action[15]; and he who has commanded, obtained a thing, or who has only consented to it in an effective manner, may say: "This thing is imputable to me, I am its cause, and I am owed it."

In sum, the difference between "acting through Christ" and "acting through Mary" in the sense that we make use of their mediation, is the same as the difference in their respective mediations. We said above, Christ is the principal, necessary, and universal Mediator; Mary is a mediatrix, subordinate to Christ, and established as such by the free will of God. Thus, when we go to God through her, Mary leads us first to Christ. ¦¦ We do not sidestep Jesus. |

ARTICLE 2: WITH MARY

Observe how a mother is with her child when she teaches him to walk or to pray. Not only does she rouse him and encourage him by gesture and voice, but she also affects him by her example, by shoring him up when he is weak, and by making up for his inexperience. For his part, the child acts towards his mother; for he watches her, is docile to her direction, and does not part from her. To act with Mary, I must first obey her impulse, then remain under her direction and influence, hold my gaze fixed on her to imitate her; I must rely on her maternal hand to support me and, if I fall, to lift me up again; and, I must follow her without getting ahead of her or falling behind to delay her.

In every instance of the practical realization of the various meanings we have given to the phrase "with Christ," we see the association and the company, the continuous cooperation, the correspondence among the thoughts, the will, and the action.

The Church clearly distinguishes the two phases in the influence of grace: the initial impulse and cooperation in the course of action.

---

[15] The Sacraments contain the merits of Christ's Passion, the price of our redemption, and confer it through their operation as moral causes, i.e. as opposed to natural or physical causes. (Cano, "Relectio de Sacramentis in Genera," 4, concl. 6, *Opera*, 488: "Morales appellamus causas liberas, quæ scilicet libere movent: ut qui consulit, qui imperat, ejus rei causa est, quæ per ejus aut imperium, aut consilium efficitur. ... At concursus hic naturalis est: non tamen illius actionis Deus est *causa moralis*, neque enim aut consulit, aut præcipit, quin potius prohibet"). Cf. Trent, Sess. 7, Sacraments, can. 6, 52.

"Go before our actions, we beseech Thee, O Lord, with Thine inspirations [that move us], and further them by Thine assistance; that every
word and work of ours may begin always with Thee, and by Thee, and
likewise ended."[16] In his recommendations, St. Louis-Marie delivers
the same idea: "In every action, we must consider how Mary has done
it, or how she would have done it, had she been in our place. ... We
must, from time to time, both during and after the action, renew the
same act and offering of union."[17] We must "begin, continue, and
finish all of our actions through her, with her, and in her."[18] At the
beginning of the action, "we must deliver ourselves to the heart of
Mary to be moved and," in the course of the action, "influenced by it
in the manner she chooses."[19]

ARTICLE 3: IN MARY

In the explanation above of how we are in Christ, we showed how
He is in us.[20] Let us do the same for the analogous formula, "in Mary,"
which is illuminated and completed by another, "Mary in us." The reciprocity is based on the nature of things, and lends itself to a more
accurate idea of Mary's presence that St. Louis-Marie urges us to
desire. As we go through the different meanings of these two phrases,
we shall specify what differentiates them from the formula "Christ
dwells in us, and we in Him."

We shall limit ourselves to the issues that matter to us, essentially
to the following four considerations: the efficient cause, the exemplary cause, the final cause, and the union by love, without repeating
the explanations already given above.

"When ... the divine Mary becomes Queen in a soul, O, there is
no marvel she would not work! ... She brings with her the purity of
heart and body, the purity in intention and design, into every interior

---

[16] ¦¦ *Missale*, §506: | ◆Actiones nostras, quæsumus Domine, aspirando præveni et ad-
juvando prosequere: ut cuncta nostra oratio et operatio a te semper incipiat, et per te
cœpta finiatur. Cf. Oratio, Dom. XVI post Pentec., ¦¦ *Missale*, §1593. |

[17] ◆*TD*, 181, 180.

[18] ◆*TD*, 77.

[19] ◆*TD*, 180.

[20] ◆Part 2.2, p. 112 ff.

where she is. ... She enlightens the mind by her pure faith; she deepens the heart by her humility, she enlarges and inflames it by her love."[21] "She conducts and directs us according to the will of her Son. ... She defends us and protects ¦¦ us against our enemies."[22] | Now every agent is present where he exerts his action; if he is not there in substance, he is, at least by his virtue or power. In this sense, therefore, we can affirm that Mary is present in us by her influence, although she is not there by her substance.

In a similar order of ideas, namely, in relation to the operation, we are in Mary, because we are subject to her influence, placed under her gaze, followed by her prayer, and protected by her assistance. We act *in her*, if, in order to act, we take on her insights and wishes as ours, and willingly fall under her guidance.

In relation to causality, there is a difference between "through Christ" and "through Mary," just as there is one between the phrases, "in Jesus" and "in Mary." As God, Jesus Christ is the principal cause of grace; as Man, He is an instrumental cause. He reaches to touch us by His divine power. Thus, we are in Him as in the *efficient* cause,[23] which directly and physically acts upon us; and, in the same manner, we are subject to His influence and operate by virtue of His grace. When we say: "Mary gives us this grace," "enlightens us," "guides us," defends us," and so on, we pass into another realm; that is, of *moral* causes and accounts of the moral order. In reality, Mary does not produce grace, but she works to have it produced in us by the Holy Ghost; she commands Angels to defend us, and so on. Thus, we are in her or act in her only insofar as we depend on her will and are influenced by her actions.

The proximate end of our devotion is "to become living copies of Mary, and to establish her life in us."[24] In the eyes of Jesus, Mary is a

---

[21] ♦Cf. *Secret*, 37, 38.

[22] *TD*, 146, 147; "against our enemies" added per the original French. Her protection, see also, 5, 26, 117, 126, 147, 185; her defense, 17.

[23] Part 1.2.1.2, p. 33.

[24] *TD*, 155; *Secret*, 33: "We must unite ourselves, through Mary, with the intentions of Jesus Christ; that is, we must become instruments in the hands of the Holy Virgin, in order that she may act in us, and for us, and that she may do with us as she it pleases her, for the greater glory of her Son, Jesus Christ, and by Him, the glory of the Father."

perfect copy. For us, she is the model from which we must be reproduced. Now, just as we say that the model exists in its copy by
resemblance, and, reciprocally, the copy is in the model which is the
cause of the resemblance; so also, do we resemble the Blessed Virgin
by imitating her virtues, and conforming to her intentions and dispositions. Thus, she is said to be in us, and we *in her*.

St. Louis-Marie summarizes these ideas in an analogy. He says
that Mary is the mold in which the God-Man came to be, and in which
the Saints were perfectly formed in the image of Christ. A mold is a
vessel that imparts its shape to the material poured into it. In other
words, it is both an instrument and a model. What the mold is to the
material encased in it, the thoughts, the wishes, the leading and providential influence of the Blessed Virgin are to our soul. They are like
the forms which shape her in the likeness of Mary, provided that we
wish to pour ourselves into the mold and meekly adapt to it[25]; that is,
to act and abide *in her*.

Let us not force the applicability of the analogy, lest we fail to
understand it. Poured material is encased in a mold, as in a specific
locality, while we are contained only by the influence of Mary's power
and will. The mold physically shapes the poured material, imprinting
its own form; while Mary's influence on us is only in the moral order.
What she produces in us is a form purely extrinsic; that is, a moral
resemblance through the conformity of dispositions, acts, and intentions. It is different from the supernatural likeness that God works in
us by grace. Such likeness may be accidental, but it nevertheless bears
a physical, intrinsic and permanent quality.

---

[25] ♦St. Louis-Marie quotes words attributed to St. Augustine: *Si formam Dei te appellem,
digna existis*, "you are worthy to be called the mold of God." No doubt, it is in Mary,
that the God-Man came to be. But there is another reason for our use of the word. All
the perfections God has distributed to creatures are found eminently in Mary. After the
Word becomes flesh, she becomes united to Him; and because of Him, she is the ideal
form according to which God created us; the same form to which He wills us to conform
in the order of grace. The text deserves to be quoted in its entirety: "Quid dicam pauper
ingenio, cum de te quidquid dixero, minus profecto est quam dignitas tua meretur? Si
matrem vocem gentium, præcellis; si formam Dei appellem, digna existis; si nutricem
cælestis panis vocitem, lactis dulcedine reples. Lacta ergo, mater, cibum nostrum; lacta
cibum Angelorum; lacta eum qui talem te fecit, ut ipse fieret in te." (St. Jerome, *Operum
mantissa*, Epistola 10, In Assump. B.V.M., §3, PL 30.149B). Cf. St. Augustine, *Sermones
supposititios*, 208, In Festo Assumpt. B.V.M., ¦¦ PL 39.2131, attributed to Fulbert de
Chartres: "Si cælum te vocem, altior es. Si matrem Gentium dicam, præcedis. *Si formam
Dei appellem, digna existis*. Si dominam Angelorum vocitem, per omnia esse probaris." |

Wherever St. Louis-Marie refers to the mold analogy in *True Devotion*, he always explains it in the rightful sense we just described.

On the question of living in union with Mary, St. Louis-Marie earnestly hopes that this glorious Queen will have supreme dominion over our hearts[26]; that is, that we be docile to her impulses and her guidance (Mary, as efficient cause). He prays the Holy Ghost find His beloved Spouse reproduced in souls that have become living copies of Mary[27] (considering her as our model). Lastly, when he writes that the principal effect of this devotion is to establish the life of Mary in a soul, so that the soul herself no longer lives, but that Mary lives in her, because Mary's soul takes her place, so to speak,[28] we understand him to mean that this is a union of thought and affection, in which two beings are become one. Let us elaborate:

We are in Mary and she is in us through the union of affection. As we explained above, the one who loves has in him the object of his love, in whom he lives and dwells reciprocally.[29] But now, even more thoroughly than elsewhere, let us note the difference of this two-fold formula "Christ in me" and "I in Him," with "Mary in me" and "I in her." In the first, we speak of a union very different from that expressed by the second; for we know that, by faith and charity, our soul attains to God Himself and that He abides in her by His substance.[30] In the second, we speak only of the presence of thought and the moral bond of affection, which establish two persons in a mutual relationship, and in a manner of speaking, make one pass into the other. When we renounce our notions,[31] intentions, our wills, to lose ourselves in Mary, as we are recommended to do, we act and abide in her, as she acts and dwells in us. In this conformity and moral union,

---

[26] *Secret*, 84; *TD*, 191. St. Louis-Marie simply writes, "empire," meaning *imperium*. He does not use the term "empire des cœurs."

[27] *TD*, 154.

[28] *Secret*, 37.

[29] Part 1.2.3.5, pp. 51-52.

[30] Eph 3.17-19.

[31] Whether our act is moral or not depends on its object, intention, and circumstances surrounding it. (St. Thomas, *Summa*, 1-2.18). Fr. Lhoumeau's "vues," translated in *TD* and *Secret* as "views," here and especially when coupled with "intentions" is rendered "notions."

we are fashioned into an *alter Maria*.

The exhortation of St. Ambrose quoted by our good Father de Montfort remains valid even if the soul of our Blessed Lady lives not substantially in ours: "Let the soul of Mary be in each of us to glorify the Lord; let the spirit of Mary be in each of us to rejoice in God."[32] The more we reflect on the unity of the Mystical Body of Christ, wherein all the members are connected and quickened by the same Spirit, the more we understand that, to be moral, the influence of Mary it is nonetheless true, effective, and of a higher order.

Closing this part of our discussion, we observe that, on the subject of "in Mary," *True Devotion* and *Secret of Mary* present but a series of metaphors. At first blush, we are tempted to see in those two works nothing but pious appeals—pure fluff—that do not go to the bottom of things; but, on reflection, we find it easy to be of one mind with St. Louis-Marie. He wrote the popular books quickly and without spending too much time pondering its finer points. Instead of definitions, he presents metaphors which, besides having the advantage of clarity, benefits from being able to suggest certain practical applications. Some, such as the towers of strength where we take refuge,[33] the garden wherein we walk, represent "to act in Mary"; others, such as the lamp which enlightens us, stand for the action of Mary in us.

By using these representations, St. Louis-Marie wishes to explain in what aspect we may consider things of the spiritual life and hopefully find in it the aid for our actions, whilst we sojourn in the interior of Mary.

ARTICLE 4: FOR MARY

§1. TO ACT FOR MARY

To the formula "through Mary, with her, and in her," St. Louis-Marie adds "for Mary." If he had been discussing the practice of the union with Jesus Christ, he would have also added "for Christ," after saying "through Him, with Him, and in Him." However, he was

---

[32] ¦¦ St. Ambrose, *In Lucam*, 2.26, PL 15.1561: "Sit in singulis Mariæ anima, ut magnificet Dominum, sit in singulis spiritus Mariæ, ut exsultet in Deo." | ◆*TD*, 154. — These last words may be understood as the Holy Ghost or the spirit of Mary, as has been shown previously, and all the more so since the Holy Ghost truly dwells in the soul of the just.
[33] *TD*, 182.

content to show that the union with Christ is the end of our devotion to the Blessed Virgin. It is only when he comes to the discussion on the means of achieving such end, that he speaks of the union with Mary in all our actions; that is, he completes the formula for the interior practice.

When we are asked: "To what end do you act?" We answer: "Mary"; that is, to serve her by fulfilling her will, to glorify her by making her known and loved. Notice that to act for Mary, to choose her for the end of our actions, is also a manner of acting in her, similar to acting for Jesus Christ that we explained above[34]; for we are encompassed in her, as the means is comprised in the end, when we rely on Mary, and subject ourselves to her according to God's plan. And within this end—assuredly not the last, but a proximate end—our will abides and rests at its aim.[35]

This is precisely what St. Louis-Marie asks us to do when he wants us to enter and sojourn in the interior of Mary.[36]

"For Mary" summarizes the practical direction of the whole formula "through her," "with her," and "in her."

Indeed, in our action, we reach our end last, but we think of it first; we set it as a point of reference, as a guide to our choice of the means to attain it, and at the outset and throughout our undertaking, we attune ourselves and adjust to it. Thus, in our acts, it suffices to hew to the purity of intention; that is, to the choice of a pure end. If we do so, we shall reap the happy consequence of exercising our acts under the impulse of grace, which we will follow obediently, and thereby unite with God.

We conclude that it is fitting to add "for Mary" to other phrases in the formula related principally to the practice of our devotion.

---

[34] ♦Part 1.2.3.4, p. 48 ff.

[35] ♦The dwelling (mansio) in the sense given in the Gospel—*In my Father's house there are many mansions* (Jn 14.2)—stands for the eternal bliss where the soul reposes and stays as in her end. But the habitual union with Mary, where our devotion leads us, is also an end in itself. It is true that Mary is a way to Jesus and that we go to her only to find Him, but it is with her and in her that we find Him. We can, therefore, take her as a subordinate end, and as such, repose in her.

[36] *TD*, 183: "Oh, what riches! what glory! what pleasure! what happiness! to be able to enter in and dwell in Mary, where the Most High has set up the throne of His supreme glory!"

§2. FOR MARY, OUT OF LOVE

One may ask, "Why do we take Mary for the end of our actions?" Because we belong unreservedly to this glorious Lady and are sworn entirely to serve her. On this account, St. Louis-Marie asks: As servants and faithful slaves, have we not the obligation to work always for her glory and according to her will?[37]

There is another motive that urges us to act for this good Mother, and that is the love we wish to show her by the practice of our devotion; for we seek to honor, to serve, to gladden the heart of those whom we love. Jesus "lived for His Father. || His plan is to communicate His Spirit to all Christians so that they, too, may live for God. |"[38] Who will tell us of how Mary lived for Jesus, and make us understand?

§3. MARY, OUR PROXIMATE END

Is it true that we may take the Blessed Virgin as the end of our actions, and in what sense may we admit of it?

There is no need for long reflections to understand how much this issue offered ample matter for the cries of the Jansenists. Cutting short the ridiculous attacks of these heretics, St. Louis-Marie, took care several times to explain his thought. "It is not that we can take her for the last end of our works," he says, "for Jesus Christ alone is such end; but we may take her for our *proximate end*, our mysterious means, and our easy way to go to Him."[39]

And why should we fear doing this? God Himself, does He not provide us an example? He did everything for His Son, says St. Paul.[40] He created the world to manifest this eminent exemplar, modeled it on that divine archetype that sums it up and crowns it; the archetype Who is its *alpha*, the beginning, as well as its *omega*, the end. Everything begins with Christ and everything ends in Him. His reign is the consummation of all things. Now, in the divine plan, Mary is

---

[37] "Prayer to Mary," *Secret*, 54: "My portion here below, I wish for no other but that which thou didst have, that is to say, ... to labor bravely for thee, even until death, without any interest of my own, as the vilest of thy slaves."
[38] Décrouïlle, *Méditations*, 2:109.
[39] *TD*, 185.
[40] Heb 2.10: It was fitting that He, *propter quem omnia*, for whom all things are, ... in bringing many sons to glory, should make the author of their salvation perfect through His Passion.

inseparable from her Son. Because of Him and in union with Him, though she may be subordinate to Him, she is *the beginning of the ways of God* (Job 40.14), and an eminent exemplar and an *intermediate end*. Thus, St. Bernard could say in truth: "All was made and every creature exists for her, after Christ."[41]

If we pass from the subject of Creation to the one of Redemption, we are taught that the Blessed Virgin is its principal end and the most magnificent trophy. Was it not for her especially that Jesus was born, suffered, and died? Many Fathers say so, and St. Albert the Great sums up the thought in these words: "Mary was predestined to be the final cause of our entire reparation; her glory, after the glory of God, to be the aim of all Redemption."[42]

Let us say again that, in religion, Mary is the proximate and subordinate end, and always because of Christ and in relation to Him.[43] If we wish to understand this, we only have to recall the universal mediation of our divine Mother. All lead to her, all is concentrated in her hands, all pass through her, before they are lifted up to Christ; and through Him, to God: be they praises, supplications, or homage of every kind. Is it then too much that we should offer our

---

[41] "Propter quam, post Christum, omnia; propter quam omnis creatura facta est." The attribution to St. Bernard is repeated in many theology textbooks since as early as the 18th century, and lately produced verbatim in Bourassé, *Summa B.V.M.*, N. 1739, 8:64: "Virgo sit causa finalis omnis rei creatæ, quia ipsa est, 'propter quam omnis creatura facta est,' uti loquitur sanctus Bernardus Serm. 3, *in Salve Regina*; item 'propter quam post Christum omnia,' ut ait sanctus Henricus Suso, c. 20, *Dialogi Sapientia*." — We find (1) among the works of St. Bernard is *In Salve Regina*, Sermo 3.2, PL 184.1069: "Concludam, de hac et ob hunc, et propter hanc omnis Scriptura facta est, propter hanc totus mundus factus est, et hæc gratia hei plena est, et per hanc homo redemptus est, Verbum Dei caro factum est, Deus humilis, et homo sublimis"; and (2) Seuse, "Dialogus," c. 20, *Opera*, 106: "Tu, Domina Mater, post Filium initium es, et medium, tu quoque finis eris." Curiously, van den Berghe, *Marie*, note 1, 13, writes: "Bernard *de Tolède*, parlant de Marie: 'Propter ~ (*In Salve*, Serm. 3)."

[42] St. Albert the Great, "Mariale," 146, *Opera* 37:209.1 : "Dominus beatissimæ Virginis opus recreationis secundum quatuor genera causarum communicavit. Causa efficiens nostra regenerationis post Deum, sub Deo, et cum Deo, ipsa fuit: quia illa illum nobis genuit, qui nos omnes regeneravit, et ipsum gignere suis virtutibus de congruo promeruit. Item, causa materialis, quia Spiritus sanctus de purissimis carnibus ejus et sanguinibus, ipsius consensu mediante, carnem sumpsit: quam in corpus transformavit per quod redempto nostra facta fuit. Item causa finalis fuit: quia per totum opus redemptionis post Deum in ipsius gloriam et honorem ordinatum fuit."

[43] ♦Finis non ratione sui, sed ratione alterius, "she is not an end by reason of herself, but by reason of something else," as expressed in philosophy. ¦¦ The reference is to Aristotle, *Nich. Ethics*, 1101b. On the dictum in the affirmative as applied to honoring Christ Our Lord, see St. Thomas, 3 Sent. 9.1.2.7, *Opera*, 9:154-157. |

life, and bear our humble actions, to this Virgin, who is blessed above
all creatures, and whom the Lord has set as the summit and purpose
of Creation, Redemption and religion? Indeed, not. Let us have the
fervor of that zeal which made our good Father de Montfort exclaim:
"We must not remain idle; but, buttressed by her protection, we must
undertake and achieve great things for this august Sovereign."[44]

---

[44] Cf. *TD*, 185.

SPIRITUAL CHILDHOOD

n the above discussion on the interior exercise we brought to light the character of the perfect devotion to the Blessed Virgin. We have pointed out ideas, made sure to outline certain characteristics, lest we misunderstand them, when we spoke of the slavery of love, the motherhood of Mary, the essence of our consecration to the Blessed Virgin; but, given the considerations in the preceding chapter, we need only briefly reflect before we find what we have not, perhaps, sufficiently examined; namely, the intimate link between the perfect devotion and spiritual childhood. *Unless you be converted, and become as little children, you shall not enter into the Kingdom of Heaven* (Mt 18.3). Yet, both are driven by the same idea. We may, no doubt, live out this spiritual childhood without the use of our special form of devotion to the Blessed Virgin. We cannot deny, however, that our devotion is the perfect practical result of such childhood, and a powerful means of establishing the reign of God in us. It is precisely because of this close link that St. Louis-Marie wrote these remarkable words: "I do not think anyone can acquire an intimate union with Our Lord, and a perfect fidelity to the Holy Ghost, without a great union with the Virgin most holy, and a great dependence on her succor."[1]

Let us now consider the object, motives, and practices of spiritual childhood so that we may easily recognize its ideas in our devotion.

§1.

¦ There is hardly a page in the works of St. Louis-Marie that does

---

[1] ♦*TD*, 23-24.

not contain some reference or allusion to the motherhood of the Blessed Virgin. We will not tire the reader with endless repetition, but we should remind him that this perfect devotion is due her because of her divine maternity. | It also bears mentioning that if we honor Mary as mediatrix, we look to her spiritual motherhood as the principal function of her mediation; and that we proclaim her Lady or Sovereign with due regard to her motherhood. In sum, the *formal* object of our devotion is Mary, Mother of God and Mother of Mankind. If such is the mother in the mystery of our spiritual childhood, what of the child?

§2.

Each one of us is that child. Next to our spiritual filiation, we shall delve into the conditions of divine life in our souls. We shall use the analogies of the infirmities, deficiencies, and needs in the natural childhood.

When we come to the explanation of the truths on which St. Louis-Marie bases his devotion, or the motives by which he draws us to it, we realize that all relates to our quality as spiritual children of Mary, and to that state of poverty and frailty, which in spiritual life is a true state of childhood. The causes are diverse:

As a result of the Fall,[2] all life on earth begins with imperfection and deficiency, requiring care and nurture. Be it life vegetative, animal or intellectual: all follow the same rule. To be born into supernatural life, we need to meet the conditions of being *as newborn babes longing for the pure spiritual milk* (1 Pet 2.2).[3] The Church applies these words of the Apostle to the newly baptized, in whom the life of grace is still weak and imperfect. They need the nourishment and care appropriate to children. Confirmation may perfect these newborns in their supernatural constitution, but they still need to grow up in faith.

Spiritual childhood is part of the ordinary course of things, and

---

[2] Fr. Lhoumeau: "Depuis la Création." Strictly speaking, all creatures (save the angels who rebelled before our first parents sinned) were in harmony with Creation, and Adam and Eve were in the state of innocence and righteousness, until they sinned. (*Catechism*, 1.2.18-19, 28).

[3] ◆Introit, Dominica in Albis, ¦¦ *Missale*, §1216: "Quasi modo geniti infantes, alleluja: rationabile, sine dolo lac concupiscite, alleluja, alleluja, alleluja." RSV, trans.; DR: As newborn babes desire the rational milk without guile. |

St. Louis-Marie does not lose sight of it in his teaching. He alludes to it, when he imagines us, sometimes borne in the arms of Mary, nourished by her milk,[4] receiving the grace of God from her in proportion to our frailty,[5] and eating the Bread of Angels formed in her for her children.[6]

Alas! If only there were no other cause for this state of infancy, its frailty and its needs than the condition inherent in all life that begins on earth! We know full well that the imperfection of our spiritual life comes from the infirmities and obstacles which trace their source to Original Sin, and which worsens the personal sins we commit here on earth. St. Paul speaks to us of this miserable childhood, when he writes to the Corinthians: *And I, brethren, could not speak to you as unto spiritual, but as unto carnal men. I gave you milk to drink, not meat; for you were not able as yet* (1 Cor 3.1, 2). Many times did St. Louis-Marie return to this thought: "Poor children of Mary," he cries, "I must admit, your frailty is extreme; your inconstancy, great; your interior nature, thoroughly corrupted."[7] In the formula of consecration, it is as sinner and unfaithful that we resort to Mary, so that she may count us among the number of those whom she loves, whom she teaches, whom she guides, and whom she nourishes and protects, as her children.[8]

Aided by his extensive experience counseling souls, and the light of higher understanding possessed by holy men, St. Louis-Marie often reflected on the condition of spiritual life in us. Steeped as he was in the glories and functions of Mary, Mother of God and Mother of Mankind; and, in his ministry, having non-stop contact with souls that exhibit (alas!) every degree of defect and frailty of children, he came to a simple and profound conclusion: If you have a mother and a child, and you put him in her arms, she cannot refuse to nurse him, protect him, and raise him. This insight is the basis of our devotion, of our system of spirituality. In sum, Mary gives birth to us in the life of grace and takes care to raise us in it.

---

[4] *TD*, 25.
[5] *TD*, 96.
[6] *TD*, 145.
[7] Cf. *TD*, 123.
[8] *TD*, 193.

❖

"To raise a child" is a beautiful and righteous word. The mother first raises the child materially, seeing to it that he develops physically and gains strength until he can stand up straight and steady, overcoming his natural frailty, which inclines him to fall to the ground. She then raises him above the animal life in which he was born, and which at first dominates him, and almost drowns his human life. Lastly, she raises him into the life of reason, by helping him to develop the faculties of his soul. Taking care to provide a Christian education, she will contribute to the growth of his supernatural life, the seeds of which Baptism sows in him.

Such is the role of Mary, and the image of our spiritual education. Indeed, we have the need of being lifted above the life of the senses, the life terrestrial and animal, to which, burdened by the weight of our vicious nature, we fall again and again. Too frail to support ourselves, to stand up straight (that is, in that rectitude of thought and will with which the Creator had originally endowed us), we, as do little children who are always falling down to the ground, we need the helping hand of a mother who holds us up, who each time puts us back on our feet, and who lifts us to the things above.

> This good Mother and Lady
> Aids me all 'round puissantly,
> And when I fall by frailty,
> She lifts me up instantly.[9]

However, as far as we are concerned, this is not the only consideration in the link between spiritual childhood and our perfect devotion. If we have the frailties and deficiencies of childhood, we must also acquire its qualities. What children are by condition and necessity, we shall be by virtue. It is the very thing that Our Lord teaches when He commands us to become like little children such that we may enter the Kingdom of Heaven.[10] That this is what is practiced in the devotion of St. Louis-Marie, we need be convinced only by briefly considering the acts and the dispositions which it inspires in us.

---

[9] ♦*Cantiques*, 77.11, 132: "Cette bonne Mère et Maîtresse / Me secourt partout puissamment, / Et quand je tombe par faiblesse, / Elle me relève à l'instant."
[10] Mt 18.3.

§3.

What most distinguishes childhood is its most striking attribute; that is, the state of dependence. A child is most often left to the care of his mother, and we may say of every child what Msgr. Gay writes about Jesus: "First of all, it is to His holy Mother, bar none, that He entrusts His childhood. In the nine months that she bears Him in her immaculate womb, He is entirely hers. He leaves not her side during the entirety of His infancy. He stays in her arms, breathes and lives in her bosom. She it is that immediately meets all his needs. Joseph is indeed the head of the Holy Family, but as with all families, the father is on the scene less than the mother during the first years; there is less for him to do in that time. Later, in Nazareth, he will exercise his authority; for it is in the fitness of things that the father should govern the adolescent son. In Bethlehem, in the Temple of Jerusalem, and at the beginning of their sojourn in Egypt, the primary role in the life of Jesus rests with Mary. She alone wakes Him up and puts Him to bed; she alone swaddles Him and clothes Him; she alone nourishes Him with her milk and keeps Him warm; and when there was need to go here or there, she alone carried Him."[11] This is why the Gospel tells us that we will find *the Child with Mary, His Mother* (Mt 2.11). What must we conclude, but that "one of the many and holy effects of spiritual childhood is to deliver our soul to the Blessed Virgin in a very special and entirely intimate way"[12]? There is no mistaking it, these words describe the main characteristic of our devotion, which is to give ourselves to Mary and be entirely dependent on her as our Mother. For what purpose? So that she may form us in the supernatural life and bring us up to its perfection: "It is by Mary that the littlest ones, without any fear, are to ascend perfectly and divinely to the Most High."[13]

This state of childhood shows us that our total dependence on the Blessed Virgin should be a slavery of love. Now observe how the child is left to the care of his mother: She guides him, motivates him to act,

---

[11] ◆Gay, *Élévations*, 19, 1:162-163.

[12] ◆Ibid. 19, 1:163.

[13] ◆*TD*, 107.

puts him to bed or wakes him up when it suits her. She may very well put him at risk of peril for her lack of care. And, would we need to question to what extent she holds an influence over his body or even his soul? In a child, such dependence is the consequence of his native helplessness; but, aided by his instinctive, if not reasoned, love, he naturally abandons himself to her. This is the mark of the slavery of love. Who, apart from his mother, could handle a child without provoking his cries? Is it not her love that always calls him back to her? He is happy and at rest, so long as he is in her arms.

Truth be told, we are compelled to depend on Mary also by necessity. We are beset by the powerlessness and needs which lay claim on her help, and without recourse to her we are at risk of being lost. There is but love, a free and generous love, that leads us to this point and makes us practice such a perfect dependence; and we may indeed call it a slavery of love.

If we cast our eye on the effects that our perfect devotion to Mary produces in the soul, we shall see that they are the same as those of spiritual childhood. On both, it is the same idea that motivates, and we need not be surprised to see it inspire in us the same acts and the same dispositions.

Do you observe humility, purity, simplicity in Christian spiritual childhood? We know them to be the fruits of our devotion to Mary; but let us add to them peace and constancy, docility, trust, and sweet surrender. Spiritual childhood is also a way of perfection, according to the words from holy Scripture: *Out of the mouth of infants and of sucklings Thou hast perfected praise*–Ps 8.3. *Whosoever therefore shall humble himself as this little child, he is the greater in the Kingdom of Heaven*–Mt 18.4. Let us recognize in them the progress in spiritual life and the perfection of our works, whose production is occasioned by the means unique to the Holy Slavery to Mary.

Jesu, tibi sit gloria,
Qui te revelas parvulis.[14]

---

[14] ◆Hymn, Transfiguratione, *Brev. Rom.*, 747, 750.

"Jesus, to Thee our praise we pay; to little ones revealed today!" We, too, O Lord, long to be as little children, left to the care of our Mother, and keen we are to be with her, that we may be humble and pure. This You do require of us that we may see You, when You say: *Blessed are the clean of heart: for they shall see God* (Mt 5.8). Is it not Mary who shows You and delivers You for all of mankind? That time, at Bethlehem, this she did for the shepherds and the Magi; now everywhere, she reveals You to the souls who seek You through her mediation. May she illumine our souls with the clear light of faith; may she teach us the knowledge of Christ, of which she is the incomparable teacher. Lastly, we pray with the Church, that after the sorrows of this exile end, to the delight of our eyes, she may one day reveal You, O Jesus, the blessed fruit of her womb: *Et Jesum, benedictum fructum ventris tui, nobis post hoc exilium ostende.*[15]

We end this part with a summary of the perfect devotion to Mary: It is the union with Jesus, the life divine, coming and growing in us by means of a Mother; it is perfection reduced to formulas we find in nursery schools, and used to teach the little ones who are still hesitant to speak, all of which are grounded on the fundamental truths of Christianity. They are sweet and profound insights, enough to give us the right idea of St. Louis-Marie. We hesitate to paint a picture of him with the characteristics of his life which have been poorly or inadequately explained. Instead, let us regard him the way he paints himself in his writings, and by doing so, we shall see him most closely resembling St. Bernard in the manner the Church has judged.[16] The conception of the system of spirituality we have described should be enough to show us the candid and affectionate soul of the man whom a multitude of people today still call "good Father de Montfort."[17] He

---

[15] Hymn, *Salve Regina*.

[16] ✦Church, S.C.R., "Decree," Feb 21, 1886, in *Béatification*, 12 ⁞⁞: "Ought we not to regard as a marvel of divine virtue the labors of his holy missions, and all that he undertook to excite the fervor of faith and charity throughout western France, to dispel the subtle errors of the Jansenist heresy by the brilliance of Catholic truth, everywhere to propagate the piety towards the august mysteries of the Passion of Our Lord, and to the Immaculate Virgin, Mother of God, especially by the habitual recitation the Rosary of Mary? In this devotion, he yields nothing to any of the valiant disciples of St. Dominic, and he is rightly considered to be the equal of St. Bernard." On the significance of Louis-Marie de Montfort's beatification, see de Fiores, "Memoria," *Quaderni Monfortani*, 1989, 6:3-5. |

[17] Quéméneur, *de Montfort*, 7: "Le peuple disait: 'Ce Bon Père de Montfort' ou le 'Père

preached this devotion. He lived it. One wonders from what visual angle anyone could have seen in him the characteristic of a rustic and an unlearned Saint.[18]

---

au grand chapelet.' Les gueux le définissaient, 'Celui qui aime tant les pauvres.'"

[18] Laveille, *de Montfort*, 126: "A number of writers saw nothing in him but a notable figure of high virtue, though almost unsociable due to his impetuousness and severity. '*Quel rude saint!*' they say after pondering portraits unbecoming of him. They wonder how this man who seems to disdain genteel virtues, who longs only for crosses, disciplines, and hair shirts, was able to gather and keep abreast of two religious families."

PART IV:

THE ASCETIC VIEW ON THE PERFECT DEVOTION

CHAPTER 1:

EXERCISES TO PREPARE FOR THE CONSECRATION

n Parts I and II we discussed the dogmatic truths that serve as the foundation of our special devotion to the Blessed Virgin. In Part III, we made an excursus on spirituality, examining the nature and substance of the Holy Slavery to Mary. We now study the practice and effects of our devotion from an ascetic point of view. We justify what we said at the beginning: That this devotion is not merely a collection of pious practices, but a complete system of spirituality that embraces the entirety of our interior life and gives it its proper form.

St. Louis-Marie advises us to prepare ourselves for our consecration by carrying out certain exercises which, although not obligatory, will assuredly render it most efficacious, given that they establish us in purity and other requisite dispositions. We cannot therefore countenance the neglect of this preparation by those who are desirous of making their consecration a serious act and a consequential influence on their Christian life. The exercises are divided into two: A preliminary period of twelve days in which one works to empty oneself of the spirit of the world; followed by a period lasting three weeks, the first of which is used to know one self; the second, to know the Blessed Virgin; and the third, to know Jesus Christ.[1]

We are generally inclined to compare these exercises favorably to those of St. Ignatius of Loyola's. There are assuredly more intimate resemblances between the two than their division into weeks; but there are also notable differences. Besides, if the preparation sketched broadly by St. Louis-Marie exhibits not the rigorous order and the

---

[1] *TD*, 160-164.

many details of *The Spiritual Exercises*, it neither seems impossible nor contrary to the thoughts of St. Louis-Marie to elaborate, by using his own writings, what he commits to us only in summary. We thus have a series of exercises suitable either for a retreat or for spiritual direction in general. With adaptations or modifications for the different categories of persons, they will be useful for the conversion of sinners, as well as the spiritual progress of the righteous.

Just like the weeks in the *Exercises* of St. Ignatius of Loyola, the periods mentioned by St. Louis-Marie do not make for a rigorous and immutable division. For instance, it is possible to prolong or abridge them, as needed.[2]

We shall briefly comment on the assertions in *True Devotion*, because our purpose here is to guide the faithful, and to suggest certain ideas for them, rather than present a comprehensive plan of spiritual exercises.

ARTICLE 1: THE TWELVE PRELIMINARY DAYS

St. Louis-Marie proposes to establish or perfect in us the reign of Christ through Mary; but whether he wishes to secure our conversion and our perseverance, or calls us to perfection, he invariably takes us back to the point of our departure; that is, to the baptismal font where we were born to grace. O how good it is to breathe the air of our rebirth, regain our strength, and heal our infirmities! Drawn near to the sacred font, we shall fill our lungs with the vivifying breath of the Holy Ghost Who delivered us unto the true life on contact with the holy water.[3]

Let us recall the formula of our baptismal promises: "I renounce Satan, his works, and his pomps, and give myself to Jesus Christ

---

[2] ♦The faithful often take just three days to prepare themselves for the annual renewal of their consecration.

[3] ♦Jn 3.5: *Nisi quis renatus fuerit ex aqua, et Spiritu Sancto, non potest introire in regnum Dei*, "unless a man be born again of water and the Holy Ghost, he cannot enter into the Kingdom of God." ¦¦ The ancient ceremonies of adult Baptism unfold in stages, successively closer to the baptismal font, beginning on Friday, third week in Lent, outside the church, with the questioning, exsufflation, and imposition of salt; then on Wednesday, fourth week in Lent, at the church door, with the exorcism and admission into the church; on Holy Saturday, in front of the baptismal chapel, with the solemn exorcism, the *ephphetha*, renunciation, and anointing; and culminating at Easter night, in the chapel, with the Baptism itself. (Church, *Rituale Romanum*, 30-63).¦

forever."[4] The same is the purpose of the devotion that St. Louis-Marie preaches, and the whole plan of his preparation is this: First, renounce Satan and the world; then, give ourselves perfectly to Jesus Christ. At the head of his preparatory exercises, our good Father de Montfort thus asks that we employ at least twelve days to empty ourselves of the spirit of the world, which is contrary to the Spirit of Jesus Christ.[5] To that end, the faithful may make use of the following considerations: 1. What is meant by the spirit of the world which is contrary to the Spirit of Jesus Christ? 2. In what form does it manifest itself? 3. What are the works and the pomps of the world and how should we recognize them?

§1. WHAT DOES THE SPIRIT OF THE WORLD CONSIST OF?

Essentially, it consists of the denial of the sovereign dominion of God; a denial that, in practice, is manifested in sin or disobedience and is the principal manner whereby the spirit of the world opposes the Spirit of Jesus, which is also the spirit of Mary.

We must thus give due consideration to the absolute dominion of God over us, as well as over all creatures, and meditate on our obligation to serve Him; for such is our end and the reason for our existence. We must regard this meditation as *fundamental*, especially given the needs of our spirituality. Clearly, the considerations and the resolutions may be qualified according to the condition of the one who makes it. As we saw in the chapter on Holy Slavery,[6] the rights and obligations of our divine membership may vary. For example, the soul committed to the states of perfection and consecrated by the vows of religion belongs more closely to God. Such a soul will thus offer herself to an ampler and more perfect exercise of divine rights over her.

Other truths of faith will converge on this fundamental insight. If need be, they may become for us the themes of complementary meditations, among which we shall mention only the consideration of Heaven and Hell, as well as Divine Providence, but always from the

---

[4] In the ceremonies of Baptism, the renunciation is followed by the anointing, in which it is the Priest who says, "I anoint you with the oil of salvation in Christ Jesus Our Lord, so that you may have everlasting life."

[5] *TD*, 161.

[6] Part 1.4, p. 70 ff.

viewpoint at issue. Everywhere and in every state in this life, God governs us by His laws, whether natural, revealed, or of legitimate
powers; we are ever in His all-powerful hand and are but His instruments, whether by will of by force. Let us not try to elude this absolute
dominion beyond this our life, because when we die we must needs
fall under one of two alternatives: Hell, where the Lord compels and
chastises those who have not voluntarily submitted to Him; Heaven,
where He grants eternal bliss to those who took up His yoke with love.
Therein lies the ideal of His reign and the perfection of our divine
belonging.

§2. THE THREE-FOLD MANIFESTATION
AND NOTES OF THE SPIRIT OF THE WORLD.

Selfishness, or the "me" opposed to God, is like a trunk whose
three branches are *the concupiscence of the flesh, the concupiscence of
the eyes, and the pride of life* (1 Jn 2.16). The acts and the end of the spirit
of the world are manifested by disobedience to the laws of God and
by the disordered use of creatures.

There we have the subjects of a meditation perfectly suited to the
character of our devotion.

Let us also not forget to examine the marks left in our soul, under
the three-fold form, by the spirit of the world. Let us then set the formal and sometimes strict teachings of the Gospel against it. We
cannot do without this examination if we desire to free our Christian
life from all adulterations. If the soul, not content merely to have
escaped the clutches of sin, aspires to perfection, she will have to pursue further the purification from the spirit of the world and seek to
root it out. We note that the religious need only make an examination
of the perfect practice of the three solemn undertakings precisely
opposed to the triple concupiscence, ¦¦ namely, the vows of poverty,
chastity, and obedience. For the layman, Dom Guéranger has this
advice: "He who yet lives in the world, but desires to be what his
Creator would have him be, without the aid of the real separation
which the religious makes, must be quite as completely detached
from his own will, and sensuality, and riches, in order that all his
intentions and aspirations may be fixed on the eternal home, where
his one infinite, beloved treasure is. If he does not bring himself, even

amidst his riches, to be as poor in spirit as the religious are in deed, his progress will be checked at the very first step he takes in the contemplative life; and, if he allows the obstacle to block up the way, he must give up all idea of rising, in light and love, above the lowly paths of the preponderance of Christians."[7] |

§3. THE WORKS AND THE POMPS OF SATAN.

By "the works of Satan" we mean sin in all its forms, and everything by which the devil induces us to sin: as to the mind, the works of error and of darkness; as to the will, seduction and corruption. Indeed, the "pomps of the devil" are all the flashes and charms by which he makes sin appear appealing to people, things, and institutions. We ought to renounce them all, to keep as far from them as we can, and to disentangle our hearts from them. How can we accomplish that if, by the light of faith, we fail to see them for the deceptions that they are? We may break the spell that holds our soul captive by discovering the horrible and frightening realities they hide. Let us convince ourselves that, despite its allures, sin is evil; and that evil is a misfortune here below, and even more so in eternity. What is Hell, if not sin committed, fixed in the soul, and all its consequences reaching their full maturity?

This consideration is fruitful for our meditation, because it is profound, binding time to eternity, shining a bright light on that true and vivid day, and making Heaven and Hell distant realities no longer, since, even in this life, we see them strike root and sprout in us, the one by grace; the other, due to sin.

One can also suggest readings on these different subjects; but it is not enough to read, to meditate, and to examine our conscience in order to empty oneself of the spirit of the world. One must also pray and act.

In any form, prayer is undoubtedly acceptable. Still, we need to choose the prayers suited to our intentions. St. Louis-Marie recommends special prayers for the later periods of preparation, but not for the twelve days. We may augment them by consulting his other writings, notably the book, *Love of the Eternal Wisdom*,[8] to meet our

---

[7] Guéranger, Dom. XIV, Post Pentec., *Liturgical Year*, 11:341.

[8] See, *Eternal Wisdom*, §§191-192, 37.

needs. We shall pray often to the Blessed Virgin most holy, in a manner befitting the substance of our spirituality, with a view towards
obtaining the gift of wisdom, and she will intercede for us before her
divine Son.

Lastly, we must practice renunciation and mortification, and seek
always to keep a pure heart, for this purity is the necessary precondition to seeing God in glory, and catching a glimpse of Him or knowing
Him better here on earth, aided by the light of faith. Divine Wisdom
dwells not in the heart that is a slave to sin. Let us then work to purify
ourselves, but in the special way that suits us; that is, by applying ourselves to the interior exercise of our devotion, of which we shall speak
below.

ARTICLE 2: THE FIRST WEEK

After the preliminary period, when the land has been cleared for
cultivation, so to speak, St. Louis-Marie wants us to take three weeks
so that we may be filled with the Spirit of Jesus Christ through the
Blessed Virgin.[9] He says "be filled," for inasmuch as we are not able to
renounce the world entirely, we cannot have the Spirit of Jesus Christ
completely. This Spirit must yet abound in us and possess us fully.[10]

"During the first week," he says, "they should employ all their
prayers and pious actions in asking for a knowledge of themselves,
and for contrition of their sins; and they should do this with a humble
heart."[11] At first glance, this first week seems to be a duplication of the
twelve days prior, for how can we empty ourselves of the spirit of the
world without examining our conscience and knowing ourselves?
However, if we take a closer look, we see that in the exercises set for
this week, we are taking a step forward, although we are not yet leaving the purgative way. To be rid of the spirit of the world, so bent on
incubating and hatching evil, is to flee from sin, and to seek conversion. However, our devotion is not concerned with merely renouncing
Satan in order to return to God; but, as we said above, it is also a path
that leads to perfection.

---

[9] *TD*, 161.
[10] Rom 15.13: Now the God of hope fill you with all joy and peace in believing; that you
may abound in hope, and in the power of the Holy Ghost.
[11] •Cf. *TD*, 161.

Now, the masters of spiritual life regard humility as the foundation of all ascetic work. We cannot acquire it, if we know not our own self. A sure sign that we have made some progress in our self-knowledge is our questioning to what degree we are imbued with the spirit of the world; and, though there may be powerful reasons for being humble, such as our physical infirmities, moral frailties, and condition as creatures lacking in many things, we cannot lay the blame for such things at its feet. In this first week, we ought to observe less the opposition between the Spirit of Jesus and the yearnings of our heart, and focus more on the miserable and humiliating state to which sin has reduced us. This is why, as soon as he mentions the contrition for sins which self-knowledge naturally excites, St. Louis-Marie adds ¦ that we should pray and do our pious acts in an attitude of abject humility.[12] ¦

Another reflection will confirm us in this way of looking at things, and enable us to better grasp the thought of St. Louis-Marie regarding the aim of his devotion, which is to unite ourselves perfectly to Jesus. He wants to lead us there *through Mary*. Given the limitations imposed by our extreme frailty and corrupt nature, the way through Mary is, for St. Louis-Marie, an easy, short, perfect, and secure one that leads to Jesus. We cannot be serious in taking this path and binding ourselves to our Mother, if we are not strongly convinced that we are miserable and powerless creatures. How can we begin our journey without even a modicum of self-knowledge? ¦¦ St. Louis-Marie shows us the way. He says that those who wish to begin our devotion should, in the six days of this week, consider themselves "snails, crawling things, toads, swine, serpents, and unclean animals; or they can reflect on the three considerations of St. Bernard, the vileness of our origin, the dishonors of our present state, and our ending as the food of worms: *Cogita quid fueris, sperma putridum; quid sis, vas stercorum; quid eris, esca vermium*.[13] They should pray Our Lord and the Holy Ghost to enlighten them; and for that end they might use the aspiratory prayers, *Domine, ut videam*, 'Lord, let me see'[14]; or *Noverim me*,

---

[12] *TD*, 161.

[13] Ps. Bernard, PL 184.1174A: "Quid fuisti, quia sperma fetidum; quid es, quia vas stercorum; quid eris, quia esca vermium."

[14] Mk 10.51, Lk 18.41.

'Lord, let me know myself'[15]; or *Veni Sancte Spiritus, reple tuorum corda fidelium,* 'Come, Holy Ghost, fill the hearts of Thy faithful'; and they may say daily the *Ave maris stella,* and the litany of the Holy Ghost."[16] | In addition, the part St. Louis-Marie devotes to the considerations on humility and the examination of our needs is sufficient testimony that | he always intended for the perfect union with Jesus Christ to be our end. | On this we may be assured by perusing through the pages dedicated to this first week, wherein we may also find the motives that ought to draw us to our devotion to the Blessed Virgin.

If we wish to determine precisely to which end and in what manner we should make the effort to know ourselves, we must recall that we shall not know how to purify ourselves and develop in our union with Jesus Christ, if we know not how to tell the movements of our vicious nature apart from the action of grace in us. A debauched soul has no self-awareness, and often is willfully blind to the movements that so easily push, pull, and sway her; never mind recognizing that, in many circumstances, she would find it difficult to sense their very different origins. Laboring to know ourselves, we shall overcome the difficulty. We shall enter into that interior life whose threshold so many souls hardly cross, but who God still calls to perfection.

Thus far, what appears to us the goal for the first week. Prayers, readings or meditations may be assigned as suggested by St. Louis-Marie. The faithful may also choose their own. What is important is that all the prayers, examinations of conscience, reflections, be done at the feet of Mary. It is from her that we await the light to know ourselves; by her side that we fathom the depths of our miseries without plunging into despair. And, keep this in mind: There are indeed degrees of self-knowledge, and it must lead us to a full understanding of our unworthiness, for the essence of humility, the highest and most profitable lesson, *sui ipsius cognitio et despectio,* is truly to know and

---

[15] St. Augustine, *Soliloquiorum,* 2.1.1, PL 32.887.
[16] *TD,* 161.

to despise ourselves, says the *Imitation*.[17] Let us not forget, however, that if we intend to go so far, we should not separate what the Lord has united; that is, meekness and humility: *Discite a me, quia mitis sum, et humilis corde*, "learn of me, because I am meek, and humble of heart" (Mt 11.29). "Humility sweetens all," said St. Teresa, ¦¦ and "true humility is not attended with trouble; it does not disturb the soul; it causes neither obscurity nor dryness: on the contrary, it consoles, ... bringing with it calm, sweetness, and light."[18] Elsewhere she says that a humble soul is "like the bee which turns all into honey."[19] | Mary will cover the bitterness of our miseries and our faults with her sweetness, such that, without disdaining or vexing others or ourselves, we shall taste the peace of the humble of heart.

ARTICLE 3: THE SECOND WEEK

St. Louis-Marie sets aside the second week for us to know the Blessed Virgin Mary, for it is though her that we unite ourselves to Jesus. Such is the defining characteristic of our devotion.

We can no more ignore the path we must take, or fail to avail ourselves of the means to perfection given to us, than a worker or an artisan can be blind to the nature and handling of his tools. The knowledge of the Blessed Virgin is a vast field of study. We should nevertheless plant some stakes to serve as markers.

§1.

Mary is our Mediatrix and Sovereign, our Mother and Lady. Let us labor to know the functions of her queenship, mediation, and motherhood, as well as the glories and prerogatives that are their foundation or which result therefrom. We should not be satisfied with the banalities bandied about in so many lesser works. We ought to approach the theology underlying our understanding of the Blessed

---

[17] Kempis, *De imitatione*, 1.2.4, 6; cf. *Imitation*, 6.

[18] St. Teresa of Avila, "Life," 30.11, *Works*, 220-221.

[19] "Foundations," 8.4, *Works*, 454; cf. *Interior Castle*, 1.2.9, 18: "Let humility be always at work, like the bee at the honey comb, or all will be lost. But, remember, the bee leaves its hive to fly in search of flowers and the soul should sometimes cease thinking of itself to rise in meditation on the grandeur and majesty of her God. She will learn her own baseness better thus than by self-contemplation, and will be freer from the reptiles which enter the first room where self-knowledge is acquired."

Virgin without trepidation. The better we know Mary, the more we shall love her; but, from what we have discussed thus far, we already know that the devotion to her called Holy Slavery presupposes a heart filled with admiration and bursting with love for her. How, then, are we to embrace it, if we have not a high regard for the Blessed Virgin? St. Louis-Marie must have had the same thought, or perhaps the concern that his discourse on the practices of our devotion in *True Devotion* would not bear fruit unless he first spoke of the excellences and glory of Mary. Is it not for the lack of knowing the Mother of God as who she truly is, that some conjure up a vapid idea of her, or that others lend her a countenance and sentiments of a Naturalism bordering on the blasphemous? Let us not make the same mistake. Let us, instead, come to know the Blessed Virgin through readings selected from among those that shed light on the points touched by St. Louis-Marie in *True Devotion* which may, not exclusively, but preferably, capture our attention.[20]

§2.

Our Mother is the perfect mold that should form us, seeing as it is her intentions and her dispositions that we should take as our own; but we cannot do so, without studying her interior life; meaning, her virtues, her affections, her actions, her participation in the mysteries of Christ, and her union with Him. She is our teacher in the science of Christ. Let us see how perfectly He dwells in her, how she serves Him, how much she loves Him. This is the vantage point from which we should conduct our study. The first place to start is the Rosary with all its fifteen mysteries; then, the mysteries of the Blessed Virgin, such as her Immaculate Conception, her Purification[21] in the Temple of Jerusalem, or the various acts of her life, such as her rapports, her conduct at the wedding of Cana—all of which are laid out for us as in a sumptuous feast.

It is impossible to condense the materials on Mary into a one volume, much less imagine that a single book could serve somehow as

---

[20] For a start, see, de Fiores, *Jesus Living in Mary*, and its French edition, *Dictionnaire*, the two invaluable resources on Montfortian spirituality.

[21] Fr. Lhoumeau: "Presentation" of Our Lord, that occurred on the same day as the *Purification* of the B.V.M. Perhaps a printer's error.

the official version of all things Marian.[22] Look at the *Spiritual Exercises*, a small work written by St. Ignatius of Loyola. It may have topics for meditation and their principal considerations already fixed, but numerous commentaries and developments of its theological underpinnings have been, and continue to be, written. In our devotion, we have a canvas just as vast. Filling it would require resorting to more than just one book. It would inspire us to labor at it. In any event, our study should be done in prayer; for through prayer we learn to know the Blessed Virgin—through prayer what we read in books will bear fruit in our hearts and nourish our souls. Let us follow the instruction of St. Louis-Marie. For this second week, he recommends ¦¦ "the Litany of the Holy Ghost and the *Ave maris stella*, and in addition a Rosary daily, or, if not a whole Rosary, at least a chaplet, for the intention of impetrating more knowledge of Mary."[23] | He then commends us to the Holy Ghost, Who, he points out, is the guardian of the Paradise that is the interior of Mary, and the divine Workman of the wonders hidden therein.

ARTICLE 4: THE THIRD WEEK

In this last period, we dedicate ourselves to knowing Jesus Christ. Since our desire is to be united perfectly to Him, we must gain as much knowledge of Him as possible. To do so, we will remain by the side of Mary, for she is inseparable from Jesus. In our devotion, we shall learn of Jesus always through her and with her, just as a disciple would be taught by the lessons and under the guidance of his teacher. We shall contemplate Him in her, just as an astronomer would first labor to be familiar with his telescope, then use it to observe the sun whose image, captured by the mirror in the instrument, is reflected back to him. Jesus is the sun and Mary is the mirror without blemish who reflects Him back to us by bringing Him closer to us.

§1.

But what is it about Christ that we ought to study? First, that He

---

[22] The compendium, *Summa aurea B.V.M,* edited by Bourrasé, lays no claim on being comprehensive. It runs into 10,500 pages in 13 volumes. Much, much more has been written on Mary since its completion 150 years ago.

[23] *TD*, 162.

is the God-Man, as well as His grace and glory. In these days of ram-
pant Naturalism,[24] people wangle to give us a Christ diminished. For
the sake of our faith and piety, we must stress His Divinity, no less
than the reality of His Humanity; and do all this without conceding a
single article of perennial Catholic doctrine. It is with this thought in
mind, as much as to be complete, that we wrote the first chapter of
this volume. It seems useful therefore to begin this third week with
some readings on the subject.

Second, let us not forget that the purpose of these spiritual exercises is for us to renew our baptismal promises more perfectly. After
renouncing Satan and the world, we take Jesus Christ for "our Lord."
We shall see under which titles He really is Lord, just as we explained
above when we spoke of Holy Slavery. In Him, we contemplate the
Word through Whom all things are created, Who is our Redeemer,
our Head, and the Spouse of our souls. In a supplementary meditation, we shall see the differences between Christ and Satan. The
former we ought to love; the latter, to despise. The one has all the
authority; the other, is a thief and a tyrant, who, says the Gospel
cometh not, but for to steal, and to kill, and to destroy (Jn 10.10).

In our meditation on the Incarnation, the Passion, and so on, we
may easily excite our love and unite the following two closely-linked
precepts: *thou shalt love the Lord* (Dt 6.5) and *thou shalt serve Him only*
(Dt 6.13). We shall also visit the scenes in the Gospel where Jesus affirms
His Divinity and His kingship, either in words or deed, such as in the
miracles, in the resurrection of Lazarus,[25] in the Transfiguration,[26] in
His affirmations before Caiaphas[27] and Pilate,[28] in the mission He

---

[24] Pollien, *Interior Life*, 2.3.3.16, 225: "As to the end, Naturalism gets rid of, or tends to
get rid of, God's glory, leaving nothing but human pleasure behind. As to the way, it
does away with, or tends to do away with, God's action, reckoning almost entirely upon
human action. As to the means, it destroys or tends to destroy grace, and puts all its
hope in human expedients. God more or less banished from man's life and work and
instruments, such is Naturalism and such are all of its tendencies." For an antidote
against Naturalism, see Leo XIII, *Humanum genus*.
[25] Jn 11.11-45.
[26] Mt 17.1-8, Mk 9.1-8, Lk 9.28-36.
[27] Mt 26.64: Hereafter you shall see the Son of man sitting on the right hand of the
power of God, and coming in the clouds of Heaven.
[28] Mk 15.2: And Pilate asked Him: Art Thou the King of the Jews? But He answering,
saith to him: Thou sayest it.

sends the Apostles,[29] and in the mantle of power He clothed them with,[30] and so on.

These considerations may indeed pry souls away from sin; but, this third week seems better to correspond to the illuminative way and particularly suited to the souls who have made progress in their supernatural life. By this time, we shall have made our choice and we wish never to waver from it. It is to serve Our Lord more faithfully, and to unite ourselves more perfectly to Him, that we labor to be suffused again with the grace of our Baptism.[31]

§2.

To lead a life united to Jesus Christ, we must have the knowledge of His external actions, but also of His interior life; meaning the entire Gospel, wherein we read of His hidden and public life, His suffering and glory, all of which must serve as the subjects of our contemplation. May we exclude anything in the mysteries surrounding His life? Indeed, not; for they all are a source of grace for us; and we all, each according to his needs, may find, in this or that circumstance in the life of our Savior, a form of holiness, a light, or a help. Even if we may not exclude anything, we may still have to limit ourselves to some aspects. Then, what are we to choose? For sure, on the one hand, those that are relevant our devotion; and on the other, those that meet our needs.

We are told that we must give up the world. Consider how the Divine Master teaches us by example at the stable in Bethlehem, in Nazareth, all throughout His Passion; how, in the temptation in the desert, He shows us how to overcome Satan and the world, and emerge victorious over the triple concupiscence. Listen to what He teaches us on the same subject in the Sermon on the Mount, especially in the beatitudes. The study of the interior life of Christ, that is, the virtues and acts of His Sacred Heart, will show us how "He lived for the Father," how meek and humble of heart He was, and to what great length He goes to show His love for us, giving Himself up for us. Lastly, if we consider the bond between Him and Mary, we will find

---

[29] Mt 28.18: All power is given to me in heaven and in earth.
[30] Act 1.8: You shall receive the power of the Holy Ghost coming upon you.
[31] Fr. Lhoumeau: "l'esprit du Baptême."

there the reason and the model for our devotion. St. Louis-Marie
especially commends our attention, first, to the mysteries of the
Annunciation and the Incarnation; then, Our Lord's holy Infancy, His
hidden life, followed by the Wedding at Cana, His Crucifixion, His
word to the Apostle St. John, *Ecce Mater tua* (Jn 19.27), on which we
should particularly meditate, if we wish to understand how Jesus
allows Himself to be subject to His Mother, and entwine her in His
work of Redemption.

We must pray, if we want Jesus to reveal Himself to us, Mary to
show Him to us, and, following His example, to converse in the secret
part of our heart with the Holy Ghost on the things we learn. On top
of the prayers for the prior week, St. Louis-Marie advises us to say the
Litany of the Holy Name of Jesus. We shall find gathered in it the titles
most especially apt to summarize the interior life of the Savior, and a
recitation of touching invocations well-designed to rouse our love for
Him.

Thus far what seems to us to be the plan of exercises in preparation for the consecration. They were tailored for it. In our
consecration, we must observe their order, their composition, and
that search for the particular fruit borne within them which distinguishes them from other more or less similar exercises. Just as a light
projecting directly onto an object may create a glow around it, so must
we not want the effect of the lights and interior movements that God
may grant us during this preparation to be restricted or focused exclusively on things of our choosing. We caution the faithful that the
considerations and the holy resolutions having a tenuous connection
to our consecration cannot serve as the proper aim of our preparatory
exercises. The rather broad canvas St. Louis-Marie has but filled with
a sketch contains a variety of thoughts and exercises to choose from;
but they are, nonetheless, already set. We shall propose a specific end
to be attained in four phases, logically organized.

CHAPTER 2.

ACTING IN UNION WITH MARY: PRACTICAL OBSERVATIONS

We have studied the consecration and the manner of its preparation. Let us now turn to how we should exercise the interior practice. Three main subjects present themselves: 1. The acts to which we must apply this practice of acting through Mary, with Mary, in Mary, and for Mary; 2. The renunciation it implies; 3. How to unite ourselves with the Blessed Virgin in our actions. We shall conclude with our responses to certain objections raised.

ARTICLE 1: APPLYING THE INTERIOR PRACTICE

We must "do all our acts through Mary, with Mary, in Mary, and for Mary."[1] These words are plump with meaning; and should we squeeze them, insights and practical consequences of great import will burst out.

§1.

What are "acts"? We take this word to mean not only our external actions, such as working, speaking, eating, and so on, but also the inner acts of the soul, such as thinking, longing, wanting, rejoicing, loving. In a word, "acts" signifies the entirety of a man's life, because our consecration encompasses it all. For our purposes, however, we shall focus on the thoughts and acts of the will that are especially to be recommended.

The thoughts, or manner of seeing. In times past, many too often

---

[1] ◆*TD*, 178.

forgot the evil brought about by detaching morality or spirituality from dogma. The Schoolmen had devised the axiom, *voluntas sequitur intellectum*,[2] from which we may derive, "we love as we see," and, we hasten to add, "we act as we love"; because love is our ¦ overriding passion.[3] | Correct the manner a wayward soul sees, and it will be easier to bring her back to the right path. How often do we vainly endeavor to act on the will, when we should have first needed to gain understanding through an enlightened intellect! It is to their enlightened faith, and hence to their unity of purpose, that the Saints owe their unity of life and love. In our moral life, we, too, must look to the onset of evil, and good, by confronting the mind first in order to set it aright and illuminate it by the light of faith. These thoughts give us some understating of what St. Louis-Marie means, when he asks that we give up "our best ideas, our light of understanding, and replace

---

[2] With respect to God, St. Thomas, "Summa contra gentiles," 1.75.6, *Opera*, 12:84.1: *voluntas consequitur intellectum*, "His Will *accompanies* His intellect." The corollary in man is "the will *follows* understanding"; that is, the object of his will is the good, which the will knows only by the intellect which recognizes it and presents it as a thing the will ought to desire, long for, and attain.

[3] The therapeutic idea of the passions as some collection of disembodied forces acting on the mind—a far cry from the *Summa* of St. Thomas—ginned up to replace the virtues, may be traced back to Descartes, who says that they are "the perceptions, feelings, or emotivities that particularly informs the soul, and are caused, maintained, or strengthened by some movement of the mind," some of which are capable of rendering the soul more "perfect" than others. ("Les passions de l'âme," Arts. 27, 137, *Œuvres*, 4:70-71, 148-149). It took Pope almost a hundred years later—the very same whose pride knew no bounds, and said that "the proper study of mankind is man"—to attempt at some order in the chaos of Descartes's thoughts, with the theory of the "ruling passion"; that is, some passions are more dominant than others, and one of which may be eminent above all ("Moral Essays," Epistle 3.53, *Works*, 3:144). A commentator called it the "master passion," which crossed the Channel and became "passion maîtresse." So loose is the concept, that one Protestant writer even called friendship, "the master-passion of humanity." Tesnière tried to regain the older tradition, by using the term in matters spiritual, saying: "Love is to the soul what fire is to matter.... Love is set in the soul as the *master-passion* or the living flame that shines, illuminates, burns, and consumes life, making the human heart a fireplace ablaze. ... Charity descends into the hearts of the Apostles in the form of a flame; we ask that our hearts be set aflame, our minds enlightened, our works come alive, the 'rust of sin' consumed in the fire of divine love. It is from the fire of pure love, quickened by the agitating wind of suffering, that we await the perfect union of our souls with God, in the final union of glory." (*Le Cœur de Jésus-Christ*, 2:48-49; "rust of sin," St. Catherine of Genoa, *Purgatory*, c. 5, 16). Cf. Camus, Bishop of Belley, *Les événements singuliers*, 3.15, 2:189: "Friendship always has the preeminence above love, inasmuch as, in friendship, *reason* is the mistress of passion, and its actions are led by prudence." Fr. Lhoumeau: "passion maîtresse," and even though he uses this term, the tenor of this his work indicates that he hews to the understanding of the passions as enumerated in *Summa*, 1-2.26–48.

them with those of Mary's."[4]

Still, there are the wants and intentions; that is, the object of our will and of our love, the end serving as the purpose of our actions, and many other things crucial for our spiritual practice that demand our attention; because after the will is led by the intellect, our spiritual acts should go towards fulfilling the holy yearnings of our soul. In sum, since the will is the faculty that commands the others, we must hark back to it in our moral life.

Lastly, we take the word "acts" to mean the acts of the other faculties of the soul or bodily senses, such as those of memory, sight, sensibility, and even the movements of our passions; that is, love, hate, desire, fear, and so on. All this pertain to our life in action; our daily life. As much as we can, we ought to consecrate our acts to the Blessed Virgin, so that she may succeed in aiding us to submit them to our will (and our will to divine grace), to direct and purify them, as much as it may be done here below. We note again that it is the whole man, and his entire life, that embraces this perfect devotion.

All our acts. In this word we hear the echo of St. Paul: *Whether you eat or drink, or whatsoever else you do, do all to the glory of God* (1 Cor 10.31), and also: *Doing the truth in charity, we may in all things grow up in Him Who is the Head, even Christ* (Eph 4.15). We must seek to have everything in our life imprinted with a supernatural character, as well as give leave for our consecration to influence all our actions, be they interior or exterior. That is the duty that we must never shirk, for St. Louis-Marie observes that there is not much difficulty enlisting in the service of Mary, in devoting ourselves to her as slave, and many do willingly; but it is well-nigh difficult to live out the idea of Holy Slavery, and very few understand and truly practice the devotion.[5]

§2.

The application of the interior practice to all our acts naturally

---

[4] *Secret*, 32-33: "We must renounce our own ideas, ... we must have recourse to the most Holy Virgin, and unite ourselves with her ... in order that she may act in us, and. for us, and that she may do with us as it pleases her, ... so that we must not undertake any kind of interior life, or perform any spiritual action except in total reliance on her."
[5] *Secret*, 32.

provokes the cry: "I think not!" For beginners, this seems to sum up all their difficulties, including losing heart. Let us quickly recall that there is a bright distinction between actual union and habitual union.

Actual union takes place by an act of will at the very moment when I act: for example, at the beginning of my prayer, I think of uniting myself presently with the intentions of the Blessed Virgin. Actual union is not necessary and, in this life, it is not even possible to have it always.

Habitual union is a permanent disposition of the soul, which makes the acts of union easy and frequent. This disposition remains, although presently we have no intention and we do nothing; for example, during sleep. As long as it is not disavowed, the habitual disposition affects virtually all acts not contrary to it.[6]

Thus, consecration makes the faithful slave "give to Jesus and Mary all his thoughts, words, acts, and sufferings of his entire life, without reserve, in such manner that whether he watches or sleeps,[7] whether he eats or drinks,[8] whether he does great things or the most insignificant,[9] it remains true to say that whatever he does, even if he had nary a thought of it, he does it for Jesus and Mary, in virtue of his offering, unless he has otherwise expressly disavowed it."[10]

Habitual union has its degrees; and the more our acts of union become easy and frequent, the more they can be perfect and meritorious. We shall return to this important subject when we speak of spiritual work; for the moment, it suffices to have touched on these principles for the benefit and comfort of souls of goodwill.

---

[6] ♦In this we follow the opinion of St. Thomas, *Summa*, 2-2.24.8c: "On the part of the person who loves, charity is perfect, when he loves as much as he can," most commonly when he gives "his whole heart to God habitually; to wit, by neither thinking nor desiring anything contrary to the love of God." See the provisos to the foregoing statement, 2-2.24.10 ad 2, 11 ad 2, 11 ad 3. See also, Terrien, *Grâce et gloire*, 7.2 [Le mérite], 2:15-25.

[7] 1 Thes 5.10.

[8] 1 Cor 10.31.

[9] Ps 113.21, Wis 6.8.

[10] ♦Cf. *TD*, 92. This is the application of St. Thomas, "De perfectione vitæ spiritualis," c. 5, in *Opera*, 2:410: "Man should refer all things to God as his end. ... One fulfills this when one orders his life to God's service, and thus all the things that he does for himself, he virtually orders to God, unless they are things that lead away from God, such as sin."

ARTICLE 2: THE RENUNCIATION NECESSARY
TO ACT IN UNION WITH MARY

"In order that the soul may let herself be led by the spirit of Mary," says St. Louis-Marie, "before she does anything, she must renounce her own spirit, and her own lights and wills, ... because the darkness of our spirit, and the malice of our will and operation, if followed, ... would become an obstacle to the spirit of Mary."[11] ¦ Commenting on the same Scripture text quoted by St. Louis-Marie, St. Thomas says: | "What inclines the spiritual man to act is not *primarily the movement of his own will*, but the impulse of the Holy Ghost."[12]

Thus, we have in the act of union positive and negative parts; and, since St. Louis-Marie devised the formula for our practice of union as "acting through Mary, with Mary, in Mary, and for Mary," in renouncing our will, we shall consider the four corresponding aspects.

1. *Through Mary*. To act through Mary, as we have said, is to be moved by her heart, to undertake an interior life, and perform all spiritual acts entirely dependent on her.[13] We must be at peace, ¦¦ a remove from all disquiet; | but while asking for divine help, taking care to be congruent with the aid granted and to understand the will of the Lord, let us not act deliberately but only under the movement of grace[14]; for it is by such movement that Mary calls us to act. To achieve this aim, we must give up the impulse of our own will, appetites, and passions; if not, there will be no dependence or spiritual childhood. An infant does very little by relying solely on his own will and power. His condition, and his job as child (gladly do we say it), is

---

[11] ◆Cf. *TD*, 179.

[12] ◆Rom 8.14. ¦¦ See note 13, p. 206. |

[13] ◆*Secret*, 33.

[14] St. Thomas, *Summa*, 1-2.114, summarized in Lynn, *Christ's Redemptive Merit*, 32: "The concept of grace as a movement of the Holy Ghost is intimately related to the notion of divine ordination. Man can merit before God only under the supposition of a divine ordination which not only determines the reward he can merit, but also equips him with the capacity for meriting. Free will is the first essential endowment required for performing a meritorious action; but if man's acts are to be directed to a higher, supernatural reward, a new principle must be introduced in order to render the act of equal dignity with the reward. That principle is grace; not merely grace as a habit of the soul, animating her with supernatural life, but grace considered as an activity of the Holy Ghost moving the soul."

to let things be, even when he acts. What is he capable of doing on his own? What will he make up his mind to do? Other than screaming at the top of his lungs for the things he needs, the best thing for him is to remain quiet in the arms of his mother and to do nothing contrary to her will. So, too, it is with us. We are children in the arms of the Blessed Mother. We shall not bother to use this analogy note for note, since its applications speak for themselves.

The initiative of our will to act, or the activity not moved by the Holy Ghost and the spirit of Mary, is opposed to the idea of Holy Slavery and our consecration; it hinders the action of God in us and impedes His dominion over us. We should not evade our dependence on Mary. We lay stress on this point because many who have been but dimly lit by the light of faith only look to their defects, perhaps thinking that those things by themselves hinder the operations of God and thwart His dominion over us. Just as a child who, though not disobedient, becomes agitated untimely in the arms of his mother, tires and vexes her; so also, do we often interfere with divine action by the eagerness and activity which we believe to be justifiable and to redound to the good. We must be watchful, the more so since, besides our individual temperament, the habits of modern life agitate for such interference on our part. Nowadays, piety has a marked predilection for exterior works. Be that as it may, we must not forget the following aphorism of St. Vincent de Paul: "I walk in the footsteps of God,"[15] that is to say, "I am become His Will and the movement of His grace, though I may not notice them." St. Louis-Marie said as much. ¦¦ He writes: "Your sure vocation is obtaining the gift of holiness from God, and all your thoughts, words, and acts—all your sufferings, and all the movements of your life—must incline towards that end; or you will defy Him by not doing the thing for which He created you and is now keeping you in His grace."[16] |

When he was consumed in fervent prayers, while on pilgrimages and journeys to establish the missionary Company of Mary, we hear him exclaim: "If man is *the first* to put his hand to the work, nothing

---

[15] A common refrain of St. Vincent de Paul; e.g., Conf. May 2659 [On Mortification], or Common Rules, 2.8-9, Œuvres, 12:227 : "The Saints are Saints because they walk in the footsteps of Our Lord, renounce themselves, and mortify themselves in all things."
[16] *Secret*, 8-9.

will come of it. If he contributes anything of his own to what you are doing, O Lord, the entire undertaking will be warped and come down in ruins."[17]

Mary herself is a beautiful model of ¦ quiet determination.[18] ¦ For instance, she knew that the Messiah was to be born in Bethlehem; but did she trouble herself, or wander off on her own, for the prophecy to be fulfilled? No. She waited docilely for God to manifest His Will in the edict of the Roman emperor. ¦ And when she was to visit her cousin Elizabeth so that John the Baptist would be sanctified in her womb, ¦ Mary was moved by the Holy Ghost, as the Gospel says: *Exsurgens Maria*, "Mary rising up ..." (Lc 1.39), on which Msgr. Gay comments: "But if she did get up, she must have been sitting down. .... Outside of work, necessary and divinely prescribed, the soul must habitually keep quiet[19] and repose in God[20]; so that in all that she does, she begins with Him, imitating Jesus Christ,[21] Who says: *The Son cannot do anything of Himself, but what He seeth the Father doing: these the Son also doth in like manner* (Jn 5.19)."[22]

2. *With Mary.* We have the starting point for our action; but during the act, we should stay with Mary to make the movements of our soul accord with her lead, and let not slip her hand heedlessly, in excessive ardor, or due to spiritual sloth. We must renounce ourselves, in order to follow those "footsteps of God" variously traced by events, the orders of our superiors, and the inspirations of grace.

---

[17] *Prayer for Missionaries*, §26, *VD*, 263.

[18] Fr. Lhoumeau: "cette conduite."

[19] Perhaps referring to the Greek ἡσυχία/*hēsychia*, "stillness, silence, contemplation, inner peace," or simply "quietude," but not "solitude." Cf. 2 Thes 3.12, Act 22.2, 1 Tim 2.11, 12 ("silence"); St. John Cassian, *Conferences*, 10.6, 11:403.

[20] Pollien, *Interior Life*, 2.3.3.15, 224-225: "*Surgite postquam sederitis*, 'rise ye after you have sitten' (Ps 126.2); we must be seated before we can rise up, and we must rise up after being seated. These three words perfectly characterize ... Christian truth. ... Christianity demands the union and submission of man's action to God's. And a wonderful thing is this sitting down and this action, this repose of leaning upon God and this acting with God: they are ever allied and combined to form the divine life in me, which is essentially made up of repose and action. Is not all life action in repose?"

[21] ♦It is among a thousand others, an example of the union of spirit and will that exists between Jesus and Mary. He who observes and imitates it, sees and imitates Jesus Christ of Whom she is the perfect copy.

[22] ♦Gay, *Rosarie*, 143.

3. *In Mary*. In order for us to act in Mary, that is, to live in her interior, to be molded to her intentions and dispositions, we must renounce ours. Any resistance, any attachment to our thoughts and longings, any remnant of the old Adam, would hinder or imperil our transformation. St. Louis-Marie teaches us the necessity of this perfect renunciation by using astute analogies. We must abandon ourselves to Mary, "like a tool in the hands of a workman, like a lute in the hands of a skillful player. We must lose ourselves in her, like a stone thrown into the sea."[23]

4. *For Mary*. It is almost superfluous to point out that one cannot act for Mary, without giving up acting for oneself. Whether it be in the end or in the intention, it is an abnegation all the same.

These recommendations are well justified, since Our Lord made renunciation the condition to following after Him: *If any man will come after me, let him deny himself, and take up his cross, and follow me* (Mt 16.24). Indeed, without renunciation what might be the outcome? Many say easily enough, and in good faith, that in their actions they unite with the dispositions of Mary and take on her intentions; but because they have yet to renounce the objects of their acts and their will seriously, the union they flatter themselves having is imperfect and a mere illusion.

To illustrate, we use the case of a worker who would enamel or gild a piece of metal. If he does not *scour* it (to use the technical term), and polish off the marks and impurities, the gold or tin will not adhere or it will be imperfect and not solid. Similarly, when we wish to put the dispositions or intentions of Mary (which are like most fine gold) on our actions, let us purify them with our renunciation, lest our coating be defective and inconsistent.

We spoke of quietude, of the soul at rest. We recommended letting things be, losing and abandoning oneself, in order to act through Mary and in Mary. Need we explain to the reader that nowhere in that is there any tendency of semi-Quietism?[24] The thoughts and

---

[23] *TD*, 180.

[24] *Quietism*, from the Latin, *quies*, "repose" is the heterodox and false mystical doctrine based on the repose of the soul which manifests itself in the indifference to salvation.

expressions in this volume are borrowed, for the most part, from the works of St. Louis-Marie. We have not pointed up to now that, in the process of his beatification, nothing in his writings was found to be deserving of censure.[25] It would horrify those who knew him and his works even the slightest, were he to be tarred with the label "Quietist" semi or not.

In preaching the union with Mary, St. Louis-Marie says not, "Do nothing"; but, "*Do nothing without her*, that is, without the movement and the grace she obtains for you. Renounce your will, but so as to follow the Will of God." Without work, or trials, or a generous coop-eration on our part—without the exercise of virtues, can we really act through Mary, with her, in her, and for her? Is it possible to conform to her intentions and wishes, to renounce oneself in the innermost core, to give oneself practically, and, at the same time, to fall into the somnolence of semi-Quietism or the stupor of complete Quietism? If so, every master of spirituality who preach recollection, the repose of

---

The author was Miguel Molinos, a priest from Spain who died in Rome at the end of the 17th century, repentant and in submission. In his *Spiritual Guide*, and in his letters, Molinos sought to establish the interior life as consisting of the annihilation of the fac-ulties of the soul (insisting that they remain entirely passive), in a total abandonment of the self to the hands of God, so as to desire nothing, to hope for nothing, to trouble not with the sanctification of the soul, salvation, eternity, Heaven, or Hell. He con-cluded, in a kind of religious sentimentality, that it was necessary only to resort to what he called "a prayer of repose" contemplating God in general, and every operation of the mind, every memory of the Trinity, of the Humanity of Our Lord, of His Passion, of His death were to be ignored; that nothing should be asked for; that there was no good work, neither confession to make; that there was no need for positively resisting temp-tation, or exercising any act of contrary virtue. Consequently, among the followers of Molinos there was a resurgence of the impieties and impurities of the ancient Gnostics. Pope Innocent XI in *Cælestis pastor*, Aug 28, 1687, declared *Quietism* heretical, suspi-cious, erroneous, scandalous, blasphemous, and so on. — *Semi-Quietism* consists in recognizing a habitual state of perfection in which hope has no part, where one loses all *interested* motive; wants no happiness for oneself, but only for God; wants no longer His Salvation to be his salvation, but merely as a thing that God desires; where the sacrifice of one's eternal bliss is no longer conditional but absolute; where pure love becomes the only principle and the sole motive for all deliberate and meritorious acts. These elements of semi-Quietism are found in *Explication des maximes des Saints sur la vie intérieure*, condemned by Pope Innocent XII in *Cum ad Apostolatus*, Mar 12, 1699. It is well-known that the author was François Fénelon, who wrote it at the instigation of Madame Jeanne-Marie Guyon. It is also well-known that, in his retractation, the great Archbishop gave an example of submission for the consolation of the Church and the confusion of her enemies. (Church, Diocese of Le Puy, *Conférences*, 11, nos. 32-33, 185-187).

[25] Church, S.C.R., *Béatification*, 7: "The Cardinals judge ... that the revised works contain nothing that may be an obstacle to the pursuit of the Cause of Beatification."

the soul in God, and the calm of her powers, are suspect. To these reflections seeking to prevent any doubt on the devotion of St. Louis-Marie from arising, we add the words of the Angelic Doctor on the text we commented previously: ¦ *Whosoever are led by the Spirit of God, they are the sons of God* (Rom 8.14).[26] ¦ "When it is said that spiritual men are primarily inclined to act by the movement of the Holy Ghost rather than by their own will, it means not that they act without their will or free will, but that the Holy Ghost gives the movement to their will and free will according to this word: *It is God Who worketh in you, both to will and to accomplish* (Phil 2.13)."[27]

ARTICLE 3: HOW TO MAKE OUR ACT OF UNION

Our union with the intentions and the dispositions of the Blessed Virgin "is done simply and in an instant, by one glance of the mind, by one little movement of the will, or even verbally, in saying, for example, '*I renounce myself; I give myself to you, my beloved Mother.*'"[28] These words summarize several practical indications which we now explain.

§1.

The union, first of all, is an act of the will. We recall the important truth that, in moral life, there are no human acts, no meritorious acts, but only acts of the will or, by another name, voluntary acts. The will commands the other faculties; and devotion, says St. Francis de Sales, is wanting to do promptly all that God commands us.[29] Thus, whether we gave ourselves or renounced our intentions by an act of will in order to act in our dependence on Mary, our donation or renunciation is a prior given, which, despite our feigned indifference, is well worth

---

[26] *TD*, 178-179. See also Part 3.3.1, p. 206, and note 13 therein.

[27] St. Thomas, ad Romanos, 8, Lect. 3, *Opera*, 20:490.1: "Non tamen per hoc excluditur quin viri spirituales per voluntatem et liberum arbitrium operentur, quia ipsum motum voluntatis et liberi arbitrii Spiritus sanctus in eis causat, secundum illud Phil 2.13: *Deus est qui operatur in nobis velle perficere.* "

[28] ♦*TD*, 180.

[29] de Sales, *Devout Life*, 1.1, 14: "Devotion is no other than a spiritual agility and vigor, by means of which charity acts in us, and we in it, promptly and lovingly. As it also appertains to charity to make us obey, generally and universally, all the commandments of God, it belongs to devotion to make us exercise such acts promptly and diligently. This is why those who observe not the commandments of God may not be deemed either good or devout; for to be good, it is necessary to have charity; and to be devout, other than charity, to have a great vigor and swiftness in all charitable deeds."

the repugnance and trials we suffer.

This act need not be explicit all the time. The implicit thought suffices,[30] as St. Louis-Marie explains when he says: "The more you look to Mary in your prayers, contemplations, actions, and sufferings, if not with a distinct and definite view, at least with a general and imperceptible one, the more will you perfectly find Jesus Christ."[31]

Now observe a child in his mother's hands. Even though he does not always think of his mother, he retains the vague sense of being with her and under her watchful eye. As soon as he realizes that his mother has left him, even for an instant, and another person holds him, he screams. The calm and joy he had from the implicit thought of his mother gives way to an explicit demand for attention.

This distinction helps us to understand what habitual union is in practice. It excludes the scruples of souls yet untutored, who believe that, to conform to the essence of our devotion, they need to think explicitly of their Mother whenever they turn to her divine Son. Having the general intention of going to God through her should be enough, provided that we retain the habitual sense of dependence on the Blessed Virgin, such that we can rightly say that our acts of faith, of love, of renunciation, and so on, are made implicitly in union with her.

The act of union in question can be done quickly, simply, by a look, or, in the expressive and charming word of St. Louis-Marie, "by a glance,"[32] evoking that simplicity of which St. Francis de Sales delightfully speaks in his *Conferences*: "Children whom Our Lord has told us should be our model of perfection, are, generally speaking, quite free from care, especially in the presence of their parents. They cling to them, without turning to consider their satisfactions or their consolations. These they presume in good faith, and enjoy in simplicity, without any curiosity whatever as to their causes or effects. Love

---

[30] ♦When we directly think of a thing which we see before our eyes, we have an explicit thought. We have an implicit thought when it is contained in another; that is, it is a consequence of that other thought. When I say, "My Jesus, I believe that Thou art truly present in the Blessed Sacrament" ¦¦ (Liguori, "Love of Jesus Christ," 3.4, *Works*, 6:351), ¦ I make an explicit act of faith in the mystery of the Eucharist. If I say, "I believe all the truths of faith," my act is implicit; for I think not directly of the Real Presence, but my thought is implied or included in my general act of faith.

[31] ♦*TD*, 114.

[32] *TD*, 180; cf. *VD*, 224: "par une œillade."

occupies them sufficiently without anything else."[33] Elsewhere the same Saint cautions that there is no need to bend the mind to find fair thoughts.[34] This concern, this excessive preoccupation with doing good, is a detriment to the peace of the soul, and quickly tires her. We must go to our union with poise, simplicity, and discretion.

§2.

Another of St. Louis-Marie's recommendation is to "beware of doing violence to ourselves for the purpose of hearing or tasting what we are saying or doing, lest we do not say or do not do everything in that pure faith which Mary had on earth, and which she will communicate to us in due time."[35]

We know how much beginners run into stumbling blocks for want of knowing the nature, origin, and effects of hardships, distractions, repugnance, and spiritual dryness, as well as the manner of conducting themselves under those trials.

We wish not to repeat here what the authors of spirituality have so abundantly explained,[36] and so have limited our discussion to a few reflections particularly relevant to the essence of our devotion.

We ought, sometimes, to attribute our dryness and repugnance to our physical condition, as St. Teresa mentions[37]; *for the corruptible body is a load upon the soul* (Wis 9.15). Other times, the devil is the

---

[33] de Sales, *Conferences*, 12, 227; cf. *Œuvres*, 6:216.

[34] de Sales, "Lettres, 2092," n.d., in *Œuvres*, 21.177-178: "We must pay attention to what we do, and not bend the mind, nor, above all, our reflections. We must receive with open hands the advice that God gives us. They need be examined only by the one counsel that governs the rest, and faithfully practice those that simplify the mind. He who does not want to keep anything for himself surrenders all to God."

[35] ♦*Secret*, 35-36.

[36] Ps 62.2: "O God, my God, to Thee do I watch at break of day. For Thee my soul hath thirsted. ... O how many ways!" For what the Saints say, see e.g., St. Augustine, *Confessionum*, 11.2.4, PL 32.810-811; St. Ignatius of Loyola, "Letter 7," Jun 18, 1536, to Sor Teresa Rejedalla, *Cartas*, 1:39-40, poignantly rendered in Bartoli, "Vita," 1.13, *Opere*, 1:59, cf. *History*, 1:54; St. John of the Cross, "Night," *Works*, 1:323-455; and St. Thérèse of Lisieux, *Story of a Soul*, c. 8, 118.

[37] St. Teresa of Avila, "Foundations," 21.3, *Works*, 532: "I was always unwell during the six months I was in Segovia; besides I had gone thither inwardly ill at ease, for my soul was in very great dryness and darkness; I had a fever upon me, and loathed my food, with many other bodily ailments which for three months oppressed me sorely."

cause.[38] "He will raise up," says St. Louis-Marie, "new persecutions and will put terrible snares before faithful servants and true children of Mary,"[39] for, in the judgment of the masters of spiritual life, Satan fears seeing a soul committed to the path of perfection more than leaving her unimpeded to undertake works of charity or the apostolate. Such works are excellent in themselves, but imperfect souls usually do them imperfectly, while those who are more advanced in interior life give even their smallest acts a purity and value most deadly to the reign of Satan. With them, there is few or none of those "imperceptible attachments"[40] that St. Louis-Marie points out, none of those secret relapses, none of those multiple intentions which the devil always manages to spy in our good works, and whose merit before God is found to be diminished. We should not be surprised that the enemy redoubles his efforts in order to turn us away from a devotion which is a secure, easy, and perfect way to perfection.

The fruits promised accounts for the attacks of the infernal adversary. St. Louis-Marie shrugs it off, saying: "But no matter! And so much the better!"[41] Let us imitate his confidence in Mary, and let Satan's efforts rouse us to do battle.[42]

In his *Prayer to Mary*, St. Louis-Marie asks us to forsake those things that are perceptible by the senses: "I ask of you not visions, nor revelations, nor gusts, nor raptures, nor even spiritual delights."[43] What follows is a quotation of his other counsels, a little more fleshed out, where he speaks of the dispositions we need to endure repugnancies and periods of dryness, whether arising from reasons given above, or that we rightly regard them as punishment for our faults, or as salutary trials that God sends us: "Say and do everything in that pure

---

[38] St. Teresa of Avila, "Life," 30.10, *Works*, 220.

[39] *TD*, 30.

[40] *TD*, 99.

[41] *TD*, 75.

[42] ◆Cf. St. Teresa of Avila, "Life," 13.3, *Works*, 77: "God seeks and loves courageous souls; but they must be humble in their ways, and distrust themselves. I never saw one of these lag behind on the road; and never a cowardly soul, though aided by humility, make that progress in many years which the courageous makes in a few. ... I was often thinking how St. Peter lost nothing by throwing himself into the sea, though he was afterwards afraid." Elsewhere (11.20, 70) she says: "The soul ... is determined not to care much, neither to rejoice nor to be greatly afflicted, whether sweetness and tenderness fail it, or our Lord grants them, has already travelled a great part of the road."

[43] *Secret*, 53. The full text of the prayer, 52-54.

faith, which Mary had on earth, and which she will communicate to you in good time. O poor little slave, leave to your Sovereign the clear vision of God, the transports, the joys, the pleasures, the riches of Heaven, and take for yourself only pure faith, full of disgusts, distractions, weariness, and dryness. Say "Amen" to whatever Mary, your mistress, does in Heaven. That is the best that you can do for the present."[44]

O the sweetness and tenderness of Saints—they that are of humble and gentle heart! In Scripture, God is compared to the eagle that entices its egrets to fly and endeavors to buttress them in their failure.[45] Does St. Louis-Marie not do the same? With an outpouring of love for humble and little people inspired by ¦ the Sacred Heart of Jesus and the Immaculate Heart of Mary,| he bends down towards the soul he wants engaged in the arduous path, he caresses her like a mother does her child, he is affectionate with her and calls her, "poor little slave,"[46] "dear soul."[47] Thus God once called His beloved nation, *paupercula*,[48] "poor dear"; and Jesus, His Apostles, *filioli*,[49] "my little children"! But what does ¦¦ the good Father de Montfort | want? To convince the soul of her misery, of her unworthiness; for her, humbly and calmly, to be dependent and confident in the hand of Mary; and to teach her to blurt out an "Amen," that is, a "yes"—like a babe's kiss—a full, affectionate and guileless acquiescence to the wishes of his Mother. By thus abasing himself, St. Louis-Marie wants the soul uplifted to love complaisant[50] to the point of self-forgetfulness,

---

[44] ◆*Secret*, 35-36.

[45] Dt 32.9-11: The Lord's portion is his people: Jacob the lot of His inheritance. He found him in a desert land, in a place of horror, and of vast wilderness: He led him about, and taught him: and He kept him as the apple of His eye; as the eagle enticing her young to fly, and hovering over them, He spread His wings, and hath taken him and carried him on His shoulders.

[46] *Secret*, 36. *Affectionate*: Fr. Lhoumeau, "il la tutoie et l'appelle." English has no equivalent for the verb *tutoyer*; no distinction between the formal and informal "you."

[47] *Secret*, 36.

[48] Is 51.21, 54.11.

[49] Mc 10.24, Jn 13.33.

[50] Faber, *All for Jesus*, 8.5, 307: "Love ¦ complaisant, | strictly speaking, is the joy we feel in the infinite perfections of God, that He is what He is," and the yearning to please Him. The idea is from St. Francis de Sales, *Love of God*, 1.7, 30-33. The original French is "amour de complaisance," often translated, "love of complacency," the same as used

content with knowing that Mary rejoices in Heaven, while she suffers here below, because this good Mother keeps her watchful eye on her and will sustain her.[51]

Is there anything that better portrays spiritual childhood and reflects more the essence of the perfect devotion to Mary? It does St. Louis-Marie great credit. Is it any wonder that, for the people, he is always the "good Father de Montfort" that he was when he conducted the holy business of souls?

ARTICLE 4: QUESTIONS AND ANSWERS

§1. SHOULD WE NEVER GO TO JESUS EXCEPT THROUGH MARY?

Going through Mary sometimes seems like a detour; always letting her speak for us may be a veritable sacrifice. At times, it seems to us good and right to go straight and spontaneously to Jesus, and speak to Him alone, freely, and without any intermediary.

No one prevents us from doing so. The objection to our devotion stems from a false idea of it and a misinterpretation of its practice. Our advice is to reflect on the facts before arguing against it.

Just because Mary presented the Divine Child to the shepherds and the Magi, and they received Him from her hands, were they prevented from approaching Him, paying Him tribute and perhaps taking Him in their arms? Surely not; for she showed Jesus, made Him known, and gave Him to them. Also, we should not think that, being attached to Mary, put under her direction, having imitated her, the holy women followed Jesus in His Passion any less closely,[52] or that they could not contemplate and testify to their love just as easily.

Consider also that even if an infant is sometimes lifted up by his mother to reach for an object or to see something, there is nothing impeding him from seeing or touching whatever and whenever he

---

by Faber. It sounds strange, and it should, even to the Victorian ear, although it is grammatically correct, and means, "love *arising out of* complaisance," and not, "love *of the thing called* complacency." Worse still is the rendering "com*placent* love," which is the very opposite of what St. Francis meant. For a synopsis of St. Francis' teaching on love, see John D. Lyons, "In Love with An Idea," in Perlmutter, *Relations*, 17-32.

[51] ♦Xavier de Ravignan, ¦¦ "the apostle of Paris," ¦ said in his last illness: "I think of the goodness of Our Lord, and how happy He is in Heaven, which thought consoles me for I am so bad and wicked here on earth." (de Ponlevoy, *Maladie*, 8).

[52] Mt 27.55-56, Mk 15.40-41, Lk 23.49.

wants. And when the mother hands him to his father, causing him to smile, and helps him to baby-talk her words, and receive the gentle caresses from his father, we can be sure that she places no obstacle for the infant to look at his father and speak to him directly.

Mary is not a barrier between Jesus and us, neither is she a screen filtering His light before the eye of our soul; rather, she is a means and a path to Him. Corrective lenses are intermediary instruments, and far from harming our sight, they are the means for us to see better. If we wish to speak to the Sacred Heart of Jesus, and pass into its interior, then Mary is the door through which we enter. A door unlocked is never an obstacle to crossing the threshold. It is the obvious and ordinary means of entry. Only thieves and robbers climb windows. ⁞ *Qui qui non intrat per ostium in ovile ovium, sed ascendit aliunde, ille fur est et latro*, "he that entereth not by the door into the sheepfold, but climbeth up another way, the same is a thief and a robber," says Our Lord. (Jn 10.1). ⁞

We could find other analogies. We say, for instance, that Mary is the sanctuary where Jesus rests,[53] the monstrance[54] that exposes Him to us, and so on. We will note, however, that many imagine risking an impediment, and indeed may have a palpable sense of it, because they think it necessary to explicitly and actually think of Mary. We said above that a habitual and implicit thought suffices. He who wears corrective lenses never dreams that he must now and always see through them; likewise, he who leads his life habitually dependent on Mary, without striking out on his own or shying away from her mediation, may very well speak directly to Jesus, unburdening his soul before

---

[53] St. Ambrose, *Inst. Virginis*, 5.33, PL 16.313C: "Non de terra utique, sed de cælo vas sibi hoc per quod descenderet Christus elegit, et sacravit templum pudoris," which, in the pen of a Redemptorist in the Age of Victoria blossoms into: "Not even Thine Only-begotten Son Himself, in coming here on earth to recover what was lost, was able to find a purer way of generation for His flesh, than to dedicate for His own dwelling the court of the heavenly Virgin, wherein might be both the sanctuary of immaculate chastity, and the temple of God." (Livius, *B.V.M.*, 260). St. Gregory Thaumaturgus, *In Annunt. B.V.M.*, Homilia 3, PG 10.1173D, says she is the sanctuary (αγίασμα, *sanctuarium*), pure chamber (καθαρὸν νυμφῶνα, *cubiculum*) of the Incarnation.

[54] *Secret*, 34, as does Fr. Lhoumeau: *ostensoir*. The word St. Louis-Marie uses (French edition of *Secret*, 29) is *reposoir*, meaning either the decorated altar along the route of a Corpus Christi procession, on which the monstrance is set to expose Our Lord; or the Repository, the Altar of Repose, where the Sacred Host, consecrated in the Mass on Holy Thursday, is reserved until the Mass of the Presanctified on Good Friday.

Him, approach Him in all liberty and spontaneity. He need not actually think that he is going to the Him through Mary; but, upon reflection, he will thank this good Mother for having brought him into the intimacy of the Savior and presenting him to His divine Majesty; he will rejoice that she has offered her prayers and, no doubt, also counseled or corrected him for his faults and clumsy mistakes.

We should recall that Mary is mediatrix between Jesus and us is not, in fact, because we thought so; for whether we think it or not, our prayer does go to Jesus through her, and through her are we granted the graces, by divine design. In Heaven she sees in God all that is done in the Church, because she is Mother to all; and her singular rapport with God is such that we cannot regard her a stranger, whose presence may harm our intimacy with Jesus. It is only through her, the Spouse's *garden enclosed and the fountain sealed up* (Cant 4.12), that we reach any degree of intimacy with Christ.

These truths, which we have already explained, show us how the universal and permanent mediation of the Blessed Virgin justifies, in all things, the practice of going to Jesus through her, since God did so ordain. Thus, it is right that St. Louis-Marie should warn us: "Beware of believing that it is more perfect to go straight to Jesus, or straight to God."[55]

We shall come back to this point when we explain that Mary is the perfect way.

§2. ANOTHER DIFFICULTY

We have another difficulty: In "doing your actions through our Blessed Lady, ... you abandon your own intentions and activities, be they good and known, to lose yourself, so to speak, in the intentions of the Blessed Virgin, although they be unknown."[56]

How can I unite myself with the intentions and operations of which I know not, and is it not preferable, lest we say it is the one and only practice, to stick to those of mine when my conscience judges them to be good?

Yes, it is possible to unite oneself to unknown intentions or activities, such as it is done when signing a blank check or giving a blanket

---

[55] ◆*Secret*, 35.
[56] ◆*TD*, 157.

approval in a formula like this: "I agree and approve all that you will do." Let us call to mind the everyday examples found in sacred liturgy. When responding with an "Amen" after a priest says a prayer inaudibly, because it is a *secret*, or it is not understood, because he says it in Latin, Christians nevertheless unite themselves with the prayer and intentions unknown to them. Liturgists have shown the profound meaning and sublimity of this acquiescence, full of faith and trust, that the faithful give to the Church's prayer, whose precise meaning and special intentions elude them. Nevertheless, they unite themselves to it, rather than seizing on to their distinct and particular notions. It is certainly in this order of ideas that St. Louis-Marie makes us say "Amen" to what Mary does.

We cannot but notice that if this practice is the basis for the mother to educate her child, why would it not serve as a way to inculcate a spiritual life? In truth, when the mother makes her child babytalk a few words in order to teach him to speak or makes him press his hands together to show him how to pray, does he understand what he is doing? With his eyes fixed on her, he adapts as much as he can to her will and her ideas, he does what he sees her doing, and acts not according to his own ideas and intentions. This is the example we must follow, and we believe that it is not impossible to do so.

"Thus," says St. Louis-Marie, "we enter by participation into the sublimity of Mary's intentions,"[57] just as the child unites with the intentions of his mother. For him, they are sublime indeed. He gains a great benefit by preferring them over those that he expends much effort to understand. And think you not it better for us to come out of the shadows,[58] quit those low places where our desires creep,[59] and rise to the brilliant peaks[60] that Mary inhabits, and say: "We believe what she sees, we want what she wants"?

But, why reject our own notions or intentions if they are good? "Because the darkness of our own spirit, and the malice of our own

---

[57] *TD*, 157.
[58] 1 Chr 29.15, Job 8.9.
[59] 2 Tim 3.6.
[60] Cant 4.6.

will and actions, if we follow them, *however good they may appear to us*, will become an obstacle for the spirit of Mary."[61] On our part, we may deceive ourselves of their worth. The child avoids errors and mistakes, by preferring the ideas and wishes of his mother over his, however good his seem to him.

One might even think that by renouncing our notions and intentions to unite with those of the Blessed Virgin's, which are unknown to us, we refrain from entertaining thoughts and wishes which are, in general, known and distinct; that we are condemned always to act with no understanding and to let ourselves be led without ever having any insight into things.[62] Nothing could be further from the truth. What the good Father de Montfort wants us to do is to avoid indulging ourselves in our own thoughts by this secret and almost imperceptible attachment which often eludes even those who lead a spiritual life. He wants our devotion to Mary to be inspired by this counsel from the Apostle: *Not that we are sufficient to think anything of ourselves, as of ourselves: but our sufficiency is from God.* (2 Cor 3.5).

We shall have lights, movements, intentions, but always from the dependence on Mary. We will attribute them to her, and not to ourselves. We will ask for them through her. We will seek them in her. And when God calls us to do so, we are ready to renounce ours for hers.

The blessed souls see everything by the divine light; so, too, in a way, shall we see everything in Mary: by looking to her, by enrolling

---

[61] ♦*TD*, 179. Emphasis added.

[62] St. Thomas, *Summa*, 2-2.48c: We are aided in our actions by the eight integral parts of prudence, of which "five belong to prudence as a cognitive virtue, namely, 'memory' (*memoria*), 'reasoning' (*ratio*), 'understanding' (*intellectus*), 'docility' (*docilitas*), and 'shrewdness' (*solertia*); while the three others belong thereto, as commanding and applying knowledge to action, namely, 'foresight' (*providentia*), 'circumspection' (*circumspectio*), and 'caution' (*cautio*). The reason of their difference is seen from the fact that three things may be observed in reference to knowledge: First, knowledge itself, which, if it be of the past, is called 'memory,' if of the present, whether contingent or necessary, is called 'understanding' or 'intelligence.' Second, the acquiring of knowledge, which is caused either by teaching, to which pertains 'docility.' ... Third, the use of knowledge, inasmuch as we proceed from things known to knowledge or judgment of other things, and this belongs to 'reasoning.' And, in order to command aright requires to have three conditions: First, to order that which is befitting the end, and this belongs to 'foresight'; second, to attend to the circumstances of the matter in hand, and this belongs to 'circumspection'; third, to avoid obstacles, and this belongs to 'caution.'"

in her school, we shall endeavor to gain an understanding of the mysteries of God and of His Will, instead of looking for it in ourselves, entrusting ourselves to the activity and the lights of our mind.

"The soul," says St. Louis-Marie, faithful in doing actions through the Blessed Lady, "counts as nothing whatever she thinks or does of herself; and only puts her trust, and takes her pleasure, in the dispositions of Mary, when she approaches Jesus, or even speaks to Him. She thus practices humility far more than the souls who act of themselves, and rely on their own dispositions, however imperceptible is their complaisance. But if the soul acts more humbly, she thereby glorifies God more highly; and He is only perfectly glorified by the humble, and those that are meek and lowly in heart."[63]

Far from wanting us always ignorant and blind, St. Louis-Marie promises us that in return for this devotion, Mary will communicate to us the light of her living faith and the ardor of her charity. He speaks at length of the qualities of this faith, and says that it will be "active and piercing, and, like a cryptic passkey, will give us entrance into all the mysteries of Jesus Christ; ... a faith which will be our blazing torch, our divine life, our hidden treasure of divine wisdom."[64]

In sum, although a child at first acts without any comprehension and imitates his mother, he must not remain in his ignorance and helplessness; little by little his understanding builds and his will is formed. This is the very purpose of his education. And since our spiritual childhood and education last our whole life, it is best that we always live and act as true children of Mary, keeping ourselves completely dependent on our Mother and Teacher.

---

[63] ◆Cf. *TD*, 158.
[64] ◆Cf. *TD*, 150-151.

CHAPTER 3

THE PERFECT DEVOTION AND THE THREE
STAGES OF SPIRITUAL LIFE

We thought it necessary to address the question of the perfect devotion and the three degrees or stages of advancement in the supernatural life of grace, lest our discussion be deemed incomplete, risks spreading lamentable misunderstandings, or exposes souls to dangerous self-deceptions. How do we set aside the differences that exist in the practice of the perfect devotion arising out of whether we are in one or the other states of spiritual life, namely, the purgative, illuminative, and unitive; that is, its beginning, progress, and perfection? How can we fail to note the many instructions offered on the three states in the writings of St. Louis-Marie? Absent our explanations, many would be left with the impression that our devotion is not only a path of spirituality special and endowed with its own qualities (which is true), but also an established one, by reason of those very qualities; or that it is apart from what is contained more fundamentally and authoritatively in traditional teaching. In short, the critics would not have spared us the accusation of having set souls on a perilous path. Thus, before moving on to the next chapter, where we treat of the qualities of our devotion, let us now speak of how it is related to the three stages of interior life as understood down the ages.

Our form of devotion to the Blessed Virgin is a path to perfection, and St. Louis-Marie presents it to us as such; but, where does this path lead us, and what route does it take? We shall see that it is short and straight. It has a beginning, a middle, and an end, and we cannot reach our destination if we do not set foot on it. It is a perfect path to union with Jesus Christ, a way of love—a union and love that will begin, progress, and be perfected with different characters and effects. Some have also observed that, in this spirituality, there is only one ascetic process to which everything converges; that it is an interior practice of acting through Mary, with Mary, in Mary, and for Mary. Nonetheless, one soul puts it not to work in the same manner as another, for each soul obtains different results, depending on whether she is more or less advanced in her spiritual progress.

St. Louis-Marie counsels us as much when he says that the practice of this devotion has several steps and that very few people rise to the last: ¦¦ "As the essential of this devotion consists in the interior which it ought to form, it will not be equally comprehended by everybody. Some will stop at what is exterior in it, and will go no further, and these will be the greatest number. A few will enter into its inward spirit; but they will only mount but one step. Who will climb to the second step? Who will get as far as the third? Lastly, who will so advance as to make this devotion his habitual *state*?"[1] |

This chapter will provide the explanation. Referencing the writings of St. Louis-Marie, we shall show that in the perfect devotion to the Blessed Virgin, a soul finds certain lights of understanding and particular assistance in the three states of spiritual life; and that the practice and effects of this devotion differ depending on what progress she has made in her spiritual life.

ARTICLE 1: THE PURGATIVE WAY

§1.

In the first stage, our main care is to guard ourselves against sin and to resist the guilty lusts that thwart divine Charity.[2] The task falling especially on a beginner is to purify himself of the sins committed and also of their vestiges, and to prevent relapses into sin.

We need not give here the reasons that stir us to us invoke Mary under the title Refuge of Sinners, though they may be well-founded and a source of consolation. Whether we speak of conversion or preservation from sin, the masters of spiritual life never fail to

---

[1] *TD*, 81.

[2] ◆St. Thomas, *Summa*, 2-2.24.9c: "For at first it is incumbent on man to occupy himself chiefly with avoiding sin and resisting his concupiscences, which move him in opposition to charity."

commend sick or frail souls to her, giving them assurances fitted to save them from being discouraged.

But are there particular reasons in our devotion that brings us hope? After our consecration, should we expect more abundant help from Mary? A resounding "yes" to both questions. To devoted slaves of Mary, confident in her mediation, St. Louis-Marie says: "She is so charitable that she rejects none of those who cry for her intercession, notwithstanding the gravity of their sinful habits."[3] From their consecration, they have a singular claim to her protection. But, by which means does St. Louis-Marie wish us to ensure that our conversion lasts; that we persevere and avoid relapses? By the one that makes us rely the more on our Mother; the one that entrusts her with the treasure of our graces and virtues; the one that faithfully fulfills all the practices of this devotion. We need not mention here the hundreds of passages that our readers, just as we, may call to mind; but better that we should recall the testimony of those who have had the sweet experience of promises fulfilled. After so many unsuccessful, feeble, imprudent efforts, and already falling prey to the enemy of salvation, how many souls have had no other recourse but to fling themselves at the feet of the Blessed Virgin? They surrendered themselves to her, body and soul, for this life and the other; they implored her to defend them as her property, save them by the power of her hand,[4] in return they promised to honor her and make her loved by all. Soon enough these poor desperate people felt that the ground beneath their feet shook no more, that they stood on solid earth, and that an invisible power has made Satan recoil, and his attacks to cease suddenly or little by little. At the side of Mary, they learned to bemoan their faults, are filled with the horror for sin, and are become open to the love of Jesus.

O Refuge of Sinners, there is none but you and the God of mercy (of whom you are the minister), who know how many are the intimate and touching dramas that unfold in each of the years of grace we owe Jesus! And when, not having descended into the depths of mortal sin, we ponder on the state where venial faults, passions, and vestiges of

---

[3] Cf. *TD*, 58.
[4] Cf. Magnificat, Lk 1.50-52.

sin trouble the spiritual life of beginners, rendering it infirm and ster-
ile in parts, who inspires the idea of a superior state, who lends a hand
to help them rise again, if not you whom we honor by the pregnant
name, *scala peccatorum*, the sinner's ladder to God?[5]

It is through the practice of holy and loving Slavery to Mary that
souls climb from the depths of sin to the summits of perfection.
Acting through Mary and in Mary, their actions become pure, and are
freed from faults. St. Louis-Marie reminds them,[6] *qui operantur in me
non peccabunt*, "they that work by me shall not sin" (Sir 24.30). Propped
up by Mary, they will not come tumbling down: *ipsa tenente, non
corruis.*[7]

§2.

We speak now of the purification of the soul, not the one that
absolution obtains, but the one that rids us of even the last vestiges of
sin.

First of all, we owe a debt which is to be is satisfied by temporal
punishment. We have already seen the generosity we may expect from
Mary in return for offering her all our spiritual goods; but we also understand that the Mother of Dolors inspires in us a resolve to do
penance. This important subject deserves a weighty consideration.

We also must cleanse ourselves of venial faults—faults we often
overlook, such as our inclination to vice, our willful ignorance, and
our timid will, which all result from Original Sin and all make the sins
we actually commit graver. In this long and hard spiritual toil, we said
that our first task is to know ourselves; but how do we cure the maladies we see not? Pointing it out to us in his discussion on the effects
of our devotion (a proof—one among many—that he never conceived
of a spiritual life separate from the three stages of our advancement
towards perfection, that is, the purgative, illuminative, and unitive,
handed down to us from the ancient Fathers), St. Louis-Marie tells us:

---

[5] St. Bernard, *de Aquæductu*, §7, PL 183.441D: "The Son will listen to His Mother, and
the Father to His Son. O my little children, she is the *ladder for sinners*. She is my greatest confidence, and the entire reason for my hope. Can the Son either fend her off, or
stand her being rebuffed; either be deaf to her, or she fails to be heard? Clearly, none
of it. ... She will always find grace, and we stand in need of grace alone."

[6] *TD*, 122, 184.

[7] ◆St. Bernàrd, *De laudibus B.V.M.*, Homilia 2.17, PL 183.71A.

"By the light that the Holy Ghost will give you through Mary, His beloved Spouse, you will come to realize your inclination to evil, ... and upon gaining the knowledge, you will despise yourself."[8] Elsewhere, he says that the soul dedicated to Mary and living in intimacy with her will find "a well of distrust, contempt, and hatred of self, and a profound confidence and total self-abandonment in the Blessed Virgin."[9] He speaks at length on the miseries of our tendency to evil: our incapacity, frailty, faithlessness, unworthiness, and iniquities, which the light of the Holy Ghost alone will make us see. He says that it is Mary who will obtain this light for us.

At times this clarity will be so vivid, the sight of our past iniquities and our present misery so sharp, that "we will look upon ourselves with horror."[10] In the higher stages of spiritual life, when the lights of faith increase, the disgust becomes so intense that we cannot find words to describe it. But, in his colorful, original and folksy style, St. Louis-Marie says that we shall see ourselves "as snails, that spoil everything with their slime; or toads, that poison everything with their venom; or serpents, spiteful, and only seeking to deceive."[11] He adds: "We are naturally prouder than peacocks, ... more gluttonous than hogs, more furious than tigers, lazier than tortoises, flimsier than reeds, and more capricious than weathervanes."[12] Many will see in his language nothing but exaggerations, because, living in the half-light of a fledgling interior life, they have no experience of the clear and frightening visions that will surely tear the soul away from lies and deceits; they have not yet come to *despise and hate themselves*. We can be forceful still. What soul, probed to the darkest folds of her life by a light hitherto unknown to her, and made to see herself in all her true colors and haunting relief—what soul, say we, so affected, will defy the precision of these turns of phrase and the accuracy of this supposedly coarse language? The Saints spoke thusly, and in this they echoed the words of Holy Scripture.

In the devotion to the Blessed Virgin, St. Louis-Marie often

---

[8] Cf. *TD*, 149.
[9] *TD*, 98.
[10] *TD*, 149.
[11] Cf. *TD*, 149.
[12] Cf. *TD*, 53-54.

returns to the need for self-knowledge and contempt of self to be the basis of the spiritual edifice and how they must not be found wanting in any soul, be it ever so high the state of perfection she has attained. ¦¦ He says that due to our devotion, "the humble Mary will communicate to us a portion of her profound humility, which will make us despise no one but ourselves and like regarding ourselves with contempt."[13] |

We repeat: in this matter, the masters of spiritual life point out two peculiarities which harken our thoughts back to Mary.

"I believe we shall never learn to know ourselves," says St. Teresa, "except by endeavoring to know God, for, beholding His greatness we are struck by our own baseness; His purity shows our foulness; and by meditating on His humility, we find how very far we are from being humble."[14] Let us apply this to the knowledge of the Blessed Virgin, and we shall enter into the mind of St. Louis-Marie, who said:

> She is my fountain clear,
> Where my ugly faults lay bare.[15]

He would have us understand that, for us to gain self-knowledge and become humble, we ought to take Mary as a spotless mirror wherein we may compare ourselves to her who is the type of eminent purity.

Concerning those who occupy the first mansion, that is, souls who are yet in the first stages of spiritual life and have need of being purified, St. Teresa adds this second observation in common with other authors: "It is very injurious never to raise our minds above the mire of our own faults. ... While we are continually absorbed in contemplating the weakness of our earthly nature, the springs of our actions will never flow free from the mire of timid, weak, and cowardly thoughts. ... This comes from not understanding our own nature. Self-knowledge becomes so warped that, unless we take our thoughts off ourselves, I am not surprised that these and many worse fears should threaten us. Therefore, I maintain ... that we should fix our eyes on

---

[13] Cf. *TD*, 150.

[14] St. Teresa of Avila, *Interior Castle*, 1.2.10, 19.

[15] *Cantiques*, 77.17, 133: "Elle est ma claire fontaine / Où je découvre mes laideurs."

Christ our only Good, and on His Saints; there we shall learn true humility, and our minds will be ennobled, so that self-knowledge will not make us base and cowardly,"[16] but raise us to the contemplation of the perfections of God.

If, in this exercise of self-knowledge and contempt, "the devil tries to bring you to despair, ... surrender to hope by considering the goodness and clemency of God, ... which surely will come and does, often, to the one who starts the journey, especially if it is a soul that God has delivered from the many dangers and grave sins that engulfed her."[17]

Let us follow the advice of St. Bernard: | "O you who find yourself tossed about by the storms of life: If you would not be overwhelmed by their raucous waves, turn not your eyes from of Mary, our bright shining Star. If the winds of temptations rise, if you fall among the rocks of tribulations: Raise your head, call on Mary. If anger, covetousness, or other passions beat on the vessel of your soul: Look up to Mary. If you begin to sink in the gulf of melancholy and despair: Think on Mary. In dangers, in distress, in perplexities: Think of Mary. Call on Mary. Let her name not depart from your lips. Let her not leave your heart. And never stray from the example of her life, so that you may win the suffrage of her prayers. Following her, you will not be lost. Imploring her aid, you will not yield to despair. Thinking on her, you will not err. Under her patronage, you will not wander. Beneath her protection, you will not fear. She being your guide, you will not weary. If she be your favorable Star, you will arrive at port safely."[18] |

This guarantee against despair that the masters of spirituality seek by wisely combining the consideration on our misery and that on divine perfections, we join to our self-knowledge, through the knowledge of Mary; but in the perfect devotion, we find something else to confirm it powerfully. Faced with the unfathomable abyss of our heart, where we risk being sunk, St. Louis-Marie casts his eye on Mary and says:

---

[16] ♦St. Teresa of Avila, *Interior Castle*, 1.2.11-12, 19-20. || "But raise us to ... God" not in the original Spanish. It is an embellishment in the French translation. The "other authors" include, | St. Albert the Great, "De adhærendo Deo," c. 15, *Opera*, 37:539-540; St. Vincent Ferrer, *Vita spirituali*, c. 5, etc.

[17] ♦Rousset, *La doctrine spirituelle*, 1.5, 50.

[18] ♦St. Bernard, Super *Missus est*, Hom. 2.17, PL 183.70-71. Moved from note, amplified.

> She's my ark come the flooding,
> Where I'm hale, not sunk and drowned,[19]

and exclaims with St. Bernard: ¦¦ *Hæc est tota ratio spei meæ*,[20] ¦ "she is the entire reason for my hope." That is why he makes us abandon all into her hands: our body, our soul, and our joy. O how this act of abandonment should calm us, if we only understood the thought that inspires it! We read in Sacred Scripture: *Libera nos propter nomen tuum*, "Deliver us, O Lord, for Thy Name's sake" (Ps 78.9).[21] For the glory of His Name! Here, we invoke neither our merits nor our care. Such is the language we are called to use in our perfect consecration when speaking to Mary. Save for the necessary cooperation that we should bring to our salvation (and we do indeed bring it by our dependence and docility to our Mother), if we may say so, it is up to her to save us. We are more hers through our consecration than we are to ourselves; we appertain to her as her property, and she is as much responsible for us as we are for her, for her honor, and for her interests. The deeper we delve into this idea in which we recede behind our Mother and Lady, the more we find there a solid base to sustain our confidence. There is no limit how far it will be raised, if we evoke longingly the special fruits of this devotion; if we are bonded lovingly to the spiritual childhood, for which she is our model.

These are the means that the Holy Slavery to Mary offers us in this first stage of our interior life. Further on in this study, we shall see more of them in the exercises for active purification.

§3.

After we have been mortified of the sins and the last vestiges of them, we must do the same to the inner and outer senses: the passions, the mind and the will[22]; we must put off the old man,[23] and die to ourselves.[24]

St. Louis-Marie speaks of this subject most forthrightly. He chose, "among all the devotions to the Blessed Virgin, the one which draws

---

[19] *Cantiques*, 77.7, 132: "Elle est mon arche du déluge / Où je ne suis point submergé."
[20] St. Bernard, *de Aquæductu*, §7, PL 183.441D.
[21] Cf. Ps 43.26 : Domine, ... *redime* nos ("redeem us") propter nomen tuum.
[22] Col 3.5-9.
[23] Eph 4.22.
[24] Jn 12.24-25. Cf. Gal 2.20, 6.14; Rom 6.6-7, 6.11-14, 12.1-2.

us the most to this death to ourselves."[25] He knows not who more empties us of ourselves and our self-love. Further on, he says: "When they have brought forward and consecrated to her their body and soul, and all their appurtenances, without exception, what does that good Mother do? Just what Rebecca did of old with the two kids Jacob brought her. First, she kills them, that is, makes them die to the old Adam. Second, she flays, and strips them of their natural skin, that is, their evil tendencies and all attachment to creatures. Third, she cleanses them of their spots, filth, and sins. Fourth, she prepares them to God's satisfaction, and for His greatest glory."[26]

We could quote other similar expressions of St. Louis-Marie's, but we need not. To him who studies the perfect devotion and wants to understand its genius, it is clear that in it is practiced the purgative way in a truly special, profound, and complete manner. When we live out the idea that we no longer belong to ourselves, how can we not sense that we are engaged in the practice total mortification? This total dispossession, this obligation to use all things only in the dependence on Mary, creates a vacuum around the *old self* and chokes it.

Let us return to the examination of the interior practice of Holy Slavery.

To act only through Mary, that is to say, by the movement according to her mind, under her direction, and not by our own, is to "renounce the operations of the powers of our soul, and of the senses of our body;" that is, "we must see, as if we saw not; understand, as if we understood not; and make use of the things of this world, as if we made no use of them at all, which St. Paul calls *quotidie morior*, to die daily"[27] This is the mortification of the bodily senses and the faculties of the soul required for progress in spiritual life, such that, with the passions reined in, we obtain interior recollection and arrive at the silence of the soul[28]; we cut short idle thoughts, curiosity, and

---

[25] *TD*, 55.

[26] Cf. *TD*, 141-142.

[27] ◆*TD*, 54. ¦¦ The Scripture quote is from 1 Cor 15.31. Cf. 1 Cor 7.30-31. ¦

[28] Is 32.17-18: The work of justice shall be peace; and the service of justice, *silentium* (quietness) and security forever. And my people shall sit in the beauty of peace, and in

voluntary and often seductively aimless drifts of the imagination and fond memories. Just as a filter well fixed to the opening of a vessel stops the slag and foreign matter, leaving only the purified liquor to drop, so also this practice, faithfully exercised, does stop at the entrance of our soul every movement, every deliberate thought, every intention of our own life, letting in only the movements of grace, purified of all foreign influence.

When we add that we must act *for* Mary to all the foregoing, we will practice the purity of heart or of intention highly recommended to us ever since the beginning of our interior life.

To act in Mary and be molded in her, we must renounce our own notions and intentions and conform to those of the Blessed Virgin. In so doing, we work particularly to purify the intellect and the will through a complete detachment in the exercise of these two faculties ¦¦ of the soul. | We must insist on this point; for one of the last strongholds of self-love is well-nigh the attachment to our thoughts and passions, either by our obstinacy or in order to take pleasure and joy of them. The Saints recommend that we come out of ourselves, that is, do away with our principle, support, and joy, which is the very thing we practice in abandoning our intentions and operations, be they good and known, to take on those of Mary's. ¦¦ Thus, we "enter by participation into the sublimity of her intentions, which are so pure, that she gives more glory to God by the least of her actions."[29] | And if, as the Saints teach, the exercise of divine love is the most efficacious means of purifying our will, do we not heed it when we act "for Mary"?

As for the dryness, repugnancies, and other sensible trials that beginners have to undergo, we refer to the explanation we provide above.[30] Suffice it so say, some observe that they lend the substance of our devotion a particular sweetness and special virtue, even though they lead us valiantly to tread the path of perfect abnegation.

§4.

We may now understand how a soul interiorly practices this

---

the tabernacles of confidence, and in [calm repose].
[29] *TD*, 157.
[30] Part 4.2.3.2, pp. 252-253.

devotion, whilst still in the purgative way. What brings her to act *through Mary* and to resort to the mediation of the Blessed Virgin is, above all, the keen feeling of her needs and the sight of her sins. The soul labors to renounce the self by following the movement of grace and Mary's lead; but, notwithstanding the goodwill and sincerity she may have, alone, the soul cannot complete her work. Only later, when she has made some progress will she gain greater knowledge of herself and the ability to discern more clearly what it is that moves her to act; it is then that she will discard many things that she has yet to perceive as unnecessary. Her recollection and interior silence are imperfect and, in general, of short duration. She is so enthralled by a multitude of extraneous notions that she is become accustomed to the night of the senses and faculties, and one might say, even satisfied to remain in the shadows.

But the thought of "acting *with Mary*," and the experience of her assistance, be it rudimentary, are invaluable to this soul; that is, in providing encouragement to endure difficulties, which seem at first to be so insuperable, and in preventing her from turning tail when faced with the prospect of daunting trials and endless struggles.

The soul acts *in Mary* by an act of will and faith; but, in spite of her acquired knowledge, she still has few insights into the interior of this admirable Mother. She cannot have the slightest glimpse of the sights and dispositions in Mary's heart most pure, because she has none of those brilliant lights that emanate from the Spirit of God and which, more than any other, lead to union.

The same soul may remain habitually *in Mary*, but only with great effort. She rightly bemoans it all through her travails, though gives it no thought. She renews her morning offering,[31] sometimes; but more often she acts contrary to the intent of her consecration, and slips from under the dependence on Mary by the rash movements of her passions, by the hardened habit of yielding to her own will. We must seek a remedy for this state of affairs in its root cause, and avoid latching on to a simple act of memory, or to a cottage industry full of

---

[31] In Montfortian spirituality, the consecration is renewed every morning upon rising, with a short prayer. There is no set formula, but the one often used is: "Je suis tout à vous, et tout ce que j'ai vous appartient, ô mon aimable Jésus, par Marie, vôtre sainte Mère." (Texier, *Manuel*, 79).

mnemonic devices, purporting to aid us in recalling the presence of God; for he who is beset by a dominant idea, who is enamored of one thing only, and moved by a sole passion, needs no aid to recall such idea or the object of his passion. Forsooth, he is obsessed with it— possessed, even. We think no more of the life of Christ in our soul, or that we have made a consecration to Mary, because in our mind we count them among ideas foreign to our thinking, even though they may take the place of honor, or at least, *prima inter pares*, first among similar thoughts; but if we come to a more resolute conviction, if our heart falls in love with the ideas inherent in our devotion, Christ and Mary will be our *dominant ideas* and all others in our mind will rally around them. This is the reason masters of spiritual life insist on the necessity to convince beginners of the obligation of perfection, of the importance of the supernatural realities, of the greatness of the goods that lead us to divine union, and so on.

We need prayer, reflection, and work, in order to obtain a living faith, deeply cherish these things, and acquire the habit of union with Mary. We shall return to the topic of prayer when we speak of it separately. For now, let us touch on reflection and work.

Reflection or meditation is generally the means in the purgative way suited to enlighten the mind and strengthen the will. As for work, we must mortify the interior and exterior senses and rein in the passions, making our soul freer and less frail; but above all, we must take care to renew our act of union with Mary every time the thought arises, or to set our intention aright, when we notice that it has taken the wrong path. Being willfully negligent on such occasions is more damaging to the progress of the soul than not thinking of Mary for a long time.

Lastly, the soul is exercised to love by acting *for Mary*; but this love is just a spark that offers neither brilliant clarity nor great warmth. It emits a lot of smoke, expends its energy to dry the moist wood, vaporizes the liquids, and requires tending. Hence, we need prayer, meditation, resolutions, and the exercise of virtues to tend to that infirm love, which may very well act for Mary, but still has mixed in it an unhealthy dose of self-interest. At this stage, the task of this love is to purify the soul. Later, it will set her afire. This gradual purification, with its effects and notes, coincides with the first degrees of the interior practice in our devotion. Few know it, and they advance in it intermittently. Most are stuck at its external practices. The Saints speak of the various states of spiritual life, using terms such as "mansions," or "mystical degrees," and other like analogies; and, like St. Louis-Marie, they are unanimous, alas! in finding that there are far too few who rise to even the initial steps of the purgative way.

ARTICLE 2: THE ILLUMINATIVE WAY

The illuminative way is that period of interior life which accords with adolescence in a man's life or Spring in the changing of the seasons. It is a stage of progress, of blossoming and of growth.[32] Its principal character is an increase of light in the soul, delivering her from the tyranny of the senses and the passions, allowing her to tend to things divine more freely, begin to perceive them better, and take joy of them. *Vacate et videte*, "be still and see" (Ps 45.11). And just as the days are longer, the sky purer, and plants sprout and grow in the Spring; so also, purified of sin, the soul emerges from the dark days of Winter to a brighter and more lasting brilliant light of faith that engenders an expansion of supernatural life and stirs us to ever greater virtues.

§1.

We can hardly speak of illuminating our soul without turning to Mary. Is it not her who says: *I made that in the heavens there should rise a light that never faileth* (Sir 24.6)? "She will illumine others throughout the world," says St. Thomas, "for which reason she is compared to the sun and to the moon."[33] "'Tis she that lights up our hearts and drive away the darkness," says St. Epiphanius.[34] Her queenship is a

---

[32] ◆We know that these divisions, like those of the ages of life and changes of the seasons, are not clearly demarcated. They overlap. We undergo purification even in the illuminative way, and in the purgative way one already receives lights. Each stage also has its degrees, but each is named after its dominant character.

[33] Note 80, p. 138.

[34] Fr. Lhoumeau credits St. John Damascene, perhaps missing the comment in St. Jean Eudes, "Le cœur admirable," 3.4.1, *Oeuvres*, 6:293, who, after quoting the Latin, says "C'est la voix de saint *Épiphane*," and gives the French of: "O virginal candle that brought to light of day those shrouded in the shadows of the night! O virginal torch that banished the murk of Hell, and caused the brilliance of Heaven to shine in our souls! O radiant lamp, ever filled with the oil of grace, that kept on the fire of divine love to light our minds and inflame our hearts! O light that spread, and spreads still, its

queenship of light. "The rays of her mercy spreads to touch even those far off, her tender consolations *brightens those who approach her with a special devotion*, her surpassing glory shines on the elect of Heaven beside her; thus, there is none that can hide from her heat, meaning, her charity and her love most fond."[35]

We must be surprised no longer that, consonant with the Doctors and the Masters of the Church, St. Louis-Marie tells us: "Our Blessed Lady will give you also a portion of her faith."[36] To whom does she make this promise? To all who faithfully practice the devotion to her. Most assuredly everyone needs the light of faith; but the qualities he lists belong only to souls advanced in spiritual progress. Of such qualities, some obtain fully in the unitive way only:

"A faith pure," he says, "that makes you care not at all for the sensible and the unexpected; a faith lively, animated by charity, that makes you act only out of pure love; a faith steady and immovable as a rock, that makes you stand fast and firm amidst the tempests and the tumults; a faith quick and penetrating, that, like a cryptic passkey, allows you entry into all the mysteries of Jesus Christ, into man's Last Ends, and into the Heart of God Himself; a faith courageous, that enables you to undertake great things for God and for the salvation of souls, against all odds; lastly, a faith that is a blazing torch, ... for you to light the way for those in darkness under the shadow of death[37]; to inflame the lukewarm in need of purification by charity, as in gold by fire[38]; to give life to those dead by sin[39]; to touch, to melt the cold hearts of stone,[40] and to humble the proud cedars of Libanus,[41] by your

---

splendor to all parts of the earth!" The Greek and Latin, in *Homilia*, 5, In laudes S. Mariæ, PG 43.495B, among the doubtful works of St. Epiphanius of Salamis. Cf. St. John Damascene, *In Nat. B.V.M*, Homilia 2.7, PG 96.694C: "Tum candelabrum, tum mensa, tum reliqua omnia legis ritu aurea, allegoriæ non ambigua significatione, de te aureis multisque neminibus celebri, accipiuntur"; St. Ephrem the Syrian, "Precatio," 4, *Opera*: 3:529E: Maria, "septem luminum candelabrum, cujus splendor solares radios superavit."
[35] Jordan, "De B.V.M.," Proœmium, in *Opera*, 117-118: "Longe enim positos illuminat radiis misericordiæ suæ, sibi propinquos per specialem devotionem, consolationis suavitates secum existentes in patria excellentia gloriæ. Et sic *non est qui se abscondat a calore ejus* (Ps 18.7), id est, a caritate et dilectione ipsius."
[36] *TD*, 150.
[37] Cf. Is 9.2, Ps 106.14, Job 12.22, Mt 4.16, Lk 1.79, which all apply to Christ.
[38] Rev 3.18.
[39] Rom 6.23.
[40] Zec 7.12.
[41] Ps 36.35.

gentle and puissant words[42]; and, lastly, to resist the devil and every other enemy of Salvation."[43]

The increase in the light of understanding, St. Louis-Marie says, is due to the Holy Ghost more abundantly acting and communicating Himself to a soul in whom He encounters Mary.[44] Thus, the deeper is our union with her, the brighter will our soul be illumined. We do not assert, however, that in the first stage of interior life, or the purgative way, the soul is not at times illumined brilliantly enough, just as we have clear and bright days in Winter; but those times are brief, and souls who take joy of them (for example during instruction, a feast, in the course of a reading, a prayer or a retreat), regret seeing them fade away. They seem to think so would go their piety. They lament the loss, for their ideal is to live in this light and under the gentle imprint of the warmth that touches their soul. Often, because these fleeting lights do not sprout strong virtues in their hearts quickly enough, they become discouraged and go so far as to doubt the truth of the grace granted them by God.[45] They mistake the time and condition, like those who expect to have Spring-time vegetation in the rare fine days of Winter. These souls, purified before this light which now is steadier and more abundant, would grow and ripen in their virtues.

St. Louis-Marie attests to this progress of faith and virtues by the influence of the Blessed Virgin, saying: "It is in the bosom of Mary that they who are youthful become elders in light, in holiness, in experience, and in wisdom; and that we arrive in a few years at the fulness of the age of Jesus Christ."[46]

In the text quoted above,[47] St. Louis-Marie mentions faith and charity. In other passages, he names the other virtues.[48] Rather than

---

[42] Ez 7.25, Mt 28.19.

[43] ◆Cf. *TD*, 150-151.

[44] *TD*, 20.

[45] Mt 5.45: "He maketh His sun to rise upon the good, and bad, and raineth upon the just and the unjust"; that is, grace is a free gift from God.

[46] ◆*TD*, 107.

[47] *TD*, 150-151.

[48] For instance, *TD*, 72: "True devotion to our Lady is *holy*, that is, it leads us to avoid sin and to imitate the virtues of Mary. Her ten principal virtues are: deep humility, lively faith, blind obedience, unceasing prayer, constant self-denial, surpassing purity, ardent love, heroic patience, angelic kindness, and heavenly wisdom."

delving into all of them, let us be satisfied with this: That if we spend any time at all pondering the interior practice of our devotion, we would be convinced soon enough that our progress in it and the increase in virtues is one and the same. Indeed, what does it mean to act in Mary, to conform to her intentions and dispositions, to be molded in her? Simply: It is to imitate her virtues as perfectly as we can.

§2.

The work of purification also takes place in the illuminative way. It is an effect of the increase of our light of understanding; for everywhere in nature, as it is in grace, light is a powerful agent of cleansing and hygiene. In this case, the work is more refined. No more is the need to scrub off the filth of sin. Here, we brush the dust of small faults, defects, and minor passions. We must then, in the words of St. Louis-Marie, *empty* ourselves[49]; that is, *wholeheartedly* renounce ourselves even down to our least and most secret attachments. The perfect devotion to Mary is a means to arrive at that state. As St. Louis-Marie assures us so many times: "There is no other practice equal to this which rids us of a certain proprietorship that has covertly crept into our best actions."[50] And, "the predestined ... even throw themselves, hide themselves, and admirably lose themselves, in her loving and virginal bosom, ... that they may be cleansed there from their least stain."[51]

§3.

In this second stage of spiritual life, the interior practice of our devotion is realized to a greater extent than in the first.

We act more faithfully *through Mary*, for our individual will no longer has dominion over us; and the soul, being more enlightened, is better able to discern the least promptings. Our faith in the mediation of the Blessed Virgin is increased by our appreciation of her and a holy familiarity with her, resulting in our greater confidence and inward peace. In return for our fidelity to keep near this good Mother,

---

[49] *TD*, 160-161.
[50] Cf. *TD*, 92.
[51] *TD*, 137.

her assistance becomes more efficacious and thorough, and as we act more *with her*, the weight of all our works in all our states is halved.

We do ever more *for Mary*, because in this stage is lit the spark of love and zeal that sets us afire which hitherto has brought us to the exercise of the most generous of virtues.

Lastly, to act *in Mary*, the soul is in a better condition than before. The light she receives, especially in contemplation, leads her to a higher understanding of things divine, serving as the means for her to pierce into the interior of Mary, to be initiated into her insights, her intentions, her acts, and her dispositions; and whereas previously in this practice the soul often acted by pure faith and will, now she begins to perceive and taste.[52]

Meanwhile, her habitual union strengthens little by little. Allow us to stress this point. We said above, that in beginners the gaps in thought and will come easily and frequently; and their union with Mary, often broken by the return of self-love. As the soul progresses, her union becomes more stable; she *abides* with our Mother more easily, and dwells in her. Mortification freed her from the things that held her captive and were a source of distractions. Illuminating supernatural realities, the light draws and steadies her within.

After the exercise of mortification has fortified the soul and disciplined her faculties, she is able more easily to resist the tendencies of her evil nature, to overcome the obstacles of the passions or the attacks of the devil, and to hew more resolutely to her initial intention. She thus ascends the hidden degrees of union with Mary, to which our good Father de Montfort refers, until she is there *by state*. This is the unitive way of which we shall now speak.

ARTICLE 3: THE UNITIVE WAY

§1.

The proper character of the unitive way is the purified soul, perfected by the practice of virtues, having for her principal care to attach herself to God and take joy of Him.[53] It is thus not just the *habitual*

---

[52] In Hebrew, "discernment" (Job 12.20) comes from the word "taste," טַעַם / *ta'am* (Ex 16.31); in other words, to taste is to be able to discern that which is good. By extension, self-knowledge or wisdom is gained by experience and not by theoretical study.

[53] ◆St. Thomas, *Summa*, 2-2.24.9c: "Man's third pursuit is to aim chiefly at union with

union of the soul with God by sanctifying grace, a union that is common to all the righteous; it is more than the *ordinary actual* union that takes place, for example, when, with the help of grace, we make an *act* of charity, or we assent to the Will of God. Well, everything happens in the obscurity of faith; and if we sense some movement of affection, if we have any taste for the union, it is generally a passing sentiment whose effects are nothing out of the ordinary. The *fruitful actual* union, or union of joy, assumes that there exist the principles of the ordinary actual union, namely, the state of grace, the supernatural movement, and an act of union of our will; but, in addition, other conditions need to be met. The soul must have arrived at a certain degree of perfection; the sense of the presence of God stirred in her, no longer by an ordinary movement, but by an extraordinary supernatural light, derived from the gifts of the Holy Ghost. This light, produced by the gifts of understanding and wisdom, causes the soul to know and taste the presence of God. She has no doubt about it, for she tastes and loves by a tender experience. It is a prelude to Heaven, where she will see and enjoy in conditions more perfect.[54]

Here on earth, this act cannot last without interruption; neither can it constitute a permanent state. If we speak of it as a state, we must understand it in the sense that souls (at least the most perfect) keep a more or less indefinite and indistinct perception of the presence of God. St. John of the Cross compares this state to the sleep of the Beloved, Whose acts of union are akin to him awakening.[55] The ease, frequency, and intensity of these acts may vary, but their effects are considerable and we shall discuss them below. They characterize the stage of spiritual life in question.

§2.

How is the unitive way and the perfect devotion linked one to the

---

and enjoyment of God: this belongs to the perfect."

[54] ♦See, Meynard, *Vie intérieure*, 2.3.1-3, 1:463-543.

[55] St. John of the Cross, "Living Flame," 4.3, *Works*, 2:303: "God is not hidden from the soul in the state of perfection, for such a soul is ever conscious of His presence. ... He is there, as it were, asleep in her embraces, and she is, in general, conscious of His presence, and, in general, has the fruition of it most deeply. If He were always awake in her, the communications of knowledge and love would be unceasing, and that would be a state of glory. If He awakes but once, merely opening His eyes, and affects her so profoundly, what would become of her, if He were continually awake within her?"

other? The intimate, perfect, fruitful union with God is the goal of our devotion. It leads us there by means of a similar union with the Blessed Virgin. It is thus not merely a practice of common piety, an ordinary Christian life, or an inferior degree that is proposed to us; it is a perfection with eminent virtues and greater lights. In a word, they are "miracles of grace."[56] It is the fullness of the age of Christ, the abundant communications of the gifts of the Holy Ghost, and especially the gift of wisdom. When he reads this list, the reader will recall certain well-known passages from the writings of St. Louis-Marie, among which is this: "If devotion to the most holy Virgin Mary is necessary to all men simply for working out their salvation, it is still more so for those who are called to any *particular* perfection; and I do not think that anyone can acquire an intimate union with Our Lord, and a perfect fidelity to the Holy Ghost, without a very great union with the most holy Virgin, and a great dependence on her succor."[57]

Moreover, what we say of the union with Mary and its effects, will demonstrate sufficiently that here we treat of a perfect union, a kind of union of joy. But let us first mention St. Louis-Marie's precious note on the phenomena that prepare us for it.

§3.

We know that in order for the soul to be disposed to the unitive way, and especially to the graces of extraordinary contemplation, God must have intervened to purify her, to strengthen her by special trials, the number, gravity, and duration of which vary according to the magnitude of the gifts He intends to grant her. The masters of spiritual life are unanimous in proclaiming the purifications called *passive* to be most painful, even terrible; and they regard the time of these trials as a critical and perilous stage of spiritual life. The Saints and the most illustrious of souls have left us ample testimony to confirm these assertions.[58] In *True Devotion*, we read the following lines which should leave those having had instruction in the ways of interior life no doubt as to their meaning and application:

---

[56] *TD*, 155.

[57] ♦*TD*, 23-24.

[58] E.g., St. Teresa of Avila, *Way of Perfection*, 18, 72: "I am well aware that the trials given by God to contemplatives are intolerable; and they are of such a kind that, were He not to feed them with consolations, they could not be borne."

"Truth be told, we may attain to divine union by ways" other than our perfect devotion, "but then we shall bear many more crosses, suffer more strange deaths, and undergo many more trials, all of which we shall find hard to overcome. We shall pass through dark nights, wage combats, endure strange torments, climb craggy mountains, walk on prickly thorns, and cross desolate deserts. But if we take the path of Mary, we shall stroll down gently and in great calm. We may indeed face raging battles to fight and great hardships to overcome; but our good Mother and Lady will draw near her faithful servants, and stand ready to light their shadows, clear their doubts, bolster them to face down their fears, and sustain them in their struggles and difficulties, such that this virginal path that leads to Jesus Christ, when compared to others, is a path ¦ fragrant and sweet, strewn with roses and flowing with honey.[59] | There have been some Saints—just a few—who traversed this path to reach Jesus, for the Holy Ghost, faithful Spouse of Mary, showed them the way by a singular grace. Such were St. Ephrem the Syrian, St. John Damascene, St. Bernard, St. Bernardine, St. Bonaventure, St. Francis of Sales, and others. The other Saints, much greater in number, did not or did only in some small way, notwithstanding their devotion to the Blessed Virgin. They thus had to undergo rougher and more dangerous trials."[60]

We quote this curious passage in its entirety, but refrain from giving it much thought, except to remark that it may contain something specific or even new in mysticism, and that we are not aware of it existing in the works of any other writer. We surmise that St. Louis-Marie speaks from experience[61]; and, as the Church, in the examination of his writings, has not contradicted it, we feel free to accept his most worthy assertions.

§4.

We now explain how this devotion leads us to the unitive way by means of a *perfect* union with Mary, a union which consists in acting faithfully through her, with her, in her, and for her.

---

[59] St. Louis-Marie, simply, "de rose et de miel."

[60] ◆Cf. *TD*, 103-104.

[61] St. Louis-Marie sometimes admits as much, as in *Secret*, 36, 39: "Experience will teach you infinitely more than I can tell you. ... It is only experience that can teach the marvels of Mary."

A. THROUGH MARY

To act through Mary is to act by the movement and in virtue of the Holy Ghost Who moves Mary. But souls yet imperfect most often act only by the movement of ordinary graces; in their actions they go not beyond the direction of reason and the ordinary degree of virtue; while perfect souls are moved and led more often by divine help in the form of the gifts of the Holy Ghost.[62] These souls then do *excellent* works due to their extraordinary character or their perfection.

Is this movement proper to the gifts that St. Louis-Marie has in mind in the perfect practice of his devotion to the Blessed Virgin? We doubt it not, so many are the indications. First, his way of speaking about the graces that this devotion provides us: "When the Holy Ghost finds Mary in a soul, He flies there. He enters there fully. He communicates Himself to that soul abundantly."[63] Elsewhere, he promises us a fullness of grace and an anointing by same divine Spirit,[64] indicating by these expressions graces extraordinary and uncommon, in addition to lights and movements of a higher order. We see the idea explicitly stated along the same lines: "The Holy Ghost, finding His beloved Spouse, as it were, reproduced in souls, will come in with abundance and fill them to overflowing *with His gifts*, particularly with the gift of wisdom, to work the miracles of grace."[65]

We may derive other conclusions from the explanations of St. Louis-Marie on the manner of acting *through* Mary, for they are the same as what we obtain from considering the actions done through the gifts of the Holy Ghost. When he explains, amongst others, that to act through Mary is to be led interiorly by her, he has in mind the words of St. Paul: *Whosoever are led by the Spirit of God, they are the sons of God* (Rom 8.14). This is true of the ordinary impulses of actual grace, as we have explained; but to St. Augustine and St. Thomas, this superior and preponderant movement appertain only to divine gifts. So also says St. Louis-Marie. He offers us the Blessed Virgin as an

---

[62] ♦On the question of the gifts, fruits and beatitudes, see Froget, *Indwelling*, 4.6, 203-227, where it is explained with as much breadth as clarity.

[63] *TD*, 20.

[64] *TD*, 116.

[65] ♦*TD*, 154-155.

example, saying: "She is always led by the Holy Ghost, Who has rendered Himself so completely master of her, that He has become her
own proper spirit."[66] Thus, "we must deliver ourselves," he says, "to
the spirit of Mary to be moved and influenced by it in the manner she
chooses. We must put ourselves and leave ourselves in her virginal
hands, like a tool in the hands of a workman, like a lute in the hands
of a skillful player. We must lose ourselves in her, like a stone thrown
into the sea."[67] We read elsewhere on the same subject: "We must
place ourselves ... in the hands of Mary, in order that she may act in
us, ... such that we do not undertake any kind of interior life, or perform any spiritual action except in total reliance on her."[68] When we
compare these words with the commentaries of St. Augustine and St.
Thomas on the text of St. Paul, we find the same thoughts expressed
almost in the same terms. They and St. Louis-Marie speak of a superior influence under which man is more passive than active, not in the
sense that he does nothing, but that he is moved rather than moves
himself, whilst remaining free, and must give his consent and cooperate with divine movement.[69]

With the ordinary movement of grace and virtues we have the
what to do. We have to decide to act, and move to execute. At this
level, it is like the condition of an insect that, warmed up and revived
by sunshine, stirs and dashes off. Introduce divine gifts, then, above
all, we need to allow ourselves be carried along by divine movement.
Such is the case of a young pupil whose tutor cups his hand and guides
his finders to trace letters on piece of paper. He is free, but should give
his consent. He co-operates by his action, and tries hard obediently
to follow the tutor's movements and proceeds to draw the letters. Still,
he is driven more than he is moving entirely of his own accord.[70] On

---

[66] *TD*, 179.

[67] *TD*, 179-180.

[68] ♦*Secret*, §1, 33.

[69] ♦St. Augustine, *de Gestis Pelagii*, 3.5, PL 44.323 : "To be *led* implies more compulsion
than to be *ruled*. For he who is ruled also acts in some measure, and is ruled precisely
in order that he should act rightly. But he who is led can hardly be understood to do
anything by himself. Nevertheless, the grace of the Savior is so far superior to our wills
that the Apostle says without hesitation: *Whosoever are led by the Spirit of God, they are
the sons of God*–Rom 8.14. And our free will can do nothing better than to commit itself
to Him, to be led by Him Who cannot act wrongly." See note 13, p. 206, for the text of
St. Thomas referred to here.

[70] ♦St. Thomas, *Summa*, 2-2.52.2: "In donis Spiritus Sancti mens humana non se habet

Mary's mode of acting, we cannot doubt that it is, to a perfect degree, that of acting by the gifts of the Holy Ghost.

We provide this rather long explanation so that the reader may grasp the thought of St. Louis-Marie, and dispel any notion that, in any way, it hews to the heterodox and false mystical doctrine of Quietism or semi-Quietism[71]; for indeed it does not.

We may also say that the practice of this devotion leads us to act under the influence divine gifts, considering their effects. Gifts, says St. Thomas, are abiding habits or qualities (essentially supernatural) whereby man is perfected to obey readily the movements of the Holy Ghost.[72] Theologians agree that the characteristic effect of gifts is that suppleness or docility which makes the soul more passive, more dependent on God, but also more active and more valiant in her divine service. As the practice of our devotion tends to set us in the same dispositions of dependence, perfect docility and generosity, is it not manifest that it also disposes us to receive the gifts of the Holy Ghost and to be in harmony with them?

Faithfully practiced, the perfect devotion allows us to accomplish works that we could otherwise do only with the assistance of divine gifts. In certain aspects, such works are always excellent. Sometimes they are extraordinary, for it is in the souls risen to the unitive way that we see the heroic virtues, the fervent and pure zeal for the glory of God and the good of souls, the passionate love of the Cross; that is, everything that excites our admiration and contrasts so sharply with our coldness, our cowardice, and our dull life. Sometimes they are common actions, but achieved with eminent perfection.

St. Louis-Marie speaks to us of each and every kind of such work. The union with Mary must bring us, he says, "into the most sublime and secret ways of perfection"[73]; she works miracles in souls—

---

ut movens sed magis ut mota."
[71] Note 24, p. 248.
[72] St. Thomas, *Summa*, 1-2.68.3c.
[73] *TD*, 25.

"miracles of grace."[74] By the faith that Mary communicates to her faithful slaves, they will do great things, both for their own sanctification and for that of others. In sum, this devotion will form those great Saints of the latter days who will do prodigious acts. He also says that in renouncing our own intentions to act in union with Mary, we shall enter into the participation of the sublimity of her intentions, which rendered the least of her actions more meritorious than the sum of all heroic actions of the Saints; and that we shall "give Jesus Christ more glory in a month than by any other practice, however difficult, exercised in many years."[75]

To conclude, we note that to act through Mary is to make use of her mediation. In this, perfect souls surpass all others. ¦¦ In the words of St Louis-Marie: | "This Mother of fair love will lift the cloud of all scruple and all disordered and servile fear from your heart. She will open and widen it,[76] that you may run the way of her Son's commandments with the holy liberty of the children of God[77]; that in it may blossom pure love, of which she has a treasure. ... [She] will fill you with great confidence in God and in herself, because: (1) you will no longer approach Jesus alone, but always through this good Mother; (2) she will communicate her virtues to you, and will clothe you in her merits, since you have given her all your merits, graces, and satisfactions for her to dispose of at will; ... (3) she, who is generous with the generous, and more generous than even the generous, in return for your having entirely given her your body and soul, will give herself to you in a manner marvelous and real."[78]

These are the dispositions which writers note as among the effects of divine union in souls advanced in their progress to perfection: debts paid, sins cleansed, and fear banished by their perfect love. And if their humility moves them resort to the mediation of Mary, she will bud forth a thousand flowers in acts of confidence and filial liberty.[79]

---

[74] *TD*, 155.

[75] ◆*TD*, 157.

[76] 2 Cor 6.13.

[77] Rom 8.21.

[78] ◆Cf. *TD*, 151-152.

[79] Galot, *Jesus*, 70-71: "In proclaiming the principle: *Where the Spirit of the Lord is, there is liberty* (2 Cor 3.17), St. Paul is speaking of the supreme liberty by which man ... is transformed by contact [with God]. ... The Christian enjoys this liberty because he has been raised by Christ to a level of [sonship with the Father] and because the Holy Ghost

B. WITH MARY

As we have seen, these words point to a relation. They tell us that the soul abides in the company of Mary, and that she receives no end of help and protection from Mary. Souls yet imperfect are not set in this amiable association. They are not diligent in keeping close to their good Mother. Too many things too easily distract them. They are divided in their loyalties. But as they are purified and progress in supernatural life, they will free themselves from things external and discard ¦¦ all selfish claims, even | ownership of themselves. Then, strengthened and truly liberated, they will steadfastly persevere in their interior life, and their intimacy with Mary will grow each day.

"See now," says St. Louis-Marie, "the habit the predestinate soul keep each day: They stay at home with their Mother; that is, they love solitude, guarding their interior life and devoting their utmost to prayer, but after the example of their Mother, the Holy Virgin, and in her company. ... It is true that they venture abroad into the world, sometimes; but they do so in obedience to the Will of God, and their beloved Mother's, to fulfil the duties of their state."[80]

In return for their devotion, such souls receive special assistance from their good Mother and Lady. Even if Mary may give to all, she is surely much more vigilant and generous towards those who are better disposed to receive her graces, because of their generous fidelity and great love for her. So explains St. Louis-Marie, giving in detail how graciously the Blessed Virgin offers her good offices to her devout and faithful servants. He summarizes them with these words, which obviously apply only to perfect souls: "After she obtains for them the benediction of the heavenly Father, and the union with Jesus Christ, she will preserve them in Jesus, and Jesus in them. ... She guards the Saints in their fulness of grace, and makes them persevere to the end."[81] Previously he had developed this thought, quoting the well-known commentary: "The Blessed Virgin abides in the fullness of the Saints, and guards against their virtues fading away, their merits

---

develops a filial life in him. ... Filial freedom finds expression in a mode of behavior marked by trust and assurance (παρρησία, parresia) before God (cf. Eph 3.12). ... It is neither egoistic or egocentric. Being filial, it is necessarily relational. It establishes man in his true relationship to the Father."

[80] ◆Cf. TD, 133.

[81] TD, 148-149. St. Louis-Marie's Latin, in plenitudine detinet, see following note 82.

perishing, or their graces being lost."[82]

C. IN MARY

§i.

Being "in Mary" means united to her by love. It is a union of the mind, the will, and operation. It is a union that renders one present by thought, affection, and relationships to the other. It is a union of two beings who love each other. Even though in this union there can never be a presence of one in the other by substance (for such presence in the soul is reserved to God alone), we still may find other notes of the perfect union of souls with God, or the notes of the unitive way.

Foremost is the transformation of the soul into Mary, causing her to live more in Mary than in herself[83]; to breathe Mary as much as the body breathes the air[84]; the soul of Mary to be communicated to her; and to be of one mind with Mary, and suited to glorify the Lord and rejoice in God.[85] In this transformation, mystic writers speak of a grand forgetfulness of the self[86]; St. Louis-Marie asks us to "lose ourselves"[87] in Mary. The same writers urge perfect conformity; he asks that we become "living copies of Mary."[88] Here we find the apt use of the mold analogy that St. Louis-Marie so often and so fondly recalls, in which we see another phenomenon of the unitive way—that of the soul melted. Being molten, she is purified, then poured into a cast,

---

[82] •Holtnicker, *Speculum B.V.M.*, ¦¦ 7, 105: "It is written: *She shall be admired in the holy assembly of Saints* (Sir 24.3, 16) , on account of which the abode of Mary is in the fullness of the Saints, not in the fullness of the impious; because Mary remains willingly with those who are full of sanctity, not with those who are full of iniquity. She not only abides in the fullness *of* the Saints, but abides in fullness *with* the Saints, lest their fullness should grow less. She takes hold of virtues, lest they fly; she takes hold of merits, lest they perish; she takes hold of demons and keeps them in check, lest they do harm." |

[83] *TD*, 39.

[84] *TD*, 154.

[85] *TD*, 154.

[86] St. John of the Cross, "Ascent," 3.1, *Works*, 1:207: "Memory cannot be perfectly united at the same time to God and to forms and distinct knowledge. And as God is without form or image, on which the memory may dwell, so when the Memory is united with God, ... it remains without form or figure, with the imagination destroyed, and itself absorbed in supreme felicity, in profound oblivion, remembering nothing. Divine union expels every fancy, and shuts out all forms and knowledge; it elevates memory to that which is supernatural, leaving it in such deep forgetfulness that it must do violence to itself, if it is to remember anything at all."

[87] *TD*, 180.

[88] *TD*, 155.

which is Mary, to be transformed into her by the will and by an affective operation.[89]

§ii.

We will now explore the topic of the presence of Mary in us and on our sojourn in her. We have spoken of its nature[90]; here, we show the different degrees to which we may practice our union and how we may take joy of such presence in Mary.

We said elsewhere that there are differences between actual and habitual unions,[91] but there are also two kinds of habit: acquired and infused.

The acquired habit is the facility to do one thing which is obtained by the repetition of acts. We experience it every day in the exercise of the trades and arts, as well as in that of virtues.

If work, aided by grace, may lead us to acquire a habitual union with the Blessed Virgin, it is reasonable to say that such habit is infused by God's gift. In such a case, this union is granted to us even before we do any exercise or preparation; that is, in one instant, grace gives us what our prior labors could not obtain. God operates, and we receive.

We have arrived at the realm of mysticism proper. We hasten to add, however, that this precious gift of union is absolutely not rare, at least not to a degree. We practice our union with a supernatural taste, and, in the unitive way, that union deepens and becomes part of our life. But St. Louis-Marie warns: "Take great care not to torment yourself, should you not immediately enjoy the sweet presence of the Blessed Virgin in your interior."[92] That St. Louis-Marie understands our union as an infused habit, ever so delectable to the soul, we read in his own words. Like all the graces of infused contemplation and mystical union, "this grace is not given to all; and when God favors a

---

[89] Gerson, "Conférences spirituelles," *Opera*, 3:886-887, summarized in Aumann, *Spirituality*, 7, 171: "In his *speculative* treatment of mystical theology, Gerson teaches that reflection leads to meditation, and meditation to contemplation; but contemplation is essentially an affective operation; it is an ecstatic love. Thus, it calls into play the higher appetite of the soul called συντήρησις / *synteresis*, leaving behind the operations of the passions (the sense appetite) and the will."

[90] See especially, Part 3.3, p. 202 ff.

[91] Part 4.2.1.2, p. 243.

[92] *Secret*, 36.

soul with this grace out of His great mercy, *it is very easy for the soul to lose it,* unless she be *faithful* in practicing frequent recollection," in addition to adhering to other aspects particular to the graces in question; "and should this misfortune fall on you, then return quietly, and make honorable amends to your Sovereign."[93] We can most assuredly not recover this grace by our own efforts, for it is a gift, although we may be worthy of it and of it being restored to us; but for that, we must be humble and we must pray.

Considered as an infused habit, together with the illumination, the movements, and the dispositions that comes with it, this union with Mary deserves to be called a "secret"; and, from this point of view, St. Louis-Marie quite rightly said that he had not "been able to find it in any book old or new."[94] We find this to be true, for it appears that it must have been in his childhood, prior to his undergoing any study, that the Holy Ghost not only instructed him on the devotion interiorly, but also taught him its practice, more perfectly than any book or master could have. We note that he commends us to the Holy Ghost when we desire to know the interior of Mary, saying: "Happy, and a thousand times happy, is the soul here below to whom the Holy Ghost reveals, that she may know, the secret of Mary!"[95] Who will, by habit, keep his union with Mary? "He alone to whom the Spirit of Jesus Christ shall have revealed the secret."[96]

So very few begin, let alone advance, in this devotion, exercising in it down to the core, often because they so very seldom implore the Holy Ghost to grant them the understanding and teach them the practice of it. We who desire to drink from the *fountain sealed up* (Cant 4.12), that is, Mary, let us not be discouraged by our thoughts of unworthiness, for it is written: ¦¦ *Omnes sitientes, venite ad aquas; et qui non habetis argentum, properate, emite, et comedite,* | "all you that thirst, come to the waters: and you that have no money make haste, buy, and eat" (Is 55.1). What an invitation! Let us all heed this call; *all,*

---

93 ♦*Secret,* 36.

94 *Secret,* 7.

95 *Secret,* 16.

96 ♦*TD,* 81.

without distinction or restriction; *all*, on condition that we be changed, that we be souls of desires,[97] excluding none, not even the wretched Samaritans, since by His acts, Jesus Himself gives meaning to this divine word and applies it.[98] It summarizes, moreover, the pressing invitations of the Wisdom Books that the Church puts on the lips of Mary.[99]

§iii.

The union with Mary and our delight in her presence may come with the extraordinary phenomena described as mystical, some of which we find in the life of St. Louis-Marie, as he expressed in a hymn:

> This passeth understanding:
> She I bear deep in my heart
> Marks of glory imprinting,
> Though faith's darkness yet to part.[100]

Grandet, his first biographer, relates that when in prayer he sometimes seemed to sleep; and that, if asked what he was doing, he would say: "I was between Jesus and Mary. I believed that one and the other were in my heart: one to my right and the other, to my left."[101] What

---

[97] Dn 9.23: *Vir desideriorum*, lit. "a man of desires"; but Hebrew, חֲמוּדוֹת, *chamudot*, and Greek LXX, ἀνὴρ ἐπιθυμιῶν, "man much beloved."

[98] Jn 4.13-14.

[99] Prv 9.4; Wis 8.13, Sir 24.26-27.

[100] *Cantiques*, 77.15, 132: "Voici ce qu'on ne pourra croire: / Je la porte au milieu de moi, / Gravée avec des traits de gloire, / Quoique dans l'obscur de la foi."

[101] ¦¦ Grandet, *Vie*, 295-296. | ♦The Jesuit de la Tour, who was his confessor, said that his life was a continual recollection and that he had a sublime gift of prayer and contemplation. De Ponlevoy describes a similar anecdote. In *Vie de Ravignan*, he tells of Ravignan. the pious and well-known Jesuit, being united to St. Ignatius of Loyola, not only by a moral bond of affection, but by something more immediate: "I see him not. I sense his presence, for he is here and I touch him in his heart. ... The thought of him quits me not, night or day. ... He responds to me in the depths of my core, with a clarity and precision that henceforth will give me an unshakable certainty of peace and immense joy." (*Vie*, 328, 441). Lallemant, also a Jesuit, who died, as did St. Louis-Marie, with a crucifix in one hand and a statue of Mary in the other, never stopped asking for the favor of being pierced by the thought of this good Mother. (Champion, *Vie Lallement*, 44). This grace he obtained, and he enjoyed the sweet presence of the Mother and the Son. Mother Marguerite Mostyn, who consecrated herself to Holy Slavery of Mary, received a similar favor. And, let us not forget Jean-Jacques Olier, who wrote: "On February 17, the Blessed Virgin did me a good turn. She came to me and stayed in the depths of my soul." As has already been remarked, these favors imply not a personal presence of the Blessed Virgin or a Saint in the soul, but a presence by action ¦¦ (*præsentia per contactum virtutis*, for which see St. Thomas, "Summa contra gentiles," 2.56.7, *Opera*, 12:174). |

mystery do these words hide? Could it be prayers of ecstatic union? Imaginary or intellectual vision?[102] Be that as it may, we thought it useful to quote here the observation of a commendable author: "In the first stage of fruitful union," says Fr. Louis Chardon, after Richard of St. Victor, "the soul is assured that nothing can alter her repose; in the second, the presence of the Beloved fills her with delightful joys; in the third, she is absorbed, engulfed, and transformed."[103]

These are extraordinary favors, at least, in that the faithfulness to graces and perseverance in prayer enable us to avail ourselves of the effects of this promise that St. Louis-Marie gives to all uncondition-ally: "If you are faithful to the little I have taught you, you will find so much riches and so many graces in this practice that you will be sur-prised, and [your soul will] be filled with gladness."[104] Perhaps here we might touch on certain points on the extraordinary ways of praying as contained in the book *True Devotion*, but we will defer speaking about them until we come to the subject of prayer in general.[105]

D. FOR MARY

These words, "for Mary," express the intention or motive that causes us to act; that is, as we said above, pure intention and motive of love. But since every virtue has its beginning, its progress, and its perfection, in this practice one can rise to a greater or lesser grade. St. Louis-Marie speaks of the motives and advantages of the perfect con-secration, in which he engages beginners by the promise of rewards and spiritual profit. Then, he shows us what pure love is, and also, the charity of perfect souls, as the end to which we must aim, but without expressly ignoring our inward calm,[106] which if we did, we would go down the errant path of the false mystics. We are familiar with these words: "We must have no pretension to recompense for our little ser-vices to Mary, except the glory of belonging to so sweet a Queen, and

---

[102] St. Teresa of Avila, *Interior Castle*, 7.2.2, 263: "In the union of the spiritual nuptials, ... God appears in the soul's center, not by an imaginary but by an intellectual vision, far more mystic than those seen before, just as He appeared to the Apostles without having entered through the door when He said: *Pax vobis* (Jn 20.19)."

[103] ◆Chardon, *La Croix*, 2.9, 330. ¦¦ Richard of St. Victor, *Mystical Ark*, 308-343. |

[104] ◆Cf. *Secret*, 36.

[105] Part 5.1.5, p. 332 ff.

[106] Fr. Lhoumeau: *Béatitude*, not as in "eternal bliss," but "the serenity of the soul that comes during contemplation."

the happiness of being united, by her, to Jesus, her Son, in an indissoluble bond in time and in eternity."[107]

Writers on Christian mysticism also speak of other effects that the perfect union with God engenders in the soul. We also find them in the perfect union with the Blessed Virgin, and we shall discuss them in the next chapter. Let us conclude this one with an important reflection:

In a passage quoted above, St. Louis-Marie recommends that we not torment ourselves, should we not so *quickly* enjoy the sweet presence of the Blessed Virgin in our interior, because *this grace is not given to all.*[108] Further on, without making any distinction, he says: "Let us labor, ... and let us act in such a way, that *by the faithful practice of this devotion*, the soul of Mary may be in us to glorify Our Lord, and that the spirit of Mary may move us to rejoice in God our Savior."[109]

There is no contradiction between these passages, and they can be reconciled according to the doctrine of the best masters, as follows: To enjoy the sweet presence of the Blessed Virgin within oneself to such a degree that it constitutes a fruitful union is the privilege of souls advanced in spiritual progress. This favor is thus not given to all. On the other hand, perfection, or ordinary perfect union, is the goal of spiritual life and the end to which all may aspire,[110] and the same must be said of a certain delightful presence of Mary in our soul, which is the fruit of our devotion. This perfect union with the Blessed Virgin, as well as with Jesus Christ, is based on absolute conformity of will and total surrender to the good pleasure of God.

---

[107] ◆Cf. *TD*, 185. Instead of "glory," St. Louis-Marie has, "honor."

[108] Part 4.3.3.4.c.iii, p. 287, and *Secret*, 36.

[109] ◆*Secret*, 36-37.

[110] ◆This applies to ordinary contemplation, which is also called "acquired." It is not the same with the "extraordinary" contemplation and the states of infused union which God dispenses at will and which cannot be desired without being temerarious. ¦¦ Butler, *Western Mysticism*, "Afterthought," §§7, 8: "'Mystical' or 'supernatural' contemplation is a divine gift, the result of God's action upon the soul, which is passive. ... 'Acquired' contemplation may be described as active. The essential difference between asceticism and mysticism, and between 'mystical' contemplation and every other form of prayer, however perfect, is the element of passivity which constitutes the former state, and that of activity which constitutes the latter. ... The name 'acquired' contemplation was devised by Carmelite theologians at the beginning of the seventeenth century in view of St. Teresa of Avila's very rigid conception of 'supernatural' contemplation." See also Garrigou-Lagrange, *Perfection chrétienne*, 2:745-769. ¦

Without going out of our ordinary way, St. Louis-Marie was able to say to all, "Let us labor," and to give us hope that we will rejoice in this presence of Mary in the manner and to the extent that it will please the Lord to grant us.

CHAPTER 4.

THE PATH IS EASY, SHORT, PERFECT, AND SECURE

pt is the title of this chapter, for, according to St. Louis-Marie, our path to perfection, our devotion to Mary, do indeed bear the qualities of being easy, short, perfect, and secure. As he speaks of them at some length in his *True Devotion*, we thought it fitting to study them here in order to complete the physiognomy, so to speak, of his spirituality. We saw in Part I that his spirituality has these qualities by the very fact that the union with Jesus is at once the goal and the means. Let us now see how they are even more heightened, because of the special means we use to unite ourselves to Jesus Christ, which is the Blessed Virgin. In short, we seek to determine how is Mary the easy, short, perfect, and secure path that leads to Jesus and unites us to Him. ¦|

ARTICLE 1: THE PATH IS EASY

That the path to perfection is easy, is a powerful motive for us to take it. St. Louis-Marie speaks of it in these terms: "Truth be told, we may attain to union with God by other paths, but then we shall ... undergo many more trials, all of which we shall have to painstakingly overcome. We shall pass through dark nights, wage combats, endure terrible torments, climb craggy mountains, walk on prickly thorns, and cross desolate deserts. But if we take the path of Mary, we shall stroll down gently and in great calm."[1] He adds: "How many devout souls do I see who seek Jesus Christ, some by one path or by one practice, and others by other paths and other practices; and after they have

---

[1] ♦Cf. *TD*, 103. ¦¦ Fr. Lhoumeau changed a few adjectives. See same passage, p. 280. |

worked hard through the night, ... we may yet say to them: *Laborastis multum, et intulistis parum*, 'You have labored much, and brought in little.' ... But by that immaculate path of Mary, ... we sweat but little,"[2] and gain much.

We now turn to the causes of this facility. We first observe that it depends not on extrinsic circumstances, which may vary or fail, but that it comes from the very nature of the means employed. It is, in a word, an intrinsic quality of the perfect devotion to Mary. This same note applies to the other qualities of which we shall speak below.

§1.

The first reason why this devotion is an easy path is that, in reality, it applies to the supernatural life the natural method that a mother uses to educate her children. We spoke of this above in the chapter on spiritual childhood.[3] Let us now speak of its effects.

Of all the pedagogical processes, of all the systems of education, the maternal is undoubtedly the easiest. Why? Above all, because, driven by her love, the mother uses the means best suited to the needs of her child, and that she takes it upon herself to shoulder the effort.

We may observe that a mother becomes a child with her child in how she condescends to his intellectual frailty and stoops to his level of understanding. She shortens words that seem too long, giving them an elementary form that could be said to be a language apart, and, like him, baby-talks them. The ideas and explanations that she suggests are of such simplicity and naïveté that they make us smile; yet, we fail not to notice that they are suited most ingeniously to the nascent intelligence of her little pupil. She causes him to yield his mind and to allow her to mold it by her insistent cajoling and endearing assurances. This method of teaching may be summed up in the insistent use of two means: imitation and assistance.

Imitation, because the mother does first what she wants to teach her child. She articulates the word that he will baby-talk; she walks in

---

[2] ♦*TD*, 155. ¦¦ The allusion is to Agg 1.6: *Seminastis multum*, ... "You have sowed much." The use of "laborastis," perhaps from Nicolas Foucault, the pastor of Saint-Michel in Orléans, in his posthumous best seller, *Prônes* (1696). *Vraie Dévotion* was written around 1712. See, Prône 49, "Qu'est-ce que travailler sans Jésus-Christ?" [What does it mean to labor without Jesus-Christ?] in Migne, *Orateurs sacrés*, 88 [21]:765. |
[3] Part 3.4, p. 217 ff.

front of him to encourage him to take his first steps; she smiles to make him smile; she folds her hands to teach him to pray; in a word, she is the model that he must imitate. Moreover, the child acts with the help of his mother. By her continual assistance, she compensates for his frailty in whole or in part. If the child cannot walk, she carries him; if he is too weak to stand up, she sustains him; if he is too short, she lifts him up to the desired height, or lowers objects to be within reach. This maternal labor knows no end. She teaches her child over and over again. Never will the inexperience, the inconstancy, or the physical and moral infirmities of her little darling ever dissuade her. In this, the mother is the one expending almost all the labor, and all to provide her child with the ease to learn. He grows up with nary a worry; he learns almost unwittingly—by surrendering himself to her care.

Here we see, step by step, but in their supernatural perfection, what makes up our spiritual formation by the Blessed Virgin; which formation would be more laborious and imperfect without true dependence on our part, and without diligence on hers; in a word, without those unbroken string of benefits derived from our spiritual childhood with Mary. If the care and the lessons of a teacher (and especially of that incomparable teacher who is also a mother) so facilitate the physical and moral education of the child, the care and the lessons of the teacher, who is also the Mother, are all the more necessary for the supernatural life which absolutely passes our understanding.[4]

Thanks be to God, we find in Mary the perfect model and the powerful help we need.[5] After giving birth to us in the life of grace,

---

[4] Phil 4.7: The peace of God surpasseth all understanding.

[5] ♦We quote the reflections of Faber, *All for Jesus*, 4.5, 181-182: "I am not saying it is easy to be a Saint, but that Saints ... are the easiest masters ... because they are more like Jesus than the rest of men, more common, more considerate, more condescending, making allowances, calculating for character, and entering into the circumstances, views, and feelings of others." Still, who among such masters is like Mary, she who has the knowledge of Jesus infused and acquired? No Doctor, no Cherub even, can teach the way she teaches. Now, the more learned and cleverer the teacher, the easier and quicker the progress of the pupil will be. On these grounds, it is hard to avoid concluding that Mary is the easy road to perfection.

she makes us grow in it by gradually forming Christ in us.

This divine Word, splendor of the Father, which she, through the Incarnation, gave us abridged and as if in miniature—this *Verbum abbreviatum*,[6] she now places within our reach by her baby-talking to us the mysteries of our Faith. "There is no place," says St. Louis-Marie brilliantly, "in which the creature can find God nearer to him, and more suited to his frailty, than in Mary, for it was for this effect that He came down to be in her womb. Everywhere else, He is the Bread of the Mighty and the Bread of Angels; but in Mary, He is the Bread of Children."[7]

So often does Mary tenderly summon us, calling at the door of our will. We hear of her invitations in the words of Wisdom that the Church puts in the mouth of this good Mother: *Come over to me, all ye that desire me, and be filled with my fruits, for my spirit is sweet above honey* (Sir 24.26-27). *Whosoever is a little one, let him come to me* (Prv 9.4). The Wisdom Books are filled with such calls.

St. Louis-Marie conveys the process of maternal education, most real and truly lived, to the order of grace when he says that the servants of Mary carry their crosses with more ease, because the good Mother, full of the grace and unction of the Holy Ghost, candies them, be they ever so bitter, reducing them in the sugar of her maternal sweetness and the unction of pure love, so that they swallow them gladly, as they would caramelized walnuts.[8]

Lastly, let us remember that St. Louis-Marie presses us to look to

---

[6] *Verbum abbreviatum* is a concept much discussed in the Middle Ages. It carried many connotations. The simplest is "the Word made flesh." St. Lawrence Justinian, *Opera*, 394.2E, "Wherefore, ... we may approach with confidence, not towards the throne of glory, but towards the haven of His humanity, where, indeed, we will recognize the Majesty emptied, the *Word abbreviated*, the One clothed with a cloud and whose face is as the sun, and who is Wisdom made a fool by an excess of love." Peter the Chanter, *Verbum abbrev.*, c. 1, PL 205.23: "If indeed He, the Word sent to us from the bosom of Father, the Son of God whose breadth and depth are unfathomable, whose entirety the world cannot begin to understand, wished to be enclosed in the narrowness of a virgin womb, how much more would He wish to abridge the Word of the sacred pages that He bestowed on us, and left to us as a token and pledge of His love? By what paths and ways might we understand, in which course might we read the short and concise way towards eternal blessedness?" Answer: Through Jesus Christ in the Blessed Sacrament.

[7] ✦Cf. *Secret*, 17. ⁞⁞ Ps 77.25, Hebrew אַבִּירִים, of the mighty ones, which St. Jerome rendered as *Angelorum*; cf. Ps 104.10: Bread of Heaven; and Mt 15.26: It is not good to take the bread of the children, and to cast it to the dogs. |

[8] ✦cf. *TD*, 104-105. ⁞⁞ *Tailler le sucre*, a baking process in which reducing sugars caramelize to form a crust. Since 1912, it is technically called the Maillard reaction. |

Mary in all our actions, and to conform to her intentions and dispositions, as would a child look to his mother before he acts and then
strives to imitate her.

❖

We should observe that, to a great extent, we owe the abundant
fruits of this devotion and the ease of passage to perfection that it
provides, to the extraordinary power and continuity of the special
assistance given by the Blessed Virgin to her faithful children and
slaves. According to St. Louis-Marie, our experience of her generosity
will take us by surprise, for she fully realizes this word of the Psalm:
Step by step, *thy mercy will follow me all the days of my life* (Ps 22.6). She
is like a mother whose child is learning to walk. She follows him, both
arms extended, to brace him, and press him against her heart, should
he stagger.

O Mother of Mercy, Our Lady, is it not that the very thing which
you do for us? In every state and situation, you are there to help us
and carry us forward, step by step, whenever we need your assistance.
We cannot count how many are the perilous passes we have crossed
with such impunity, and even unwittingly, thanks to you! True are the
words of St. Bernard which St. Louis-Marie recounts in his treatise:
"Following her, you will never go astray. ... Under her patronage you
will never wander; beneath her protection you will not fear; she being
your guide, you will not weary."[9]

It is most sweet for the soul to find all the touching traits of maternal education in our spiritual formation by Mary, of which we shall
mention one last thing:

As we said, the child surrenders himself to his mother and grows
up without noticing having done so. Let us listen to this remark of St.
Louis-Marie: "When ... Mary becomes Queen in a soul, ... she works
there in secret, without even the soul knowing it, for were the soul to
know, she would destroy the beauty of Mary's works."[10] Such is the
sincerity, the guilelessness of childhood that the humility of the soul

---

[9] *TD*, 146. — St. Bernard, *De laudibus B.V.M.*, Homilia 2.17, PL 183.71A : "Ipsam sequens
non devias. ... Ipsa tenente non corruis; ipsa protegente non metuis; ipsa duce non fa-
tigaris." More amply quoted on page 267.
[10] ◆*Secret*, 37-38.

recreates. In turn, under the guidance of Mary, the soul becomes oblivious to herself, and she thinks less often of herself, and more of her good Mother.

We ought also to speak of the reciprocal love between the mother and the child, which love lightens the burdens of education and lets the results come in more easily. The words of St. Augustine find their natural application here: "Where there is love, there is no labor; and if there were labor, we would think it precious."[11] In the mother, the love is deep, thoughtful, untiring, and inspires her to heights of devotion, even unto devising ever cleverer methods of teaching. In the child, although instinctive, the love is the source of his docility and his attachment, and lends credence to his intuitions.

§2.

We find the second reason why this devotion is an easy path in the abundant communication of the Holy Ghost, and especially in grant of the gifts of wisdom and understanding. The Holy Ghost is called *Spiritualis unctio*,[12] the "spirit of unction." As spiritual oil, He penetrates our soul and her faculties, and consecrates her interiorly; | and, just as oil coats contact surfaces in the cams and gears and other parts of an engine and makes it run smoothly, so also the anointing of the Holy Ghost gives us the ease to do acts that the rust of routine, the causticity of spiritual dryness, the dust of our faults, or the resistance of our vicious nature, would otherwise make it too grueling to exercise, or that they may even grind our spiritual progress to a halt. | Our good Mother does not let this divine unction penetrate our soul drop by drop, parsimoniously, for St. Louis-Marie tells us: "It is an easy path, because of the fullness of the grace and unction of the Holy Ghost, Who fills her to overflowing."[13] And elsewhere: "They

---

[11] St. Augustin, *De bono Viduatis*, 21.26, PL 40.448: "Fastings and watchings help the prayers of widows, so far as they disturb not health, if they be spent in praying, singing psalms, reading, and meditating in the Law of God, even the very things which seem laborious are turned into spiritual delights. For no way burdensome are the labors of such as love, but even if of themselves they delight. ... It matters therefore what is loved. *In eo quod amatur, aut non laboratur, aut et labor amatur*, 'for, in the case of what is loved, either there is no labor, or the labor also is loved." Cf. St. Bermard, *In Cantica*, 85.8, PL 183.1191D: "Ubi amor est, labor non est, sed sapor."

[12] Hymn, *Veni, Creator Spiritus*.

[13] *TD*, 116.

have such ease in bearing the yoke of Jesus Christ, that they are almost oblivious to its weight, for the oil of devotion has made it rot ¦¦ and fall away |: *Jugum eorum computrescet a facie olei*, 'the yoke shall putrefy at the presence of the oil' (Is 10.27)."[14]

We should call to mind the most consoling and confident words of St. Louis-Marie's concerning the special assistance that the Blessed Virgin gives to her faithful servants in their gravest trials. We have already quoted a portion of the delightful passage which readers know so well. We now add these affirmations: It is true that those most devoted to Mary, are the ones "who carry their crosses with more ease, more merit, and more glory." And, "a person ... will never carry heavy crosses, neither do so joyously nor to the end, without a tender devotion to the Blessed Virgin, for it is the sweetmeat of crosses."[15] The entire life of St. Louis-Marie bears out as a striking example of this teaching. ¦¦ One man wrote: "The works of [St. Louis-Marie] took such a heavy toll on his body and spirit, his pious spiritual exercises never did stop, and his mortifications were so relentless, that I always thought it a kind of miracle that he did suffer so much, yet did not die a thousand deaths."[16] No doubt, he was able to sustain his efforts for love of the Blessed Virgin. | We have here the secret of this ease by which he lifted the heaviest of crosses, and would sooner carry them.

The third reason souls undertake and work great things with ease is that they are robustly strengthened by divine gifts; for the Spirit of God is power, whilst also unction and sweetness. Frail as we are, we would be overwhelmed by the works that perfect souls exercise with pluck, and sometimes as if being at play, for they possess the gifts of the Holy Ghost in abundance, and we still do not. Nevertheless, we know that the practice of Holy Slavery disposes us to receive such gifts, and that by "surprises of grace" it presents us with outcomes to which our infirmity would otherwise not even allow us to aspire.

> She makes me pure and fertile
> By her true fecundity,

---

[14] *TD*, 146.

[15] ♦Cf. *TD*, 104-105.

[16] Mr. Dubois, almoner to the Poitiers general hospital, in Pauvert, *Vie*, 482-483.

She makes me strong and docile
By her deep humility.[17]

§3.

We said that one of the distinctive processes of the spiritual method called living the life in union with Christ is to leave behind abstractions in order to come face to face with His Person, to realize in Him our supernatural life and our practice of virtues.[18] We can be sure, that this, too, eases our spiritual progress. The system of maternal education, applied to our life of grace in the exercise of our perfect devotion, gives tangible form to everything more than any other and, consequently, makes our every spiritual endeavor easy. As we know, in his mind, the child reduces everything to his mother: Who is the authority? His mother. Who teaches him? His mother. Who looks after his welfare and safety? His mother. He cannot conceive of being loved or loving, except in relation to his mother. It is she who provides for all his needs. In short, we can safely say that she means the world to him.

Now, when St. Louis-Marie urges us to act through Mary, with her, in her, and for her, to abide in her interior, and so on, he is saying that, for the child, the bonds and tasks of daily life take their concrete form in the union. Grasp that and we will have the practice of the purity of intention in conformance to that of our Mother's; we will have hope, in throwing ourselves into her arms; Mary shall be our world, ¦ and, in the apt and cogent expression of St. Louis-Marie, our soul shall breathe her, as the body breathes the air.[19] ¦

The workings of the life of union place us first and foremost on the bright side, or at least they keep us in the shadowy side the briefest. Such a life is more appealing and easier, as is also a mother's process of education. Every mother, for example, offers recompense for making sacrifices and practicing obedience. Mary it was who revealed to ¦¦ St. Louis-Marie, ¦ her devoted servant, the positive side of the Cross, so full of mystery which, without the luminous lights of

---

[17] ♦*Cantiques*, 77.16, 132. Elle me rend pur et fertile / Par sa pure fécondité, / Elle me rend fort et docile / Par sa profonde humilité.

[18] Part 1.3.1.1, p. 61.

[19] *TD*, 154.

understanding, may not be fathomed.[20] It was she who repaid him for his sacrifices with her maternal loving-kindness. But we cannot linger among these considerations, for we must move on to one last and important reason for why this devotion is an easy path.

§4.

The method used by St. Louis-Marie is simple. Elsewhere the processes are more complicated and, as a result, more laborious. There are rules for one action, others for another; the workings of spiritual life are analyzed, and detailed piece by piece. Some have duly ordered the work of sanctification as a series of ingenious tactics designed for a battle set in stages, yet ends only in life itself. Many multiply the acts, carefully tailoring them to suit the times, the places, and the circumstances. All this is real, respectable, and deserves attention all the more because we find in them the fruit of a worthy experience and a goodly reserve of traditional teaching. We cannot disdain what the Church has approved and what many souls have found helpful. We only wish to say that there is something else; that many have a particular need for a simple practice, and being simple, it would afford them an easy path. Indeed, simplicity is what distinguishes the method set down by St. Louis-Marie, since it consists in the application of a *unique* process suited to all acts and states. Everything is reduced to this one practice: Acting through Mary, with her, in her, and for her. Whether I pray, work or eat; whether I am joyful or sad, I have only one thing to do, and that is to unite myself with the dispositions of Mary, to abandon myself to her wishes. A single goal, a single process. It is simplicity itself. ¦¦ As St. Louis-Marie says: "There is a great difference between carving a figure in relief by striking the chisel with a hammer, and making one by pouring molten metal into a mold. Sculptors labor much to make statues in the first manner; but in the second, they work but little, and finish quickly."[21] | — ¦ In one manner, there is a great variety in the way of working, depending on the material used and the desired result; in the other, it is always the same

---

[20] *Cantiques*, 19.1: "La croix est un mystère / Très profond ici-bas, / Sans beaucoup de lumière / On ne le connaît pas."

[21] Cf. *TD*, 156. Technically, it is also laborious to make the clay pattern and plaster master. The time saving is in the process of replication by casting in the mold.

process, whatever the object to be molded and its shape. |

This consideration will be particularly agreeable to beginners. What director has not had to fight the despair of souls confronted with their faults and imperfections? Long is the progress and many are the amendments that must be made to be transformed in Christ Jesus, and all require great effort! Where to start and what resolutions need to be made? There is so much to do, yet souls are capable of so little! One thing only will meet their needs: When the child is born into this world, does he not have much work to do before he grows up and becomes a perfect man? If he were capable of thinking about it and realizing the challenge, would he not be discouraged? But, if all is reduced to the one thing that he practices, that is, submitting himself obediently to his mother and remaining in her dependence, in this condition alone, will he be nourished, and grow, and learn. So also, in in our spiritual life, where all is reduced to living docilely in reliance on Mary. This is our sole resolution, or, if you will, one which contains the others and to which we can reduce. If we are ever faithful to it, whilst on earth, our spiritual life will increase, we will carry on the fight against our enemies, we will grow in virtues, and we will arrive at the fullness of the age of Christ.

Let us take care not to think that this path is easy in the sense that we can avoid running into either trials or struggles. St. Louis-Marie seeks to shield us from making this mistake. He was not one to attempt minimizing the import of this word of the Gospel: *Regnum cælorum vim patitur, et violenti rapiunt illud*, "the Kingdom of Heaven suffereth violence, and the violent bear it away" (Mt 11.12), or to conjure up a way to follow Jesus other than the royal road of the Cross. Indeed not. He proclaims that, more than others, the faithful servants of Mary have to ¦ fight more battles, face more hostilities, and bear more crosses,[22] | as he himself can testify.[23]

With its total dependence, and continual and intimate self-denial, the devotion to Mary may be considered a narrow path, though its ease remains undiminished; for the ease and narrow strait

---

[22] *TD*, 30.
[23] See, Pauvert, *Vie*, 131-142.

are not necessarily in opposition. With a gauge of mere inches (but from which wheels swerve not), our railroads are but narrow tracks, especially when compared to the national routes. But, friction amply lessened and other improvements provided, no one would deny the ease of carriage on our tracks. Yes, ours is an easy path and, in a sense, broad; that is, it is one on which we may be at ease.[24] Whence this particular effect that St. Louis-Marie noted: | "To those that practice it faithfully, this devotion affords an awesome interior liberty, which is the liberty of the children of God. For, as in this devotion we make ourselves slaves of Jesus Christ, and, as such, consecrate ourselves entirely to Him, our Good Master removes all scruple and servile fear from our soul, along with everything else that tends only to diminish, enslave, or confound her, and enlarges the heart by a firm confidence in God, in recompense for the loving captivity in which we put ourselves."[25] | Ours is an easy path. It is also short, and the one that leads us promptly to our goal. We shall now explain why this is.

ARTICLE 2: THE PATH IS SHORT

No doubt the above title will fascinate a soul seeking a means to quickly attain spiritual perfection. The desire to act quickly and to attain a goal rapidly, even when it comes to sanctification, is peculiar not only to the age of steam and electricity, because in the sixteenth century, with his accustomed finesse St. Francis de Sales did say: "I see that you want me to teach you a sort of ready-made way of perfection, one that you have only to put your head into it, or put it on like a dress, and thus be perfect, without taking any trouble. ... Certainly, if that were in my power, I should be the most perfect man in the world; for if I could give perfection to others without their having to do anything, I assure you that I should take it first of all for myself. You fancy that perfection is an art of which, if you can only discover the secret, you will instantly obtain possession, without any trouble. Certainly, this is a great mistake, for, in aspiring to union with the Beloved, there is no other secret than to do what we aspire to; that is,

---

[24] Ps 118.96: *Latum mandatum tuum nimis*, "Thy commandment is exceeding broad."
[25] ◆Cf. *TD*, 116-117; see also, 149, 151, 152. Fr. Lhoumeau credits the cause of the effects to the devotion. Quotation extended to show that St. Louis-Marie attributes it to Christ.

to labor faithfully in the exercise of divine love."[26] His conclusion lies in this advice: "Walk always, ... walk in the way of your vocation with simplicity, more intent on doing than on desiring; that is the shortest path."[27]

Many a soul are shocked by this counsel, for they dream of obtaining splendid and complete outcomes in just a few weeks, if not a matter of days. Such is the cause of the puerile and disordered despair that occurs in their perfervid moments. We should realize that, here below, all life begun in time needs time to grow. The principle equally applies to the life of the body, the life natural, and the life supernatural of the soul. We note that, in speaking of the marvelous fruits of the perfect devotion, St. Louis-Marie insists on its faithful and persevering practice.[28] To this Tree of Life, which is Mary, we must apply the word of the Psalm: *It will bring forth its fruit in due season* (Ps 1.3). The time of the fruits is preceded by Summer when they ripen, which in turn is preceded by Spring when the flowers appear, and Winter, when everything seems dead.

Now that we have forewarned the reader against a false understanding of the term "short path," we turn to the consideration of why it still is a suitable description. We have no need to restate the motive we gave earlier; namely, that an easy path is short, because we advance faster on it. We end this section with these two considerations: Mary is a short path that leads to God, first because of her eminent holiness and her union with Him; second, because her mediation shortens the distance that separates us from God.

§1.

We should here meditate on the marvelous prerogatives of the Blessed Virgin which we call her Immaculate Conception, her impeccability,[29] and on the states that consequentially flow from them. This

---

[26] ♦de Sales, *Conferences*, 9, 159; cf. *Œuvres*, 6:150-151.
[27] Ibid.
[28] *TD*, 154.
[29] The absolute inability to sin. God owed it to His own dignity and holiness, so to speak, to bestow the grace of perfect perseverance (as against mortal sin) and confirmation in grace (as against venial sin) upon her from whom His Divine Son was to assume human nature; meaning, the impeccability of the B.V. Mary rests upon the grace of her divine motherhood. (Scheeben, *Dogmatik*, n. 280, 3:558-570, in Pohle, *Mariology*, 80-82).

daughter, in whom everything ascends to God without effort or delay; that soul which, like a well-polished mirror, faithfully reflects all that strikes it, that is to say, all the graces granted her, all the gifts which are her prerogative, may be but an easy and short path for us. St. Louis-Marie likes to say that Mary is only the echo of God, that in her everything says "God"[30]; that she cannot be an obstacle that turns us away from God, as would other creatures. Thus, through her, "without pulling back or delay, with giant strides ¦ and in the quickstep, ¦ we shall march towards Jesus Christ."[31]

§2.

Mary is the mediatrix between Jesus and us. She brings Him closer to us, she shortens the distance that separates us from Him. She is thus the short path to Him.

Mary brings Jesus Christ closer to us: "There is no place," says St. Louis-Marie, "in which the creature can find God nearer to him, and more suited to his frailty, than in Mary, for it was for this effect that He came down to be in her womb."[32] ¦ In every age, men dreamt of having God with them. It was realized in Mary, who carried His Only-Begotten Son in her. ¦ Jesus is the God made Man, born of the Blessed Virgin, and he who comes to her comes to Him. Seek Him not in the sublime ¦ heights ¦ of Heaven.[33] His Heaven is the bosom of Mary; His throne, the arms of His Mother. There it was that the shepherds found the Word made flesh[34] and Whom the Magi adored. We, too, let us go to Mary, for we are sure to find the Divine Child with His Mother.[35]

As soon as we come near her, she will bring Him to us, and place Him in our arms. And much do we need that it be so, for Msgr. Gay says that to us, Jesus is so far in His states, yet so near in His mysteries![36] We thus stand in need of a mediatrix before the principal and

---

[30] *TD*, 159.

[31] ♦Cf. *TD*, 105-106.

[32] *Secret*, 17.

[33] Fr. Lhoumeau: *profondeurs de*, "depths of."

[34] Jn 1.14. Fr. Lhoumeau: Made "man."

[35] Mt 2.11.

[36] Gay, *Élévations*, 44, 1:385, speaking of the Holy Sacrifice of the Altar: "If the sun had a heart, would it not take great joy of that lighting, warming, and lending life to all in Creation which its solitary placement high in the firmament made it possible for it to do? So it is that You, O Jesus, are pleased to be our divine Sun, to be Jesus our sole

prime Mediator. Such is the teaching of St. Bernard in the words that
have become classic in the field: ¦¦ *Opus est mediatore ad mediatorem
istum, nec alter nobis utilior quam Maria*,[37] "We have need of a Mediatrix to Christ the Mediator, and there is none more to our profit than
Mary." | We may yet want to start off on our journey to Jesus by means
natural, frail though we are and wounded by Original Sin, but remember the words of the Psalmist: *Blessed are they who are undefiled in the
way of life!* (Ps 118.1); for by our personal faults, we have indeed set ourselves apart from God. We should never cross the threshold of interior
life without being fully conscious of those unbearable distances which
our past faults and their consequences have put between us and the
Lord. They do remain even after absolution ¦¦ in the Sacrament of
Penance. | *And he went abroad to a far country* (Lk 15.13), said the Divine
Master of the prodigal son. When we turn away from God, our pace
quickens because we go downhill, but we notice not our downward
direction, nor the path we take, nor if there is a path. But how great
will be the distance that separates us from our heavenly Father, when
we wish to climb back and return to Him, less perhaps to obtain a first
pardon, than to regain (if it pleases His mercy) a certain degree of
union and intimacy out of which we have fallen!

Even so, Mary is there to bring us closer to Jesus, to give Him to
us. In going out to meet the prodigal son, the father shortened the
distance he needed to travel and hastened ¦ the reunion. | Closer still
Jesus will have walked towards us on the path through Mary; and if
we take the same path to return to Him, our route will become all the
shorter, and we will risk neither starving and fainting nor succumbing
from the blows of our enemies.

§3.

The puissant help of Mary's also shortens our route by removing
obstacles. *I will make crooked paths straight*, said the Prophet Isaiah
in one of his messianic visions (Is 42.16). This prophecy is meant for
¦¦ St. John the Baptist, | the Precursor, for he fulfilled it by preparing

---

Heaven, so full of mystery, yet are everywhere; so evidently a King, yet so lowly; so far
from us by Your states, yet so near in Your mysteries."
[37] ¦¦ St. Bernard, *Sermo*, Dominica infra Octavam Assumptionis B.V.M., §2, PL
183.429D. | ◆St. Louis-Marie often referred to this aphorism and commented on it.

hearts for the coming of Christ. ¦ She who, on the day of the Visitation, brought Jesus to the Precursor to prepare *his* soul for His coming, ought to be called the first missionary, which is an eminent honor. In this respect, she preceded St. John, bringing with her the Good News.[38] | As the dawn heralds the rising of the sun, where she appears, there Christ will be, and through her, He will come. When thoughts of Mary and love for her begin to dawn in a soul, the hope for justification will shine, and Jesus will come near; when they increase, the sun of spiritual advancement will rise, and Jesus will grow in us; for "Jesus is everywhere and always," says St. Louis-Marie, "the fruit and the Son of Mary."[39]

Mary straightens our paths. When we act through her and in her, our intentions are purified and they ascend straight to God; all the imagined twists and turns on our path tend to disappear; our pride is beaten down by her abject humility; she fills the valleys,[40] meaning the depths of our miseries or the gaps left by our imperfections, in becoming our supplement.[41] Then, if our enemies come to hinder our advance, or make us pull back or trip us, ... with the support and aid of Mary, and under her guidance, without pulling back or delay, with giant strides ¦ and in the quickstep, | we shall march towards Jesus Christ."[42]

ARTICLE 3: THE PATH IS PERFECT

This devotion is a perfect path to divine union, first because we have in Mary the perfect means, as she is a most perfect creature; second, the manner of uniting to her in our devotion is equally perfect.

§1.

Our proximate goal is to conform to Mary. She, a copy of Jesus,

---

[38] In the original French, Fr. Lhoumeau has the Virgin Mary preparing the soul of St. John, and claims for her the title of "Precursor of the Messiah." De Fiores, *Jesus Living in Mary*, the comprehensive handbook on Montfortian spirituality, only goes so far as calling the Blessed Virgin "the first missionary," for bringing the Word Incarnate at the Visitation. (p. 214). It is the Holy Ghost Who sanctified St. John in the womb of his mother, Elizabeth, upon her hearing the greeting of the Blessed Virgin Mary. (Lk 1.41).

[39] *TD*, 24.

[40] Bar 5.7.

[41] *TD*, 98.; see note 53, p. 193.

[42] ◆Cf. *TD*, 105.

our divine exemplar; but a copy so faultless that she surpasses in perfection all other Saints put together. Of this St. Louis-Marie reminds
us, for example, when he explained the title of *forma Dei*, "the mold
of God,"[43] where Christ first became man and by which we are conformed to Him. Now, the more perfect the mold, the more perfect will
be the reproduction.

Mary is our teacher who teaches us to live imitating Christ better
than anyone. We know of many a pupil taught by a teacher of excellent manners, correct language, and the purest diction, who not only
received an excellent education, but also acquired good behavior and
enunciation from her. Similarly, we shall profit under the guidance of
that incomparable teacher whose words and deeds so perfectly speak
of Jesus. We realize that we cannot attend a better school than Mary's,
when we see the depths to which she has pierced the divine mysteries,
living as she does in the ineffable bonds with the adorable Trinity,
without offending the ardent jealousy of divine holiness.

 ¦ In the absence of a mother, the child suffers a gap in his education that we sooner sense than define, because it exists in the depths
of his soul. Mothers recognize it, for their heart is a special school
where intuitions, tender cares, devotions, exquisite sensibilities, delicate operations come naturally. Now, Mary is a teacher, and also the
Mother, which means that she is the most perfect of teachers—one
that no other may best. Her Immaculate Heart guides the soul to that
exquisite sense of things divine, to that supernatural and delicate sen-
sitivity to the touches of grace, without which we hardly can be
perfect. The soul is indebted to Mary for leading her and for filling the
gaps in her progress. | This is at least one of the reasons why St. Louis-
Marie says that the devotion to Mary, and a complete dependence on
her, are most necessary to those who strive for perfection.

We are thus not surprised to see him solemnly affirm, with
repeated oaths and declarations, that he prefers the immaculate path
alone with Mary, to the road on which all the Angels and Saints come
to assist. ¦¦ Says he: "Make for me, if you will, a new road to go to Jesus,
and pave it with all the merits of the Blessed, adorn it with all their

---

[43] *TD*, 156.

heroic virtues, illuminate and embellish it with all the lights and beau-
ties of the Angels, and let all the Angels and the Saints be there
themselves to escort, defend, and sustain those who are ready to walk
there; and yet, in truth, in simple truth, I say boldly—and I repeat that
I say truly—I would prefer the immaculate way of Mary to this new
path, even if it were perfect."[44] |

But it is also by the very manner by which this devotion makes us
practice the union with Mary that it appears to us as a perfect path.

§2.

St. Louis-Marie repeatedly states that he knows of no practice in
which we empty ourselves, that rids us so easily of a certain proclivity
towards proprietorship that surreptitiously creep into our best
actions.[45] While it may be true that such practice does not positively
constitute holiness, it surely is an indispensable precondition for it.
The soul may live in God only so long as she dies to herself; she can
follow Christ inasmuch as she renounces herself. A perfect path,
therefore, is one that leads to the perfect practice of self-abnegation.

We saw in our discussion on the consecration according to the
formula of St. Louis-Marie's that it is a total and absolute donation.[46]
Total, because, we give all that we have and all that we are, without
exception; absolute, because in consecrating ourselves as slaves, we
profess that we belong to God and His Mother, in the strictest sense.
This is the perfect dispossession.

As to the interior practice, we said that the overwhelming evidence points to our devotion leading us to a self-abnegation in its
totality, where the immolation is so perfect that Fr. Olier compares it
to a continual martyrdom.[47]

We also observe that the process used to unite us to Jesus through
Mary is eminently suitable to stave off the impulse to self-regard.
With our gaze fixed on Mary, and steadily looking to her as our model
for conforming our intentions and dispositions, we go out of ourselves
by thought and affection, and are separated from ourselves to be lost

---

[44] ♦Cf. TD, 108. ¦ [Quotation moved up to text above]. |
[45] ♦TD, 92.
[46] Part 3.2.1.2, p. 182.
[47] ♦Olier, "De quel nom faut-il appeler cette dévotion ?" in Le Règne de Jésus par Marie,
July 1901.

in Mary. On this, St. Francis de Sales says: "He whose one desire is to please the divine Lover, has neither inclination nor leisure to turn back upon himself; ¦¦ his mind tends continually in the direction whither love carries him."[48] |

Other methods leave more latitude in the exercise of the will, initiative, and personal labor, in respect of personal intentions, thoughts, practices, direction, as is the case in the work of sculptors. In our devotion, Mary leads in everything. Our job is to be docile and to bend to her will—to let her do as she wills, that is, to let her do her work of molding the soul in which there is less of the "me."

It may be said that in the practice of this devotion the attention to oneself is reduced to a minimum, for there is less self-regard the more one gazes at Mary and Christ, and when one does need to turn one's eye to oneself, it is only to lose oneself in Mary. In contrast, when one faces oneself, as the sculptor stands before his work, to look at one's vices and virtues in search of perfection, is to risk the return of self-love. He who looks at his reflection, even it was for a purpose, soon becomes a narcissist, or at least is led there. This explains why the masters of spiritual life stress so much the perils that beginners run with self-love; which perils are partially shed in our devotion.

The idea of spiritual childhood allows us to delve deeper into this consideration. The child is wont to forget himself, be oblivious to himself, and to surrender himself, for which reason he has no guile, is forthright, and is marked by an absence of introspection. In his talk on simplicity, St. Francis de Sales has these fine and judicious remarks to say on the subject: "An infant is in a state of such simplicity that he has no knowledge but of his mother. He has only one love, which is for his mother; and in that love only one aim and desire—his mother's breast; when he is upon that beloved breast, he wants nothing more. The soul which has attained perfect simplicity has only one love, which is for God. In this love, she has one only aim—to rest upon the bosom of the heavenly Father, and there to abide like a loving child, leaving all care of self to that good Father; anxious about nothing except to maintain this confidence; not even disquieted by any desires

---

[48] de Sales, *Conferences*, 12, 227; cf. *Œuvres*, 6:216.

for those virtues and graces which seem necessary to her. It is true that such a soul never neglects any good opportunity which she meets with on her way, but she hunts not about eagerly for means of perfecting herself other than those which are prescribed."[49]

And further on: "Children, whom Our Lord has told us should be our model of perfection, are, generally speaking, quite free from care, especially in the presence of their parents. They cling to them, without turning to consider their satisfactions or their consolations. These they presume in good faith, and enjoy in simplicity, without any curiosity whatsoever as to their causes or effects. ... In its absolute simplicity and purity, this exercise of continual self-abandonment into the hands of God comprehends the perfection of all other exercises; and while God leaves us the use of it, we ought not to change it. Spiritual lovers, spouses of the heavenly King, from time to time do indeed contemplate themselves, as do the *doves upon brooks of pure waters* (Cant 5.12), in order to see if they are adorned so as to please their Beloved. This is done by examinations of conscience, by which they cleanse, purify, and beautify themselves as well as they can, not in order to be perfect, not to satisfy themselves, not from a desire to make progress in virtue, but out of obedience to the Spouse, out of the reverence they have for Him, and the fervent desire which they have to please Him. ... These simple doves do not give a very lengthy or very anxious study to the work of cleansing and adorning, for the confidence which their love gives them of being greatly loved although unworthy—I mean the confidence that their love gives them in the love and goodness of their Beloved—deprives them of all anxiety and mistrust as to their not being beautiful enough. Besides, the desire to love, rather than to adorn and prepare themselves for love, takes away all anxious solicitude."[50]

This quote is long, but it goes a long way towards explaining how spiritual childhood is, amongst all others, a perfect path.

St. Louis-Marie guarantees us that it is the peculiar character of our devotion to the Blessed Virgin, and that there is in it more than an enthusiastic affirmation and fanciful considerations, when he says:

---

[49] Ibid. 226.
[50] Ibid. 227-228.

| "O what a difference there is between a soul formed in Jesus Christ by the ordinary ways, that is, like a sculptor, trusting her own skill and counts on her own ingenuity, and another, wholly malleable, truly free, melted down, and, in no way relying on herself, that suffers herself to be cast in Mary and be shaped by the operation of the Holy Ghost! | Many are the stains, the defects, the darkness, the self-deceptions, the things pertaining to the natural or to the human in the former; and how pure, how divine, and how like unto Jesus Christ, is the latter!"[51]

§3.

Lastly, we say that this path is a way of perfection, because it is a way of love. To act always for Mary, is to make our actions be acts of love. What other motive than extraordinary love would lead us to a total and absolute donation, as does our perfect consecration? It is the pure and perfect love which stays so simple, regards itself so little, seeks less its own good than the satisfaction of the beloved.

Spiritual life principally consists in charity. In our path, to grow and be perfected in one, is to do the same for the other, and when we allow our devotion to hold sway over our practice of other virtues, we will acquire the habit of marching to the cadence of a perfect love.

ARTICLE 4: THE PATH IS SECURE

How precious is the benefit of walking securely in the path of perfection! To take the grueling and difficult ways without going astray, to find a prized guide amidst the thorny and touchy trials of interior life, is assuredly a foretaste of paradise and a glimpse of the repose in Heaven. Even so, | there is no denying the necessity for holy fear, for humility, in the work of our salvation, but lest we tremble at the enormity of the task, let us listen to these reassuring words: | "It is fitting that the Blessed Lady should surely lead us to Jesus, just as it is that Jesus should surely lead us to the Eternal Father."[52] Let us examine what makes "the way of Mary" perfectly | secure. |

---

[51] ◆Cf. *Secret*, 15. ¦¦ [Corrected to conform with original.] |
[52] ◆Cf. *TD*, 113.

§1.

Do demons threaten us with external perils and attacks? We need not fear, for we are safe in that Tower of David and under the care of her who, to Satan, *is terrible as an army set in array* (Cant 6.9). Her name alone fills him with dread and makes him recoil. It is the name of she whom God has set in opposition as the personal enemy of that serpent; the same who crushes his head.[53] The Saints and Angels assist us, but according to the order and power they receive from their Queen, which is why, in a passage quoted above,[54] St. Louis-Marie affirms that he preferred the path where Mary alone would protect us, to the way where all the Angels and Saints are gathered to defend and assist us.

> Strike him, strike the enemy,
> Bearing down on me, tempting me,
> Strike him, strike the enemy,
> Crush, trample him beneath thy feet.
> Thy po'erful hand, my Lady,
> Fills all Hell with fear and trembling.
> Strike him, strike the enemy.[55]

§2.

Sometimes, the cause of our perils is within us, namely our frailty, our self-deceit, our ignorance of divine intentions, or the blindness to our own needs.

The continual and maternal assistance of the Blessed Virgin is the surest safeguard against our frailty; for he who is as feeble as a newborn finds no place more secure than in the arms of his mother. Filled with this sentiment, St. Louis-Marie sings:

> This good Mother and Lady
> Aids me all 'round puissantly,
> And when I fall by frailty,
> She lifts me up instantly.[56]

A discussion on self-deceit is an uncomfortable chapter in a book

---

[53] Gn 3.15.

[54] Part 4.4.3.1, p. 308.

[55] ◆*Cantiques*, 145.6, 134. Frappez, frappez, / L'ennemi me presse et me tente, / Frappez, frappez. / Écrasez, foulez à vos pieds, / Sous votre main toute-puissante, / Tout l'enfer prendra l'épouvante, / Frappez, frappez.

[56] ◆Ibid. 77.11, 132. See note 9, p. 220.

on spirituality. Fr. Faber, who is otherwise so generous and encourag-
ing, betrays an exactitude almost to the point of being dispiriting. In
his *Conferences*, he speaks of self-deceit by describing the consequences of frail human nature in excruciating detail. ¦¦ He says,
amongst other things, that men are corrupt and incapable of being
truthful with themselves, with others, and with God. They are prone
to sloth, have no drive for self-knowledge, and go about life in a haze
of ignorance, which they seek to cover in self-deceit, of which he iden-
tifies seven fundamental kinds:

First, the one that takes no advice. "A man neglects the duties
which God has given him to do, and spends all his day in church, and
yet imagines himself a special favorite of God. Even monks and nuns
can mistake singularity for perfection. There is a false modesty, and a
false humility, a deluded penance and a deluded prayer. Delusion is
everywhere, and yet to us looking on, it is unaccountable how the
victim does not at once see through the delusion."

Second, the self-deceit that is "always taking advice, and, what is
perhaps worse, always taking it of everybody. This vice belongs to men
... who are always undertaking things, and who never succeed in anything they undertake."

Third, complacent self-deceit, in which the deluded man, cannot
conceive the possibility of doubt, and finds "an external reason for
every failure, which no foresight could have calculated, and against
which no prudence could have guarded."

Fourth, the censorious self-deceit, belonging to those "who
always are so sure they are in the right, that they set themselves up as
a standard by which to judge others."

Fifth, ambitious self-deceit that "confounds single actions with
formed habits; and if by a more-than-common impulse of grace a man
has been able in one instance to do something generous for God, it
leads him to suppose that he has already acquired a saintly habit."

Sixth, the scrupulous self-deceit. "It perversely fixes its attention
on the wrong things, that is, on things which it need not particularly
attend to, and it does this exclusively. Meanwhile, it is perfectly
unscrupulous in things which are a scandal, or a ruling passion, or an
occasion of sin, or a besetting temptation."

Seventh, the falsely humble self-deceit. "A man in this state is ignorant of that which of all things in the spiritual life is most necessary for him to know—his own want of courage. This is because his false humility never allows him to try himself. He thinks, in his artificial self-abjection, which has now become real without becoming true, that he ought only to attempt low things for God; and therefore, he does what is below his strength, without trying what is level with it or above it."

Fr. Faber ends his long discussion on the varieties of self-deceit by saying: "There is in fact no entanglement in Creation like the entanglement of self-deceit; and there is this peculiarity about all its varieties, that they are all of them swift diseases, tending to become so very soon and at such early stages very difficult to cure."[57] |

Even if we approached the subject of self-deceit with compassion, we cannot study it without having to probe into the darkest folds of our soul and becoming uneasy. Still, there is none that suffers not from self-deceits. The best that we can aim for in our life here below is to reduce the number, guarding ourselves against them and being in the best possible condition to be rid of them, while we wait for | the dawn of eternity where, with the rising of the brilliant the Sun of Justice,[58] | every error and every lie shall be no more.

Let us meditate on the following words, and we shall see that the devotion to Mary according to St. Louis-Marie gives us the desired results. "Where Mary is," said he, "there the evil spirit is not. One of the most unmistakable signs that we are led by the good Spirit is that we are most devoted to our good Mother, and that we oft think and speak of her."[59] Then he adds: "Just as respiration is a certain sign [of life], so also is the frequent thought and loving invocation of Mary a certain mark that the soul is not [separated from God] by sin."[60] Further on, he asserts that "no faithful client of Mary will ever fall into heresy (at least formal heresy) or self-deceit. He may very well err materially, take falsehood for truth, and evil spirit for the good; but, notwithstanding his facing more difficulty in doing one than in the other, sooner or later he will acknowledge his material fault and error;

---

[57] Faber, *Conferences*, 156, 185-195. The talk on self-deceit takes up 82 pages in total.
[58] Mal 4.2.
[59] Cf. *TD*, 114-115.
[60] Cf. *TD*, 114.

and when he does, he will no longer—not in the least—persist in the belief of what he once thought to be true, neither will he tolerate it."[61]

Another cause of self-deceit, as we said, is our ignorance of God's plans for us, or the blindness to our needs, which more often than not causes us to blunder in our supplications and undertakings. We find the best guarantees against them in our total abandonment to Mary, our adherence to her views and intentions in preference to ours, our donation of the fruits of our prayers and our satisfactions; all the more so, because such guarantees ¦ point us to the security in the freedom born of obedience to divine Will.[62] |

§3.

Lastly, if we seek it in the perfect conformity of our will, as we must, our union with Mary will shelter us from our many self-deceits. As all masters of spirituality have proclaimed, we shall find in such conformity a sure and open path on which all may ascend to the highest degrees of spiritual life. This is a promise good even for those in states extraordinary. In truth, St. Louis-Marie could very well have said that no other practice of devotion to Mary more faithfully preserves the soul in grace and more perfectly and easily unites her to Jesus Christ.

We might venture to apply to the Blessed Virgin the words of the Prophet Isaiah: *"And a path and a way shall be there, and it shall be called the holy way: the unclean shall not pass over it, and this shall be unto you a straight way, so that fools shall not err therein. No lion shall be there, nor shall any mischievous beast go up by it, ¦¦ nor be found there: but they shall walk there that shall be delivered* | (Is 35.8-9).

---

[61] Cf. *TD*, 115.

[62] On obedience, see St. Ignatius of Loyola, Letter 3304, Mar 26, 1553, to the Jesuits of Portugal, *Letters*, 287-295; critical Spanish edition, Letter 304, *Cartas*, 3:184-206. The summit of all obedience, Phil 2.8-11.

PART V:

THE LIFE IN UNION WITH MARY

PROLOGUE

o round out the ascetic part of our work, we shall show the application of the perfect devotion in certain acts of Christian life. Even though a number of books on the life of union with Mary have been written, there is still much to be said, for many have yet to take the special viewpoint of St. Louis-Marie's, and fewer still have fully lived the teaching of Holy Slavery. Its principle of dependence and dispossession gives the life of union with the Blessed Virgin a specific expression, which does not arise from honoring her only as Mediatrix.

We shall not review every act of Christian life. We shall limit ourselves to prayer, examinations of conscience, holy works, the Holy Mass, and Holy Communion, as we deem these the most important for our purposes.

CHAPTER 1:

ON PRAYER

§1. THE NECESSITY OF PRAYER

od gave man a law of prayer for his life supernatural, as He did of nourishment for his life corporeal. We must pray, just as we must eat, for each is a necessity. Our Lord says to everyone: *Oportet semper orare et nunquam deficere*, "we ought always to pray and not to faint" (Lk 18.1). We may not actually be able to pray all the time, but we certainly can continually, if we be faithfully in setting aside the same times during the day, or choose to keep the disposition and attitude of prayer.

This we do when we lift up our thoughts and intentions to God, and, under the influence of charity, offer Him all our acts; for the purpose of prayer is this elevation of ourselves to God. In other words, we ought to pray always by faithfully observing the interior practice of our devotion.

But as we grow in perfection, fervent prayers become a necessity to nourish a more intense supernatural life. Some people are sometimes said to be "great eaters," meaning they have a great need for a giant meal after a grueling exercise in manual labor. Souls that need to pray often are also "great eaters," so great is their hunger for God; for the exercise of the highest virtues, and leading a life of continual sacrifice, require much energy. Also, many are the things they need to obtain for others, and so much have they to do in the Church. For these souls, prayer is not an infrequent act, it is a habit, and, in the apt and pregnant word of St. Teresa, prayer is like their supernatural respiration.[1]

Above the Saints stands the Queen of all the Saints. To a more excellent degree, prayer for her is a state and an office. It is a state, because, with the veil of her interior life here below lifted in the Gospel, we know that she treated with the Holy Ghost in her heart. On earth her life was so divine, that she prayed as she loved, that is, with all the strength. If she was filled with grace, if "full of grace" barely describes the unfathomable depths of her holiness, we can hardly imagine the fervor of her prayer; for of her it was said that, to receive, she only had to ask.[2] Indeed, Mary is the faithful imitator of Jesus. She is associated to His actions and participates in His states. She is thus united to the prayer of Christ; that is, not only with the acts of prayer He did (of which we may read in the Gospel), but above all to the adoration in spirit and in truth, to the interior worship that He

---

[1] In another work, Fr. Lhoumeau says without citation: "Ste. Thérèse voulait que l'oraison fût comme la respiration surnaturelle de l'âme." (*Les actes*, 11). That St. Teresa of Avila calls all faithful to pray always is well attested in her writings, but "*respiración sobrenatural*," or some-such, is not found in her published works. For the use of the term in French, see e.g. the Jesuit Fr. Ramière, *L'Apostolat de la prière*, 189; the Dominican, Fr. Minjard, "La prière," *Enseign. cath.*, 1867, 17:137; and the Marianist Fr. Simler, *Guide*, 2.48, 29, wherein he brought up the same points highlighted in the first two paragraphs of this chapter.

[2] Note 48, p. 129.

rendered the Father without end in living by the Father.[3] This prayer He began in Mary, and continues, ¦ *semper vivens ad interpellandum pro nobis*, "always living to make intercession for us" in glory (Heb 7.25). ¦

We also say that Mary prays because it is her office to do so, since she is the Mother of Mankind and the universal Mediatrix. We saw above that her mediation is one of intercession,[4] as every communication of grace, every work in the soul by Holy Ghost, and the entire life of the Church, is subsumed under this great law of prayer. She prayed at Calvary. She prayed in the Cenacle. If you could but look, you would see that she is praying in glory.

It impossible to live at the side of this Orant,[5] to be taught by this Mother and Lady, and not acquire the taste and habit of prayer. Recall the promise God made through the Prophet Zechariah, who says that He will *pour out upon the house of David, and upon the inhabitants of Jerusalem, the Spirit of grace, and of prayers* (Zec 12.10).[6] Now, if we dwell in Mary, in the heavenly city here represented by Jerusalem, the Spirit of prayer will be poured out on us; but in what abundance we hardly need say, since we know that where Mary is, there the Holy Ghost not only shall come, but shall hasten to come, and fill us to overflowing with His gifts, as St. Louis-Marie assures us.[7]

§2. THE RECOLLECTION OF THE SOUL

Let us now speak of the recollection that should accompany our prayer.

The first act of prayer is to approach God, because prayer is the raising up of the mind to Him,[8] that is, what we call in the common tongue, "putting ourselves in His presence." But to approach God, we must isolate ourselves from creatures that distract us; and if we are weighed down by the things that captivate us here below, our soul will be unable to ascend to Him. In a word, we must gather our

---

[3] Jn 6.58.
[4] Part 2.2.3.2, p. 124.
[5] Note 54, p. 131.
[6] ¦ Officium Lanceæ et Clavorum D.N.J.C., Lectio 1, in certain approved breviaries. Fr. Lhoumeau mistakenly attributes it to the Prophet Joel (2.28-29). ¦
[7] *TD*, 154-155.
[8] ◆St. Thomas, *Summa*, 2-2.83.17.

thoughts. Does our devotion offer certain special insights on this topic? We only need to listen to St. Louis-Marie:

> She's my divine house of prayer
> Where I always find Jesus.[9]

The interior of Mary is a holy place, an oratory, a house of prayer,[10] where we are set apart, isolated from the noise of this world. We may remain there habitually, but during prayer, we must delve deeper and be even more fully shut up from the world.

What a wondrous place to recollect the soul! And, see, how close we come near to God when we are there! Every righteous soul is a temple of God; but He reigns ever so marvelously and acts ever so expansively in those whom we call Saints that, when we are near them, we sense being more in contact with God, and we forget the things of this world. Now, just as the sanctuary is the sacred space of the temple, so also is Mary the holy refuge of all Saints. By her states, her functions, and her privileges; by her grace and, now, by her glory, she is an enclosure the furthest from creatures, the most sealed up and protected against all that would assault from without, the most reserved to God Who sojourns there as in His own world, His paradise,[11] and His tabernacle. There, in the interior of Mary, we "always find Jesus." Has He not come down to be there? Has He not appeared closer to us in the Incarnation, more accessible and more available than anywhere else?

St. Louis-Marie also likens Mary to a mountain and, following the commentators, he says that she is depicted as the fertile and bountiful mountain,[12] where God is well-pleased to dwell.[13] He says that she is the mountain where Jesus Christ teaches and ever dwells, where we

---

[9] *Cantiques*, 77.6, 132: Elle est mon divin oratoire / Où je trouve toujours Jésus.

[10] ✦In Dedic. Ecclesiæ, *Brev. Rom.*, 77: "Locus iste sanctus est in quo orat sacerdos."

[11] Given by Fathers, East and West, e.g., St. John Damascene, *In Dorm. B.V.M.*, Homilia 1.8, PG 96.711B: "You are a spiritual Eden, holier and more divine than Eden of old. That Eden was the abode of the mortal Adam, whilst the eternal Lord came down from Heaven to dwell in thee."

[12] St. Gregory, *In 1 Reg*, 1.1.5, PL 79.25C: "Under the name of mountain may also be signified the most Blessed and ever Virgin Mary Mother of God: since a mountain she was, who, by the dignity of her election, transcended all height of elected nature. ... With just reason, too, is she called 'a fruitful mountain,' since of her the best fruit, that is, the New Man, is generated."

[13] ✦Ps 67.16, 17: The mountain of God is a fat mountain. ... A mountain in which God is well-pleased to dwell: for there the Lord shall dwell unto the end.

are transfigured with Him, where we die with Him, where we ascend to Heaven with Him.[14] To go to Mary, to unite with her in our prayer, is thus to scale the holy mountain, and make our ascent to God. Whether we make use of the images of the mountain of God or the oratory, they both mean the same thing: creatures set apart, the soul in solitude with God, when all around her is muted, and she herself is silent. Such are the delicious moments that we, alas, savor so seldom, says the *Imitation*,[15] for we catch there a glimpse of the divine embrace, and savor a little morsel of Heaven. Let us pray that we may, with the help of our Mother, gather out thoughts and meditate more often.

How do we proceed so that we may meditate on Mary, gain entry into her interior and come near to Jesus? We can, without much effort, and many are the ways.[16]

A simple act of faith, for example, is enough to put us in her presence, under her gaze. We need only think that she sees us in the light of glory.

St. Louis-Marie offers a process useful for beginners in focusing their mind, and that is, "little by little gaining the habit of interior recollection for forming a small idea or spiritual image of the Blessed Virgin."[17] For this purpose, we use metaphors that represent her excellences, her states, and her different functions, such as an oratory, a sacred monstrance,[18] a tower,[19] a paradise,[20] a banquet hall,[21] an

---

[14] ◆*Prayer for Missionaries*, §25, VD, 261.

[15] Kempis, *De imitatione*, 4.1.6, 287; cf. *Imitation*, 387.

[16] ◆Clearly, in order to be recollected and meditate, we need ample time and care, and adapt ourselves to the circumstances or obstacles we face. A man rocked by a lively desire or beset by worries, cannot begin his recollection as quickly as another who leads a calm life or does not allow himself to be absorbed in things exterior.

[17] *Secret*, 33.

[18] Note 54, p. 256.

[19] Cant 4.4.

[20] Note 11, p. 322.

[21] Rupert of Deutz, *Comment. in Joan.*, lib. 2, PL 169.290B: "Ipse namque harum nuptiarum architriclinus est, qui et beatæ Virgini superveniens, uteri ejus *triclinium* præparavit, ut in illo divina natura humanæ naturæ uniretur." St. Bonaventure, "Laus B.V.M.," 1.5, 16.5, *Opera*, 14:181, 185: *Triclinium Deitatis*, the "Banquet Hall of the Godhead." The poem of eighty-three *ottava rima* (14:181-188), is replete with names for our Blessed Mother, using the brilliant symbols of the Old and New Testaments. Some

enclosed garden,[22] and so on. Or, meditate on Mary in some mystery of the life of Christ in Bethlehem, at Calvary; and there, by her side, our gaze fixed on her, we will pray to Jesus with her.

St. Teresa advises us to undergo a similar process of making a mental representation[23] at the beginning of our prayer to facilitate the recollection of the soul, followed by reciting the *Pater Noster*, in union with Jesus Christ, the divine Master. It was for the same purpose that St. Louis-Marie sought to help the faithful by recommending them certain external representations, and, following his example, we may make use of pious images.

§3. DISPOSITIONS OF THE SOUL IN PRAYER.

The issue of distractions is foremost in the mind of many, and their main concern is to do away with them. In this, they are mistaken. A complete suppression of distractions is well-nigh impossible; but more to the point, we should rather use the effort in removing them as an indirect (but most effective) means to stop the fruitless wanderings of our imagination, than as a way to set ourselves firmly in holy dispositions.

These dispositions are closely linked to the conditions of prayer, which we may reduce to four: humility, trust, love, and perseverance. Let us see how our devotion aids in exciting them in us.

Humility is the basis of prayer. There is none that can pray if he is not humble, if he is oblivious to his needs, and refuses to confess his indigence. Our devotion leads us to pray in a disposition of singular humility.

St. Louis-Marie tells us that it is humbler to go to Jesus through Mary than to approach Him by ourselves and through our own

---

doubt St. Bonaventure's authorship of the poem, but that he used the metaphor is indisputable (see, 3 *Sent.* 3.1.2.1, *Opera*, 4:69.1). Note that *triclinium* also means a three-person couch used in ancient Roman festive repasts.

[22] Cant 4.12.

[23] St. Ignatius of Loyola, *Ejercicios*, passim: "composición viendo el lugar," no relation to the English "composition." We must look to Latin for its meaning. St. Gregory, in *Hom. in Ev.*, 23.1, PL 76.1182C, explains that the verb *componere* means "to model" as in modeling with clay (*compositio luti*). The meaning of St. Ignatius of Loyola's expression is best rendered today as "a representation of the place by seeing it in the imagination," or briefly, "a mental representation of the place." In St. Teresa of Avila, "Relations," 7.4, *Works*, 373, her *representación* ("Relaciones," 4, *Obras*, 2:21) is rendered "a sort of making things present." Fr. Lhoumeau: *représentation intérieure*.

effort.[24] In making use of her mediation, we recognize our unworthiness and powerlessness, we join the lowly ranks of those who are humble of heart, ¦¦ of the solitaries such as the publican who dared not look up to Heaven,[25] and the woman with an issue of blood who was sore afraid to approach Jesus,[26] | but who all will ever fall under the propitious gaze of God. It is truly an act of humility to renounce our notions and intentions to take on those of Mary's, and to surrender to her all the fruits of our supplications. Who is our model, again? No other than she, the Blessed Virgin, the incomparable teacher of humility, who trains us to approach God merely by ¦ repeating her word to the Angel: | *Behold the handmaid of the Lord;* ¦¦ *be it done to me according to thy word* | (Lk 1.38).

The faithful slave of Mary also prays with confidence and love. He surrenders himself to her in a goodly act of love, entrusting to her care his particular and powerful motives during his consecration, as also when he seeks her mediation.

Let us not forget ¦ St. Luke's word in the Acts of the Apostles, where he says that, | in the Cenacle, the entire Church persevered in prayer *with Mary*.[27] So also shall we, guided and aided by the same Blessed Virgin who, in her unending prayer, sets a powerful example for us.

The spiritual childhood in our union with Mary leads us to persevere. Who better than a child knows how to insist, again and again, and repeating non-stop the same demand, until he turns into a darling pest? As Fr. Faber says: "A child with his mother is full of innocent respectful liberties. He never doubts of gaining his end. He never anticipates a refusal, till it actually comes, no matter how often it has come before. He was refused yesterday, so he feels sure today. If refused, he persists with the persuasions of a not-disobedient love, and argues with a playful smile. When he is definitively refused, he goes up to her, and kisses her, and runs away as happy with his mother's affectionate will, as if he had gotten what he wanted."[28] He

---

[24] *TD*, 56.
[25] Lk 18.13.
[26] Lk 8.43-44.
[27] Act 1.14.
[28] Faber, *Conferences*, 303-304.

is right, of course. To that child, this maternal kiss is a gift far better than what he had originally wanted. Despite how it may appear, his perseverance did indeed bear fruit. We see that St. Louis-Marie had similar thoughts, if we reflect again on the consoling words of his poem, part of which we quoted earlier:

> She's my divine house of prayer
> Where always I find Jesus.
> There I pray in glory greater
> Never knowing her rebuff.[29]

§4. DISTRACTION IN PRAYER

As we are sure to run into difficulties in prayer, we propose certain considerations. We spoke above of the repugnancies and dryness faced by beginners and would refer the reader to the relevant part if he needed a refresher.[30] Here, we shall speak only of distractions. We must pray that our devotion to Mary obtains for us the wherewithal and patience in the struggle that would otherwise tire us to the point that we lose heart.

Distractions can be divided into two classes: those which have a passion or an affection as their cause, and those which come from our wandering mind.[31] Let us call them the distractions of the heart and the distractions of pure imagination, respectively.

The first may have its beginning in injured self-love, a desire of some kind, curiosity, natural activity, a movement of affection or antipathy, and so on. *For where thy treasure is, there is thy heart also*, says Our Lord (Mt 6.21); and we would add: "as are thy thoughts."

To fight distractions of this kind, without digging deep to find

---

[29] ¦¦ *Cantiques*, 77.6, 132. Elle est mon divin oratoire / Où je trouve toujours Jésus. / J'y prie avec beaucoup de gloire, / Je n'y crains pas de refus. — In Dedic. Ecclesiæ, *Brev. Rom.*, 75*, quotes a sermon (Sermo 229, PL 39.2166-2168), attributed by Migne to Paul the Deacon (see PL 95.1457A), which says that all that we say and do in Temple is for our spiritual edification, and, as much as we can, with God's help, we must strive to keep our conscience clean when we are there. Mary is the Ark of the Covenant, a spiritual vessel that bears our impetrations to Heaven. Let us thus aim for the same when we pray in union with our Blessed Mother. ¦

[30] Part 4.2.3.2, pp. 252-253.

[31] ♦Those which come from the devil, or are a test of God, or have a natural cause, such as fatigue and illness, may belong in the second class, since we give them the same treatment.

their causes, and equipped with the mattock of empirical methods, is to be like a farmer who mows the weeds instead of uprooting them, as they will inevitably grow back. Imagine what happens if the passions and distractions in our soul grow as fast as the plants in lands hot and humid!

We weed out and uproot distractions by renouncing our will, otherwise all that we do for prayer will be in vain. If creatures enthrall us, they are obstacles in our path to God. We have no true and intimate recollection without making some sacrifice. Recall the dictum: *sacrificium laudis, hostiam laudis*, "a sacrifice of praise, is a sacrifice of prayer,"[32] for if we cannot pray without recollecting, or recollect without renouncing ourselves, prayer becomes an act of immolation. He who prays not only offers God an act of religion,[33] which, in a broad sense, is an interior sacrifice; but also renounces things external, and to a greater extent, that inner little world of thoughts, unjust desires, passions, and movements, where we live and which we unjustly deem more dear than anything else.

Consider also that, by our perfect renunciation, our dependence on Mary makes it easier for us to be wholly in the place where her will presently calls us to prayer. Remember that in praying through Mary, with her, in her, and for her, we shed our notions and dispositions to take on those of our Mother's, from the start to the completion of our action. Nothing is more apt to decrease our distractions than tearing off the ground the roots of the "me" and letting them wither in the scorching heat of the noon sun. Nowhere else is Fr. Faber's observation more appropriate than here. He says: "Everything that

---

[32] Gihr, *Mass*, 1.1.3, 31-33: "Only such acts of divine worship as contain in themselves all the essential requisites and characteristics of the idea of sacrifice ... are and may be called sacrifices in their proper sense. In the religious and ascetical life, virtuous acts, differing essentially from sacrifice, are often called by that name. The term sacrifice applied to such acts is to be taken ... in a derivate and improper sense: acts of virtue are and are called sacrifices in a broader sense. ... Prayer stands in intimate relation and connection with sacrifice; for the spirit of prayer and the sentiments of the heart constitute the intrinsic being of sacrifice, the soul of the exterior rite of sacrifice. Hence, as sacrifice is called effective or real prayer, *oratio realis*, on the other hand, prayer is also called sacrifice. Thus, the Prophet designated the prayer of praise and thanksgiving as the 'sacrifice of the lips,' *vituli labiorum* (Hos 14.3). Referring to this, the Apostle writes: 'Let us offer *hostiam laudis*, the sacrifice of prayer, always to God that is the fruit of lips confessing His name' (Heb 13.15). In the Psalms we are invited to 'offer to God *sacrificium laudis*, the sacrifice of praise' (Ps 49.14)."

[33] Note 32, p. 188.

contributes to the increase in our purity of intention also helps us to master our distractions!"[34]

When this renunciation is not only done in prayer and but also habitually practiced in all our actions, it nibs the causes of our distractions in the bud, disciplines our faculties by the good habits which eases our recollection. ¦¦ St. Albert points to self-abandonment as a powerful means to prevent distractions from overtaking us. Says he: "Happy is the man who, by continual removal of fantasies and images, by turning in within, and raising the mind to God, finally manages to dispense with the products of the imagination, and by so doing, nakedly and simply, and with a pure understanding and will, works within on the simplest object of all: God."[35] | We will never be able to free ourselves from our wandering imaginings if we wait until we pray to fight them, or if we spend no time trying to fend them off.

Fr. Faber, also makes these remarkable observations: "There is none to whom the devotion to Our Lady (her shape of spiritual life) cannot be applied with abundant blessings: I mean the attempt to do our ordinary actions perfectly. This is the most excellent of practices, and walks in a clear air that delusions seldom can obscure; and our power over our distractions grows in proportion to our perseverance and our skill in this [salutary] exercise."[36] And in order to perfect our ordinary actions, he says that, as an interior practice, we should do all in her presence, in the sight of Jesus, that is, through Christ, with Christ, and in Christ.[37] We see here the spirituality of St. Louis-Marie most fully expressed.

---

[34] ♦Faber, *Growth in Holiness*, ¦¦ 377: "No man short of a real contemplative will ever reign like a despot over his vast hordes of distractions. He is a happy man, and has done much, who has set up a constitutional monarchy among them." | Read the entirety of this fine and thorough study ("Distractions," ¦¦ 365-377), summarized in a poem, "Distractions in Prayer," *Hymns*, 334-336. | The reader will find that, on many points, they resemble the teaching of St. Louis-Marie.

[35] ♦St. Albert the Great, "De adhærendo Deo," c. 4, ¦¦ *Opera*, 37:525-526: "Felix ergo qui per abstersionem continuam phantasmatum et imaginum, ac per introversionem et inibi per sursum ductionem mentis in Deum, tandem aliquando obliviscitur phantasmatum quodammodo, ac per hoc consequentes operatur interius nudo ac simplici ac puro intellectu et affectu circa objectum simplicissimum Deum." |

[36] Faber, *Growth in Holiness*, 375.

[37] Ibid. 377.

Do distractions of pure imagination beset us; that is, those that are caused by no other than the involuntary wanderings of the mind? Some notes unique to our perfect devotion allow us to understand their nature, make remedies, and derive a benefit from them.

In a certain aspect, we were describing the recollection of the soul beside the Blessed Virgin, when we said that to act through Mary, with her, and in her, is to renounce practicing our devotion by our own movement, and instead, take her guiding hand and rest in her interior. St. Louis-Marie illustrates this in the conduct of Esau and Jacob towards their mother Rebecca, who, he says, is the figure of Mary for both the reprobate and predestinated.

Following Jacob's example, the faithful and devout children of Mary, "stay at home with their Mother; that is, they love solitude, guarding their interior life and devoting their utmost to prayer, but after the example of their Mother, the Holy Virgin, and in her company. ... It is true that they venture abroad into the world, sometimes; but they do so in obedience to the Will of God, and their beloved Mother's, to fulfil the duties of their state. The things they do outside may seem great, but they esteem much higher the acts within themselves, deep in their interior, in the company of the most holy Virgin, because it is there that they do the great work of their perfection."[38] On the other hand, the reprobates "do not stay put, or are hardly at home in their own interior. ... They cannot bear seclusion, or spiritual life, or interior devotion."[39]

The willful wanderings of our imagination and external agitations trouble the life settled or recollected interiorly. In contrast, the habit of acting by Mary and living dependent on her is its perfect realization. Our soul is like a child that keeps calm and cavorts beside his mother and under her watchful eye. But, as we well know, a child is never long at rest. Listen to the remarks of St. Francis de Sales about distractions. He says that we must "be careful to restrain our minds as far as possible from running after these flitting butterflies [meaning, distractions], as a mother restrains her child. If she sees the little one longing to run off after them, hoping to catch them, she holds him

---

[38] Cf. *TD*, 133-134.
[39] Cf. *TD*, 130.

back and says: 'My child, you will only exhaust yourself by running after these butterflies in the glare of the sun. You had much better stay with me.' The child stays with her, indeed, until he sees another, after which he fain would run as ever, if his mother did not hold him back as before."[40]

This fickleness and the need for movement are the defects of childhood. Adults are not immune from them. They are the cause of our distractions. There are many a book on how to deal with them, and we wish not to reject of the wise counsels proffered in them, but we are content with the few lines of the charming story told by St. Francis de Sales; for he accurately describes our frailty and suggests a remedy, which exists in maternal education. We all were that child. We all needed to be constantly on the move. We all were quick to anger. We all had the difficulty of not being able to sit still by our mother. But, little by little, by being docile, by acceding to her repeated coaxing (and aided by a measure of reflection), we became well-behaved children. We may apply the same process to our interior life. How much simpler, more appealing and effective can it be?

To be recollected is to be still beside our good Mother; it is to think and do calmly under her gaze. If, at some moment, our mind or heart jumps at the things that flit before our inner eye, listen to Mary. She will bridle us or beckon us, if we have started running. Lay down at her feet that desire, that musing, that attachment to an idea or the will, that pleasure which lures us. Prefer instead the joy of bringing her gladness and remaining with her. A hundred times during our prayer we should return, humbly and trustingly, to her side. Humbly, because long will that fickleness and excessive ardor make us suffer. They grip our nature, they pester us, and will not allow us a moment's respite from involuntary distractions; but humility, a salve for all ills, will put them to good use, earning us Mary's compassion. So, too, will our confidence, because we know that she will recoup our losses, if there are any; that, under her care and with our docility, we shall acquire the habits of recollection and silence, and that our distractions will be less frequent and less prolonged.

---

[40] ◆Cf. de Sales, *Conferences*, 9, 157. Original French at, *Œuvres*, 6:149.

Another thought may further bolster our confidence. There is but little that we shall not obtain from the Blessed Virgin by our filial and persevering prayer and in return for our faithful dependence.

Grace stills the powers of the soul in the various states of infused contemplation. Without needing to go so far, without even aspiring to favors, let us ask that it moderate, calm and discipline our powers, in the manner of St. Louis Marie, who in the Prayer to Mary bid us say: "May your sublime contemplation arrest the distractions of my wandering imagination; may your continual sight of God fill my memory with His Presence!"[41]

These words of St. Louis-Marie remind us of one of the privileges of the Blessed Virgin: the one in which her contemplation was continual and her act of charity, uninterrupted. We have no such privilege. Actions and objects external distract us from the contemplation of things divine. Sleep interrupts it, because our ideas spring from what our senses perceive; because our soul cannot know but by means of the senses, and even if it were their wont to aid the intellect, they would also hinder its application when they untimely excite its activity. That is why, during the recollection of the soul, we choose to bar our senses and to regulate the movements of our imagination and of our passions. We often fail; hence, distractions assail us.

It was not the case for Mary. Her infused knowledge, independent of the senses and the use of them, allowed her to praise God and to love Him from the instant He created her soul; and, by the grace of this superior mode of knowing, her contemplation was neither interrupted by sleep nor hindered by external action or by fatigue or by any other condition of the body. In addition to this prerogative, every movement of the passions was absent in the Blessed Virgin, and no act of the powers of the soul (such as thought, imagination, and so on) prevented her will from exercising its dominion. Is it any wonder that much has been written of the uplifting realities expressed by the representations of her as "sanctuary" and "mountain" of which we spoke above?[42] They recount for us in what air of celestial calm and

---

[41] *Secret*, 52-53.
[42] Part 4.2.4.1, and note 53, p. 256; Part 5.1.2, p. 322.

pure clarity did Mary live so near to God by her unending and sublime contemplation. How touching and ingenious a thought that St. Louis-Marie gave us, so that when we are beset with sorrows and frailties, we would seek consolation in the venerable privileges of our Mother! There is none that would bar us from hoping that, by her maternal kindness, she will repay our love by relieving our misery and, through her longer-lasting and more fruitful contemplation, obtaining for us the grace of resembling her, albeit remotely. In any case, let us ponder these words of St. Germanus: *Nemo cogitatione Dei repletur nisi per te*, "There is none that may come to know God but through you, ¦¦ O Mary most holy. ¦"[43]

§5. NOTES ON THE STATES OF PRAYER

We just spoke of prayer in general terms. Let us now turn to see some notes on prayer in the writings of St. Louis-Marie. We know that there is a close link among the various modes or states of prayer and the three stages of spiritual life.[44] Meditation is regarded as the form of prayer most common to beginners. As the soul progresses, prayer becomes more affective,[45] and it is in the illuminative way that contemplation predominates. Lastly, to the unitive way is the so-called prayer of union. There are also certain acts of extraordinary contemplation that many also call *infused*.

---

[43] Fr. Lhoumeau credits St. Bernard, but it is from St. Germanus of Constatinople, Sermo 7, [In Dorm. B.V.M., 2], PG 98.350BC: *Nemo Dei cognitione repletus est nisi per te, O sanctissima*, etc. "There is none that may come to know God but through you, O Mary most holy; none that may be saved but through you, O *Deipara*; none that may be delivered from perils but through you, O Virgin Mother; none that may be redeemed but through you, O Mother of God; no gift is by mercy obtained, but through you, O most worthy of knowing God." Cf. St. Bernard, *de Aquæductu*, §§6, 8, PL 183.431A, 442A: "Desiring to redeem all mankind, He placed the entire ransom in the hands of Mary, ... and the plenitude of all good. ... Let us seek grace, and let us seek it through Mary."

[44] The nine levels of prayer grouped into three "ways" are: (I) Ascetical Prayer, *Purgative Way*, consisting of: 1. Vocal Prayer, 2. Meditation, 3. Affective Prayer, 4. Acquired Contemplation, with Dark Night of the Senses, in which the soul is purged of all consolation of the senses, as bridge to: (II) Mystical Prayer: (A) *Illuminative Way*, whose levels are: 5. Infused Contemplation, 6. Prayer of Quiet, Dark Night of the Soul, in which the soul is purged of all consolation of the intellect, mind and memory, as bridge to: (B) *Unitive Way*, with: 7. Simple Union, 8. Conforming Union, 9. Transforming Union.

[45] St. Teresa of Avila, "Life," 8.7, *Works*, 49: "Mental prayer is nothing else, in my opinion, but being on terms of friendship with God, frequently conversing in secret with Him Who, we know, loves us."

❖

We spoke above of the process St. Louis-Marie invites us to take to be recollected at the side of Mary.[46] When we say our prayer, does our Mother play no role other than placing us in the presence of God? Is she a mediatrix who introduces us to the Lord and then withdraws?

Indeed, not. Listen to St. Louis-Marie: "Be persuaded that the more you look to Mary in your *prayers, contemplations, actions, and sufferings,* if not with a distinct and definite view, at least with a general and imperceptible one, the more perfectly will you find Jesus Christ."[47] The words intentionally emphasized in the foregoing quote show that St. Louis-Marie's counsel applies to all levels of prayer. ¦¦ He explains the importance of Mary in our spiritual life, saying: "A devotion to our Blessed Lady is necessary for salvation. ... It is still more so for those who are called to any particular perfection. ... No one can acquire an intimate union with Our Lord, and a perfect fidelity to the Holy Ghost, without a very great union with the most holy Virgin, and a great dependence on her succor. It is Mary alone who has found grace before God. ... It is only by her that all those who have found grace before God have found it at all; and it is only by her that all those who shall come afterwards shall find it. She was full of grace ... in such sort that the Most High has made her the sole treasurer of His treasures, and the sole dispenser of His graces, to ennoble, to exalt, and to enrich whom she wills; to give the entry into the narrow way of Heaven whom she wills; and in spite of all obstacles, to pass whom she wills through the strait gate of life; and to give the throne, the scepter, and the crown of the King to whom she wills." In sum, | "it is to Mary alone whom God has given the keys to the storehouse of divine love, and the power to enter into the most sublime and secret ways of perfection, and the power likewise to make others enter in there also."[48]

Msgr. Gay expresses the same thought in his beautiful *Elevation,* "Mary and the Mysteries of Jesus." We quote only those reflections which are consistent with St. Louis-Marie's thoughts: "As God willed that Mary be the Queen of all creatures, so also must she be their

---

[46] Part 4.3.3.4.c.ii, p. 287 ff.

[47] ♦*TD*, 114.

[48] *TD*, 22-25.

Mistress, that is, to teach them and illumine them. As a matter of principle, those beneficent illuminations will come to creatures from God, be they the visions which the Angels and Saints in glory do have, or the somewhat clear, though exalted, notions men will have whilst pilgrims on earth. Either way, they will all come to creatures through Mary, who is the Seat of wisdom,[49] the Mother of Divine Knowledge,[50] the Light of Angels,[51] and the Beacon of Doctors.[52] Only after pouring them in His Mother (and only because He has begun by pouring them in her), will He then cause them to flow to all other creatures; for we are only served at the banquet of God, or may drink from His chalice, after she is served and has partaken."[53]

The learned writer explains in the same *Elevation* how, for Mary, the mysteries of Christ were not only revelations of God, but also objects of worship, which mysteries provoked her adoration, just desires, and love, as they were forms of sanctity to which she conformed her entire life, and sources of grace from which she drew through her prayer. This is precisely what we must attain in prayer, following the example of Mary.

¦ We refer the reader to the Fathers and Doctors for their testimonies of the Blessed Virgin as an incomparable teacher of prayer.[54] For our purposes, it would enough to read the "Prayer to Mary" set down by St. Louis-Marie, and usually appended to *Secret of Mary*, which we cannot recommend enough to souls who wish to progress in prayer. ¦¦ We quote a small portion: "I give myself once again wholly to you, as your eternal slave, without reserve. ... If you still see in me something not belonging to you, pray take it away this moment,

---

[49] Litany of Loretto, in Christopher, *Raccolta*, n. 319, 217.

[50] Ibid. n. 765, 608.

[51] Litany of the Immaculate Conception, allowed for private use by Pope Pius VI, in Anonymous, *Path to Heaven*, 340.

[52] St. Jean Eudes, *Méditations*, 2:175, called the B.V. Mary the same "Flambeau des Docteurs" translated above. Jordan ("De B.V.M.," 7.3, *Opera*, 107), and St. Antoninus (*Summa*, 4.15.2, 4:1011E), called her, *Doctrix doctorum*. The title *Lux doctorum* exists, but it is not ascribed to her. The early Renaissance poet Giuseppe Brivio called St. Jerome by that name. ("Laudes s. Hieronymi," 150, in Canellis, "Le *S. Jérôme* de Brivio," *RET*, Suppl. 5, 7 [2017-18]:65). A few decades later, the Augustinian friar and preacher, Simon of Cremona, ascribed it to St. Augustine. (*Opus epist.*, Mc 329:7r).

[53] Gay, *Élévations*, 101, 2:289.

[54] Bourassé, *Summa B.V.M.*, 4:1414-1417 (Magistra solitudinis); 4:1419-1422 (Magistra orationis); 9:26-27, 361 (Magistra apostolorum).

and make yourself absolute Mistress of the faculties of my soul. ... May the light of your faith dispel the darkness of my mind; ... may your sublime contemplation arrest the distraction of my wandering imagination; may your continual sight of God fill my memory with His Presence."[55] |

    In the celebrated pages of her *Life*—the ones where we can sense the burst of joy of a bird freed from the net in which it was caught— St. Teresa, once held captive by the error of considering the Humanity of Our Lord an obstacle, realized that she was wrong and instead saw it as a way to attain higher contemplation. ¦¦ Says she: "Because I was conscious of the profit and delight which [the prayer of quiet] furnished me, no one could have brought me back to the contemplation of the Sacred Humanity; for that seemed to me to be a real hindrance to prayer. ... I did not continue long of this opinion. ... Who is there so proud and wretched ... that, even after laboring all his life in penances and prayers and persecutions, can possibly imagine himself not to be exceedingly rich, most abundantly rewarded, when Our Lord permits him to stand with St. John at the foot of the Cross?"[56] | St. Louis-Marie affirms the same thing of Mary's thought: "It is quite true that the view of other creatures, however holy, may perhaps at certain times retard divine union. But this cannot be said of Mary, as I have remarked before, and shall never weary of repeating. ... Thus, so far from the divine Mary, all absorbed in God, being an obstacle to the perfect in their attaining to union with God, there has never been up to this point, and there never will be, any creature who will aid us more efficaciously in this great work, whether by the graces she will communicate to us for this effect," ¦| or by the care she will always have in guaranteeing us against "the illusions and trickeries of the evil spirit."[57]

    St. Louis-Marie lays emphasis on this last thought: He says that if

---

[55] Cf. *Secret*, 52-54.

[56] St. Teresa of Avila, "Life," 22.3, 4, 7, *Works*, 151, 152.

[57] ◆*TD*, 113, 114. [For the text of St. Germanus in *True Devotion* and which Fr. Lhoumeau quoted at the place marked "¦|" but was deleted, see note 43, p. 332].

anyone longs to advance in the way of perfection, and surely and perfectly find Jesus Christ, he should put aside the fear of self-deceit which dogs men of prayer,[58] and embrace the devotion to our Blessed Lady ¦ *corde magno et animo volenti*, "with a great heart and a willing mind"[59] (2 Mac 1.3). ¦

Let us close this chapter with this reflection: The masters of spiritual life recommend that we prepare ourselves for divine operations by renouncing all sense of proprietorship in our soul. "If you yield yourself with all your faculties to God, offering up all your being and its attributes," says Fr. Johannes Tauler, "then must God enter into your being and into your faculties, ¦¦ because you have renounced all self-ownership and made your soul like a desert wasteland." ¦[60]

Francisco Suárez notes that contemplation elicits in the soul a sense of profound respect and absolute submission.[61] Giving due regard to these words, let us attune the practices of our devotion, as we know them, to its substance. We shall then see that it admirably and assuredly disposes the soul for divine union, even for the highest degree of contemplation, if indeed God so wills.

---

[58] ◆St. Louis-Marie is alluding to the false mysticism which, in his day, made followers of many in society and academia.
[59] *TD*, 115.
[60] ◆Tauler, "Sunday after New Year's," *Sermons*, 93.
[61] ◆Suárez, De oratione, 2.9.12, ¦¦ *Opera*, 14:159.2 : "Ex ... reverentia ad Deum statim nascitur devotio per affectum submittendi se illi, et omnem cultum ac honorem illi exhibendi." ¦

CHAPTER 2:

THE EXAMEN AND THE WORK

he examen, or examination of conscience and work have, after prayer, a particular importance among the various acts of Christian life. We will explain some ideas on how to practice these exercises according to the tenor of our devotion.

ARTICLE 1: THE EXAMEN

To examine our conscience at Mary's feet; to invoke her that, by the light of the Holy Ghost, she may dispel the self-deceit which plague us, and we may probe the unfathomable depths of our heart; to implore her the graces of contrition and firm purpose of amendment, are praiseworthy practices, but it is superfluous to say it, for reason alone will lead us to think so.

There are specific considerations that call our attention, and though they are applicable to any general examen,[1] we shall narrow our focus to a discussion on the guided examen. For the purpose of confession, it is enough to identify our faults and to be contrite; but we need something more in order to acquire self-knowledge and make fruitful use of direction. Just to see the fruits is not enough; we need to study the plant, to cultivate it, to cure it of diseases or to tear them down to their causes. Such is the goal and the scope of the examen we envisage.

---

[1] St. Ignatius of Loyola makes a distinction between general and particular examens. (*Ejercicios*, 21-25 and 17-18, respectively; in the Puhl translation, nn. 32-43 and 24-26). In the general examen we survey all the morally significant actions of the day; in the particular, we focus on one fault that the Holy Ghost prompts us to overcome with the corresponding virtue.

337

§1.

The examen is a guided exercise to cast our eye on our actions in order to maintain their integrity.

The first question is: *What must I watch?* Answer: All my acts. My Christian life encompasses them all. As we explained, we must take the word "action" to mean any external or internal thought, wish, desire, and so on; any movement of our passions or any of their causes; any object of our acts or ideas; and any intention or end for which we act. Thus understood, the examen extends to all that comprise the interior practice of acting through Mary, with her, in her, and for her. This is the first concordance of note.

§2.

Second question: *Why?* What is the purpose of my examen? Answer: In order to direct my life in accordance with the essence of my consecration; that is, to keep to my dependence on Mary and my union with her, or to reduce myself to that state, if I have strayed from it. In the expression of the Scholastics, this is the *formal* reason[2] for the examen.

As we would in other cases, we shall give due regard to our good deeds and our faults, our victories and defeats, along with their circumstances and causes; but all reduced to the unity of view and purpose proper to our devotion. For example, I see in me a lack of kindness towards a neighbor. It is not enough just to see my fault. I must also consider how I have shunned my dependence on Mary by acting, not by her impulse and for her glory, but by my own movement and for my own satisfaction. I must ransack through the roots of my act to discover the part my will plays in the causes and circumstances of this fault, in opposition to the Will of God or the will of the Blessed Virgin.

And we shall remove them by coming under the dependence of Mary, who will lead us back to the divine Will, since all virtue consists in radically submitting ourselves to God and serving Him. Thus, we may say that we shall have only one resolution to take; namely, to determine, as the case may be, how we shall act being more

---

[2] Note 1, p. 4.

dependent on Mary, being better in accordance with her insights and dispositions, in order to honor and please her.

In those considerations and prayers which must strengthen our resolution and revive our fervor, without excluding other truths, we must always return to this fundamental one: "I belong not to me, but to the Lord; it is Christ alone that has the right to live in me; I must therefore renounce all that pertains to my life, all that sustains it, and all its operation, that I may abandon myself into the hands of Mary and allow myself to be possessed by her spirit."

§3.

We close our reflections on the examen with two remarks: First, we find that this spirituality is one and simple. We have seen that it has the unity of purpose, process or practice. Now, in the examen as we envisage it, we find *one* prominent resolution, *one* special purpose, *one* preeminent way of considering things. Second, that the interior practice of the Holy Slavery to Mary necessarily requires watching our dispositions, intentions, and actions. Thus, this practice is a summary examen of which we can, in due course, develop its various phases; that is to inspect the acts and state of our soul, excite her contrition, rectify the will by firm resolutions, and strengthening it through reflection and prayer.

It is hardly bears saying that our observations apply to the particular examen.

ARTICLE 2: THE WORK

Beginners lament that, in general, it is difficult to reconcile exterior occupations with interior life. Yes, it is quite true that advanced souls know how to engage in exterior works, without prejudice to their recollection. We see these purified souls mingling with the things of this world with impunity, yet are not caught like fowls in birdlime; but since everything may co-operate for our good and serve our advancement, why should our use of them, especially when divine Will imposes them on us, not serve to unite us to God? If we can renounce and sanctify ourselves in our other acts, why not in our work?

Making work willed by God a sort of scapegoat laden with all its distractions, restlessness, and other faults, frequently occurs among pious men. We have an aphorism of the Saints to counter it: "Working in silence recollects the soul and quickly warms her." From our particular vantage point and with the help of our practices, let us see how we could make external work serve the interior life.

Many say work is irreconcilable with recollection because they want the impossible. Here on earth, the mind cannot be applied to one thing without being distracted by another, given its ordinary condition. It is thus naturally impossible to pay attention to work whilst continually having *actual* thoughts of God. But, we know it is not necessary to do so, and that our acts are truly directed to God and are meritorious when, without actually thinking of Him, we act with a customary disposition to serve and love Him. And if we either have no intention or do nothing deliberately to contradict this disposition, we are indeed working for the Lord and in union with Mary.

However, it is not sufficient just to ensure that our actions are good and meritorious by avoiding sin. It is necessary to sanctify our work as much as we can. In order to achieve this, we must maintain a purity of intention, and through frequent acts of faith, we should also safeguard our habitual union with Mary, by removing all that prevents us from strengthening it.

Our intention will be righteous if we renounce our notions and dispositions to take those of the Blessed Virgin's. What are they? As in everything, Mary is *the handmaid of the Lord* (Lk 1.38). She works to serve Him. She uses the faculties of her soul, the forces of her body, and all her time, in perfectly fulfilling His Will. Such is how we must work; that is, in a spirit of belonging to Jesus and His Mother, renouncing all pretense at independence, all whims of our will, which often guide our endeavors. Let us serve God as He wants to be served. Let us be ready for the labors He imposes on us; our repugnancies and desires, notwithstanding. Let us be meek, let us remain at peace amidst the waves of work, in the face of the demands and burdens which makes us a servant to all.

It will serve us well to work for Mary, with a view to glorify her, to extend her reign and, through her, the reign of the Lord. Even so, we may yet face secondary notions mingling with our principal intention, altering its purity, and diminishing the merits of our work. Sometimes it is a feeling of pride or of vanity, the desire for an excessive pleasure in the work itself, which goes so far as to make us neglect our other duties; sometimes it is a motive of unbridled ambition, an immoderate attachment to our passions. Thinking of our consecration will help us to correct these deviations from our intention.

When we act for Mary, we are inclined to act only through her; that is, under the impulse of her grace, according to the indication of her will. In this manner, we prevent the excesses of natural activity, the impetuosity of passion, or an overly eager solicitude. To act through Mary is also to expect her help and to surrender to her guidance in the conduct of our work; it is to put in her hands the fruits of our labors. If we do all this, we will set our soul in a detachment most perfect and a peace most profound. She is rid of those exaggerated concerns, that unquiet yearning which confidence tempers not sufficiently. We see her no longer longing for success, beaten down in failures, or chafing under difficulties. Now that she is fully abandoned in Mary, and given that she honors and serves her, she is content just to have the love of the good Mother.

We sense how much in these dispositions is the soul free to remain with Mary, and in Mary during work; how, finding herself discarded, a mere "glance of the mind"[3] away from Mary would, as it is capable of doing, vex her habitual union and prevent her from making acts of faith. Just as a spring stretched to the limit, *tends* to return to its original position, and does indeed end up there, as soon as it is released, so also a soul in these dispositions may be distracted from thinking of God and the Blessed Virgin for some length of time, as a result of an intense dedication to work, yet at bottom she maintains a tendency or habitual position to return to such thoughts; and, in fact, easily makes reference to them, as soon she relaxes her dedication. By acting through Mary, with Mary, in Mary, and for Mary, we remove the imperfections and faults that stand in the way of this easy return to union, and our soul will be absorbed in her work even more, or

---

[3] *TD*, 180.

shall we say better, for work enslaves no more.

We will complete these discussions with examples drawn from the Gospel. We see a difference between the eagerness of Martha receiving the Divine Master and the promptitude, *cum festinatione*, of the Blessed Virgin to visit St. Elizabeth. Both hasten to their task with joy. At first blush, it seems that not all eagerness and joy of work are prohibited. The peace of the soul and exterior modesty do not call for the deliberate slowness, the regularity of the pendulum, the calculated measure that does not let us break a sweat for the Gospel, or run to minister to the dying. ¦ Martha, though intent on honoring the Divine Master, has *several* secondary notions mixed in. The intention should be her only preoccupation, because only *one thing*, honoring Him, *is necessary*.[4] Her desire to succeed is excessive. She wants all to go according to her desires. This is the cause of her worrisome solicitude and her anxiety, and the ensuing slight discontent that ends up hollowing her prayer. Mary, our Mother, hastens, but her intention is absolutely pure because she only wants to serve the Lord. Before getting up, *exurgens Maria*, she waits for the movement of the Holy Ghost. She acts through Him, with Him, and in Him, which is why she keeps calm and remains holy in her eagerness. | Such is how the practice of Holy Slavery aids us in sanctifying our work.

---

[4] Lc 10.42.

CHAPTER 3:

ON HOLY COMMUNION

t is worthy of note that, of all the acts of Christian life which he could have chosen to provide us with an example for the practice of this devotion, St. Louis-Marie picked Holy Communion.[1] It is the greatest, the one in which every faithful is bound together; that is, even greater than the reception of all the other Sacraments. Under the conditions that characterize our pilgrim life, Holy Communion realizes the union with Christ, and prepares for the union in glory; aye, 'tis a pledge of it.

Our perfect devotion is a singularly important application of Holy Communion; and, more than elsewhere, it is to our advantage not to go to Jesus but through Mary. Let us learn from St. Louis-Marie the way of communicating in union with the Blessed Virgin.

It is true that what he sketched for us is not a rigorous and detailed method. St. Louis-Marie intends not to limit us to a certain number of thoughts and acts; for "there are," he says, "an infinity of other thoughts which the Holy Ghost ... will furnish you, if you truly have an interior life, are mortified, and are faithful to this great and sublime devotion."[2] The important thing is to know how to apply this fundamental maxim: "Always remember that the more you give Mary leave to act in your Communion, the more Jesus will be glorified."[3] Many an act and reflection may be presented on the order of these ideas, and dare we add, a delightful book written on Holy Communion to regale our heart.[4] We shall try, at least, to elaborate on certain

---

[1] Note 26, p. 42.
[2] Cf. *TD*, 190.
[3] ♦Cf. Ibid.
[4] ♦In addition to several pamphlets and manuals of the pious associations, read Fr.

evocative thoughts of St. Louis-Marie's by incorporating considerations drawn mostly from his own writings.

In her Eucharistic liturgy, Holy Mother Church teaches us not to separate Jesus from His Mother. She shows us that in this mystery, as in every other, Mary's role is unique. First, we owe the Eucharist to the Blessed Virgin, and that, in instituting it, Our Lord first thought of her. We shall better understand the reason for the acts proposed by St. Louis-Marie for Communion in union with Mary, and we shall see that they are essentially the application of its interior practice: to act through Mary, with Mary, in Mary, and for Mary. She is here also as our Queen and Lady, our Mediatrix and our endearing Supplement. Lastly, it will be easy for us to show that to live in Mary's dependence, in accordance with the tenor of our devotion, is an excellent disposition to prepare ourselves for Holy Communion and to preserve its fruits.

ARTICLE 1: THE VIRGIN MARY AND THE EUCHARIST

§1.

¦ Let us sing with the Church adoring the Sacred Host: *Ave, verum corpus, natum de Maria Virgine*,[5] "Hail, true Body, truly born of the Virgin Mary mild"! ¦ Jesus could have been born of Mary and not institute the Sacrament of the Altar; but if He had not become man in the womb of the Virgin, we would not have had His adorable flesh to eat, nor His precious blood to drink. Thus, the Eucharist comes to us from Mary,[6] its first source, and we must all the more affirm that she intended to give Jesus, with all His mysteries and all His states, to the world when she consented to be the Mother of Christ. We owe her the Eucharist, as much as we are indebted to her for the Nativity and Passion of Christ.[7]

Bernardin de Paris, *La Communion de Marie*, a small book, complete with sound theological underpinnings.

[5] Fourteenth century hymn, sung at the elevation, attributed to Pope Innocent I.

[6] ♦St. Peter Damian, *Sermo* 44, In Nat. B.V.M., 2, PL 144.743: "What tongue could worthily praise such a Mother, who feeds her children with the immaculate flesh of her womb, that is the one Who said, speaking of Himself: *I am the living bread which came down from Heaven* (Jn 6.41)."

[7] ♦By placing the doxology of the B.V.M., *Jesu, tibi sit gloria, qui natus es de Virgini,* ¦¦ in the office of the most Holy Sacrament ¦¦ (Corporis Christi, *Brev. Rom.* 1942, Æstiva,

§2.

Let us attend to another consideration: In His mysteries, Christ gave Himself first to Mary, then to us, through her. He instituted the Eucharist first and foremost for Mary, who received the graces of this Sacrament in their fullness, in order thereafter to distribute them to us. As new as this may seem to certain ¦ souls ǀ who are yet unfamiliar with the prerogatives of the Blessed Virgin, we say that it is but the application of a principle whose several consequences we have already seen; for is it not also first and foremost for her that Jesus became incarnate, ¦¦ suffered, ǀ and died? For God, Mary alone, apart from the rest of the Church, would have been sufficient reason for the Incarnation and a magnificent fruit of Redemption. To which we may add that Jesus would have instituted the Eucharist just for her.

Then, why did He institute this Sacrament? Simply, out of love for us, says St. John: *In finem dilexit eos,* "He loved them unto the end" (Jn 13.1); *convescens in edulium,*[8] to nourish our souls; *contristatis absentia solatium singulare reliquit,*[9] to be "the special consolation to them that would grieve His absence"; and, *in me manet, et ego in eo* (Jn 15.5), to abide in us, and we in Him, and united to us, and at one with us. These are the very same reasons why we say that, in the institution of the Eucharist, Jesus thought of Mary in the first place. He loved her more than ¦ the rest of the Church. ǀ She was His Mother and the Mother of all the faithful, and it was necessary to nourish the Mother so that she, in turn, might nourish her children. There was the need to assuage this blessed Virgin for the absence she sorely felt; she who even in death, was bursting with love. In sum, there was none else to whom He should or could have been united as He was with Mary.

The Eucharist is therefore Mary's good. We need not speak of the Host she might have received on the evening of Holy Thursday in the rooms adjacent to the Cenacle, nor insist on the privilege that she could have had of keeping in her sacred bosom the ¦¦ graces of the ǀ

---

297), ǀ the Church affirms the relationship of this Virgin with the Eucharist, founded on her divine motherhood. Jesus in the Sacred Host is the fruit of this divine Mother, as is the child Jesus or the glorious Jesus.

[8] St. Thomas, Laudes, Hymn, Feast of Corpus Christi, *Opera,* 29:340.2.

[9] Ibid. Matins, Lectio 4, 29:337.2.

consecrated species from one Holy Communion to the next, nor rely on other facts and prerogatives, before we may piously believe, not without some basis, it is certain that Mary did communicate. Serious theologians, such as Suárez, assert that she did, daily.[10]

We spoke there of the externals. Who, apart from God and Mary herself (and St. John to some extent), is aware of the prodigious effects that this Sacrament has on her soul? St. Louis-Marie was fond of saying God made her to be His world, His paradise, His garden of delights where He was well-pleased to be, where His beloved and all-powerful Wisdom reveled more freely and more marvelously than in all Creation. Probe the depths of the insight, the depths of grace that may be uncovered from these words: "God, Who is at liberty to act, communicates to a creature"! It is the formula that summarizes the effects of Holy Communion in union with Mary. We thus say that all graces that has been given down the centuries, or will be given, to the faithful in this Sacrament were first vested in Mary for them to overflow on to us. We are here only applying to the Eucharist the general insight of St. Bernard: "Let us see with what sentiments of tender devotion the Lord would have us honor Mary, in whom He has placed the plenitude of all good, so that if there is anything of hope in us, if anything of grace, if anything of salvation, we may feel assured it has overflowed unto us from her who *cometh up from the desert, flowing with delights* (Cant 8.5)."[11] If it were otherwise, Mary would not be Queen and Lady in this Sacrament, the summary and crown of the mysteries of the Incarnation, and she would cease to be what God has made her to be everywhere; that is, Treasurer and Mediatrix ‖ of grace. |

It is right for the Church to put these tender words on her lips: *Venite, comedite panem meum, et bibite vinum quod miscui vobis*, "come, eat my bread, and drink the wine which I have mingled for you" (Prv 9.5). The Virgin invites us, and she has the right to invite us, for this bread is *panem ⸢ suum, ⸤* "her bread," the same that she prepared for us in the Incarnation: Jesus, Who, at the altar, as on the

---

[10] Suaréz, Summæ S. Thomæ, q. 37.4, d. 18.3.3, *Opera*, 19:288.2.

[11] •St. Bernard, *de Aquœductu*, §6, PL 183.441A: "Altius ergo intueamini, quanto devotionis affectu a nobis eam voluerit honorari, qui totius boni plenitudinem posuit in Maria: ut proinde si quid spei in nobis est, si quid gratiæ, si quid salutis, ab ea noverimus redundare, *quæ ascendit deliciis affluens.*"

Cross, is her Son. And this wine that she prepared for us, is the pure wine of the Divinity, a strong wine to buttress us in our frailty, but which Mary has diluted for us in His Humanity. In Jesus, God is within our reach and we dread Him no longer.

All these insights, therefore, perfectly justify the ¦¦ devotional | practice of our good Father de Montfort. They allow us to suck the marrow out of it; that is, to draw the truth and unction it contains. If Mary gave us the Eucharist, after she had received it, then it is fair that we should ask her for it, especially since, in the words of St. Louis-Marie, Jesus is everywhere the Bread of the Mighty and the Bread of Angels; but in Mary, He is the Bread of Children.[12] Indeed, it is from their mother that children seek ¦ nourishment. |

ARTICLE 2: HOLY COMMUNION THROUGH MARY

§1.

To communicate through Mary is not just to ask her for Jesus and receive Him as she gives Him, but also to take her as mediatrix between her Son and us.

As Our Lord did first look upon her and love her when He instituted the Eucharist, it is she (that is, her titles of ownership over us, and her dispositions reproduced in our soul) whom we shall offer to Jesus to draw Him nearer within us. When He comes, He will first greet Mary, whilst we hide behind her, with her merits and her name draped over us. By a tactic as profound as the ways of God, as delicate as love, St. Louis-Marie brings us to the complete abnegation of ourselves, of our notions and dispositions, to be at one with the Blessed Virgin. Happy is the appropriation that allows us to say of Jesus: "We shall bid Him enter the house of His Mother and she will receive Him in us and for us!" This is the manner of Holy Communion through Mary and in Mary.

That was a beautiful and consoling thought. It is indeed fitting that we should expand our soul,[13] often stifled by the profound sense

---

[12] Cf. *Secret*, 17. See also note 7, p. 296.

[13] St. Thérèse of Lisieux, *Story of a Soul*, c. 10, 162: "With me prayer is an uplifting of the heart; a glance towards Heaven; a cry of gratitude and love, uttered equally in sorrow

of our powerlessness, and afflicted by the sight of our faults, our somnolence, and our coldness!

How is it then that, for this Eucharist, where His love is generously given *in finem*, up to the limit of our capacity to take, and
accumulates works of wonder in our soul, Jesus gets only the little we
give Him? Mean we are in charity, and we know full well the bitter
taste of such a paltry return, for it seems a mockery even to us misers.
But imagine this: Add up all that all the souls give Him, past, present,
and future, in their adoration, their self-abandonment, their ardor,
and praises most pure, what we come up with still pales in comparison
to one gift God gives a single soul.

Eternal thanks be to Him! We have Mary standing at the start of
our path, ready to assist, as she does in all the other ways by which
God comes to us. She can receive all that Jesus gives her, and after
receiving them, she will give them to us one hundred percent. It is
right, then, that we should invite the blessed Virgin to come and abide
in us, that we should make her Queen regnant of our souls, that our
dispositions and acts be hers, so that Jesus may be more in her home
than in ours. Mary will welcome her Son, adore Him, love Him, glorify
Him, and pray to Him for us, all in her own name. Who better to ac-
custom Him to the shadows of our soul, to recompense Him for our
coldness, to take from her abundant treasures to supplement what is
wanting in us, and what we fail to surrender?

And there we have the substance of the acts that St. Louis-Marie
tells us we must do before and at the moment of Holy Communion.

§2.

It is not enough just to be in the disposition for Holy Communion,
nor to receive ¦¦ the Eucharist | through Mary and in union with her.
The period subsequent to Holy Communion is most precious; and, in
accordance with the theological import of the Eucharist, the Saints
have recommended the good use of the moments, which are far too
short.[14] We have much to do, and much, much more *to let things take*

---

and in joy. In a word, it is something noble, supernatural, which *expands my soul* and
unites her to God."

[14] St. Ignatius of Antioch, *In ad Ephesios*, c. 20, PG 5.662A: The Eucharist is "the one
bread, that medicine for immortality, that antidote for our dying, which allows us to
live forever in Jesus Christ." Ps. Dionysius, *De eccl. hierarchia*, 3, PG 3.423, 426:

their course. In spite of our goodwill, we know not always how to ac-
cede to one or the other of these important things, and our excessive
eagerness is often at odds with divine operations.

We have the security, and the peace of mind, in knowing that we
will make our thanksgiving through Mary, with Mary, and in Mary!

Recall the family feasts where an infant, sitting beside his mother,
indulges in his antics. He flails his arms in the air, he babbles, he questions, he wants to seize the objects he spies. The poor little thing!
What would he do without his mother! He is ignorant of most of the
things before his eyes, he knows not what is good for him, and he
cannot help himself. The best dishes and the biggest pieces are laid
out before him, still he cannot choose the food that would nourish
him. He would go off hungry during a veritable feast, but for his
mother. She is there to make him eat; she chooses what he needs, fills
his plate and serves him. All the while, she watches, lest he break or
spill something.

And we, so often seated at the Eucharistic banquet of infinite
opulence where God is made our food, what would we do if ¦ our
Mother ǀ were not there? We may be her true children in spiritual life,
but we still are ignorant and helpless. What do we know of the divine
food offered us? With the manna of heaven laid out before us, we
might as well repeat to our Mother the cry of the Israelites at seeing
the manna of the desert: *Manhu,* "What is this?" (Ex 16.15). If we cannot
tell which is best for us, do we not know less what to take and how to
be nourished? If we want to act, risk we not making mistakes; that is,
of doing the very opposite of what Jesus does? We invariably end up
going hungry, not partaking of the rich feast, and complain of it, when

---

"Without the most Holy Eucharist as the beginning of the consecration, rarely is the
communion with God achieved." Innocent III, *De sacro altaris,* 4.44, PL 217.885B, "By
the mystery of the Cross, He snatched us from the power of sin; by the Eucharistic
Sacrament, He delivers us from the will to sin." St. Vincent Ferrer, *Sermones œstivales,*
224.2, "We prevail in grace through communion more than by any other work." Trent,
Sess. 13, Eucharist, c. 2, 72: "The Eucharist is the antidote, whereby we may be freed
from daily faults, and be preserved from mortal sins." In sum, the feeding upon the
Eucharist has a mediate effect upon our body through its intimate union with Christ's,
and to some extent restoring us to our original integrity; for the union diminishes and
tempers concupiscence, or desire, and so enables the intellect and will to maintain their
supremacy over the lower nature. Cf. Kempis, *Imitation,* 4.12.4, 448.

we seek the fruit of our many Holy Communions.

But if Mary is with us, everything changes. She leads us to the Holy Table and bids us sit there. Let us docilely entrust ourselves to her. This Mother and Lady knows what is right for us in the three-fold service of this divine banquet: the human life, the glorious life, and the divine life of Christ. She will give it to us, after choosing it and preparing it according to our needs. She will watch us, so that the un-bridled activity of our thoughts and our just desires hinder not the action of Jesus. Thanks to her motherly care, we will come out of the prayer of thanksgiving nourished and satisfied, provided that we trou-ble not ourselves to see, to taste, or to feel, but live purely by faith ¦¦ especially here in Holy Communion. ¦[15]

Understand: it is the spiritual childhood that we practice here; and if we have not advanced further in the Kingdom of Heaven on earth, which Holy Communion is, is it not for want of becoming as little children beside our divine Mother?

St. Louis-Marie suggests a certain number of acts of thanksgiving. We need to have a grasp of their purpose and tenor, if we wish to derive benefits from their practice. We need not, nor is it advanta-geous to do them all after each Holy Communion, nor should they be used indifferently. However, we must follow the interior appeal to taste one practice at one time; and another, at a different one. This variety of tastes and this diversity of choice of pious exercises, accord-ing to the states and times, are noted by the author of the *Imitation*.[16]

Sometimes it is the sense of our helplessness, the need to have a mediatrix who carries us to let Jesus and Mary speak in our soul, while "we go in spirit to Heaven and over all the earth, praying all creatures to thank, adore, and love Jesus and Mary in our place."[17] With this in mind, the Church has the priest recite the canticle *Benedicite*,[18] as he comes down from the altar. Even so, we have better than the voice of Creation entire, be it of the redeemed, or even the glorified, to praise

---

[15] *TD*, 190.

[16] Kempis, *Imitation*, 4.6-9, 418-432.

[17] *TD*, 189.

[18] Dn 3.57-88, 56: Canticle of the Three Children, in the Act of Thanksgiving after Mass.

Jesus in the sacred Host. We have the voice of Mary and her *Magnificat*, which St. Louis-Marie urges us to pray in thanksgiving. And when we do, her soul will praise the Lord in us, and through her spirit we shall tremble with joy in God our Savior.[19]

At other times we ourselves shall ask Jesus, although always in union with Mary, for the graces we need, and "the coming of His Kingdom on earth through His holy Mother."[20]

Above all else, what St. Louis-Marie presses us to do is "to give Jesus to His Mother, who will receive Him lovingly, ... adore Him profoundly, ... and will render to Him, ... many homages which are unknown to us who are shrouded in dense darkness."[21]

To give Jesus to Mary is to communicate not only *through* Mary, *with* Mary, and *in* Mary, but also *for* Mary. It was so ordained for justice and our benefit. It was ordained, because God gave us His Son through Mary, and through her also we offer Him back, as the Host of praise and of our salvation. For justice, because Jesus appertains to His Mother; and giving Him back to her is an act of reparation on our part. Think about those painful separations our sins inflicted on Jesus and Mary on the way to Calvary, at the foot of the Cross, and at the sepulcher. Think also that between them there should have existed only bonds of unalloyed joy; but because of our sin and action, imagine how many reservations, sorrows, and griefs, have cut them short! It is right that we should recompense the Virgin and her divine Son, by returning one to the other. And while they rejoice together, says St. Louis-Marie,[22] in one of those movements of humility that the Holy Ghost inspires, we shall stand as at the door of our heart, assured that we shall at least gather the crumbs of this incomparable feast of joy and love, ¦ which poor Lazarus did partake in Heaven.[23] ¦

Lastly, many are the benefit of giving Jesus to Mary; that is, of surrendering the value and fruit of our Communion to her. And there lies our treasure; but as we hold it in our hands, we risk it being

---

[19] Cf. Ps 94.1: *Jubilemus Deo salutari nostro*, "let us joyfully sing to God our Savior."

[20] TD, 189.

[21] Cf. *TD*, 188-189.

[22] *TD*, 189-190.

[23] Lk 16.25.

wasted, stolen, or misused. Mary will keep watch and provide for its safety, and this security will lead us to remain in our humility, peace, and silence, which are sorely needed during our thanksgiving ¦¦ after Holy Communion. ¦

O Blessed Virgin, sometimes we imagine the blessedness of St. John and of those who have seen you here below. If we knelt by your side to receive the Eucharist, could we also not cast a discreet glance and see reflected on your countenance and in your attitude something of your dispositions and your inner acts? At the very least, make the eye of our soul see, in the light of faith, further than it is otherwise capable. Give us leave, like a child daring to do all with his mother; give us leave to see well into your ¦¦ immaculate ¦ heart, O Mother most admirable; give us leave to understand a little what passes there during your Communions. May Jesus living in you come and live also in our souls by the Eucharist, the source and summit of all the other mysteries![24] And, at the end of the Eucharistic banquet, we will repeat with you: *Esurientes implevit bonis,* "He hath filled the hungry with good things" (Lc 1.53).

ARTICLE 3: HOLY SLAVERY
AND THE EFFECT OF HOLY COMMUNION

We have just seen the marvelous benefits flowing from our union with Mary in Holy Communion. Let us now see how the habitual practice of our devotion disposes us most excellently to receive the divine Sacrament, whilst securing its fruits. In other words, we will give a brief account of the links between the devotion of Holy Slavery to Mary and the proper effect of Holy Communion.

St. John tells us what that is when he ¦ reports the word of Our Lord: ¦ *I am the bread of life. ... He that eateth my flesh, and drinketh my blood ... abideth in me, and I in him* (Jn 6.35, 55; 15.5). It is the spiritual transformation of a man in Jesus Christ, through charity, that must beget the Eucharistic communion. On this subject, Fr. Louis Billot remarks: "Every Sacrament, by the grace which is the salve proper to it,

---

[24] ◆Olier, "Prayer to invoke the Life of Jesus in oneself," *Règlements*, 118: *O Jesu, vivens in Maria, veni et vive in famulis tuis, ... in communione mysteriorum tuorum,* "O Jesus who dost abide in Mary, come and abide in Thy servants, ... in the communion of Thy mysteries." For the variations of this prayer, see his, *Pietas seminarii,* 357-368.

heals the wound in our fallen nature that directly opposes its special effect. We may say, therefore, that the curative action of the Eucharist is exercised over that wound of corrupt nature which makes each one of us relate everything to himself as to his end; and there we have, in effect, that which is most directly opposed to the union with God and with neighbor."[25] This selfishness, says the same author, is the radical injury inflicted upon us by Original Sin[26]; and our other infirmities proliferate from it, like branches from the trunk or brooks from the spring.

Now, the sacramental grace of the Eucharist gives us a special double dose of aid to remedy this selfishness. It is at once a contrary *habitual* disposition, and an actual help that stirs us to do acts of charity.

Dig deeper into this effect of the Sacrament on the dispositions wherein we establish the perfect Consecration and the acts it stirs us to exercise, and we will see a remarkable correspondence. There is no other preparation for the curative action of the Sacrament than to diligently renounce every thought of proprietorship, even in its subtlest manifestation, and to live habitually in perfect subjection to the operations of grace. Besides Holy Communion, there is no other favorable condition to preserve and multiply the fruits.

Consider also that in order to transform ourselves into Jesus Christ,[27] we must emerge from ourselves through love, break the chains that holds us back, strip away the form of our life, and put on that of Christ. We know that Mary is the perfect and divine mold. Let us throw ourselves into her when we communicate. Let us renounce our notions and intentions to take on hers and to unite ourselves to her acts. This is the most excellent way of despoiling ourselves in order to conform to Christ. What St. Louis Marie says bears repeating: "No devotion unites us to Jesus Christ more perfectly and easily or

---

[25] ◆Billot, *Sacramentis*, q. 49. 1:546 : ‖ "Omne sacramentum per gratiam sibi propriam alligat vulnus naturæ lapsæ suo proprio fini contrarium. Consequenter ergo dicendum videtur medicinalem Eucharistiæ ligaturam apponi contra illud naturæ corruptæ vulnus, ex quo provenit ut tam facile unusquisque ad suam modicam personam omnia referat ut ad finem, cum nihil sit quod magis directe impediat charitatem Dei et proximi." ‖

[26] Ibid. Proœmium, 1:5.

[27] St. Thomas, 3 *Sent.* 27.1.1 ad 4, *Opera*, 9:421.2; Billot, *Sacramentis*, q. 79, Th. 51.1, 1:548-549.

keeps us in the state of grace more faithfully."[28]

It is thus not a vain and pious fiction to communicate in union with Mary. The more we lose ourselves in her, the more she lives in us, the more Jesus Christ will delight in our souls. We shall then become a domain secured for Him, where He will dwell as master and be at home. He will stroll there, as in a spacious place where one comes and goes to act with perfect liberty, ⫶ fulfilling what Holy Scripture says: *Inhabitabo in illis, et inambulabo inter eos, et ero illorum Deus, et ipsi erunt mihi populus,* "I will dwell in them, and walk among them; and I will be their God, and they shall be My people" (2 Cor 6.16) ⫶.

---

[28] ◆*TD*, 81.

CHAPTER 4:

MARY AND THE HOLY SACRIFICE OF THE MASS

e should not be surprised that St. Louis-Marie did not outline a method for assisting at Mass in union with Mary. If he has given some notes on Holy Communion, perhaps it was with an eye to giving us an example of how he practices his devotion to the Blessed Virgin, and not because he intended to teach its application to the principal acts of our Christian life.

To fill this this gap, we may use several opuscules in keeping with the tenor of our devotion.[1] However, we shall follow a different path from theirs by emphasizing the liturgy, which is the teaching of the Church through prayer, acts, and the symbolism of things. The liturgy of Holy Sacrifice, in particular, is commended by its remote antiquity, its dignity, its profound meaning, and its sacred character. Liturgy holds our hand to guide us all through ¦¦ the ceremonies of | the adorable sacrifice. Which safer guide should we seek? Where do we find more fruitful thoughts? And which method is more natural, easier, and more approved to pray Holy Mass? We need only look to, and unite ourselves with, the action of the priest and the prayer of the Church to follow the Spirit of God. The same is true of following Mary, Queen and Mother of the Church, and in whom the same divine Spirit resides with a special fullness. Here we see the similarities and affinities between Mary and the Church, making it possible for us to pass from one subject to the other.

---

[1] ◆Of note, "Prière du Matin" and "Méthode pour entendre la sainte Messe en union avec Marie," in The Daughters of Charity, *Manuel*, 430-440, 449-474; "Les Biens du Cœur de la Sainte Vierge," a spiritual exercise for assisting at Mass in union with the dispositions of the Immaculate Heart of the Blessed Virgin Mary at the foot of the Cross during the Sacrifice of her Divine Son, in Jeanjacquot, *Simples explications*, 194-200.

355

Is the transition even necessary, so much do we see them united, and so much is Mary present in the liturgy of the Sacrifice? In many places she is identified by name; elsewhere, we may glimpse her under the veil of symbols. She plays a prominent role in the Eucharistic sacrifice, above and beyond the role of ¦¦ the rest of | the Church. We can thus follow the liturgy of the Holy Sacrifice in union with Mary, in keeping with the tenor of our devotion.

Seeing as liturgy is the expression of faith, we shall seek a better understanding of its meaning in theology, specifically to explain how the Mother of God participates in the Holy Sacrifice of the Altar.

Mary is associated with the Eucharistic sacrifice, because she is bound in the sacrifice of the Cross. In her capacity as Mother of God, she exercises an important priestly function in both instances. This is how she earned the title of "Virgin Priest." Let us have her as our guide to assisting at Holy Mass.

ARTICLE 1: THE "VIRGIN PRIEST"

Mary holds this title ¦¦ of honor | in Catholic tradition.[2] It is not that she has received the character and power conferred by priestly ordination, for her sex was an impediment. But she is also not just of

---

[2] ♦See, van den Berghe, *Marie*, ¦¦ especially c. 4, 83-126. The characterization of the B.V. Mary as "priest" belongs to the realm of speculative theology. Lest the faithful be confused, it bears repeating that Mary is not a priest in the sense of having a ministerial office by virtue of ordination. The priesthood is a state ordained by God for men. (Nm 1.49-50). Christ chose His Apostles from among men. St. Paul affirmed that the practice continued in Apostolic times. He would that the high priest be *taken from among men* (Heb 5.1), and would not *suffer a woman to teach, nor to use authority over the man* (1 Tim 2.12). The exclusivity is an immutable teaching of the Church, taught and practiced throughout the ages (St. Thomas, *Summa*, Suppl. 39.1c). Van den Berghe stands on this teaching (pp. 85-86). It was formally declared by Pope St. John Paul II, *Ordinatio sacerdotalis*, May 22, 1994. He writes that "the Church has no authority whatsoever to confer priestly ordination on women and that this judgment is to be definitively held by all the faithful of the Church." (*AAS*, 86, 1994, 548; as deposit of faith, 87, 1995, 1114). [*Emphasis added*]. The speculations arose out of a laudable effort to render honor to our Mother by the Spanish and French schools of spirituality during the 17th to late 19th centuries. (Laurentin, *Marie, l'Église et la Sacerdoce*, and Neubert, *Marie et Notre Sacerdoce*). Nonetheless, Lépicier, would rather that our Blessed Mother be called "Priestly Virgin," as her office refers to the priesthood of Christ, and not to the hierarchical and sacramental priesthood of the Church: "Excellentissima ratione, licet non proprie, dici potest, Maria *Virgo sacerdos*, aut melius *sacerdotalis*, ut hac denominativa appellatione deficientia a vero sacerdotio innuatur." (*Tr. de B.V.M.*, 1906 ed., 537). The Church proscribes pictures of Mary in priestly or liturgical vestments (*AAS*, 8, 1916, 146), as well as all devotions to *Virgo Sacerdos* (*Doc. Catholique*, 19, 1928, 809). |

the universal priesthood as understood from what St. Peter said of all Christians: *You are a kingly priesthood* (1 Pet 2.9). In receiving the grace of Christ, every individual Christian to a certain extent participates in His kingship and His priesthood; for in his prayers, his works, and especially by his sacrifices, he offers God an interior worship of a private order. So did Mary, and most perfectly; but she fulfills other functions eminently more priestly, first on Calvary, then every time the sacrifice of the Cross is re-presented on the altar.

§1. ON CALVARY.

The Blessed Virgin was on Calvary, and there is no doubt that she was. ¦ We know she was there because the Gospel explicitly says so. How do we list all the reasons for her presence on Calvary? | In what quality do we see her at the foot of the Cross, where the holy women and St. John, not to mention the others, were also?

Stabant autem juxta crucem Jesu Mater ejus, "there stood by the Cross of Jesus, His Mother" (Jn 19.25). As we have often said, she is inseparable from her Son because of her divine motherhood. She participates in His prerogatives, His acts, and His mysteries to the degree of which she alone is worthy. Now, Jesus is ¦¦ High | Priest and victim; she, too, will be priest and victim. ¦ Jesus is priest in virtue of His human nature, | which He took in His Incarnation in Mary's virginal womb. There He became the Man Who would save the world. In virtue of her motherhood, Mary participated in His divine priesthood, since she it was who received and gave birth to Him, her Son, the Redeemer and victim. Subsequently, when the hour of ¦¦ the supreme | sacrifice came, she followed Jesus to Calvary, not just in body, but also by will. She was a victim in union with Him, and the sword pierced her soul.[3] She was also a priest, ¦¦ in the sense that | she participated in a *priestly manner* in the offering that Jesus, the Supreme Pontiff, made of Himself to His Father. With the authority and power of a mother, through an act whose worth was equal to her incomparable love, the Virgin also offered her Son, and delivered Him to untold suffering and death. For this reason, she stood up—*stabat*— taking on the posture of a High Priest.[4] She stood there as Mother of

---

[3] Cf. Lk 2.35.

[4] Fr. Lhoumeau: *sacrificateur*, taken to mean the Hebrew הַכֹּהֵן הַגָּדוֹל *ha'kohen ha'gadol*,

Jesus, which is what the other women who accompanied her at the foot of the Cross were not.

We surmise that, in a role subordinated to the priesthood of Jesus, and in a distinct order, ¦ Mary took on certain priestly characteristics ¦; for she truly offered a holy victim acceptable to God, with that special power which she held from Him, and for the same purposes as in a sacrifice—a sacrifice in which she offered Him Who had received from her His passible and mortal human nature.

§2. THE HOLY SACRIFICE OF THE ALTAR

What we said of Mary's role on Calvary we may apply to the Eucharistic sacrifice. It is fair to ask: Is she associated in the Sacrament in the same manner as she is at the foot of the Cross? We propose to examine that question. She was present at Calvary, as the Gospel tells us. We say that she is also present in what occurs on the altar, as the Church affirms in her liturgy. If she is not present corporally as she was at the foot of the Cross, at least we may say that, from Heaven, she sees the sacrifice that is being made on the altar; that she is associated with it in such a way that she is in a communion of action, thought, and intention with the priest and the faithful. This is expressed in the words of the Canon: *Communicantes et memoriam venerantes in primis gloriosæ semper Virginis Mariæ*, "in union with and honoring the memory, first, of the glorious, ever Virgin Mary." By what title do we invoke her? As always, Mother of Jesus. Just as the Evangelist had been careful to represent her on Calvary in this quality: *Stabant. ... mater ejus*, so also the Church says at the Canon of the Mass: *In primis gloriosæ semper Virginis Mariæ, Genitricis Dei et Domini nostri Jesu Christi,* ¦¦ "first, of the glorious, ever Virgin Mary, Mother of our God and Lord Jesus Christ." ¦ We therefore call her at the position that befits her; that is, *in primis*, in the first rank, before the Apostles and Saints. It is she, above all, to whom we must look; she, with whom to unite ourselves; because, after Jesus, she is here at the altar the first, and through her must we go to Him.

Mary participates in the sacrifice of the altar. She could hardly be absent. She is the inseparable associate,[5] the Spouse ¦¦ of the Holy

---

the High Priest of the Temple in Jerusalem.

[5] St. Albert the Great, "Mariale," 42, *Opera*, 37:81: "Beata Virgo non est assumpta in

Ghost | and the faithful helper of Jesus in all His mysteries, of which the Eucharist is the continuation and the summary of the others. We read in the Office of Corpus Christi: *Memoriam fecit mirabilium suorum*, the Lord "hath made a remembrance of His wonderful works" (Ps 110.4).[6] If Mary was present at, and is associated with, the mysteries of the Incarnation, the | Presentation,[7] | Calvary, the Resurrection, and the Ascension, why would she be excluded from the mystery of the Eucharist? The fact that Jesus was present in all those circumstances is sufficient reason for His Mother to be a participant, regardless of the manner in which she did. But there are specific reasons we associate the Blessed Virgin with the Eucharistic sacrifice, for it is none other than the sacrifice at Calvary re-presented, at which the Mother of Jesus should cooperate, as she did in the immolation of her Son on the Cross. At Holy Mass, Jesus offers Himself, but the priest also offers Him in the name of the Church. How would Mary, Queen and Mother of the Church, participate in this oblation? The sacrifice of the altar applies the merits of the One on the Cross. Should not Mary, the treasurer and universal dispenser of all graces, have an interest in it?

All these reasons explain why sacred liturgy gives Mary a place of honor, as Mother of Jesus, in the Eucharistic sacrifice.

When we look further into Mary's participation in Holy Mass, we see that, in a manner of speaking, her priestly role is superior to that of the priest's.

Mary has not the power to consecrate; but, all things considered, consecration does not give Jesus a new existence or nature. It only makes Him present under the species of bread and wine in the way proper to the Eucharist, in what we call a "sacramental state," while the Blessed Virgin gave the Word His human existence, another nature, without which we would not have had the Sacrament or the

---

ministerium a Domino, sed in consortium et adjutorium, juxta illud: *Faciamus ei adjutorium simile sibi* (Gn 2.18), ... non est vicaria, sed *coadjutrix et socia* [Christi]."

[6] *Brev. Rom.*, 388, 85.

[7] Fr. Lhoumeau: "Purification," that refers to Mary, and occurred on the same day as the Presentation of Our Lord. Likely a printer's error.

sacrifice.[8] Her *fiat* to the Incarnation ¦ made possible │ every word of consecration ¦ said by priests everywhere. │

The priest offers sacrifice; but his action, however official, is that of a minister. He lends his cooperation to Jesus Christ and the Church. Mary acts not in that capacity, nor in that manner, for she makes the offering, and immolates Jesus in her name; she offers Him by virtue of a power which undoubtedly comes from God, but is not an extrinsic and accidental prerogative, as is the priest's, since hers is founded on her divine motherhood.

And as for the ends of the sacrifice, we need to say how much Mary was inspired by the oblation on Calvary. The first two ends are adoration and thanksgiving. But what priest has ever delved deeper into the things of God as Mary did? Like a lyre, her soul, always in perfect agreement with Jesus, wafts sweet melodies of adoration and ineffable praise under the touch of the Holy Ghost. Her *Ecce ancilla Domini* and *Magnificat* overwhelm the praises of all heavenly choirs and Creation entire. How far did the adoration and the thanksgiving of Mary ascend on Calvary and still do before our altars? Peruse the offices of Compassion and the Seven Sorrows, which honor the coop-eration of Mary at the sacrifice of Calvary, and you will find these words that the Church applies to her: ¦¦ *Recordare, Virgo Mater Dei, dum steteris in conspectu Domini, ut loquaris pro nobis bona, et ut avertat indignationem suam a nobis,* │ "Be mindful, O Virgin Mother of God, when thou standest in the sight of the Lord, to speak good things for us, and to turn away His anger from us."[9] And in the eighth response of the Office of the Seven Sorrows, ¦¦ we say to Our Lord: *In toto corde tuo, gemitus matris tuæ ne obliviscaris* (Sir 7.29): *ut perficiatur propitiatio, et benedictio,* │ "With all Thy heart, forget not the groan-ings of Thy Mother, that Thine offering and Thy blessing may be perfected."[10] That is where we ask Mary to procure for us the other purpose of sacrifice, which is propitiation.

He who owns an ingot of most pure gold certainly does not have

---

[8] ♦See, Terrien, *Mère de Dieu,* ¦ 1.1, 3.2, 1:253, et 1.2, 5.1-8.5, 2:1-426. │ The book is a good resource on Marian theology.

[9] *Missale,* Ant., §3063; cf. Jer 18.20.

[10] Septem Dolorum, Sep 15, *Brev. Marianum,* 348.1.

it ¦ in coins of legal tender,[11] | but he nevertheless possesses its value. Similarly, for Mary, her divine motherhood is worthy of a grace and priestly functions which, in truth, do not confer on her the character and faculties given to priests of the New Law, but which nevertheless are superior. At the Cross, as at the altar, she participates in her name and in the name of the Church; above her there is only Jesus. It is from Mary, as from the source, that priestly grace flows into souls, by virtue of which they make offerings to God, immolate, and distribute the very same Jesus Whom she brought into this world, and offered, and immolated, and gave to the world for the very first time.

The Blessed Virgin is the "Priestess of Justice,"[12] the "first after Christ at the altar of sacrifice,"[13] and the "Queen of the clergy," as the devout founder Saint-Sulpice was pleased to call her.[14] It is thus not a question of pious imagination to want to pray Mass in union with her and under her guidance. Here again, in going to Jesus through Mary, our devotion rests on Catholic dogma, our piety opens to new vistas, and we have a method as fruitful as it is easy to witness the Holy Sacrifice of the altar. What help to the pious women, do you think, was the presence of the Blessed Virgin who supported them and led them to the Cross? Was it not enough for them just to cast their eyes on Mary, to unite their acts and dispositions with hers, as much as they could understand them, so that they might offer the divine Victim a perfect tribute of religion and love?

And we, let us have confidence that being in communion with the acts and dispositions of our divine Mother during the holy mysteries,

---

[11] Fr. Lhoumeau: "une pièce de cinq francs dans la forme qui lui est propre." The 5-franc coin, 1.61 gr., 0.900 fine, struck between 1862-1868, was the smallest gold denomination.
[12] ◆St. Antonin, ¦¦ *Summa*, 4.15.3.3, 4:926-927: "Fuit et *sacerdotissa justitiæ*, quæ proprio Filio suo non pepercit, sed stabat juxta crucem Jesu non ut ... mortem Filii aspiceret, non ut dolorem Filii consideraret, sed ut salutem humani generis exspectaret, parata ipsa offerre Filium Deo pro salvatione mundi." |
[13] ◆Jan Mombaer, Abbot of Livry, *Rosetum*, ¦¦ Pars. 2, Tit. 24, 601H : Gratias etiam sacramentales perfectissimæ tenuit; quæ omnia Sacramenta, suo tempore omnibus hominibus generaliter observanda instituta observavit; ita ut nihil ei de illorum efficaciis, et perfectione deperiret; ita quod omnes (juxta Albertus) in vita præter ordines suscepit; quos tamen per æquipollentiam tenuit, quia dignitatem, potestatem, et administrationem in Ecclesia habet, et *summa Sacerdos post Christum fuit*. |
[14] Olier, "La journée chrétienne," 2, *Œuvres*, 223.

our worship may be less unworthy; our love, more ardent; and our
spiritual benefits, greater than in the past.

Before going through the *sacred act* most excellent, which is the
sacrifice of the altar, we may cast a glance at the liturgical objects or
instruments of worship. These objects which the Church uses for her
sacred functions, are also symbols of invisible realities. Since we seek
to unite ourselves with Mary during the Holy Sacrifice, is it not natural to study how the objects may represent it to us and symbolize its
august functions?

The altar and the tabernacle primarily grab our attention. The
altar, say the liturgists, represents Christ; but Christian tradition also
tells us that Mary is an altar and a tabernacle. "The ark of the
covenant, the living temple or tabernacle of the deity, the golden urn
containing the true manna,"[15] are, among others, the metaphors
befitting the Blessed Virgin, who carried the Son of God in her virginal
bosom. "Mary is [also] an altar of pure gold on which the great Victim
Himself is offered, ... the quickened altar of the bread of life; the altar
of holocausts on which the Lamb of God was consumed; ... the altar
of reconciliation, where the Seraphim most excellent, Jesus Christ,
took the burning coal with which He purified humanity of its stains.
Mary is [also] the divine and mystical table on which the living Host
rests, Whose flesh is distributed to the faithful. ... If the Fathers say
that the hearts of all the faithful are altars, even more so must it be
affirmed of the heart of this Virgin, the most similar to the Heart of
Jesus."[16] Is it not in the arms of Mary, and on her heart, that Jesus
offered Himself, and laid down in Bethlehem, in the Temple, and on
Calvary? This is the same altar where we shall also lay down our
offerings, our acts of religion, and especially ourselves, to be worthily
presented, in union with Jesus, to the eternal Father.

There is no contradiction between the two symbols of the altar. If
it represents Mary, it is not with Jesus absent. On the contrary, it is

---

[15] van den Berghe, *Marie*, 117.

[16] ♦Ibid. 117-118, where there is an extensive list of sources used. They form a collection
of authoritative testimonies from antiquity.

insofar as she carries Him, and through her, that He offers Himself to God ¦¦ the Father. |

The Cross itself is not unrelated to the Blessed Virgin. ¦ The remarkable paintings of ancient times, beginning with of the Virgin of the catacombs of St. Agnes, depict Mary with Jesus on her heart, and in the attitude of prayer and sacrifice, her arms raised in the shape of a cross,[17] imitating the holy Victim spread on the Cross for the sacrifice. Elsewhere, the Virgin is often represented alone in the same Orant posture. |

The candlesticks. We would not be refuting the representation of the Christian people in the candlesticks accorded by liturgists, if we saw Mary also as the mystical candelabrum that brought Jesus Christ, the Light of the world. Through Him and because of Him, she is also the light of our souls.

We shall have occasion to speak of the chalice and the sacred vessels, but there is much to say about the vestments of the priest, minister and figure of Christ. Mary, say the Fathers, is like the *sacrarium*, where Christ took His sacerdotal vestment; that is, His Humanity in which He was to offer Himself as a sacrifice.[18] The priest should put on the sacred ornaments with his mind entering the interior of the Blessed Virgin. He will then emerge to ascend to the altar, accompanied always by Mary, just as Jesus came out of His mother's womb, and then, and not without her, to ascend the altar of the Cross.

There are many other aspects of the Eucharistic sacrifice associated to Mary that we may discuss at great length, but we shall summarize them with the words of Fr. Faber on the Crucifixion: "The Immaculate Heart of Mary is the living altar stone on which the Sacrifice is offered; it is the Server, the beatings of whose broken heart are the responses of the liturgy; it is the Thurible, in which the world's faith, the world's hope, the world's love, the world's worship, are being burnt like incense before the slain Lamb that taketh away the sins of

---

[17] The Orant of the *Cœmeterium Majus*. See also note 54, p. 131.

[18] St. Ambrose, *Inst. Virginis*, 17.105, PL 16.331B: "Sed ipse quoque unigenitus Filius tuus venturus in terras suscipere quod amissum est, puriorem carnis suæ generatione reperire non potuit, quam ut habitationi propriæ cælestis aulam virginis dedicaret; in qua esset et immaculatæ castitatis *sacrarium*, et Dei templum." For an extensive list of references of Mary to *sacrarium*, see Ippolito Marracci, "Polyanthea Mariana," in Bourrasé, *Summa aurea B.V.M*, 11:236-238; ibid., Index V, 13:1029;

the world; and finally, the same Immaculate Heart is the Choir, the more-than-angelic Choir of that tremendous Mass; for did not the silence of her beautiful sufferings sing unutterable, voiceless songs into the ravished ear of the Bleeding Host?"[19]

ARTICLE 3: THE LITURGY OF THE MASS

Holy Mass begins with the priest chanting the Psalm *Judica me.* He soon sees himself in the presence of infinite holiness, and, before approaching the awesome mystery, the priest humbles himself, confesses his sins. After him, the faithful do the same, followed by him pronouncing the words of forgiveness. In reciting the *Confiteor,* we bow to the most holy things in Heaven and on earth. Twice we invoke the name of Mary, the refuge and advocate of sinners, and both times ahead of all others. Then, confident in that blessed name, we lift up our heads to beg mercy and help from God.

The *Introit* generally expresses the just desires of the patriarchs and of the righteous for the coming of the Savior. It is also the song of the soul that groans, prays, and hopes in the Lord. On rare occasions, as in certain festivals, we hear a note of triumph. We should unite ourselves to the sighs and supplications of Mary, that we may hasten the coming of the Redeemer. We may also think of the *Introit* as an entrance ⁞ hymn, | because we sing this antiphon at the entrance of the priest, signaling the beginning of the Holy Sacrifice. It should serve to remind us of Jesus, the Eternal Priest, entering into this world, to offer Himself as the Victim to His Father. Let us associate ourselves with Mary's sentiments, for it was in her that He was incarnated, and hers the *Ecce* that accorded so well with the same of Jesus Christ's.[20]

The *Kyrie eleison* is a prayer in honor of the Holy Trinity, for the first three *Kyrie* address the Father; the three *Christe,* the Son; and the last three *Kyrie,* the Holy Ghost. If we wish to say it well, we should think of Mary, who is bound to the Holy Trinity under many titles. We will laud her worthily and implore here efficaciously, she who is the Daughter of the Father, Mother of the Son, and Spouse of the Holy

---

[19] Faber, *Foot of the Cross,* 364.
[20] ✦Heb 10.5, 7: *Ideo ingrediens mundum dicit: Hostiam et oblationem noluisti.* Ecce *venio,* "Wherefore when He cometh into the world, He saith: 'Sacrifice and oblation Thou wouldest not. *Behold* I come.'"

Ghost.

Dom Guéranger says that these nine invocations show us that the Church on earth is associated with the nine Choirs of Angels before the throne of the Lamb.[21] During this litany we shall raise our eyes to their Queen, through whom the praises and supplications of the heavenly hierarchies pass, before ascending to Christ.

After this prayer there follows ¦¦ the *Gloria*, | the hymn which Rupert of Deutz says is at the same time the song of Angels and of men,[22] for the Church here on earth repeats it having received it from the heavenly spirits.

Bethlehem, the house of bread, announced the Eucharist, and the Eucharist, in turn, prepares for the glory to come. There, in a mean trough for animal feed, and here in the ciborium at Mass, it is the same Jesus, our living Bread. He is also the Bread of Angels that He fills with His glory. The ox, says Scripture, utters not a plaintive bellow when its crib is full,[23] so it was a song of praise and joy that the Angels chanted before the manger. There Jesus filled the crib; here He is laid abundantly on our Eucharistic tables, as if in the fullness of the heavenly feast. Let us sing before our altars as the Angels did in Bethlehem and as they do in Heaven; but above all let us not forget Mary. She it is who filled our crib. When she laid her divine Child down in it, she understood the meaning of her act and, better than the Angels, knew who Jesus was. We will sing with her in a more perfect mode and at a higher tone every parts of this hymn. It unfolds in praise, blessings, and thanksgiving; then it bids us sinners bow down for a moment that we may humble ourselves in a triple supplication; finally, the hymn rises to burst into three solemn acclamations to confess the supereminence of Christ: *Quoniam Tu solus Sanctus, Tu solus Dominus, Tu solus Altissimus,* ¦¦ "for Thou alone art holy; Thou alone art the Lord; Thou alone art the Most High"! |

The priest kisses the altar, as a sign of communion with Jesus Christ, the Saints and, consequently, Mary; then, turning to the

---

[21] Guéranger, *Liturgical Year*, 2:58.
[22] Rupert of Deutz, *De divinis officiis*, 30, PL 170.27C.
[23] Cf. Prv 14.4.

faithful, he greets them: *Dominus vobiscum,* "the Lord be with you."
We heard it from his lips, before he went up to the altar, and he will
repeat it again; but each time this greeting strikes our ears, it reminds
us of the Archangel's, *Dominus tecum,* "the Lord is with thee."[24] May
the Lord be with us, and may He steer the spirit of the priest praying
on our behalf! His prayer brings together the prayers of all the assembled faithful, and is addressed solemnly to Jesus Christ, Who offers it
to His Father; but it is Mary who presents it to Jesus. Let us say "Amen"
from the bottom of our hearts to all that she asks for us before the
throne of the Lamb.

During the *Epistle,* let us implore Mary for the understanding of
Holy Scripture and its teachings. And before the Gospel is read, bowing our heads with the priest, we may say something along the lines
of the following prayer, which is like the *Munda cor meum,* "cleanse
my heart":

> O Virgin faithful and holy,
> Tender Spouse of the Holy Ghost!
> Amend my heart most contrary,
> Be it made humble and contrite.
>
> Do thou give me a heart most meek,
> Ever more faithful to His voice,
> That in the Gospel will I seek,
> His counsel and His laws to keep.[25]

Let us make the sign the cross, the sign of the Christian whom the
Blessed Virgin marks as her true children; for without the Cross, how
would she form Christ in us, and what would be the doctrine of Jesus
crucified mean for us? We will listen to the Gospel by standing beside
our incomparable Lady, so that, following her example, we may know
how to keep in our heart the words which we will afterwards confer
with the Holy Ghost to nourish our soul.

When we recite the *Credo,* let us think of the faith of Mary, the
faithful Virgin most excellent. She conceived the Son of God by an act
of faith. It was through her prayer and influence that the miracle of
Cana was wrought, which then strengthened the faith of the disciples.

---

[24] Lk 1.28.

[25] ♦*Cantiques,* 141.16, 2: O Vierge sainte et fidèle, / Épouse du Saint-Esprit! / Changez
mon cœur si rebelle / En un cœur humble et contrit. / Donnez-moi ce cœur docile / Et
bien fidèle à sa voix, / Pour pratiquer l'Évangile / Dans ses conseils et ses lois.

The Holy Fathers call her "Queen of the Apostles and Disciples,"[26] and the Church sings: "She hath cast asunder all heresies."[27] We know that she will make her devout servants participate abundantly in her incomparable faith. Surrendering our mind to her, let us pray with ardor that it be so.

With the *Offertory*, the sacrifice begins. Recall the secret offering that Jesus made in the womb of Mary before coming into the world, and His public offering in the Temple through the hands of His Mother. In a certain way, the offertory is the life of Christ. ¦ The consecration and elevation in this solemn Mass is akin to His immolation on the Cross. | The golden paten on which the Host is offered remains far from the golden throne which is Mary. Jesus rests in her arms and wants to offer Himself though her hands. This is where we must place ourselves, in order to be offered up with Him.[28] That is how it must be. If the priest cannot avoid confessing his unworthiness during the oblation of the immaculate Host to the living and true God, imagine how much our unworthiness begs for the mediation of our divine Mother!

The priest then pours water and wine mixing them in the chalice, to symbolize the union of the divine and human natures in Jesus Christ, as well as the union of the faithful with Him. We cannot ask to participate with the Church in the divinity of the One Who deigned to take our humanity, without thinking of Mary, in whom and through whom this mystery was accomplished. She is the Mother of this people reborn, out of whom the Church is formed.

Returning to the middle of the altar, ¦¦ during the *Offerimus tibi*, | the priest raises the chalice and beseeches divine clemency to accept the oblation as a savor of sweetness for his salvation and that of the whole world. If our offerings are always pleasing to God, when we make them through Mary, it will please Him to receive this Victim of infinite value through her hands, as He undoubtedly did of old at the

---

[26] St. Thomas of Villanova, "In Assump. B.V.M.," 3.7, *Conciones*, 1:322: "Apostolorum omnium et Discipulorum Christi Ecclesiarumque Magistra."
[27] *Brev. Rom.*, In Festis B.V.M., Ant. 7, 35: Gaude, Maria Virgo, cunctas hæreses sola interemisti in universo mundo.
[28] ◆This is the moment to renew our consecration and promises.

Temple and on Calvary.

Then the priest bows in humility and contrition asking the Lord to accept the sacrifice. In great part, this prayer is borrowed from that recited by the three children in the fiery furnace.[29] To repeat it, let us enter into the heart of Mary, amidst the flames of divine love. Then, we shall be pierced by the sense of humility that animate this prayer: *In spiritu humilitatis*,[30] which fill the soul of the "handmaid of the Lord."

Then raising his hands, the priest invokes the Holy Ghost ⁝⁝ in the *Veni, Sanctificator*, | to change the bread and wine to the Body and Blood of Christ, as He once formed His body in Mary's womb. It is always with the help of His faithful Spouse that He works on the altar and consume our life with the fire of charity, so that Jesus may live in us. It is thus useful to remember Mary in this invocation.

When the priest, as a sign of perfect purity, washes his fingers, let us pray to the most pure Virgin Immaculate, Queen of Angels, to obtain a greater purity for us to participate in the august mysteries.

Then comes the prayer, ⁝⁝ *Suscipe, sancta Trinitas*, | by which the Holy Trinity is entreated to accept the offering of the sacrifice in memory of the Passion, the Resurrection, and the Ascension of Jesus Christ. These three mysteries make Redemption complete. Then the priest invokes the Saints to whom, after God, is due some honor in this sacrifice. First, we call on the name of the Most Blessed Virgin. "Not a single Mass is offered," says Dom Guéranger, "that does not bring glory to our Blessed Lady, who is, in herself, a whole world apart."[31]

Then let us pray in silence with the priest. This prayer, called the *Secret*, reminds us of one of the fondest ideas of St. Louis-Marie's, who urges us to say "Amen" to all that Mary does in Heaven. We hear not what the Church and Mary ask of God in this prayer; however, we should associate ourselves to it confidently.

We now arrive at the *Preface*, the song of thanksgiving and jubilation. "May your soul, O divine Mary, be in me to praise the Lord, and your spirit, too, that I shall tremble with joy in Him," for far above

---

[29] Dn 3.39.

[30] *Missale*, §1033.

[31] ✦Cf. Guéranger, *Explan. of Holy Mass*.

the heavenly hierarchies quivering with fear, adoration, and love, O Lady of the heavenly Choirs, you appear to us to be directly leading them to Christ. We who are yet sojourners here on the earth, we lift up our eyes and our hearts to you. You are the straight path on which our prayers ascend to the Lord, to render Him just and worthy thanksgiving. *Sursum corda*, ⫼ "We lift up our hearts to the Lord!" |

The triple *Sanctus*, resounds. Let the spirit of adoration that fills our Mother pierce us, and notice how the memory of her sheds a deeper meaning on the very words of this solemn confession: ⫼ *Sanctus Dominus, Deus Sabaoth*, | "Holy Lord, God of hosts." But these hosts are not made up only of the legions of Angels; they have at their head this woman, who was ordained to crush the serpent, and who alone to him is *terrible as an army set in array* (Cant 6.9). ⫼ *Pleni sunt cæli et terra gloria tua*, | "Heaven and earth are full of Thy glory." Indeed, so is she who is "full of grace," and is said to be the paradise of God, His own world, and "the splendor of the Lord of lords!"[32] *Hosanna*, then, and praise in the highest Heaven; that is, may God have His glory in her who, surpassing all the choirs of Angels, sits at the right hand of Christ.

Now begins the great prayer, the central prayer of the Holy Sacrifice. Until the *Pater Noster*, the entirety of Canon of the Mass must be viewed as forming one whole action in the sacrifice.[33]

Here everything gravitates around the consecration, everything relates to it and is one with it. From that moment, the soul is so bathed with the scenes on Calvary that one must kneel before the altar in the company of Mary, Mother of Jesus. We will find among the Angels and men none whose dispositions are more perfect and whose help more efficacious to unite one's self with Jesus in the Eucharist. Let us learn from her how to regard the Holy Victim, to understand what is happening before our eyes, to offer ourselves with Christ, to finally stand at the foot of the Cross. We know how necessary it is that this universal Mediatrix, Mother of the Church, should substitute our

---

[32] *Cantiques*, 76.9, 128: "La magnificence du Seigneur des seigneurs."

[33] ◆Franzelin, *SS. Eucharistiæ*, Th. 7, 79 : ⫼ "Tota ea pars sacræ liturgiæ quæ a Latinis vocatur *Actio, Canon* (a Græcis, ἀναφορά, *anaphora*), spectatur ut una actio sacrifica." |

prayer, too often straitened and feeble, with one that encompasses the entire Church, ¦¦ Militant, Suffering, and Triumphant, | fully aware of the infinite value of the divine sacrifice.

Shortly before the consecration, the priest extends his hands to the Host and the chalice to offer them to God, our sovereign Master, in an homage of dependence: ¦ *Hanc igitur oblationem* servitutis *nostræ, sed et cunctæ familiæ tuæ, quæsumus, Domine, ut placatus accipias,* "we therefore beseech Thee, O Lord, graciously to accept this oblation of our *servitude,* so also of Thy whole family." | Here we find the devotion of Holy Slavery reflected in depths of religion and first among the ends of sacrifice. If we live habitually in this manner, we will keep an excellent disposition to assist at Mass.

When the solemn moment of consecration comes, the genuflections of the priest, the elevation, and the deposition of the Host or chalice, will remind you that, in Bethlehem, Mary adored Jesus Who came forth from her womb, presented Him to the heavenly Father, and laid him down in the crib; that, at the Cross, if she could not have the body of Jesus in her arms as she did in Bethlehem, at least by her attitude and by her interior acts, she adored Him, offered Him to God, and soon after laid Him down in the sepulcher.

Now Jesus Christ is present on the altar. The bread and wine apart signify the separation of His Body and His Blood. Imagine seeing through Mary's eyes and what thoughts she had when she looked on Cross and saw the separation at work; the Divine Blood flowing out gradually from the broken Body of her Son. May she deign to apply to us the fruits of this *immolatio!* We should hope and take courage when we ask ¦¦ for some part and fellowship with all the Saints in Heaven: | *Nobis quoque peccatoribus.* Mary's help ranks first, ¦¦ after God's, | in "the multitude of Thy mercies," which is the bedrock of our hope.

Let us follow the action of the priest, ¦¦ now at the oblation of the Victim to God. | Standing, facing the ¦¦ consecrated | Host, he raises his arms again to pray; and, it bears noting, after the consecration, as before, he presents his offering to the Divine Majesty as a tribute of our dependence: *Unde et memores, Domine, nos* servi *tui* ... "wherefore, O Lord, we Thy *servants* ..."

Then he begs God to look favorably on this sacrifice, recalling that once it pleased Him to accept the sacrifices of Abel, Abraham, and Melchizedek.[34] This evocation of the ancient sacrifices reminds us how they are bound to the sacrifice of the altar. Those of the Old Law were but a prefigurement of the New, which is superior, and by bringing together all the ends of the ancient sacrifices, has by itself an infinite worth.

But it is not only on earth and in time that the Mass is a center where the worship of times past finds its true end, and a summit that dominates the history of the ages; for the sacred liturgy raises our eyes all the way up to Heaven, even to the sublime altar where the divine Lamb stands immolated.[35] Bowing deeply towards the altar, and prostrate in spirit before the throne of God, the priest asks that the sacred gifts be carried to the heavenly altar, and placed there, by the Angel of the Great Counsel, the Divine Messenger, Who is Jesus Christ. For it is this same Jesus Christ, immolated on our altars, Who in Heaven offers His Father His glorious wounds and intercedes for us. But on the right hand of her Son, Whom she assists on high as she did on Calvary, we see Mary offering Him to the Divine Majesty and praying with Him.

The past and the future converge on Jesus in the sacred Host; above our altars, Heaven opens up to show us in their glorious liturgy the splendor of ours, saying to us again and again that Christ was yesterday, is today, and will remain for ages to ages. Where else can we find thoughts more profound, more orthodox, and more fruitful for pious devotion?

We must not forget that the blood of the Lamb should bring refreshment, light, and peace even to Purgatory. The intercession of Mary compassionate follows souls in this place of trials, also part of

---

[34] ♦When we pray to God to accept the sacrifice offered to Him, it must be remembered that the Mass has by itself a value independent of the dignity of the minister and is a sacrifice always agreeable to God. (Trent, Sess. 22, ¦¦ Sacrifice, c. 1, 142: The sacrifice is "pure oblation, which cannot be defiled by any unworthiness, or malice of those that offer it." ¦). It is insofar as it is offered by us that we beg the Divine Majesty not to take offense at our unworthiness and to apply the fruits to it.

[35] Rev 5.6: Behold in the midst of the throne and of the four living creatures, and in the midst of the ancients, a Lamb standing *tanquam occisum*, as it were slain.

her realm. May our suffrages reach there through her mediation and may she deign to add hers to ours!

Lastly, let us pray *Nobis quoque peccatoribus*, for ourselves, wretched sinners, relying less on our merits than on divine mercy: ¦¦ "To us sinners also, Thy servants, O Eternal Father, hoping in the multitude of Thy mercies, vouchsafe to grant some part and fellowship with Thy holy Apostles and Martyrs, ... and with all Thy Saints, into whose company we pray Thee to admit us, not considering our merits, but of Thine own free pardon." | Our merits and the value of our works, we have surrendered into the hands of Mary; but we count on her to obtain an abundant share of this mercy and to gain entrance into the glory of the Saints. ¦ How can this prayer not stir us to a greater devotion to our good Mother? |

Then when we say with the priest: ¦¦ *Per ipsum, et cum ipso, et in ipso, est tibi Deo Patri omnipotenti, in unitate Spiritus Sancti, omnis honor, et gloria,* | "through Him, with Him, and in Him be to Thee, God the Father Almighty, in the unity of the Holy Ghost, all honor and glory," we shall rejoice in the thought that ¦ this is hymn of praise is said | in a surer and more and perfect manner, through Mary, with Mary, and in Mary.

Lord, teach us to pray (Lk 11.1), said the Apostles to the Divine Master; and He taught them the Lord's Prayer. At the school of Jesus, Mary was, in every respect, the first disciple, and no one said and understood the *Pater Noster* as she did. Let us say it again under her guidance.

The prayer ends with the last appeal: *Libera nos a malo,* "deliver us from evil," and implores peace, the peace that Jesus alone can give. The Church asks for peace by the intercession of the Saints, some of whom she names, placing at their head, as everywhere else, the Blessed Virgin Mary, Mother of God.

After this prayer, the priest kisses the paten, an *instrument of peace*, because it receives the Body of Jesus Christ, Who is the author of peace. The same paten symbolizes Mary, who not only received Christ and in whom He was borne, but who also gave Him His Body. For this reason, she became the sign and the minister of peace.

The *Agnus Dei* is borrowed from St. John the Baptist. He said it in faith when he identified Jesus to the multitude, but also with love in proclaiming His quality as Savior. We may imagine how much more enlightened Mary was, and how much more perfect her love, when she often contemplated Jesus. Surely, better than anyone, especially after Simeon prophesied, she saw Him as the Lamb of God.

Do deign, O Mother, to illumine our souls and touch our heart, that we may devoutly recite this three-fold invocation.

We refer to the preceding chapter and the practices suggested by St. Louis-Marie, as regards the prayers that precede Holy Communion as well as for Communion itself. After the last prayers and the *Ite Missa est*, we are left with the final prayer, ¦¦ said by the priest, | which begins with these words: *Placeat tibi, sancta Trinitas obsequium servitutis meæ,* "may the performance of my homage be pleasing to Thee, O Holy Trinity." In the formula of consecration, St. Louis-Marie has a prayer similar almost to the letter: "Receive, O benign Virgin, this little offering of my slavery." Thus, down to its very end, the words of the liturgy brings to life the essence of our consecration.

May this final homage also pass through Mary; and when time comes for us to depart this life, which will have been merely a long Mass in union with the crucified Jesus and a true immolation, we shall then call on the Holy Trinity to accept again, in homage of adoration and loving dependence, the last act that will consummate our sacrifice: *Placeat tibi, sancta Trinitas, obsequium servitutis meæ.* Let us bow our head for the blessing by the priest in uniting ourselves with the one who is "blessed among all creatures"[36] to partake of the benediction more abundantly. The priest blesses as minister, but it is Mary who obtains for us and gives us this blessing because it comes to us from Christ, in Whom the Father *hath blessed us with spiritual blessings in heavenly places* (Eph 1.3). And, indeed, we need to remind ourselves that Jesus, in turn, is given to us by Mary.

We shall conclude this volume by repeating the words of St.

---

[36] Holtnicker, *Speculum B.V.M.*, 17, 257: "When, by the blessed fruit of the Virgin all the faithful in general are blessed, rightly the chaste are specially Blessed by Him, by Whom also the blessed Queen of the chaste is blessed above all."

Louis-Marie on Holy Communion: "There are numberless other thoughts with which the Holy Ghost will inspire you."[37]

Our purpose was to pave the way and mark the trails enough so that we could walk without much difficulty. It will be observed that we have expounded views and suggested motives rather than given formulas; for, in the opinion of the masters, it is most profitable to ourselves and agreeable to God to draw thoughts and deeds from our wellspring. We must not think that minds less cultivated are incapable of understanding. One is often surprised and touched to hear with what simplicity and truth the least learned often express what they grasp of things supernatural. For the rest, far be it for us to believe that formulas are useless; but as the various works quoted at the beginning of this chapter, not to mention many others, contain excellent ones, we thought it wiser to go down a different path.

THE END

---

[37] *Secret*, 74.

BIBLIOGRAPHY

For a free copy of the pdf file containing active links to all sources, please send in your request on the contact page of the website, www.ubicaritaspress.com/contact.

———————

AA—*Acta Sanctorum*, Jean Bolland, et al., 68 vol., Paris: Victor Palmé, 1863–1940.

AAS—*Acta Apostolicæ Sedis*, Vatican: Typis Polyglottis Vaticanis, 1909–.

Alacoque, St. Marguerite-Marie. *Vie et œuvres*, Paris: Poussielgue, 1876.

Albert the Great, St. *Opera omnia*, 38 vol., ed. Émile Brognet, Paris: Louis Vivès, 1890-1899.

Alet, Victor. *L'esprit et l'œuvre de Ste. Thérèse*, Lille: Desclée, 1883.

Ambrose, St. *De institutione virginis*, PL 16.305-335.

___ *Expositio in Lucam*, PL 15.1527-1850; *An Exposition of the Holy Gospel of St. Luke*. Tr. Theodosia Tomkinson, Etna, CA: Center for Traditionalist Orthodox Studies, 2013.

Anonymous. *The Path to Heaven: A Complete Collection of Devotions*, London: Burns, Lambert, 1866.

Anselm of Canterbury, St. *Cur Deus Homo*, PL 158.359-432.

___ *Meditationum et orationum*, PL 158.709-820; *Meditations and Prayers*. Tr. Martin Rule, London: Burns and Oates, 1872.

___ *Proslogion seu alloquium de Dei existentia*, PL 158.223-248; *Proslogion, Discourse on the Existence of God*. Tr. Sidney Norton Deane, Chicago: Open Court, 1903.

Antoninus of Florence, St. *Summa*, 4 vol., Verona: Agostino Carattoni, 1740.

Arnauld de Chartres. *De laudibus B.V. Mariæ*, PL 189.1725-1733.

Augustine, St. *Confessionum*, PL 32.659-868.

___ *De gestis pelagii*, PL 44.319-360; "Proceedings of Pelagius," *Four Anti-Pelagian Writings*, The Fathers of the Church, vol. 86, Washington, DC: Catholic Univ., 1992.

___ *De sancta virginitate*, PL 40.395-429; *Of Holy Virginity*. Tr. C.L. Cornish, NPNF1-3.

___ *Enarrationes in Psalmos*, PL 36 (Ps 1–79), PL 37 (Ps 80–150); *Expositions on the Book of Psalms*, 6 vols. Tr. John E. Tweed, The Catholic Church in England, Oxford: Henry Parker, 1853.

___ *Sermones supposititios*, PL 39.1735-2354.

Aumann, Jordan. *Christian Spirituality in the Catholic Tradition*, San Francisco: Ignatius Press, 1985.

Bachelier, A. "Le Père de Montfort et le Jansénisme," *Recherches et Travaux*, Angers, Université Catholique de l'Ouest, 2 (sep-déc 1947):5-30; 3 (avr-jun, 1948):21-42.

Baillet, Adrien. *De la dévotion à la Sainte Vierge et du culte qui lui est dû*, Paris: De Laulne, 1693.

Bartoli, Daniello. *Opere*, 39 vol., Turin: Giacinto Marietti, 1825-1856, of which first two volumes, *History of the Life and Institute of St. Ignatius de Loyola*, 2 vol. Tr. Frances Erskine Inglis, New York: P.J. Kenedy, 1903.

Beleth, Jean. *Rationale divinorum officiorum*, PL 202.13-166.

Bernard, St. *De gradibus humilitatis et superbiæ*, PL 182.941-973.

___ *Sermones*, PL 183.35-1198.

Bernardin de Paris. *La Communion de Marie, Mère de Dieu*, ed. J.M. Félix Simounet, Paris: Jacques Lecoffre, 1860.

Bernardine of Siena, St. *Opera omnia*, 5 vol., Venice: Andrea Poletti, 1745.

Billard, Félix-Arsène, Bishop of Carcassone. *Œuvres choisies: sermons, prônes et instructions*, 6 vol., Paris: Vic et Amat, 1903-1905.

Billot, Louis. *De Ecclesiæ sacramentis*, 2 vol, Rome: Inst. Pii IX, 1914-1937

___ *De Verbo Incarnato: In IIIa Summa S. Thomæ*, Rome: Polyglotta, 1895.

Boethius, *In Categorias Aristotelis*, PL 64.159-293.

Bonaventure, St. *Opera Omnia*, 15 vol., ed. Adolphe Charles Peltier, Paris: Louis Vivès, 1864-1871.

Boudon, Henri-Marie. *Dieu seul: le Saint esclavage de l'admirable Mère de Dieu*, Marseille: Jean Mossy, 1836.

Bourassé, Jean-Jacques. *Summa aurea de laudibus B.V. Mariæ*, 13 vol., Paris: Migne, 1862-1866.

Bourgoing, François. *Méditations pour tous les jours de l'année sur les vérités et excellences de Jésus-Christ N.-S.*, 3 vol, Paris : Téqui, 1892.

___ *Méditations sur les litanies de Jésus et de la Sainte Vierge*, Paris: Téqui, 1891.

Boussac, Louis. *Les vertus du Cœur de Jésus*, Paris: Douniol, 1903.

Butler, Cuthbert [Edward Joseph Aloysius]. *Western Mysticism: The Teaching of Sts. Augustine, Gregory, and Bernard on Contemplation and the Contemplative Life*, San Diego: UbiCaritas Press, 2020.

Camus, Jean-Pierre. *Les événements singuliers de M. de Belley*, 2 vol., Paris: Pierre Rocolet, 1660.

Cano, Melchior. *Opera*, Padua: Johannes Manfrè, 1734.

Cassian, St. John. *Collationes*, PL 49.477-1328; *Conferences*. Tr. Edgar C.S. Gibson, NPNF2-11:293-546.

Catherine of Genoa, St. *A Treatise on Purgatory*, 4Ed., London: Burns and Oates, 1858.

Champion, Pierre. *La vie du Père Jean Rigoleu*, Paris: Pierre de Bats, 1698.

___ *La vie et la doctrine spirituelle du Père Louis Lallemant*, Lyon: Pierre Valfray, 1735.

Chanoinesses régulières du Saint-Sépulcre de Jérusalem. *Règles et Constitutions*, Charleville: Hubert Raoult, 1631.

Chardon, Louis. *La Croix de Jésus, ou les plus belles vérités de la théologie mystique*, Paris: Antoine Bertier, 1647.

Chavin, François É. *Histoire de S. François d'Assise*, Paris: Debécourt, 1841.

Christopher, Joseph O., Charles E. Spence, and John F. Rowan, eds. *The Rac-colta, or Enchiridion indulgentiarum preces et pia opera*, New York: Benzinger, 1957.

Church, Diocèse du Puy. *Résultat des conférences ecclésiastiques du diocèse du Puy, tenues en l'année 1838 sur les vertus théologales*, Le Puy: Jean-Baptiste Gaudelet, 1839.

Church, S.C. of Propaganda. *Analectu juris pontificii*, 29 vol., Rome: Librairie de la Propagande, 1855-1891.

Church, S.C. of Rites. *Béatification du Serviteur de Dieu, L.-M. Grignion de Montfort*, Luçon : Rideaux, 1897.

Church. *Breviarium Marianum, ex Indultu S.C. Rituum*, ed. José Escolá, Lérida: José Sol, 1859.

___ *Breviarium Romanum ex Decreto Sacrosancti Concilii Tridentini*, Lyon: Périsse Frères, 1847; *Supplementum*, Kempten: Joseph Koesel, 1848; 4 vol., Rome: Desclée, 1942.

___ *Canons and Decrees of the Council of Trent*. Tr. Theodore Alois Buckley, London: Routledge, 1851.

___ *Catechism of the Council of Trent*. Tr. Theodore Alois Buckley, London: Routledge, 1852.

___ *Missale Romanum*, Editio Typica, Rome: Vatican, 1962.

___ *Pontificale Romanum Clementis VIII*, Rome: Giacomo Luna, 1595.

___ *Rituale Romanum*, Paris: Le Clere, 1850.

Conradi, Gabriel María Verd. "Santa Teresa de Jesús y el soneto 'No me mueve, mi Dios, para quererte,'" *Archivo teológico granadino*, 76 (2013) 191-239.

Contenson, Vincent. *Theologia mentis et cordis*, 4 vol., Paris: Louis Vivès, 1875.

Croiset, Jean. *Devotion to the Sacred Heart of Jesus*, London: Burns and Lambert, 1863.

Cros, Léonard J.M. *La prière du Père Zucchi ou Prière O ma souveraine*, Le Puy: Marchessou, 1861.

Cyril of Alexandria, St. *Homiliæ diversæ*, PG 77.931-1118.

Daughters of Charity. *Manuel des enfants de Marie*, Paris: Le Clere, 1870.

de Bérulle, Pierre Cardinal. *Œuvres complètes*, Paris: Migne, 1856.

de Chantal, St. Jeanne. *Sa vie et œuvres*, 2 vol., Paris: Plon, 1875.

de Condren, Charles. *Œuvres complètes*, 4Ed., 2 vol., ed. Louis-Marie Pin, Paris: Guyot et Roidot, 1857-1858.

de Fiores, Stefano, et al., eds. *Dictionnaire de spiritualité montfortaine*, Outremont, QB: Novalis, 1994; *Jesus Living in Mary, Handbook of the Spirituality of St. Louis Marie de Montfort*, Bayshore, NY: Montfort Publications, 1994.

de Fiores, Stefano. "Per une 'memoria' monfortana profetica ed ecclesiale," in *Quaderni Monfortani*, 1989, 6:3-48.

de La Broise, René-Marie. "Toutes les grâces nous viennent par la sainte Vierge," *Études religieuse, philosophiques, historiques, et littéraires*, May 1896, 68 (5):5-31.

de Lestonnac, St. Jeanne. *Maximes et paroles*, Poitiers: Baudoux, n.d.

de Monfort, St. Louis. *Cantiques des missions*, Nantes: Mazeau, 1845; Poitiers:

Felix Faulcon, 1779.

___ *The Love of the Eternal Wisdom*, Bristol: Burleigh Press, 1949; Tr. A Sommers, Bayshore, NY: Montfort Publications, 1960.

___ *Life and Select Writings*. Tr. Alexander P.J. Cruikshank, London: T. Richardson, 1870.

___ *The Secret of Mary, with Preparation for Total Consecration*, London: Art and Book, 1909.

___ *A Treatise on the True Devotion to the Blessed Virgin*. Tr. Frederick William Faber, London: Burns and Lambert, 1863; *Traité de la vraie dévotion a la Sainte-Vierge*, 18Ed., Paris: Oberthur, 1906.

de Ponlevoy, Armand. *Maladie et mort du R. P. Xavier de Ravignan*, Paris: Charles Douniol, 1858.

___ *Vie du R.P. Xavier de Ravignan*, 3Ed., 2 vol., Paris: Charles Douniol, 1860.

de Rhodes, Georges. *Disputationum theologiæ scholasticæ*, 2 vol., Lyon: Huguetan et Barbier, 1671.

de Sales Chappuis, Marie. Pensées de la Vénérable Mère Marie de Sales, Paris: Annales Salésiennes, 1895.

de Sales, St. Francis. *Introduction to the Devout Life*. Tr. Harry Oesman, San Diego: Ubi Caritas Press, 2016.

___ *Œuvres*, 27 vol., Annecy: Nierat, 1892-1964.

___ *The Spiritual Conferences*. Tr. Henry Benedict Mackey, London: Burns and Oates, 1909.

___ *Treatise on the Love of God*. Tr. Henry Benedict Mackey, London: Burns and Oates, 1909.

Décrouille, Romuald. *Méditations selon l'esprit de l'Église pour toute l'année liturgique*, 2 vol., Paris: René Haton, 1900.

Denis the Carthusian. *Opera omnia*, 42 vols., Mostrolii: Cartusiæ S.M. de Pratis, 1896–1912.

Denis, Gabriel. *Le règne de Jésus par Marie*, Poitiers: Oudin, 1873.

Descartes, René. *Œuvres*, 11 vol., ed. Victor Cousin, Paris: Levrault, 1824-1826.

Documentation catholique, La. ISSN: 0012-4613, Paris: Bayard Presse, 1919–

du Manoir de Juaye, Hubert, ed. *Maria: Études sur la Sainte Vierge*, 8 vol., Paris: Beauchesne et fils, 1949-1971.

Eadmer of Canterbury. *De excellentia B. Virginis Mariæ*, PL 159.557-578.

EC—Glaire, Jean-Baptiste, et al., eds. *Encyclopédie catholique*, 18 vol., Paris: Parent-Desbarres, 1840-1848.

Encyclopédie catholique, Edouard Alletz, et al. Paris: P. Desbarres, 1840-48.

Encyclopédie Grolier, eds., John Barrett McDonnell and Edmond Labelle, Montreal: La Société Grolier, 1947-1948.

Encyclopédie ou dictionnaire raisonné des sciences, des arts et des métiers, 28 vol., eds., Denis Diderot and Jean le Rond d'Alembert, Paris: Briasson et al., 1751-1772.

England, John. *The Works of the Right Rev. John England, First Bishop of Charleston*, 5 vol., Baltimore: John Murphy, 1849.

Enseignement catholique, Journal des prédicateurs, [cont., *Tribune Sacrée*], Paris: 1851-1890.

Ephrem of Syria, St. *Opera omnia, Græce et Latine*, 3 vol., Rome: Salvioni, 1732-1746.

Études religieuses, historiques et littéraires. ISSN 2418-9774. La revue de la Compagnie de Jésus, Paris: Bureau des Études, 1856 –.

Eudes, St. Jean. *Méditations selon l'esprit du V.P. Eudes*, Besançon: Monastère de N.-D. de Charité de Refuge, 1902-1903.

___ *Œuvres complètes du Vénérable Jean Eudes*, 12 vol., Paris: Gabriel Beauchesne, 1905-1911.

Faber, Frederick William. *All for Jesus or the Easy Way of Divine Love*, 5Ed., London: Richardson, 1855.

___ *Growth in Holiness, or, The Progress of the Spiritual Life*, Baltimore, MD: John Murphy, 1855.

___ *Hymns*, 2Ed., London: Thomas Richardson, 1871.

___ *Spiritual Conferences*, 2Ed., London: Thomas Richardson, 1860.

___ *The Foot of the Cross, or, The Sorrows of Mary*, 4Ed., London: Thomas Richardson, 1872.

Ferrer, St. Vincent. *Sermones*, 3 vol., Lyon: Jacobi Giunta, 1550.

Francis of Assisi, St. *Œuvres*, Paris: Poussielgue-Rusand, 1863.

___ *Opera omnia*, Cologne: Heberle, 1849; [Medii ævi bibliotheca patristica, vol. 6], Paris: Bibliothèque Ecclésiastique, 1880.

___ *Works of the Seraphic Father*, London: Washbourne, 1882.

Franzelin, Johann Baptist Cardinal. *De Deo Trino secundum Personas*, Rome: S.C. Propaganda Fidei, 1869.

___ *De Deo uno secundum naturam*, Rome: Polyglotta, 1870.

___ *De SS. Eucharistiæ, sacramento et sacrificio*, 3Ed., Rome: Polyglotta, 1878.

___ *De Verbo Incarnato*, 4Ed., Prati: Giachetti, 1893.

Froget, Barthélemy. *The Indwelling of the Holy Ghost in the Souls of the Just*. Tr. Sydney A. Raemers, Westminster, MD: Newman Press, 1955.

Gaffney, Patrick, ed. *Jesus Living in Mary: Handbook of the Spirituality of St. Louis de Montfort*, Bayshore, NY: Montfort Publications, 1995.

Galot, Jean. *Jesus, Our Liberator: A Theology of Redemption*. Tr. M. Angeline Bouchard, Rome: Gregorian University, 1982.

Garrigou-Lagrange, Réginald. *Perfection chrétienne et contemplation selon S. Thomas d'Aquin et S. Jean de la Croix*, 2 vol., Saint-Maximin: De La Vie Spirituelle, 1923.

Gay, Charles Louis. *The Christian life and virtues considered in the religious state*, 3 vol. Tr. Abbot Burder, London: Burns and Oates, 1878-1879.

___ *Conférences aux mères chrétiennes*, 2 vol., Poitiers: Oudin, 1877.

___ *Élévations sur la vie et la doctrine de N-S. Jésus-Christ*, 6Ed., 2 vol., Poitiers: Oudin, 1908.

___ *Entretiens sur les mystères du Saint Rosaire*, 2Ed., Paris: Oudin, 1888.

Gerson, Jean de. *Opera omnia*, 5 vol., The Hague: Petrus de Hondt, 1728.

Giacomo da Milano. *Stimulus amoris* [Bibliotheca Franciscana Ascetica Medii Ævi, vol. 4], Quarachi: Typ. Collegii S. Bonaventuræ, 1905.

Gihr, Nikolaus. *The Holy Sacrifice of the Mass: Dogmatically, Liturgically, and Ascetically Explained*, St. Louis, MO: Herder, 1902.

Goethe, Johann von. *Goethes Werke*, Hamburger Ausgabe, 24 vol., ed. Erich Trunz, Hamburg: Wegner, 1948-1960.

Gonet, Jean-Baptiste. *Clypeus theologiæ thomisticæ contra novos ejus impugnatores*, 16 vol., Bordeaux: Guillaume de la Court, 1659-1669; 6 vol., Paris:

Louis Vivès, 1875-76.

Grandet, Joseph. *Vie de M. de Montfort*, Nantes: Verger, 1724.

Gregory the Great, St. *Homiliæ in Evangelia*, PL 76.1075-1314.

Guéranger, Dom Prosper. *Conférences sur la vie chrétienne*, 2 vol., Solesmes: S. Pierre de Solesmes, 1880, 1884.

___ *Explication des prières et des cérémonies de la sainte messe*, 6Ed., Paris: Victor Retaux, 1906.

___ *The Liturgical Year*, 3Ed., 15 vol., Tr. Laurence Shepherd, and the Benedictines of Stanbrook, London: Burns and Oates, 1908-1924.

___ *Marie d'Agreda et la cité mystique de Dieu*, San Diego: UbiCaritas Press, 2020.

Holtnicker von Sachsen, Konrad. *Speculum Beatæ Mariæ Virginis*, Quarachi: Typ. Collegii S. Bonaventuræ, 1904; Bonaventure, *Opera*, 14:232-292; *Mirror of the Blessed Virgin Mary*, Dublin: Gerald Bellew, 1849.

Hugh of St. Victor. *De sacramentis Christianæ fidei*, PL 176.173-681; *On the Sacraments of the Christian Faith*. Tr. Roy J. Deferrari, Cambridge, MA: 1951.

Ignatius of Antioch, St. *Epistolæ genuinæ*, PG 5.643-728.

Ignatius of Loyola, St. *Cartas de San Ignacio de Loyola*, 6 vol., eds. Antonio Cabré, Miguel Mir, and Juan José de la Torre, Madrid: The Society of Jesus, 1874-1889.

___ *Ejercicios espirituales*, Madrid: De Burgos, 1833.

___ *Letters of St. Ignatius of Loyola*. Tr. William J. Young, Chicago: Loyola Univ., 1959.

Ildefonso of Toledo, St. *De virginitate perpetua SS. Mariæ*, PL 96.53-111.

Innocent III, Pope. *De sacro altaris mysterio*, PL 217.775-916.

Innocent XII, Pope. *Cum alias*, Condemnation and Prohibition of Fénelon's *Maximes des Saint*, Mar 12, 1699, Rome: Camara Apostolica, 1699.

Irenæus of Lyon, St. *Adversus hæreses*, PG 7.433-1225; *Contre les hérésies*. Tr. Adelin Rousseau, Paris: Cerf, 1984.

Jan Mombaer [Jean Mauburne]. *Rosetum exercitiorum spiritualium et sacrarum meditationum*, Milan: Girolamo Bordoni, 1603.

Jeanjacquot, Pierre. *Simples explications sur la Coopération de la T.-S. Vierge à l'œuvre de la Rédemption*, Paris: Joseph Albanel, 1868.

Jerome, St. *Operum mantissa, continens scripta supposititia*, PL 30.

Jewish Encyclopedia, 12 vol., New York: Funk and Wagnalls, 1901-1906.

John Damascene, St. *De Fide orthodoxa*, PG 94.790-1227; *Exposition of the Orthodox Faith*. Tr. E.W. Watson and L. Pullan, NPNF2-8 and 9.

John of the Cross, St. *Nueva edición de las obras del beato Juan de Ávila*, 4 vol., ed. José Fernández Montaña, Madrid: S. Francisco de Sales, 1901; *Complete Works*. Tr. David Lewis, 2 vol., London: Longman Green, 1864.

John Scotus Eriugena. *Periphyseon, seu De divisione natura*, PL 122.439-1022.

Jones, Hugh Percy. *A New Dictionary of Foreign Phrases and Classical Quotations*, London: Charles W. Deacon, 1900.

Jordan, Raymond (Idiota). *Idiotæ opera omnia*, Paris: Jacques Quesnel, 1654.

Journet, Charles Cardinal. *L'Église du Verbe Incarné*, 5 vol., Villars-sur-Glâne, Switzerland: Fondation Charles Journet, 1998.

Justinian, St. Lawrence. *Opera omnia*, Lyons: Michel Chevalier, 1628.

Kempis, Thomas à. *De imitatione Christi*, ed. Jean-Baptiste Gence, Paris: Treuttel et Würtz, 1826; *The Imitation of Christ*. Tr. Richard Challoner, Dublin: James Duffy, 1845.

Klopstock, Friedrich. *Werke*, 12 vol., Leipzig: Göschen, 1798-1817

Lapide, Cornelius à. *Commentaria in Sacram Scripturam*, 23 vol., ed. Augustin Crampon, Paris: Louis Vivès, 1868-1880.

Lattelais, Wandrille. *Marie et l'enfant de Marie ou Nouveau manuel des enfants de Marie*, Paris: Pensionnat des S.C., 1899.

Laurentin, René. *Marie, l'Eglise et la Sacerdoce*, Paris: Nouvelles Éditions Latines, 1953.

Laveille, Auguste Pierre. *Le bienhereux L.-M. Grignion de Montfort, d'après des documents inédits*, Paris: Poussielgue, 1909.

Lawrence, D.H. *Apocalypse and the Writings on Revelation*, ed. Mara Kalnis, Cambridge: University Press, 2002.

Le Doré, Ange. *Les Sacrés Cœurs et le vénérable Jean Eudes*, Paris: Lamulle et Poisson, 1891.

Le Maistre de Sacy, Louis. *Histoire de l'Ancien et du Nouveau Testament*, Paris: Louis Curmer, 1835.

Le Rohellec, Joseph. *Marie, dispensatrice des grâces divines*, Bruges: Desclée, 1926.

Lehmkuhl, Augustin. *Theologia moralis*, 10Ed., 2 vol., Friburg: Herder, 1902.

Leo XIII, Pope. *Humanum genus*, Encyclical letter on freemasonry, April 20, 1884.

Lépicier, Alexis Cardinal. *Tractatus de Beatissima Virgine Maria, Matre Dei*, Paris: Lethielleux, 1901.

Lhommeau, Antonin. *Les actes de l'oraison d'après St Thomas*, St. Laurent-sur-Sèvre: Règne de Jésus par Marie, 1913.

Liguori, St. Alphonsus. *The Complete Works*, 24 vol., ed. Eugene Grimm, New York: Benzinger, 1888-1897.

Livius, Thomas. *The Blessed Virgin in the Fathers of the First Six Centuries*, London: Burns and Oates, 1893.

Lynn, William D. *Christ's Redemptive Merit: The Nature of Its Causality according to St. Thomas*, Analecta Gregoriana, vol. 115, Facultatis Theologicæ, Sectio B, n. 37, Rome: Gregorian University, 1962.

Marian Studies. ISSN: 0464-9680. Dayton, OH: Mariological Society of America, 1950 –.

Mary of Agreda, Ven. *The Mystical City of God*, 4 vol. Tr. Fiscar Marison [George J. Blatter], Hammond, IN: Conkey, 1902.

Massoulié, Antonin. *Traité de l'Amour de Dieu*, Brussels: Goemaere, 1866.

_____ *Traité de la véritable oraison*, Paris: Lethielleux, 1901.

Maucourant, François. *La vie d'intimité avec le Bon Sauveur*, Nevers: Mazeron, 1899; *A Pocket Retreat for Catholics*, Manchester, NH: Sophia Inst., 2000.

Mectilde du S. Sacrament. *Le véritable esprit des religieuses adoratrices perpétuelles du T.-S. Sacrament*, Paris: Normant, 1817.

Meinert, John M. *The Love of God Poured Out: Grace and the Gifts of the Holy Ghost in St. Thomas*, Steubenville, OH: Emmaus Academic, 2018.

Meyers Konversationslexikon, 19 vol., Leipzig: Verlag des Bibliographischen Instituts, 1885-1892.

Meynard, André-Marie. *Traité de la vie intérieure*, 2 vol., Paris: Amat, 1899.

Migne, Jacques-Paul, ed. *Collection intégrale et universelle des orateurs sacrés*, 99 vol., Paris, 1844-1866.

Milton, John. *Paradise Lost*, 2 vol., ed. Edward E. Hale, New York: Longmans Green, 1896.

Monsabré, Jacques. *Dimanches et fêtes de l'Avent*, Paris: Lethielleux, 1902.

Moréteau, Olivier, Aniceto Masferrer, and Kjell A. Modéer, eds. *Comparative Legal History*, Cheltenham, UK: Edward Elgar, 2019.

Neubert, Émile. *Marie et Notre Sacerdoce*, Paris: Spes, 1952.

Olier, Jean-Jacques. *Œuvres complètes*, Paris: Migne, 1856.

___ *Pietas seminarii sancti Sulpitii*, Bourges: Hyp. Sire, 1879.

___ *Règlements de la Communauté de MM. les prêtres*, Paris, 1782.

Origen Adamantius. *Homiliarium in Jeremiam et Ezechielem*. Tr. St. Jerome, PL 25.583-786.

Palmieri, Domenico. *In epistolam ad Galatas*, Gulp, Holland: M. Alberts, 1886.

Paquet, Louis-Adolphe. *Disputationes Theologicæ*, Rome: Pustet, 1905.

Paulinus of Nola, St. *Poemata*, PL 61.437-743.

Pauvert, Charles. *Vie du vénérable Louis de Montfort*, Paris: Oudin, 1875.

Pepe, Francesco, SJ. *Grandezze di Gesù Cristo, e della gran madre Maria*, 8 vol., Naples: Muzia, 1746-1749.

Pérennès, François, ed. *Dictionnaire de biographie Chrétienne*, 3 vol., Paris: Migne, 1851.

Perlmutter, Jennifer Robin, et al. *Relations and Relationships in Seventeenth-century French Literature*, Tübingen: Gunter Narr, 2006.

Pétau, Denis. *Dogmata theologica*, 8 vol., Paris: Louis Vivès, 1865.

Peter Damian, St. *Sermones*, PL 144.505-925.

Peter the Chanter, *Verbum abbreviatum*, PL 205.21-555.

Pie, Louis Cardinal. *La Vierge Marie d'après Mgr. Pie*, Paris: Oudin, 1881.

___ *Œuvres de Monseigneur Évêque de Poitiers*, 12 vol., Poitiers: Oudin, 1868-1883.

Pinamonti, Giovanni Pietro, SJ. *Opere*, 2Ed., Parma: Paolo Monti, 1710.

Pius XII, Pope. *Ad Cæli Reginam*, Encyclical on the Queenship of Mary and the Institution of the Feast, Oct 11, 1954.

Pohle, Joseph. *Mariology: A Dogmatic Treatise on the Blessed Virgin Mary, Mother of God*, 2Ed., St. Louis, MO: Herder, 1916.

Pollien, François de Sales. *The Interior Life Simplified and Reduced to Its Fundamental Principle*. Tr. William Henry Mitchell, London: Burns and Oates, 1912.

Pollock, Frederick, and Robert Samuel Wright. *An Essay on Possession in the Common Law*, Oxford: Clarendon Press, 1888.

Pope, Alexander. *Works*, 10 vol., ed. John W. Croker, London: John Murray, 1871-1889.

Ps. Dionysius Areopagite. *De ecclesiastica hierarchia*, PG 3.369-586.

Quéméneur, Mathieu. *Saint Grignion de Montfort*, Paris: Bloud et Gay, 1961.

Ramière, Henri. *L'apostolat de la prière*, Lyon: Perisse Frères, 1861.

Règne de Jésus par Marie, Le. ISSN 1271-5727, Poitiers: Oudin, 1900-2017.

RET—*Revue des études tardo-antiques*. ISSN: 2115-8266 Nantes: Association THAT, 2011 –.

Ribet, Jérôme. *L'Ascetique chrétienne*, Paris: Poussielgue, 1888.

Richard of St. Victor. *De gratia contemplationis, seu Benjamin Major*, PL 196.64-192; *The Mystical Ark*. Tr. Grover A. Zinn, New York: Paulist Press, 1979.

Roubaud, Pierre. *Synonymes français*, 4 vol., Paris: Bossange, Masson, 1796.

Rousset, Matthieu-Joseph. *La doctrine spirituelle des saints: Manuel d'Ascétisme*, Paris: Lethielleux, 1893.

Rupert of Deutz. *Commentariorum in Joannis*, PL 169.205-827.

Rylaarsdam, David. *John Chrysostom on Divine Pedagogy: The Coherence of his Theology and Preaching*, Oxford: Clarendon, 2014.

Sauvé, Charles. *Jésus*, 9Ed., 3 vol., Paris: Ch. Amat, 1907.

Scheeben, Matthias Joseph. *Handbuch der katholischen Dogmatik*, 4 vol., Freiburg: Herder, 1873-1903.

Seuse, Heinrich. *D. Henrici Susonis Opera*. Tr. Lorenz Sauer, Cologne: Arnold Quentel, 1615.

Siemering, Lucia Marie. "Capital Grace of the Word Incarnate According to St. Thomas Aquinas," *Studia Gilsoniana*, Apr-Jun 2016, 5 (2):327-343.

Simler, Joseph. *Guide de l'homme de bonne volonté dans l'exercice de l'oraison*, Paris: L'Oeuvre de S. Paul, 1885.

Simon of Cremona. *Opus epistolarum dominicalium*, University of Tübingen, MS Mc 329.

Smith, George. *The Chaldean Account of Genesis*, ed. Archibald H. Sayce, London: Sampson Low, 1880.

Sohm, Rudolf. *The Institutes: A Text-book of the History and System of Roman Private Law*. Tr. James Crawford Ledlie, Oxford: Clarendon Press, 1907.

Spinelli, Pierantonio. *Maria Deipara Thronus Dei*, 2 vol., Cologne: Johannes Busse, 1663.

Suárez, Francisco. *Opera omnia*, 28 vol., Paris: Louis Vivès, 1859-1878.

Tauler, Johannes. *The Sermons and Conferences*. Tr. Walter Elliott, Washington, DC: Apostolic Mission, 1910.

TCE—Habermann, Charles G. et al., eds. *The Catholic Encyclopedia*, 17 vols., New York: Robert Appleton, 1907-22.

Teresa of Avila, St. *Escritos de Santa Teresa*, 2 vol., [Autores Españoles, 53 and 55], ed. Vincente de la Fuente, Madrid: Rivadeneyra, 1861-1862.

___ *Obras de Sta. Teresa de Jesús*, 9 vol., Burgos: Typographía El Monte Carmelo, 1915-1924;

___ *The Interior Castle*. Tr. Benedictines of Stanbrook, New York: Benzinger, 1912.

___ *Works: Life, Relations, Maxims and Foundations*. Tr. David Lewis, ed. John J. Burke, New York: Columbus Press, 1911.

Terrien, Jean-Baptiste. *La Grâce et la gloire, ou la filiation adoptive des enfants de Dieu*, 2 vol., Paris: Lethielleux, 1901.

___ *La Mère de Dieu et la Mère des hommes*, 4 vol., Paris: Lethielleux, 1900-1902.

Tesnière, Albert. *Somme de la prédication eucharistique: Le Cœur de Jésus-Christ*, 2 vol., Turcoing: Revue Eucharistique, 1904.

Texier, Jean-Marie. *Manuel de la Confrérie de Marie reine des Cœurs*, Paris: Oudin, 1899.

Thérèse of Lisieux, St. *Sœur Thérèse of Lisieux*, ed. T.N. Taylor, London: Burns, Oates and Washbourne, 1922.

Thomas of Villanova, St. *Conciones, in dominicis totius anni, et feriis quadrasimalibus*, 2 vol., Milan: Giuseppe Marelli, 1760.

Thomas, St. *Doctoris angelici divi Thomæ Aquinatis, Opera Omnia*, 47 tom., Paris: Louis Vivès, 1871-1880.

Thomas, St. *Summa Theologiæ*, 2Ed. Tr. Fathers of the English Dominican Province, London: Burns and Oats.

Turano, Girolamo. *Vita, e virtù della venerabile serva di Dio suor Maria Crocifissa della Concezione*, Venice: Marino Rossetti, 1715.

Ubertino da Casale. *Arbor vitæ crucifixæ Jesu Christi*, Venice: Andreas de Bonetis, 1485.

van den Berghe, Oswald. *Marie et le sacerdoce*, 2Ed., Paris: Louis Vivès, 1875.

Vega, Cristóbal de. *Theologia Mariana*, 2 vol., Naples: Bibl. Catholicæ, 1866.

Vincent de Paul, St. *Œuvres complètes*, ed. Pierre Coste, 14 vol., Paris: Lecoffre, 1920-1925.

Vincent Ferrer, St. *Tractatus de vita spirituali*, ed. Mathieu-Joseph Rousset, Paris: Lethielleux, 1900.

Weitzmann, Karl Friedrich. *A History of Pianoforte-playing and Pianoforte-literature*. Tr. Theodore Baker, New York: G. Schirmer, 1897.

Wiedenfeldt, Adam. *Monita Salutaria B.V. Mariæ ad cultos suos indiscretos*, Ghent: François d'Erckel, 1673;*Wholesome Advices from the Blessed Virgin, to Her Indiscreet Worshipper*, London: Randal Tayler, 1687.

Wilhelm, Joseph, and Thomas B. Scannell, eds. *A Manual of Catholic Theology*, 3Ed., 2 vol., New York: Benzinger, 1906. [Condensed translation of Scheeben's original German].

Made in the USA
Columbia, SC
06 March 2021